Passage to Byzantium: The Romanov-Habsburg Feud that Led to World War I

Maggie Ledford Lawson

DEDICATION

To Don Hill,
my late husband and best friend,
whose kindness, generosity
and patience brought joy to my life
and made this book possible.

CONTENTS

ACKNOWLEDGMENTS vii

PHOTOGRAPHS AND MAPS ix

A NOTE ON USAGE xv

INTRODUCTION xvii

1 Paradise Lost 1

2 Greek Project 23

3 Supping with the Devil 49

4 Politics Pleasing to God 65

5 *"Vive la force!"* 82

6 When Paris Sneezes 95

7 Royal Brothers' Feud 102

8 The Turkish Sick Man 119

9 Pan-Slavs 142

10 Incitement to Riot 157

11 Crossing the Rubicon 170

12 On the Way to Tsarigrad 185

13 Outside Byzantium 199

14 Master Juggler 212

15 Battenberg 231

16 Bosnia and Herzegovina 242

17 Serbs, Pigs and Russians 251

18 Eve of Complications 260

19 The Poison Tree 287

20 Hollow Chimes of Peace 309

21 Death in Sarajevo 333

22 *C'est ma Guerre!* 360

23 The Putin Factor 387

Afterword: Later Developments 398

Notes to Chapters 401

Bibliography 435

Index 442

ABOUT THE AUTHOR 475

ACKNOWLEDGMENTS

I wish to thank my many friends who have waited so long for me finally to have something to show for my years of research on this book.

I am particularly grateful to Archduke Markus Habsburg, the great-grandson of Emperor Franz Joseph, whom I met years ago during a visit to Bad Ischl, an Austrian spa town of historical significance as the site where the Emperor signed the papers that led to the Great War. The archduke has been a regular correspondent ever since, offering invaluable help in finding documents for my research and encouraging me to persevere in this project.

Among those who provided helpful suggestions for improving the text are Professor Robert M. Saunders, Professor Hugh Agnew, John Robbart and Margot Patterson. Additionally, I am lucky to have had excellent help in preparing the manuscript for publication. Pete Baumgartner offered expert assistance as a proofreader and wordsmith. Krysti Brice, with her eye for details and expertise in formatting, has been invaluable in creating the finished project. Ryan St. James has contributed his skill as a designer, providing the cover art and illustrations for the book.

PHOTOGRAPHS AND MAPS

Habsburg Emperor Franz Joseph

Romanov Czar Nicholas I

The Czar of Russia (Nicholas II) is manipulating the rulers of France, Austria, Italy and Germany, as well as John Bull, representing England.

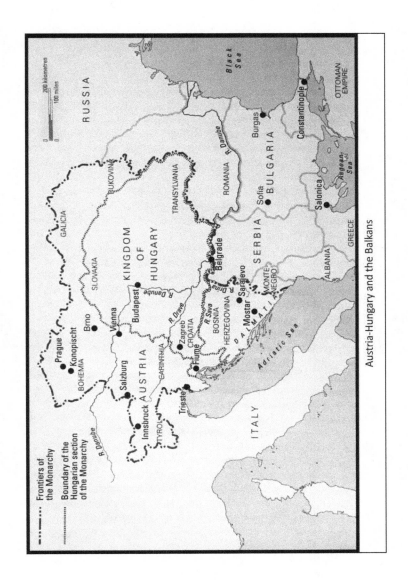

Austria-Hungary and the Balkans

A NOTE ON USAGE

This book covers a large geographic territory that comprises many languages. Furthermore, the languages spoken by the persons and places named in this book are written in different alphabets (Latin and Cyrillic). Like all languages, they have changed over time both in terms of usage and spelling in the original language itself, as well as in English translations and transliterations.

The spellings of proper names and place names used here conform to current adaptations of each language into the English language.

INTRODUCTION

On April 28, 1919, two trains with some 200 German officials left Berlin for a Paris peace conference, marking the end of the First World War. Upon entering battle-ravaged areas of northern France, the trains slowed to a crawl in a French attempt to force the Germans to confront the devastation their army had caused. When the German delegates arrived at the Hôtel des Réservoirs in Versailles, they found that their baggage had been dumped in the hotel courtyard. The high-ranking dignitaries had to search for their suitcases and take them to their rooms. The drafty old hotel had no central heating and the weather was cold. The Germans were virtual prisoners in their hotel, which was surrounded by barbed wire and patrolled by sentries.

A week went by. Finally, Georges Clemenceau, the president of the peace conference, summoned the Germans to the Trianon Palace at Versailles to receive a treaty drawn up by the Western Allies. It was no accident that the French statesman chose the Hall of Mirrors at Versailles for this dramatic occasion. In that same room on January 18, 1871, Prussian King Wilhelm I had become Kaiser of a united German Empire, following a victory in an unprovoked war against France instigated by Prussian Chancellor Otto von Bismarck. Germany had acquired the French provinces of Alsace and Lorraine at that time. Clemenceau intended to have his revenge.

While the Germans were of course aware that the French wanted to humiliate them, they persisted in the belief that they would be able to negotiate a just peace. On May 7, 1919, when the German plenipotentiaries stepped into the dazzling light of that famous room at Versailles, they arrived expecting to mount a defense against claims they were responsible for the Great War. They had reason to expect leniency. They hadn't started the war. They also had not surrendered unconditionally to the allies. Germany was now a republic. Kaiser Wilhelm II had gone into exile. The Germans had been led to believe that U.S. President Woodrow Wilson would see to it that they got a fair peace settlement.

The ailing American President, however, lacked the ability to persuade his allies to temper their judgment with mercy. Clemenceau and his supporters at the conference intended to see that the Germans were severely punished for what the Western leaders considered sins against humanity. There were to be no negotiations. The Germans, uniformly dressed in black morning coats, filed into the hall and took their seats facing their accusers. Clemenceau addressed the delegation in sonorous tones: "Gentlemen, plenipotentiaries of the German Empire, this can be neither the time nor the place for superfluous words.... The hour has struck for the weighty settlement of our accounts." He was to dictate the conditions of peace. "I am compelled to add that the second Peace of Versailles (referring to the first peace in 1871) has been too dearly bought by the people represented here for us not to be unanimously resolved to secure by every means in our power all the legitimate satisfactions which are our due." The Germans were given 15 days to present their "observations" on the agreement in writing. They were being found guilty without a trial. This was a prescript for future war rather than a peace conference.

The German delegates, handed copies of the treaty, twisted nervously in their seats. The conditions of peace were harsh. The German army was to be reduced to hardly more than a police force. The Germans were to lose large swaths of territory in the country's industrial areas. They were to forfeit their foreign colonies. Not surprisingly, Alsace and Lorraine were to return to the French. The Germans were to pay exorbitant reparations. Worst of all, in the eyes of many Germans, they were to acknowledge that they were solely responsible for the First World War. The German lead plenipotentiary, Ulrich von Brockdorff-Rantzau, a thin, sickly-looking man with a monocle, demanded to be heard. His request was granted. He remained seated as he spoke, apparently because he feared that his knees would give way. Many in the hall took his failure to stand as a sign of disrespect. His voice sounded like someone scratching on a blackboard. Acknowledging that having been vanquished the Germans expected to be punished, he went on to say that "the demand is made that we shall acknowledge that we alone are guilty for having caused the war." His voice reached a rasping crescendo. "Such a confession in my mouth would be a lie." He spoke for most of an hour, making a generally unfavorable impression on those present. The Germans, seeing no way out, signed the treaty. Clemenceau had exacted his revenge.

The Austrians, who had fired the first shots in the war, behaved with exquisite courtesy toward the Versailles war tribunal. Partly as a result, they were spared the kind of harsh punishment foisted on the Germans. The monarchy had ceased to exist by the end of October, 1918, after the Poles, the South Slavs, the Czechs, and the Hungarians proclaimed their independence. Austria survived as a state although its territory was vastly diminished. It would never again be a great power.

At the Versailles conference the question of Russian war guilt came up but was quickly dropped. Czar Nicholas II, the last of the Romanov rulers, had been forced from power by revolutionaries in February 1917. He and his entire family would be assassinated at Yekaterinburg in July 1918. The Bolsheviks controlled St. Petersburg. The delegates weren't sure how to negotiate with them. Undoubtedly, the fact that the Russians had fought on the side of France and Britain in the war made the representatives from those countries reluctant to scrutinize their ally's involvement in igniting the conflict.

For an entire century, most students of the war's origins focused their attention on German war guilt. Scholars spent endless hours in the archives poring over dusty documents generated by officials close to the Kaiser. They sacrificed whole forests of trees for books attempting to explain how the Germans were to blame for the war. Their attempts failed. They were looking for the war's origins in all the wrong places.

For one thing, Wilhelm II, and not his government, retained the sole authority to take his empire to war. There is no evidence that the German Kaiser wanted the war of 1914 or started it. (It is true that he plunged into the conflict with untoward enthusiasm once it started). For another, there is ample evidence that the responsibility for the outbreak of World War I lies in St. Petersburg.

Passage to Byzantium: The Romanov-Habsburg Feud that Led to World War I provides a coherent explanation of how and why the Great War actually started. It tells the largely ignored story of a clash between the Russian Romanovs and the Austrian Habsburgs over the czarists' attempts to expand their empire in Turkish regions to their south. These efforts destabilized the Balkans, threatening the peace and stability of the neighboring Habsburgs. The regional unrest caused by the Romanovs' repeated military adventurism near the Austrian frontier escalated in intensity over the years and ended in the tragedy of 1914. The Germans' war aims were still being drawn up weeks after the Great War started. In contrast, by July 1914, the Romanovs' war aims had been firmly in place for more than two centuries. When Czar Peter I (the Great) invaded the Ottoman Empire in 1695 in search of an ice-free port for his new navy, he set in motion a series of events that would put the world on the road to the Great War. The Czar's scheme for imperial aggrandizement included control of the Black Sea and beyond that, the conquest of Constantinople and the Turkish Straits. (Constantinople, formerly Byzantium, fell to the Ottoman Turks in 1453.) In 1711, Peter I involved the Balkans' Orthodox Slavs as proxies in his quest, urging these ethnic groups to rise and meet him in a victory celebration in Constantinople. Future Romanov czars would wage war after war in the effort to realize the dream of Peter the Great. The Great War, seen in that context, is merely the last of the Romanovs' mad attempts to plant their banner at the Hagia Sophia – the seat of the Orthodox church in Byzantium.

The Romanovs never wavered in their belief that the time would come when they would realize their God-given destiny in Byzantium. They held to their dream even during long periods when external events, including the Napoleonic Wars and the continental revolutions of the 1830s and -40s, prevented them from actively pursuing their imperial ambitions.

What the Romanovs needed most were allies. Czar Nicholas I was delighted when, in December 1848, 18-year-old Franz Joseph became Habsburg Emperor. The following year, at Franz Joseph's request, the Czar sent his army into Hungary where the Russians quickly put down a revolution that threatened the monarchy. Nicholas I assumed that the Emperor understood that he was obligated to repay this blood debt in kind. Without discussing matters with Franz Joseph, Nicholas I prepared to march against the Ottomans. The Emperor refused to join the Czar in his war of aggression. The Russians suffered a humiliating defeat in the conflict, which became known as the Crimean War. The Romanovs, who lived by a feudal code in which loyalty was a cardinal virtue, never forgave Franz Joseph for his perfidy. When Czar Nicholas I died during the Crimean War, his relatives blamed his death on Franz Joseph. Alexander II carried on the feud. So did his son, Alexander III, and his grandson, Nicholas II, the last of the czars.

In their desperation for success in Constantinople and their anger at the Habsburgs for blocking their way – as they thought – Alexander II and his successor czars increasingly used the Balkan Slavs as proxies against the monarchy. The Russians' effort to undermine the Habsburgs sharpened into a campaign for revenge after 1908, when Franz Joseph annexed the twin provinces of Bosnia and Herzegovina, which had been occupied by the monarchy since 1878. Seeking revenge, Russian agents encouraged their vassals, particularly the Serbs, to carry out hostile acts against the Austrians.

The Russians organized a Balkan Alliance of four Balkan Slav nations – Serbia, Bulgaria, Montenegro and Greece – who were expected to drive the Ottomans out of Europe, and then to take on the Austrians. Two Balkan wars, masterminded by czarist agents, soon followed, posing a direct threat to the Habsburgs' territorial integrity.

Serbia emerged from the second of these conflicts with her size almost doubled, posing an imminent threat to the monarchy. The country's ultranationalist leaders, advocates of a Greater Serbia, bragged that they intended to acquire Habsburg lands. For Emperor Franz Joseph, the June 28, 1914, assassination of Archduke Franz Ferdinand in Sarajevo was one terrorist act too many. Hoping to limit the war to a conflict with Serbia only, Franz Joseph opened hostilities against that nation on July 28.

Perhaps Franz Joseph's real mistake was his failure to take punitive action against Serbia earlier when the Russians, still reeling from their defeat in the 1904-05 war with Japan, were in no position to come to the aid of their rogue ally in the Balkans. The feud between the House of Romanov and the House of Habsburg ended on the battlefields of Europe. It brought down both imperial houses and left the continent in ruins.

Author's Note

The story of Romanov military adventurism, which led to war after war, including the tragedy of 1914, provides a cautionary tale for our time.

Russian President Vladimir Putin has made it clear that he views himself as the legitimate successor to the autocratic rulers of the House of Romanov. But he is more powerful than any czar. He controls a vast intelligence apparatus from the days of the KGB, expanded to include all the latest weaponry of digital warfare. The stakes, of course, are raised by the fact that this self-anointed czar commands a formidable arsenal of nuclear and conventional weapons.

Putin is a grand master of intrigue, capable of making fools of enemies and friends alike. Even a few years back, Kremlin watchers might have dismissed, as a pipedream of fringe Russian academics, any notion that Russia would one day try to take back Alaska – sold to the United States in 1867. Now these observers aren't so certain. The Russians have recently built an installation in the frozen reaches of the Arctic – in Alaska's backyard. It appears that the intruders' immediate goal is to establish a monopoly for mining the seabed's vast natural resources, including oil and LNG (liquefied natural gas). However, the facility includes a state-of-the-art military installation, with 250 soldiers stationed on the site. The base is equipped with high-powered radar and other technical devices. Nobody knows what Putin has in mind, but one thing is certain, the Russian ruler should never be underestimated.

1 PARADISE LOST

On a fateful summer day in 1688, the boy who became known as Peter the Great chanced upon an old boat moldering in a forgotten shed. The 16-year-old Romanov Czar had never seen anything like it. Crafts that plied the Russian rivers were flat-bottomed barge-like contrivances pulled by men or animals from the banks. This vessel, some 20-feet long and six-feet wide, had a pointed bow and rounded hull. Franz Timmerman, a Dutch merchant who often accompanied Peter on his jaunts in the Muscovy countryside, explained the advantages of the boat's design.[1] "He told me," Peter recalled, "that it (the boat) goes by sails not only with the wind, but against the wind; which speech threw me into great surprise and even disbelief."[2] On a lark Peter ordered the boat refurbished and relaunched. He spent long happy days that summer sailing nearby waterways until his royal duties called him back to Moscow.

Peter I's small boat changed the course of European history. The Czar said later that finding the dust-covered vessel inspired him to establish the Russian navy. Lacking a Russian port that was ice-free year-round, Peter looked to the south, aiming to build a harbor on the Sea of Azov or

1

the Black Sea. He ignored the fact that the territory he coveted was part of the Ottoman Empire. The Sultan, however, made it clear that he wouldn't be pushed around. He considered the Black Sea his private lake. He was prepared to defend his territory. His Tatar vassals were equally unenthusiastic about relinquishing their seaside paradise to Russian intruders.

As a member of the ancient House of Romanov, Peter viewed himself as a warrior king. For him the Muslim Ottomans (Turks), hereditary enemies of Orthodox Russia, were a logical target for territorial expansion. Peter relished the thought of the coming fight.

The Czar dreamed of planting the Romanov banner in Constantinople, a fabled city whose loss to the "infidel" Ottoman intruders had long been mourned by Eastern Orthodox believers. In ancient times the site of a Greek colony known as Byzantium, the city had been renamed Constantinople in AD 330 when Roman Emperor Constantine moved his seat there from Rome. After the Great Schism between the Roman Catholic and Orthodox faiths in 1054, Constantinople became known as the spiritual center of the Eastern Orthodox Church. The conquest of the city by the Ottoman Turks in 1453 forced Orthodox believers to flee. Many of them sought shelter in the arms of Mother Russia, who took on the role of protector of the Eastern church. Moscow became known as the "third Rome." A prediction of the Romanov court poet, Simeon Polotsky, based on astrological calculations, portrayed Peter as "the future conqueror of Constantinople and the 'new Constantine.'"[3] While this was a literary commonplace for praising Muscovite princes, it undoubtedly served as a kind of mental icon for the Czar as he prepared to lead his army into the Balkans.

Young Peter, feeling the wind on his face as he turned his little sailboat this way and that, wasn't thinking about the future. Even dynastic considerations that cast shadows on his future as a Romanov ruler were hardly on his mind as he experienced the pleasures of sailing. Soon, feeling confined by the narrow river, Peter moved to Lake Pleshcheyevo, some 85 miles northeast of Moscow, where he participated in hewing and hammering the timber needed for half a dozen boats. He would have happily stayed for months at the lake if he hadn't been receiving frantic messages from his widowed mother in Moscow. She was terrified that members of a rival branch of the royal family would take advantage of her son's absence from the Romanov court and brazen their way to power.

Peter's father, Czar Alexis, had died in 1676, leaving an uncertain legacy. Feodor, his father's heir, died six years later. Two rival male heirs remained, Feodor's 15-year-old brother, Ivan, and his half-brother, Peter, the first child from Czar Alexis' second marriage. Ivan had claims to succession, but he was lame, half blind and had trouble speaking.[4] Peter, not quite 10, towered over his half-brother physically and intellectually. In 1682, court elders chose Peter as Czar and named his mother, Natalya, regent. Sophia, Ivan's older sister, was determined to prevent her brother from being pushed aside for a sprig from his father's second marriage. In late May 1682, Sophia, supported by fierce Kremlin guards (the *strelsky*), forced the court elders to agree to joint rulership by Ivan and Peter. Pushing Peter's mother aside, Sophia assumed the role of regent. She became, literally, the power behind a specially constructed double throne. It had a peephole high in the back allowing her to oversee – and control – the proceedings.[5] It was clear that she wanted power for herself.

Sophia is among myriads of brilliant women cheated out of a chance to shine by a male-dominated culture into which she was born. She sought to defy Romanov tradition in which females, thought to threaten the line of imperial succession, were forced to spend their lives cloistered from court society. She managed to get an education at a time and place in which book learning was a male-only preserve. She might have set an example as an enlightened ruler had she had the chance. However, her relevance in the context of this book concerns her participation in a coalition known as the Holy League, in which the Romanovs and the Habsburgs became allies for the first time in history. The alliance was to be short-lived. Its failure provides an early example of a repeated pattern in which the Romanovs, expecting feudal loyalty from the Habsburgs, found their hopes dashed by Vienna. The Romanovs' anger at the Habsburgs for putting the monarchy's interests above those of their Russian brothers created a residue of bad blood between both imperial houses.

Three Catholic powers, Venice, Poland, and Austria, had formed the Holy League in 1684 to fight back against Turkish raiders.[6] The biggest threat came from the Sultan's vassal Crimean Tatars, who regularly made seasonal forays northward across the Ukrainian steppes, terrorizing the local populations. The wiry horsemen, whose ancestors were Mongols known for their ferocity in battle, swarmed whole villages, making off not only with golden vessels and earrings and horses and cows but also with prisoners. The daring agenda of the Holy League, later adopted by the Romanov czars as a cornerstone of their foreign policy, called for driving the Turks out of Europe. In an effort to make the league ecumenical, the Catholic powers asked those of other faiths to participate. Only Regent Sophia joined, after being promised Kiev, a city to which Russia had historic claims. Under the treaty, for offensive purposes, the Russians and the Austrians were to take joint action against the Crimean Khan.[7] [8]

Sophia's decision as regent to join the coalition, undoubtedly intended to further her political ambitions, led to her downfall. Her two military campaigns against the Sultan's forces ended in disaster. Sophia chose her married lover, Prince Vasily Golitsyn, as commander of the forces against the Tatar khan. Golitsyn, a bewigged gentleman who cut a dashing figure in his fur-lined cloak and precisely trimmed beard, was for Sophia an ideal adviser and lover. He was, however, no warrior.[9] He also was a poor liar. Following each defeat he returned to Moscow claiming victory. His mistress showered him with praise and valuables, including estates. The Russian people weren't fooled. They were incensed.

Peter, sickened by the sham, infuriated Sophia by refusing to participate in ceremonies in Golitsyn's honor. His relationship with his half-sister, which never had been good, was now beyond repair. Matters came to a head in August 1689 when Peter, who was at the village of Preobrazhenskoye, learned that Sophia was plotting against his life. He fled in the middle of the night, taking refuge behind the high walls of the Trinity Lavra of St. Sergius, the spiritual center of Russian Orthodoxy. Peter's supporters rallied around him. In September, acting in his behalf, they took Sophia prisoner and removed her to the Novodevichy Convent, where she was forced to renounce her position as a member of the royal family. She remained at the convent until she died, in July 1704, aged 46.

Returning to Moscow on October 16, 1689, Peter went to Uspenski Cathedral, where he embraced his ailing half-brother, Ivan. Then, dressed in imperial robes, he stood at the top of the Red Staircase,[10] the master of his own fate and that of the Russian people. Physically, the Czar was a commanding presence. At six feet, seven inches, he towered above his companions. He had strong features, fierce dark eyes and black hair. He was a study in perpetual motion. Sitting still was impossible for him. He intended to see that Russia was similarly on the move.

Peter was heir to a backward empire where communication was almost nonexistent, roads were scarce, and most people could not read or write. Peasants made up the majority of the population. Such information as they got came from their local priests, who more often than not were themselves illiterate. Not only did these ignorant men of God nourish fears of the Turkish "infidels," they also were suspicious of fellow Christians in the West. Lutherans and Roman Catholics were shunned as dangerous radicals. Western customs and beliefs were sinful. Men who shaved their beards were shamed from the pulpit. In Moscow, foreigners were forced to live in a so-called "German suburb," an enclave of English-style houses and carefully tended gardens. The population included foreign craftsmen, as well as diplomats, merchants and Jesuits. By segregating Westerners in this fashion, xenophobic Russians hoped to keep these strange visitors, with their smoking, their snuff dipping and their bizarre habit of eating "grass" (salads) from spreading contagion to the general public.[11]

To the extent that the boyars and church leaders who backed the Czar expected their young ruler to serve as a bastion against the corrupting influence of foreigners, they were to be disappointed. Peter, instead, sought to introduce Russian society to European culture and technology. He made friends with foreigners of all social classes. Peter adopted western dress and insisted that his subjects do the same. He refused to wear a beard and demanded that others abandon the custom. Believers in the old ways howled. They said that with their hirsuteness diminished to only a few whiskers they looked like cats and dogs. Some of his subjects seriously believed that they might be denied entry into heaven for want of a beard. Word circulated that Peter was the Antichrist.

The Czar often used mockery as a weapon against these throwbacks to an earlier age. He gathered around him a large group of friends from all ranks of society known as the Jolly Company. They amused themselves by making fun of the mores of the church and aristocracy. Their drinking bouts have rarely been surpassed in history. However, the Czar never let his rowdy companions interfere with the serious business of moving his empire forward.

Pursuing his interest in boats and the sea, the Czar in 1693 traveled where no Russian ruler had been, to his country's only seaport, Archangel. Located not far below the Arctic Circle on the Northern Dvina River, about 30 miles from the White Sea, the port was frozen six months of the year. The Czar and his entourage, which included eight singers, two dwarfs and numerous drinking companions, arrived during the summer's white nights, enjoying 20 or more hours of daylight. The port was buzzing with life. Typically during the warm weather at least 100 ships were docked at the port, loaded with fine woolen cloth, silks, art objects and wines. Barges regularly arrived from Russia's vast interior bringing furs, caviar, wheat and tallow.

Peter was disappointed that among the ships in the port not one was manned by Russian seamen. He intended to remedy the situation by creating his own imperial fleet. Upon returning to Archangel in the spring of 1694, he named a number of old comrades to high naval positions. It appears that only one of them, Patrick Gordon, had ever been on a ship, and his experience was limited to several crossings of the English Channel. But who cared? Peter intended to create a new world and daring was required.

Peter made plans to build ships. That was easy enough. The hard part was finding an outlet for his navy. The Baltic Sea offered geographic advantages but political difficulties. The Swedes were a floating menace in those waters. The Black Sea, a gateway to the Mediterranean, beckoned.

The Czar's imagination took flight. He believed he might be able to make good on Russia's historic claim to Byzantium – just as the court poet, Simeon Polotsky, had said.

Peter I had other reasons for turning his attention to the south. The Holy League's efforts to stop Ottoman raiders weren't working. Reports of trouble on Russia's southern border arrived with disturbing regularity. In 1692, Tatar cavalry burned the town of Nemirov (now in western Ukraine) to the ground and made off with 2,000 prisoners. The following year, fierce Tatar horsemen took 15,000 prisoners, to be sold into slavery. In every port in the eastern Mediterranean, Russian men could be seen wielding the oars of galleys. Russian boys were presented to the Crimean khan as gifts.[12]

When Peter's allies in the Holy League complained that he wasn't doing his share in fighting the Tatar menace, the Czar geared up for a major campaign against the Ottoman vassals. The Czar's military plan called for some forces to proceed down the River Dnieper to the west of Crimea, and others down the River Don to the east (both of which flow into the Black Sea), forcing the Sultan's Tatar vassals to fight on two fronts. Other troops were to head for Azov, a fortress near where the Don flows into the Sea of Azov. Control of Azov was key to Russian access to the sea by the same name. The Czar named three supreme commanders, Count Fyodor Golovin, Francis Lefort and Patrick Gordon, but reserved to himself the right to settle disagreements between them. This was a serious error since it slowed the operation dramatically. Peter ordered a second army, commanded by Boris Sheremetev, to head down the Dnieper to attack Turkish forts at Ochakov and Kazikerman.

Gordon left first, taking his troops south in March, following a route across the steppes, which he described in his diary in lyrical terms, saying the wayside was "full of flowers and herbs, asparagus, wild thyme, marjoram, tulips, pinks, melilot and maiden gillyflowers."[13] The two other commanders left in May, using rivers to transport their troops. They reached Azov in late June, where Gordon's troops were encamped. The fortified town had been the site of an ancient Greek settlement. Strategically located some 15 miles from the Sea of Azov, on the River Don, it was a major deterrent to invasion from the north.

There was nothing lyrical about the campaign. The troops bombarded Azov for 14 weeks, then ran short of food. A Dutch sailor in the Russian camp defected to the Turks, giving the enemy secrets, including information that the Russians generally napped after the noon meal. The Turks attacked the dozing troops. Before going over to the enemy the saboteurs also drove nails into the touchholes of the Russians' guns, so that the czarist forces could not fire them.[14] Before the Turks were forced back, they killed 400 Russians and wounded another 600. Many more lives were lost because of failures to bring trenches closer to walls, which left the men unprotected. The Russians abandoned their effort in the autumn, slogging north through torrential rains, hounded by their enemies. Rivers overflowed their banks, supplies were lost as barges overturned. An Austrian diplomat named Pleyer, who was on the trip, said that on the entire steppe, which stretched for 500 miles, "men and horses lay half-eaten by wolves," and villages were filled with the sick and the dying.[15] When the Russians' eastern army staggered back into Moscow in December, Peter, in a moment of inexplicable stupidity, marched in proclaiming victory, with a single Turkish prisoner stumbling in front of him. Peter fooled no one, most of all himself.

Peter realized that the eastern operation had been crippled by the divided command. He would not repeat that error. The army that had taken the western route, traveling down the Dnieper, had successfully stormed two fortresses on the river, giving the Russians control of the river almost to its estuary at the Black Sea.

Acting quickly, the Czar decreed that 25 galleys and 1,300 river barges were to be built by May, just five months away. Never mind that the days were short, the weather biting, and that no shipbuilding site existed. As the Czar's Pulitzer prizewinning biographer, Robert K. Massie, says, "Peter's plan, then, was to build the shipyards, assemble the workmen, teach them to mark, cut and hew the timber, lay the keels, build the hulls, step the masts, shape the oars, weave the ropes, sew the sails, train the crews and sail the whole massive fleet down the River Don to Azov. All within winter months!"[16]

The Czar had one major advantage over most modern rulers. His word was the law. Czar Ivan, who had played a limited ceremonial role at the court, died in February 1696. Peter I was now absolute ruler of his massive empire.

Peter chose the town of Voronezh on the upper Don, some 500 miles from Azov, for his shipbuilding operation. It lay in the midst of a thick virgin forest, a site used previously for building simple barges. The Czar was present to oversee the project, rising before daylight and spending the whole day in a whirl of action. By mid-April hundreds of barges were ready, and three galleys were launched. The troops set out in May for the long journey down the Don, their forces doubled from the previous year.

Nearing the mouth of the river, the Russians found 30 Turkish vessels at anchor. The Turks had not expected the Russians to revisit the scene of their earlier humiliation. After Russian Cossack raiders captured 10 of the smaller boats of the enemy, the Turks took their fleet back to the open sea. The Russians eventually occupied Azov, where they transformed the town's mosques into Christian churches. The literary commonplace of the past – the quest for Byzantium – seemed about to be realized under Peter's scepter.

Now that the Russians had access to the Azov Sea their next goal was to take Kerch, the stronghold controlling the narrow passage between the Sea of Azov and the Black Sea. For that the Czar needed a real navy – and he needed allies.

Peter found a harbor appropriate for his Don River fleet on the north shore of the Azov Sea, at Taganrog, not far from the mouth of the Don. After celebrating his triumph in Moscow, Peter summoned his council of boyars, telling them he intended to colonize Azov and Taganrog. The

Russian Boyar Duma on October 20, 1696, approved plans for creation of a Russian fleet. "Let there be ships!" was the rallying cry, echoing the biblical account of creation.[17]

Numerous edicts put the seal on plans to establish a military colony in the region. Three thousand peasant families were sent to Azov. Twenty thousand Ukrainian workmen were ordered to Taganrog to construct the naval harbor. The ships were to be built at Voronezh, then floated down the Don. Participation in the vast project was required from all quarters. The state was to build 10 large ships. Every large landowner as well as every large monastery was to build one ship, or – more often – pay for its construction. The government would provide the timber. The estate owners and church officials were to provide everything else. Peter imposed an 18-month deadline for completion of the project. Those who failed to comply with the order were to have their property immediately confiscated.

In March 1697, having issued his edicts and put the shipbuilding effort in motion, Peter left on a grand tour of Western European courts. The Czar not only wanted to study advanced technology and shipbuilding techniques; he also hoped to recruit allies for the war with the Turks. The Czar attempted to travel incognito, an absurdity for a man who not only towered above other mortals but who also was accompanied by some 250 helpers and advisers.

In many courts, Peter was viewed as more of a curiosity than a serious head of state. The Russians didn't help their cause with their hard drinking and boisterous behavior. In England, the Czar, hoping to evade the crowds, took refuge in the elegant house of John Evelyn, the famous diarist, at the British government's expense. During their stay, the Russians wrecked the house and grounds. The floors and carpets were so smeared with grease and ink they had to be replaced. Tiles were missing in the Dutch stoves, and so were more than 50 chairs, which apparently were used for firewood. Priceless portraits were used for target practice.

Evelyn's famous garden, whose plantings had taken the owner 45 years to perfect, was trashed.[18] The British government later was forced to compensate Evelyn for damages with what was then the exorbitant sum of 350 pounds and ninepence.

While Peter acquired much useful knowledge of technology, his efforts to find western allies for his campaign against the Turks got nowhere. The Czar and King William III got along well personally, but the English ruler refused to commit troops for war with the Ottomans. Other rulers were equally reluctant to become involved.

Determined to renew his offensive against the Turks, the Czar turned to the Austrians for support. However, developments in the East were to bring an abrupt end to the first-ever Romanov alliance with the Habsburgs. During the Czar's months-long absence in the West, the war between the Holy League and the Ottomans had dragged on. In the late summer of 1697, Sultan Mustafa II had led his troops into the Hungarian heartland (now Serbian Vojvodina), encountering the Austrian army near the confluence of the River Tisza and the Danube. The Turks rigged a pontoon bridge across the swiftly flowing Tisza. As the Ottoman army attempted to cross the river, the Austrians cut their forces in two. The ensuing battle, near the small town of Zenta, ended in a dramatic victory for the Austrians under the brilliant command of Prince Eugene of Savoy. "Clusters of corpses formed 'islands' in the river," the Prince reported to Vienna.[19] As many as 30,000 Ottoman troops died at the hands of the Austrian troops or drowned in the river's roiling current. The Ottomans were badly weakened by their defeat.

The Turks responded to the Habsburg victory by offering to open peace negotiations with the Austrians. The Ottomans did not invite Russia to participate. The Austrians, worried about a possible war with King Louis XIV of France, agreed to peace talks. Peter wanted the war to continue until he had taken Kerch. He knew that if he could break through that heavily fortified barrier, he likely could take Constantinople. Arriving in Vienna near the end of his 18-month tour, the Czar explained his situation to Count Kinsky, the Austrian foreign minister. Kinsky replied that if Peter wanted Kerch he should seize it himself, and quickly, since the Turks surely wouldn't voluntarily surrender one of their key fortresses. The foreign minister assured the Czar that Russia would be invited to the upcoming peace conference, but promised nothing more. Peter felt betrayed.

The Treaty of Karlowitz was signed on January 26, 1699, between Holy League members Austria, Poland, and Venice, on one side, and the Ottoman Empire on the other. The Habsburgs came out well in the peace settlement, receiving Transylvania and most of Hungary. Additionally, the Ottomans confirmed the right of Roman Catholics to worship freely within the Sultan's lands. Although this concession was vaguely worded, it formed the basis for later Habsburg attempts to intervene in Ottoman affairs on behalf of the Sultan's Roman Catholic subjects. With the Romanovs claiming similar rights on behalf of Orthodox Catholics in the Ottoman Empire, a potential for friction was created between St. Petersburg and Vienna. The Russians signed a two-year armistice with the Turks.

For Peter I there was irony in his Austrian ally's decision to make peace with the Ottomans at that moment. By the spring of 1699 the Czar's new fleet was ready to sail. His navy had been built for war with Turkey. It had 86 ships, 18 of which were men-of-war, as well as 500 barges for troops and supplies. The fleet headed down the Don for the Sea of Azov in May with the Czar as captain of a 44-gun frigate, the *Apostle Peter*. The voyagers found that work was progressing well at Taganrog for what would become Russia's first real naval base. New fortifications at Azov had held. Peter led his fleet in maneuvers in the Sea of Azov.

The Czar knew that without the help of the Austrians, he could never take Kerch. The Austrians had wrecked his carefully laid plans.

Peter I never forgave the Austrians for deserting him at Karlowitz. "They take no more notice of me than they do a dog," the Czar is reported to have said.[20] The rift widened in 1716 after the Austrians attempted to help the Czar's ill-fated son, Alexis, who had fled to Vienna in panic after a falling out with his father. The Romanovs, who were quick to take offense whenever they felt crossed, undoubtedly harbored this early example of Habsburg perfidy among remembered insults, to be dragged out of the closet by the Czar's descendants whenever they wanted to remind themselves of why they hated the Austrians so much.

Knowing that without allies his chances of further military gains were slim, the Czar turned to diplomacy. He prepared to send his foreign minister, Emilian Ukraintsev, to Constantinople with a list of demands. In the summer of 1699 a flotilla of 12 ships, with the Czar and the emissary among the passengers, headed for Kerch, where the Czar asked the commanding pasha to allow one ship, the 46-gun frigate *Krepost* (Fortress), with the envoy on board, to proceed to Constantinople. The pasha refused the Russian ruler's request. The Czar, threatening force, finally got his way: The *Krepost* could proceed, on condition that four Turkish ships went along as minders. The Czar drew back. The *Krepost* entered the Black Sea. Once in open waters, the Russian ship outdistanced its bothersome escorts. "The moment was historic," Massie writes. "For the first time, a Russian warship, bearing the banner of the Muscovite Czar, was sailing alone and free on the Sultan's private lake."[21] Upon arriving at the Bosphorus on September 13, Ukraintsev sought and received permission from the Sultan to bring the *Krepost* into the Golden Horn, the inlet dividing the city of Constantinople.

Diplomatic negotiations with the Porte began in

November. Ukraintsev demanded the right to sail Russian merchant vessels on the Black Sea; the right to keep Azov and the fortresses on the lower Dnieper that Russian troops had conquered; and the right to a permanently accredited Russian ambassador in Constantinople. He also asked that the Orthodox clergy receive special privileges at Jerusalem's Holy Sepulchre.

The Turks brooked no discussion regarding rights to the Black Sea. As they explained to the Russian envoy, "From time immemorial no foreign ship has sailed its waters, nor ever will sail them ... the Ottoman Porte guards the Black Sea like a pure and undefiled virgin which no one dares to touch, and the Sultan will sooner permit outsiders to enter his harem than consent to the sailing of foreign vessels on the Black Sea."[22]

Nevertheless, the Russians' diplomatic initiative worked to their advantage. A 30-year treaty with the Turks, signed in July 1700, allowed the Russians to keep Azov and certain other territory in the vicinity of the fortified town. The Sultan agreed to help the Russians gain access for Orthodox believers to holy places in Jerusalem. Also Russia for the first time was to have a permanent envoy in Constantinople. An extended Russian presence, like a camel's nose under the Ottoman tent, offered innumerable possibilities for pursuing the Romanov dream of Byzantium.

In a strange twist of fate, a disagreement between Peter I and the Sultan over the continuing presence of Swedish King Charles XII in the Ottoman Empire was to cost the Czar his hard-fought gains from the Turks. The Sultan had granted Charles XII asylum after Russian forces had crushed the Swedish army at Poltava. The Czar was worried that the king would strike again, possibly in tandem with the Turks. The Swedish king was not your everyday warrior. He was a natural phenomenon, unpredictable and dangerous.

Charles XII had never lived by normal rules. After coming to the throne in 1697 at age 15, he quickly earned a reputation as an *enfant terrible*. The king's drunken feats of daring, usually on horseback, led some people to conclude he was mad. The king is said to have abandoned the bottle after an embarrassing episode in which he and his friends forced a bear to drink so much Spanish wine that it staggered to an open window and fell to its death. Foregoing marriage – indeed, he seemed repelled by female flesh – he spent his passions on a single calling, war.

As a warrior Charles XII seemed invincible. He stormed across northern Europe winning battle after battle. But then, in late autumn 1707, he marched on Russia. At that point the Swedish king's luck turned. The Russians' scorched earth strategy forced him to abandon his hopes of taking Moscow. The king led his army southward into Ukraine. And there, in the person of Peter the Great, he met his match.

The showdown between the army of Charles XII and that of Czar Peter I came on July 8, 1709, at Poltava, some 200 miles south of Kiev. The Russian forces were firmly entrenched in the fortified town, situated high on two bluffs overlooking a swampy tributary of the Dnieper River. The Swedish troops were in terrible shape, having endured the ravages of an unusually harsh Ukrainian winter. Then, shortly after military action started, Charles XII was severely wounded in the foot. For the Swedish soldiers, whose fearless leader had seemed larger than life, the king's injury was a serious blow. The Swedish army became trapped. Defeated and in disarray, the troops fled southward to Ottoman territory, taking their king along in a wagon.

The laws of Turkish hospitality required the Sultan to treat Charles XII, and his entourage, as valued guests. The Sultan welcomed his visitors with melons, other fruits and lamb. The Swedes soon moved to a site on the Dniester River, setting up tents in a flowery meadow, where they settled in for an indeterminate stay at Ottoman expense.

Czar Peter tried to bully the Ottomans into sending the

northern interlopers home. Although the Swedish presence was a thorn in the flesh for the Sultan as well as the Russian Czar, Peter's constant haranguing caused offense. The Ottomans felt honor bound to offer hospitality to their guests, even those they didn't like. Finally, on November 21, 1710, the Turks declared that the Czar's behavior regarding the presence of the Ottomans' royal guest was "insulting to the dignity of the Shadow of God" (the Sultan). They expressed their displeasure by declaring war. So much for the 30-year truce.[23]

This was to be Peter's last war with the Turks. In early 1711, shortly after the conflict began, the Czar made a move that, in retrospect, marks a significant milestone on the road to the First World War. That was when Peter I took the unprecedented step of calling on the predominantly Orthodox populations of Serbia, Montenegro, and the Danubian Principalities (Moldavia and Wallachia) to join him in a holy war against the Turks, with the stated goal of driving the "heathen Mohammedans" back to their ancient homeland in Asia. The Balkans were already a hornet's nest of rival ambitions, nationalistic strivings, religious fanaticism and revengeful primitivism. Now, Peter I, ignoring Habsburg interests, put the volatile region in play on behalf of czarist strivings. Two centuries later, the Balkans were still in play. On June 28, 1914, Bosnian nationalists, encouraged in their terrorism by the Russians, would assassinate Archduke Franz Ferdinand, the heir to the Habsburg throne, and his wife, Sophia, in Sarajevo.

Peter I, ordinarily cautious in preparing for war, seems to have plunged into this conflict without giving military matters much thought. The Czar launched his campaign in the spring of 1711 with pompous ceremonies at the Kremlin. Russian guards stood outside the Assumption Cathedral holding large banners, inscribed with the ancient motto of the Emperor Constantine: "By this sign you shall conquer." The grandiosity implicit in the Czar's departure suggests that he already envisioned himself at Constantinople, having forgotten what was required to get there.

Peter's overreliance on his new Balkan allies proved a major error, even though the Czar wasn't totally at fault for counting on their help. Envoys representing Balkan Christians had regularly shown up at the Romanov court, pleading for the Czar's aid against their cruel Muslim lords. These envoys assured Peter that if the Russian army appeared on their soil, local volunteers and supplies would be plentiful. The hospodars (governors) of the Danubian Principalities even signed agreements promising substantial numbers of troops once the Russians arrived. Buoyed by such ill-placed hopes, the Czar went to war with only 50,000 troops, finding himself vastly outnumbered by the Ottoman army.

The Czar's call for Balkan recruits got spotty results.

The Montenegrins did not disappoint. Echoing what would become a familiar Pan-Slav[24] refrain, Peter I sent an envoy to the little nation's capital, Cetinje, reminding the inhabitants that "Montenegrins are of one blood and one faith with Russia." He urged them to join the fight against the Turks and to meet him (the Czar) in Constantinople where together they would "glorify the Slav name, destroy the brood of the Agas[25] and build up temples to the true faith." Edith Durham, a British author with first-hand knowledge of the Balkans, writes that, upon receiving the Czar's message, the Montenegrins went wild. They engaged in a fierce battle, "The Field of the Sultan's Felling," entangling the Turks in thornbushes and slaying them as they struggled.[26] From that time on, the Montenegrins remained the most loyal of the Russians' Balkan friends. The Russians rewarded them, in turn, with generous financial help. Romanov involvement in the affairs of that tiny mountain kingdom would be significant in destabilizing the peninsula.

The hospodars of Walachia and Moldavia, allies on whom the Russians also counted, were not as reliable as were the Montenegrins. This presented problems for the Russians, since the war's theater of operations was centered in the Principalities, to the north of the Danube River. Dimitrie Cantemir, the hospodar of Moldavia, at heart a timid man, fell into a panic when he heard that the Turks were approaching. The Czar tried unsuccessfully to calm the hospodar's nerves with a message full of the kind of overblown rhetoric that was to become a commonplace as future Romanov czars urged their Balkan vassals to fight the Ottomans: "You know how the Turks have trampled into the mire of our faith, have seized by treachery all the holy places, have ravaged and destroyed many churches and monasteries, have practiced much deceit, and what wretchedness they have caused, and how many widows and orphans have been seized upon and dispersed as wolves do the sheep. Now I come to your aid. If your heart wishes, do not run away from my great empire, for it is just ... Shake off fear, and fight for the faith, for the church, for which we shall shed our last drop of blood."[27]

Cantemir persisted in his frantic pleas for help. Finally, Russian General Boris Sheremetev gave in and headed for Jassy, the Moldavian capital. This was a major blunder on the commander's part. His military plan called for him to station his army near the point where the River Prut joined the Danube. Had he done this, the Turks could have been kept from moving into the Principalities. Taking advantage of the opening left by Sheremetev's failure to stick to the military plan, the Turks crossed the Danube at Isaccea and marched into Wallachia with 200,000 troops. The Russians now had little hope of victory.

Cantemir did, it is true, remain loyal to the Czar, fighting the Turks on his home territory. Moldavia suffered huge losses in blood and treasure. On the other hand, Constantine Brancovo, the rich and powerful hospodar of

Wallachia, forgot his promises to the Russians the moment the grand vizier arrived intending to arrest him for treason. The hospodar claimed the Czar's "tone" offended him. His about-face would not, however, save his life. The Sultan's forces kept advancing, forcing the Russians to retreat. Tatar fighters galloped in and out among the Russian wagons, making off with provisions and whatever else was loose. The Czar's troops, trapped at the river Prut, found themselves staring into the barrels of cannons. Peter's cause was lost. The terms of peace were harsh. The Czar was forced to surrender almost everything he had gained in his previous campaigns, including Azov and Taganrog. The Russians were required to destroy their forts on the lower Dnieper. They lost their rights to a permanent ambassador in Constantinople.

The treaty was to be signed on July 21, 1711. However, there was a problem. The grand vizier had made the handing over of Cantemir one of the conditions of peace. The gentleman had hidden under the baggage of Catherine, (Czar Peter's cool-headed second wife), who had accompanied her husband into battle. Only three men knew where he was, and Baron Shafirov, the Russian negotiator, was not one of them. The grand vizier said, finally, that he was not going to prolong the hostilities "for a coward's sake." He predicted that the hospodar would soon enough meet his just deserts. As it turned out, Cantemir's deserts were quite satisfying. He escaped to Russia with his family and 24 Moldavian boyars. He received large estates, a title as Russian prince, and had a son who served as Russian ambassador to England and France.

Brancovo, the Wallachian hospodar who had betrayed the Sultan and then the Czar, was not so lucky. In the spring of 1714 he was arrested and brought to Constantinople, where on his 60th birthday he was beheaded along with his sons.

There was to be no Black Sea Fleet during Peter's

lifetime. Russian ships were forbidden to use those waters. The mouth of the Don was closed. Peter's southern strategy had failed, but the Czar's march to the Prut had opened a major new chapter in Russian history. In Massie's words: "A Russian Czar had invaded the Balkans; Russian infantry had marched to within forty miles of the Danube; Russian cavalrymen had watered their horses in the Danube 500 miles southwest of Kiev. A further presage was Peter's summons to the Balkan Christians to rise against the infidel and welcome his Russians as liberators."[28]

The Czar's later remarks about Azov were to resound for future Russian generations: "The Lord God drove me out of this place like Adam out of paradise."[29] For the rest of the Russian Empire's history, there was to be the attempt, futile in the long run, for paradise regained.

Peter the Great's legacy is not so much what he accomplished as what he caused. The Czar set a precedent for Romanov military adventures in European regions of the Ottoman Empire that led to chronic political unrest. Peter I involved the Balkan Christians in the fight against the Turks, urging them to rise against the infidel and to welcome the Russians as liberators. Later czars used vassal states, particularly Serbia, as proxies for their mad ambitions. They encouraged radical nationalists to conspire not only against the Turks but also against the Habsburgs, whom the Russians increasingly blamed for preventing them from realizing their dream of seizing Constantinople and the Bosphorus Straits. Over time, the Russian-inspired Balkan nationalists posed an existential threat to the Habsburg Empire. The decision of Habsburg Emperor Franz Joseph in July 1914 – just short of his 84th birthday – to declare war on Serbia, a vassal of Russia, is best understood in this historical context.

After Peter I's death in 1725, the Czar's descendants contended for power with their cousins from the rival family of Ivan V, the sickly young man who had briefly ruled alongside his cousin, Peter. Elizabeth, Peter the Great's daughter, ultimately settled the secession question with a successful coup against Ivan's great-grandson, Ivan VI, who was imprisoned for life.

Early in her reign, Empress Elizabeth focused on stabilizing her empire. Although her extravagance drew criticism, her domestic accomplishments were significant. She founded Russia's first university, in Moscow, and banned capital punishment. On the foreign front, Elizabeth had her hands full fending off Prussian King Frederick the Great, who threatened his Russian neighbors as well as the Austrians. During the Seven Years' War the Empress's army fought alongside the Austrians and French against Frederick, seriously weakening the Prussian forces. The Russian army's heroism in battle was widely acknowledged. Elizabeth, who was childless, died in 1762. Her successor, the grandson of Peter the Great, quickly alienated most of his subjects, particularly his army, by repeatedly expressing his admiration for the Prussian King. Catherine, realizing that her husband was dangerously close to bringing down the House of Romanov and taking her down with it, knew she had to act.

2 GREEK PROJECT

Early on July 9, 1762, Count Aleksei Orlov arrived at Monplaisir, a summer palace near St. Petersburg where 33-year-old Catherine, the wife of Romanov Czar Peter III, was in residence. Orlov came with an urgent message. He and a handful of other military officers were involved in a plot to overthrow the Czar and to put Catherine on the throne. One of the conspirators had been arrested. She must seize power that day, Aleksei told her, before the Czar learned what had occurred.

Catherine had become involved in the conspiracy after concluding that her husband – the grandson of Peter I (the Great) – was unfit to rule. Peter III had many failings. Among them was his hero worship of the Romanovs' arch enemy, King Frederick II (the Great) of Prussia, with whom the Russians had been in engaged in a long war. Catherine knew she faced certain death if her role in the plot were found out. She quickly donned a simple black dress, in respect for the former Romanov ruler, Empress Elizabeth, who had died in January. She and Aleksei rushed off to St. Petersburg where Aleksei's brother, Grigory, joined them. Grigory, who was Catherine's lover, had organized the coup.

Grigory, an imposing figure in the green and red uniform of the powerful Preobrazhensky guard regiment, escorted Catherine to the wooden barracks of the Ismailovsky regiment. The drummers beat a call to arms. The officers, who favored the coup, rallied the guards. The regiment's priest administered an oath in which the men swore their allegiance to the woman who would be known to history as Catherine the Great.[1]

The guardsmen followed Catherine's carriage through the St. Petersburg streets to the quarters of the Semenovsky regiment. Those guards also were eager to see Peter III removed from power. They discarded the hated Prussian-style uniforms that the Czar had forced them to wear, exchanging them for those of the Russian army. They joined the procession behind Catherine's carriage.

The crowd, swelling in size, pushed through St. Petersburg's narrow streets to the cathedral of Our Lady of Kazan, where the archbishop proclaimed Catherine as sovereign of all the Russias. Seven-year-old Paul, Catherine's son, was blessed as his mother's heir. Bells pealed. A priest took the lead, carrying a tall cross, as Catherine proceeded to the Winter Palace, where she issued a manifesto. She had come to deliver Orthodoxy from danger and to save Russia's military from being compromised by an alliance with the Prussian enemy, her manifesto said.

The next day, wearing a green and red uniform borrowed from a colonel of the Preobrazhensky regiment, Catherine II mounted a white horse and, brandishing a sword, she rode out to inspect her troops as commander in chief. This flamboyant gesture suggested the direction that Catherine intended to take. She was in many respects the spiritual heir of Peter the Great. Later she acknowledged his legacy, declaring that she frequently invoked his shade when confronted with a difficult decision. Like Peter I, Catherine would attempt domestic reforms to bring her empire in line with similar developments in Western Europe. But also like

Peter, the Empress thought of herself in epic terms, as a Romanov warrior seeking military glory. She envisioned the day when a Romanov heir would occupy the throne in Constantinople (Byzantium). The Empress's predatory forays against her Ottoman neighbors, along with those of Peter the Great, were to establish a precedent for Romanov military adventurism in the Balkans. The quest for Byzantium, which Catherine named her Greek Project, would dominate the foreign policy of future czars, to the empire's detriment and, ultimately, in 1914, to the detriment of the world.

Princess Sophia Augusta Frederica of Anhalt-Serbst, the future Catherine the Great, was born on May 2, 1729, in Stettin, a Pomeranian seaport in Prussia (now Szczecin in Poland). Sophia showed an early penchant for independent thinking and a tendency to defy convention. Her father, Prince Christian August, belonged to an ancient but impoverished German family. Her mother, Princess Johanna, had ties to various European royal houses, including that of the Romanovs. When Princess Johanna heard that the childless Empress Elisabeth of Russia was seeking a bride for Grand Duke Charles Peter Ulrich of Holstein – the only surviving grandson of Peter the Great – she launched a campaign to get her daughter noticed at the Romanov court.

Empress Elisabeth eventually invited Princess Johanna to bring her daughter, not yet 15, to Russia for a visit. In St. Petersburg and then in Moscow, Sophia made an excellent impression at the court. The Empress soon gave her blessing for the match with the Grand Duke, who was Sophia's second cousin. Unlike Charles Peter, who clung to his German heritage, Sophia embraced the opportunities she found in her adopted land.

Sophia faced difficulties in her new life that would have sent most young women into a permanent decline. However, from the day she arrived in her adopted country, she had a sense of destiny. Recalling her feelings just before her wedding, she wrote in her memoirs: "My heart did not foresee great happiness; ambition alone sustained me. At the bottom of my soul I had something ... that never for a single moment let me doubt that sooner or later I would succeed in becoming the sovereign czarina of Russia in my own right."[2] She began grooming herself for her future role. She studied Russian and soon became proficient in the language – except for spelling. A requisite for her future marriage was that she become Orthodox Catholic. Having had any incipient religiosity drummed out of her at an early age by a Protestant fanatic who was her tutor, Sophia changed faiths with few qualms of conscience. On June 28, 1744, at a ritual celebrating her conversion, Sophia affirmed her devotion to her new religion in clearly enunciated Russian. During the ceremony she was given a Russian name, Catherine (Yekaterina). The next day she and Peter were betrothed, and she received the title of Grand Duchess.

The marriage was celebrated on August 21, 1745. Catherine was 16, Peter was 17. As was the royal custom, Catherine was officially put to bed at around 9 p.m. The groom was nowhere to be found. After a couple of hours a lady in waiting appeared to inform Catherine that her new husband would arrive after he had finished his dinner.

Even considering the high misery index of most politically arranged royal marriages, this one was among the worst. Some say Peter was deranged; at the very least he was neurotic. Catherine wrote that she once heard the pitiful whining of a dog. Going to investigate, she found her husband holding up the little animal by its collar while a young servant boy gripped its tail. Peter was flogging the poor creature with the handles of a whip.[3] On another occasion Catherine found a large rat in Peter's room, hanging from a small gibbet, with signs of its having been tortured. He explained that the rodent had been punished according to military law.[4]

These bizarre aberrations aside, for Catherine there were far more troubling issues. Peter failed to consummate the marriage. Eight years passed. This caused a terrible problem for a young grand duchess whose sole role in the royal marital scheme was to produce an heir. Showing a profound streak of pragmatism, Catherine took lovers, ultimately bearing four children.[5] To the extent that those at the court knew that these were not Peter's offspring, they mostly ignored it. The important thing for the Romanovs was that some sort of heir, legitimate or not, had been produced. Within hours after Catherine gave birth to her son, Paul, the Romanov heir, the child was put in Empress Elizabeth's care. Catherine only rarely was allowed to spend time with her son.

While her husband drank himself into a stupor almost every night and railed against his fate, Catherine came into her own. Her portraits suggest a commanding presence. She was not beautiful. Her features were rather exaggerated, but so was her personality. Her clear eyes reflect a certain depth. She read Tacitus and corresponded with Voltaire. She pleased Orthodox clerics by her devotion to the faith. Catherine made friends with would-be enemies. Influential members of the court realized that she was a born ruler, with abilities her husband totally lacked.

Peter III, having succeeded Empress Elisabeth to power in January 1762, wasted no time in proving himself unfit to rule. He showed disdain for the imperial court, for the army and for the Orthodox Church, traditional pillars of support for the Romanov dynasty. Ignoring the fact that since 1756 the Russians had been fighting Prussia in the Seven Years' War,[6] Peter III tried to turn his army into a Prussian-style fighting force. Enamored of the much reviled King Frederick[7] II (the Great), Peter III wore his hero's picture on a ring.[8] The Czar spoke German at court, making enemies every time he opened his mouth.

Worst of all, in the eyes of many, he showed disdain for the Orthodox Church, with its richly-garbed priests, its droning liturgy, its profusion of icons. He ordered the confiscation of vast expanses of land held by the church. He refused to be crowned in the religious ritual that was traditional for those ascending the Romanov throne; this denied him the legitimacy he might have had otherwise.

Catherine, realizing that her husband was destroying the House of Romanov, attempted to persuade him to change his ways. The Czar brooked no interference with his decisions as absolute ruler. When Catherine invited high-ranking clerics to bless a small chapel she had installed in her quarters, Peter III threatened to lock her away in a convent for life.

An episode in early June, 1762, convinced Catherine that the Czar wished her harm. Peter III had arranged a lavish banquet in the large hall in the new Winter Palace to celebrate a peace treaty with Frederick II, ending Russian involvement in the Seven Years' War. The treaty, which was highly unpopular, called for the Russians to give back all the territory that had been seized from Prussia during the long war. Peter sat on a raised dais with his mistress, Elisabeth Vorontsov, by his side. Catherine was at the other end of the hall. During the evening Peter III repeatedly praised Frederick II, the enemy Russians hated most. Then, staggering to his feet, the Czar proposed that the guests toast his own imperial family. Observing that Catherine remained seated during the toast, the Czar sent someone to inquire about her behavior. Catherine explained that she considered it inappropriate to drink a toast to herself. Peter, learning of the reply, startled those present by gesturing toward his wife and calling out loudly, "Fool! Fool!"[9]

Catherine knew the situation could not continue its present course. In her memoirs, she wrote that she had three choices. She could perish "with him (the Czar), by him," or she could assume power in hopes of saving herself, her children and perhaps the Romanov empire from certain disaster.[10]

Catherine turned to a group of supporters who had been scheming to overthrow Peter III almost from the moment he had ascended to the throne. They included Grigory and Aleksei Orlov and their three brothers, all of whom were guardsmen. Nikita Panin, a diplomat with an appreciation for constitutional government, was involved, as was Catherine Dashkova, the sister of Peter's mistress.

On the day of Catherine's coup, the Czar was with his mistress at Oranienbaum, a Romanov summer palace on the Gulf of Finland, where he undoubtedly was sleeping late. When he finally learned what was transpiring in St. Petersburg, Peter III hesitated, seemingly confused about what to do. Later he tried to flee, but Catherine's supporters blocked his way. Confronted by the conspirators, Peter pathetically begged to be allowed to go into exile, in company of his mistress. They refused the Czar's request, imprisoning him instead. He died a few days later in mysterious circumstances. While it is doubtful that Catherine was directly involved in Peter's assassination, it is certain that she was glad to be rid of her erratic and spiteful husband.

Catherine was now ruler of a realm that stretched some 5,500 miles from St. Petersburg to the east, a vast distance in the days of primitive methods of transportation. Icebound in the north, the empire touched on subtropics in the south. Its population of 19 million included some 80 ethnic groups. The Empress was mistress of far more than she could survey, yet for her, this inscrutable vastness, this babble of voices, whetted rather than slaked her thirst for lands to conquer. Like Peter the Great, she considered the Ottoman lands to Russia's south as ripe for expansion. But she needed an excuse for war.

A little more than a year after her ascension, Catherine instigated a crisis in Poland that led, eventually, to the

Turkish conflict she desired. After the Polish ruler, Augustus III, died in the fall of 1763, a struggle had ensued for the throne. Catherine, manipulating the kingdom's political process, got her former lover, Stanislaus Poniatowski, elected as king. She sent in Russian troops to fortify her favorite's hold on the throne. She then encouraged the kingdom's dissenting Orthodox Catholics and Lutherans to rise against the Roman Catholic majority. The Turks, who shared a long border with Poland, became anxious about Russian meddling in the neighboring kingdom. In July 1768, after fighting among the Polish factions spilled over the border into a region under Turkish protection,[11] the Porte repeated earlier demands that Catherine pull her troops out of Poland. When she failed to act, the Turks locked the Russian envoy, Aleksei Obreskov, in the Castle of the Seven Towers in Constantinople, effectively declaring war.[12]

Catherine II was thrilled. "My soldiers are off to fight the Turks as if they were going to a wedding ..." she wrote her friend Voltaire. "Wherever the Turks or the Tatars[13] show themselves, we send them away with a sound thrashing ... " she boasted.[14] "We are at war, it is true, but Russia has long been used to that occupation and emerges from each war in a more flourishing state than before."[15]

Catherine II understood the difficulties that the conflict presented. The Ottomans controlled Crimea and its vassal khan. From that strategic location they could push back invaders from the northern steppes with relative ease. They also controlled the mouths of the three mighty rivers that emptied into the Black Sea – the Dnieper, the Bug, and the Dniester.

In November 1768, someone in her inner circle, most likely Grigory Orlov, approached the Empress with a daring proposal. It called for engaging the Turks by sea as well as by land. While the Russian army pursued the Ottomans in the Balkans and other regions near the empire's south, the imperial navy would sail all the way around Western Europe, passing through the Straits of Gibraltar to engage the Turks in the Mediterranean.[16] It was 10,000 miles there and back. It was Catherine's kind of project.

While the naval operation was being organized, the Russian army moved into Ottoman territory, making significant inroads. Czarist forces recaptured Azov and Taganrog, where Peter the Great had enjoyed his spectacular success. This allowed Russian ships access to the Sea of Azov, where construction immediately began on a flotilla. Other troops headed for the Turkish provinces of Wallachia and Moldavia (the Danubian Principalities). By early October 1769, the Russian army had occupied the Moldavian capital of Jassy. Catherine jubilantly informed the ex-marshal of the Russian Legislative Commission, General Aleksandr Bibikov, "The new princess of Moldavia greets you."[17]

Moldavia and Wallachia were backward provinces with little to offer an invading army. Geography, however, gave the Danubian Principalities strategic importance for the Russians, but also for the Austrians. For Russia the only viable overland route to Constantinople lay through the Principalities (an overland route to the east of the Black Sea, with its rough terrain and great distance, was impractical).

The presence of Russian troops near the monarchy's southern frontier raised inevitable alarms in Vienna. The Danube, flowing through both Vienna and Buda/Pest and emptying into the Black Sea near the monarchy's border with Moldavia, was a vital trade corridor for the empire. The threat to Habsburg economic interests was serious. However, Austrian Empress Maria Theresa wanted to avoid a quarrel with the Russian Empress. She protested through diplomatic channels and waited to see what the Empress would do next.

Catherine II's plans for her grand naval expedition continued apace. On January 29, 1769, the Empress informed Aleksei Orlov that he was to lead the expedition. He had no experience whatever in naval warfare. Nevertheless, Catherine's faith in him was unbounded, and, as it turned out, justified. The project was supposed to be a secret, but such extraordinary news soon got out. The Empress, who loved to make a stir, was "bursting with glee at the thought of the 'noise' she was going to make in Europe," writes Madariaga.[18]

Catherine participated in every phase of the planning for this unprecedented maritime endeavor, even seeing to the diets of the seamen. The crews were to get meat and vegetables four days a week, salt fish, black biscuit and butter the other three. A daily ration of brandy also was included in the fare. In August 1769, Catherine waved goodbye as the first squadron left the port of Kronstadt, in the Gulf of Finland.

Catherine's plan called for her navy to sail into ports on the Aegean and Adriatic and to raise the Orthodox banner against the Turks. The Russians intended to follow Peter the Great's example by recruiting the Balkans' oppressed Christian populations for their cause. Already in the fall of the previous year, the Russians had dispatched Major General Yuri V. Dolgoruky to Montenegro to stir up a rebellion against the Turks. However, upon arriving in the Adriatic, the Russian commander found himself sailing in unfriendly political waters. The Republic of Venetia, alarmed at news that the Russians were encouraging insurrection so near its shores, prohibited warships of any nation from using its Adriatic ports. This left the Russian fleet unable to support Dolgoruky in Montenegro, and he was forced to abandon his proselyting effort.

The expedition did offer moments of comic relief. Upon arriving at Cetinje, Montenegro's rocky little capital, Dolgoruky was surprised to find a certain Stepan Maly (Stephen the Little) ruling there as Czar Peter III of Russia. The impostor, said to be an Italian named Bandini, had spent time in Russia and then fled to escape criminal charges. Having initially decided to arrest the faux Czar, Dolgoruky later changed his mind. Before departing, he decked out "Peter III" in a Russian officer's uniform and allowed him to continue his reign.[19]

Aleksei Orlov, having arrived in the Mediterranean with the first of the Russian squadrons, also encountered difficulties. Persuading the Sultan's unhappy Christian subjects to join him in driving the Turks out of Europe wasn't as easy as he had expected. His efforts to recruit the Greeks failed totally, partly because of language differences. The Russian commander, angry at being repulsed, lashed out, describing the Greeks as "flatterers, deceitful, unstable, bold and cowardly ... they profess their faith only with their lips and have no trace in their hearts of Christian virtue."[20] The Romanians, who boasted a Latinate culture, also were reluctant to join the Russians. The Balkan Slavs (Serbians, Montenegrins and Bulgarians) were more inclined to join Mother Russia in fighting the Turks.

The Russian navy, reinforced by the arrival of more ships, chased the Turks' Aegean fleet in and out of Greek islands. Then, on July 5, 1770, the Turkish commander made a fatal error, deciding to accept battle in the channel between Khios and the Anatolian coast, near the port of Chesme. Upon coming under heavy fire, the Turks panicked, withdrawing to the harbor. The Russians set fire to the Ottoman fleet on the night of July 6-7. The entire Turkish navy was destroyed, with some 11,000 seamen lost.

The Russians went wild with self-congratulation at their first naval victory in 900 years. Chesme became part of the Romanov myth, inspiring dreams of glory at sea as well as on land. Catherine wrote joyfully to Voltaire: "They say that the earth and sea trembled with the huge number of exploding ships. The quakes were felt as far as Smyrna, twelve leagues away .... Count Orlov tells me that the day after the burning of the enemy fleet, he saw with horror that the water in the harbor of Chesme, which is not very large, was stained with blood, so many Turks had perished there."[21] The Empress organized a special memorial service, paying tribute to Peter the Great, the father of the Russian navy, as was his due.

In a surreptitious attempt to establish a permanent presence in the Principalities by means of a peace treaty with the Turks, Catherine almost brought on the war she wanted to prevent. Her proposal to the Porte, drawn up in September 1770, was to give her soldiers the right to occupy the Danubian Principalities until the Russians were repaid for their entire war costs with funds generated from those provinces. This marked a transparent attempt to establish a permanent Russian stronghold on the Habsburgs' southern doorstep. A Russian occupation could be stretched out for years on grounds that the indemnity hadn't been fully paid.

Upon receiving a copy of the peace demands from Catherine, Frederick II denounced them as "a declaration of war." He warned the Empress that Austria would never agree to such terms. Catherine II replied that her demands were addressed to Turkey and had nothing to do with Austria.

The Austrians thought otherwise. They made their views clear in February 1771 by amassing troops on the Hungarian border next to Wallachia and Moldavia. Then, on July 6, 1771, the Austrians negotiated an unprecedented treaty with the Porte, in which Vienna promised to force, or to persuade, the Russians to return Ottoman territory they had seized during the war. The Habsburgs also were to guarantee Poland's independence and territorial integrity. If the Austrians fulfilled their obligations, they were to receive part of Wallachia.

Realizing that the Austrians were serious about stopping the Russians from establishing a military stronghold on the monarchy's southern border, the Empress agreed to return the Principalities to the Turks. The Austrians, having gotten what they wanted most, began having second thoughts about their treaty with the Turks, which they had not yet ratified.

Frederick II, always an opportunist, now came forward with what he envisioned as a permanent solution to the Polish problem. He intended to dismantle the troubled kingdom. In the interest of fairness, he offered the Romanovs and the Habsburgs shares in the territorial pie. While Habsburg Emperor Joseph II found the Prussian king's proposal tempting, his mother, Maria Theresa, who was co-ruler, thought otherwise. From her customary perch on high moral ground, the Empress viewed with horror the behavior of predators such as Frederick II and Catherine II. The Habsburg Empress found any talk of dividing Poland abhorrent.

Frederick II was not one to let Maria Theresa's tender conscience interfere with his roguish scheme. Bypassing Vienna altogether, he dispatched his brother, Prince Henry, to Russia in the winter of 1770 to make the case for partitioning Poland. Catherine was eager to collude in wiping Poland from the map. This left Maria Theresa with three undesirable options. She could ratify the treaty with the Porte and try to defend Poland against Russia with Ottoman help; she could watch while her powerful neighbors, Prussia and Russia, had their way with the hapless kingdom; or she could join in the partition.[22] Wenzel Anton von Kaunitz, a practitioner of realpolitik who was chancellor, finally persuaded the Empress to take her share of Poland. In May 1772, the Austrians informed the Porte that they would not ratify the previously negotiated secret treaty. Maria Theresa, previously considered beyond reproach, had lost her political virginity. She became the butt of jokes. Frederick II's mocking words stung: "She cries, but she takes always." (*'Elle pleure, mais elle prend toujours.'*)[23] Two later partitions of Poland wiped the kingdom off the map.

With the peace process with the Turks stalled, Catherine laid plans for an attack on her enemy's main army south of the Danube. Pyotr Rumyantsev, her most brilliant general, wasn't enthusiastic about the project. He knew that the region was thickly dotted with Turkish forts but he had only a vague idea where they were. The Russian military had no maps of the area. However, the Empress's will was the General's command. The Russian main army crossed the Danube in mid-June 1773, but fell back after failing to take Selestra, a key fortress on the south bank of the lower Danube.

The following year, the Empress sent Rumyantsev to try again, taking care that he had the maps and reinforcements he needed. Catherine made her orders clear to the General: He was not permitted to fail. Logistics were difficult, since there were no bridges at the point on the Danube where the troops needed to cross.[24] However, on June 20, 1774, Rumyantsev and the main Russian army were ferried across the Danube. The Russian forces swept southward into the Balkan mountains. When the advance guard came within 250 miles of Constantinople, the Ottomans sued for peace.

The Russians were richly rewarded during the peace negotiations conducted in July 1774 at Kuchuk Kainarji, a village in Bulgaria. Although the Danubian Principalities were returned to Turkish sovereignty, the Russians received the right to intervene with the Porte on behalf of the Principalities' subjects. This guaranteed a continued Russian presence in the region. The Russians gained control of Kerch and Enikale, the fortresses guarding the exit from the Sea of Azov into the Black Sea. Peter the Great's failure to occupy Kerch, which he blamed on the Austrians, had prevented him from taking his Russian navy all the way to Byzantium.

And, in a development that would have serious complications in the future, the Russians won the right to represent a particular Orthodox church before the Porte.

The Russians later claimed this gave them the right to protect all Orthodox people under Turkish rule. Future czars would invoke these "rights" to justify invading the Balkans for the "holy cause" of Orthodoxy and Slavdom. In July 1775, Catherine celebrated the Russian land and sea victories with a triumphalist extravaganza. Her letter to Voltaire reflects the grandiosity of her vision:

"To provide a treat for the people, a fairly large open space was chosen, which we called 'the Black Sea' and covered with ships. The approach was by two roads, one called the ... Don and the other the Dnieper. Following the map, on the little hills overlooking the plain, ballrooms were set up, which were called Kerch and Yenikale (Enikale) .... There were fireworks on the other side of the Danube; feasts, fountains flowing with wine, rope dancers, and other popular amusement.... [There were kitchens set up] so that between sixty and one hundred thousand people could have all their wants supplied for between ten to twelve hours." Catherine ended by telling Voltaire, "I would love to have danced with you there, Sir, and I am sure you would have honoured me with your choice."[25]

During the ceremonies, the Empress showered Rumyantsev with praise and presents. These included a diamond encrusted baton and sword, a crown of laurel leaves and an olive branch, 5,000 serfs, 100,000 rubles for a house, and paintings. However, the most significant honor bestowed on Rumyantsev by his sovereign was a laudatory charter that styled him Zadunaisky ("Beyond the Danube"). Not since the time of Svyatoslav in the 10th century had Russian forces appeared across the Danube, writes the Empress's biographer, John Alexander.[26]

For Catherine, the peace settlement provided only a pause on the road to Constantinople – the ultimate destination for her "Greek Project." Her next move called for building a network of settlements in the sparsely populated Ukrainian steppe lands, stretching southward to the Black Sea. For this complicated mission she needed the brilliance of someone who shared her grandiose vision. She found him in Grigory Potemkin, who had "swaggered into Catherine's court,"[27] in the words of her biographer, Vincent Cronin, not only finding a warm spot in the Empress's bed, but also winning a permanent place in her heart.

Potemkin fascinates in part because of his eccentricity. He often arrived at Catherine's apartments with nothing on under his brocade dressing gown. He was even said to have entertained dignitaries similarly clad. He loved oysters, champagne and spiced dishes, which he prepared himself; he seemed always to be munching on something – radishes, carrots, or, in a pinch, his fingernails. His large fingers were garnished with diamonds. A few years after he met Catherine he lost an eye, due to a badly treated infection, which gave him a ferocious look.

For the Empress, however, it was Potemkin's intellect and his daring that set this strange man apart from her numerous other lovers (by some accounts Catherine had more than 50, although a couple of dozen is more likely). Potemkin's personal qualities made him ideal for the Empress's Greek Project. Like Catherine, he regarded impossibilities as challenges to be overcome. Like the Empress his thoughts ranged freely in unfamiliar terrain. Like her, he loved to cause a stir, and often did just that. He rarely worried about what people said about him, and they said lots, much of which was negative. Nobody, however, denied that he was brilliant. If his imagination sometimes got the better of him – his dream of creating an Israelsky regiment that would march on the Holy Land and bring about the union of Roman Catholic and Orthodox believers was a bit much – his actual accomplishments were numerous and impressive.

In 1775, Catherine named Potemkin Governor of New Russia (southern Ukraine) and Azov. His main job was to colonize territory, acquired by the Empress in the Treaty of Kuchuk Kainarji, lying between the Bug and Dnieper rivers and between the lower Don and Yaya rivers. In addition, he was to oversee cornfields and grazing lands of the Zaporozhian Cossacks. Potemkin, until then a late riser, became a changed man. Arriving in the steppe lands he was to colonize, he wasted no time in getting to work. Casting aside his silk dressing gown, he donned an open necked shirt, riding breeches and boots. He familiarized himself with every mile of his territory. Then he dealt with the Cossacks, whose brigandage had so often terrorized their neighbors. Potemkin settled a few of these wild horsemen in villages. He forced the rest to join a special army known as the Kuban Host, which he sent to defend an area northwest of the Caucasus.

Into the territory emptied by the Cossacks' removal, Potemkin brought colonists – peasants of various stripes, fugitive serfs, convicts, who were pardoned for all crimes except murder; German immigrants, 32,000 strong, as well as Christians from Crimea. Each colonist received 142 acres and certain tax advantages. Those who were particularly successful were rewarded with more land.[28]

Many of the new settlements were fortresses that commanded strategic rivers. The southernmost strongpoint of the territory was Kherson, on the lower Dnieper River, where Potemkin in 1778 began building a port. Situated only a few miles upstream from the shallow Bug-Dnieper delta, there had been little on the site except a building where beehives were stored in winter. Using imported workers who spoke a patchwork of tongues and making do with improvised tools, Potemkin created a multipurpose military base, a citadel, a fortress, a dockyard and naval station. Barracks were built to house 10,000 soldiers.[29]

With the Ukrainian steppes flourishing as a result of Potemkin's tireless efforts, Catherine's next goal was to annex Crimea. The Russians had occupied the peninsula in mid-1771. They later had installed a vassal khan, Shagin-Girei, who was kept loyal by generous infusions of cash. In the summer of 1778 the Ottomans made one last attempt to reassert control over the peninsula. The Russians repulsed the Ottoman fleet at Akhtiar (the future Sevastopol). In January 1799 the Porte recognized Shagin-Girei as ruler for life and declared Crimea independent except in religious matters.

Although the Romanovs and the Habsburgs avoided war over the Principalities, the relationship between the two courts was cool. Already in 1774 Joseph II had pushed back against the Romanovs by sending troops into the Bukovina region of Moldavia shortly after the Russians withdrew from the region. In May 1775, Catherine got word of an Austrian attempt to seize territory in Bessarabia (western Ukraine), not far from the Russian border. "The impudence of the Austrians is great," she told Field Marshal Rumyantsev, admonishing him to watch for any sudden move by the monarchy's troops. "I do not desire to have the imperials as neighbors," she added.[30]

On the other hand, Empress Catherine was more than willing to have the imperials as allies for her Greek Project. Aware of the potential for pitfalls in proceeding with her plans for the Balkans unilaterally, Catherine let it be known that she needed help in driving the Turks out of Europe. She knew that Frederick II would never participate in fighting the Ottomans. On the other hand, she thought Joseph II might be willing to join her.

The Emperor was a man with something to prove. He had disappointed his Habsburg relatives by failing to produce a male heir. Undoubtedly hoping to compensate for his failures in the bedroom with conquests on the battlefield, Joseph II put great stock in his army. He customarily wore a military uniform, something that previous Habsburg emperors had rarely affected. He fancied himself as another Frederick the Great, whom he envied and feared.

In the spring of 1779, Joseph II sent the Empress word that he wanted to meet her, incognito, during a tour she planned in the Russian provinces. Catherine was thrilled. She thought if she could get the Habsburgs on board, the Balkans would be theirs. Before setting out on her journey the Russian sovereign even ordered an adviser to draft a plan for Russo-Austrian cooperation in the dismemberment of the Ottoman Empire.

Joseph II, traveling under the improbable and incongruous name of "Count Falkenstein," met Catherine at Mogilev (in eastern Belarus) after morning mass on May 24, 1780. In spite of swarms of mosquitoes and sticky heat, the two sovereigns got along splendidly. It seemed to Catherine that she had found her partner in conspiracy. The Empress "teased her guest about making Rome the capital of his empire, while he touted Constantinople as the natural capital of the Orthodox world,"[31] writes biographer John Alexander.

But bantering about future conquests was one thing; transmuting casual talk into action was another. When Joseph II realized that Catherine was serious about her plans for Balkan aggression, he was taken aback. He agreed to her proposal that the two rulers mutually guarantee their imperial possessions. This protected the monarchy from further attempts by Frederick the Great to seize Austrian territory. But when the Empress pressed him for a solid promise of help in fighting the Turks, Joseph II refused to commit himself. "Her project of establishing an empire in the East rolls around in her head and broods in her soul," he told his mother in amazement.[32]

Maria Theresa (whom Catherine referred to disparagingly as "Saint Theresa") saw to it that her son refrained from engaging in foolish alliances with the Russians. But then in November 1780, Maria Theresa died. Freed from the burden of obedience, Joseph embarked on a dangerous course, promising Catherine his support for all Russian treaty relations with the Ottomans. If the Porte declared war, Austria was to "enter the conflict with forces equal to her ally's and within three months of Russian notification."[33] There were technicalities about a treaty, so the two rulers merely exchanged private letters spelling out their obligations. They were to keep these letters strictly secret, locked in their private cabinets. As Habsburg scholar C. A. Macartney remarks, Joseph II was pursuing a foreign policy that was "uniformly unfortunate."[34]

Catherine soon put her new ally to the test. Shagin-Girei, her vassal khan in Crimea, kept taking money from St. Petersburg while ignoring her orders. She decided the time was right to annex the peninsula. Seeking an excuse for opening a conflict with the khan, she made demands of him that she felt certain he would refuse. On September 21, 1782, Catherine wrote Joseph II, asking him to join her in preparing for war if Shagin-Girei rejected her ultimatum. It was at this juncture that Catherine unveiled to Joseph II the details of her Greek Project, which she now expanded to include Austria as her partner.[35] The scheme was nothing less than a mutual aggression pact against the Ottoman Empire. Making a claim that future czars would trot forth regularly during arguments for invading the Balkans, Catherine declared that the Porte was steadily declining (the "Sick Man" syndrome). The time seemed ripe, she told the Emperor, to drive the Ottomans back to Asia. Once they were forced out, the Turks' former European provinces were to be reorganized, with two Christian buffer states between Austria and Russia. One state was to encompass the Danubian Principalities and Bessarabia. The second state was to be a restored "Greek Empire" under the suzerainty of her grandson, Constantine.[36] Russia would expand its borders to the Black Sea. Austria was to receive Turkish territory in the western Balkans (Serbia, Bosnia and

Herzegovina). "No matter how remote and grandiose these views may appear," the Empress told her startled ally, "I think that little exists that is impossible for the might of our two states, in the close unity between them."[37] For Joseph this must have been a telling moment. So-called "greatness" was being thrust upon him. But perhaps he now had the good sense to confront an unwelcome truth. He was no Frederick the Great. At any rate he refused to commit.

Accepting Joseph II's noncommittal response with equanimity, Catherine pared down her scheme, returning to the immediate goal, the annexation of Crimea.[38] While Joseph agreed to use political pressure at the Porte to help the Empress achieve her goals, he refused to join her in invading the peninsula. At that, Catherine lost patience, declaring that she would make this move with or without help from her Austrian ally. On April 14, 1783, she sent Potemkin a note, saying "When the cake will be baked, each will have an appetite."[39]

Crimea had been colonized by the Greeks, occupied by the Romans, overrun by Genghis Khan's hordes. Now the Russians took their turn at the territory. The annexation was accomplished on July 19, 1783, without significant bloodshed.

Potemkin was given the job of developing Catherine's newly acquired territories. Having transformed a frontier region inhabited by bandits and pirates into a relatively prosperous part of the Russian Empire in just seven years, he was expected to perform similar miracles in Crimea. Among other things, he was to build roads, organize agriculture and modernize the ports. Goaded by the Empress, Potemkin rose to the task. He brought in thousands of colonists, provided them with what they needed to live and thrive, including livestock, plows, melon seeds, mulberries and silkworms.

The crown jewel among the Russians' southern

acquisitions was to be a port and shipyard at the village of Akhtiar, which Potemkin renamed Sevastopol. Catherine put Admiral Thomas Mackenzie, who had helped destroy the Turkish fleet at Chesme, in charge of building the port. Potemkin was to oversee construction of the Black Sea Fleet. Since the region lacked quality timber needed for the ships, Potemkin used barges to bring oak logs down the Dnieper from Poland. He built vineyards, established botanical gardens and organized a 65-piece orchestra consisting of hunting horns, each of which sounded only one note.[40]

Naturally the colonization didn't always go smoothly. Many of Crimea's Muslim inhabitants engaged in a silent protest against the alien lifestyle being imposed on them. Substantial numbers of Tatars fled the region, taking their herds with them.[41] As one might imagine, the Ottomans were furious at the Russians' theft of much of their European territory.

And then Catherine had the audacity to set out on a triumphal journey to Crimea to inspect her new naval base at Sevastopol – only a day's sailing from Constantinople. The Empress departed from Kiev in 1787 just after Easter, in a procession headed by seven Roman-style galleys, specially ordered by Potemkin. Catherine's galley was decorated in red brocade and gold. It had its own orchestra. The entourage was followed by 80 support crafts.[4243]

At Kherson, just north of Crimea, seamen from 200 merchant ships greeted the Empress. Many of the ships were Russian vessels. Peter the Great would have been proud. At the Empress's urging, on May 7, Joseph II joined the group although he was in poor health. The Austrian Emperor's presence raised rumors that the two monarchs intended to partition Turkey in Europe, which was, of course, not the case.

The Greek inscription above the gate where Catherine departed gave silent testimony to where she was heading. It said: "This is the way to Byzantium."

The royal procession arrived at Sevastopol where the port swarmed with Russian troops. Seamen stood in formation aboard the vessels that had crowded into the harbor. Soldiers watched the spectacle from nearby hills. Potemkin presented Catherine with her own Black Sea Fleet – three 66-gun ships, three 50-gun frigates and 10 smaller vessels.[44] Even as the ceremony proceeded, the air was filled with the sound of more warships under construction.

The Russians' audacity was more than the Turks could bear. Here was the Empress watching a display of naval strength on what, until 1774, had been the Sultan's lake.[45] The Turks presented Catherine with an ultimatum. She was to remove her troops from the region permanently, give up her claims to territory, and allow the Porte to search Russian ships in Turkish waters. On August 16, 1787, the Sultan's representatives demanded the return of Crimea and declared war the same day. Catherine wept when she signed her own war declaration, her secretary noted in his diary. She may have had a premonition that her second conflict with the Turks would not go her way.

The Russian winter campaign of 1787-88 got off to a bad start. Some of the ships came out of the Sevastopol port to engage the Turks and got caught in a gale, scattering their forces. One vessel was lost to the Turks. Catherine promised Potemkin more ships. Potemkin complained of feeling poorly and said he wanted to resign. There was no way she would agree to that. By now the two were acting like an old married couple.[46] Sounding like Dame Pertelote in Chaucer's "Nun's Priest's Tale," who dismissed her rooster "husband's" disturbing dreams by advising him to take a laxative, she told Potemkin he simply had gas in his stomach.

Casting about for ways to salvage her war effort, Catherine recruited foreign commanders, including John Paul Jones, the Scottish-American "corsair," known for "multiplying fear and trembling in the foe," as the Empress told Potemkin. Jones' service to the empire failed to produce the desired results. In 1789 he was accused of raping a young girl. Although the case never came to trial, he soon left Russia for good. John Paul Jones, declared Catherine, was "a wrongheaded fellow ... very worthy to be celebrated by a rabble of detestable creatures."[47] (Meaning, one assumes, Americans.)

Although Joseph II viewed the campaign against the Ottomans with foreboding, he was tired of watching Catherine catapult from one victory to another while Austria got nothing. A *casus foederis* did exist, for, although all the real aggression was coming from Russia, it was the Porte, skillfully egged on by Prussia, that had opened hostilities.

Joseph II, honoring his treaty obligations with Russia, on February 9, 1789, declared war on Turkey. Then, writes Macartney, "a sort of madness" seemed to seize the Emperor. While he was only bound to provide an auxiliary corps of 30,000 men, Joseph II sent 200,000 troops to the Turkish frontier.[48] The Austrians took Belgrade on September 27, 1789, and occupied Bucharest on November 4. These early successes were, however, followed by a series of defeats.[49] Frederick II mobilized on the Habsburg frontier. Joseph II, who had allied himself with Russia hoping to protect the monarchy from Frederick II, now found himself in danger of being thrust into the jaws of the Prussian monster. A Prussian attack on Austria seemed imminent.

Joseph II and Austria were spared this likely disaster as death claimed the Emperor on February 20, 1790.

The days of cooperation between Austria and Russia were soon past. The new Habsburg Emperor, Leopold II, "bowed to the Prussian menace," in Macartney's words, (and to worries about the situation in France, where Marie Antoinette, the youngest sister of Joseph and Leopold, was in danger of losing her head to revolutionaries). Leopold II signed a convention with the Prussians on July 27, 1790, agreeing to start peace talks with the Porte, essentially restoring the prewar status quo. Wenzel Anton von Kaunitz, the Austrian Chancellor, and others, viewed the convention as a diplomatic retreat. It did bring an end to the alliance with Russia but, in Macartney's opinion, Emperor Leopold made a wise move. "It marked ... a retreat from forward positions which Joseph had tried to occupy, but most of those had been entirely untenable,"[50] Macartney wrote.

In August 1791, with Russian troops so close to Constantinople that guns could be heard in the city, the Turks opted for peace. The Porte accepted the Russians' annexation of Crimea and agreed to their acquisition of Ochakov. The Treaty of Jassy, between Russia and Turkey, on January 9 of the following year, advanced the Russian frontier to the Dniester River.

Catherine the Great was never to realize her Greek Project, but it would continue to roll around in the heads of her successors. She set the bar high for future Russian rulers who felt compelled to try for the gold, wasting their empire's blood and treasure in the quest for Constantinople and the Straits.

Catherine died on November 6, 1796, after suffering a stroke. She was 67 years old. Her son, Paul, succeeded his mother to the throne. Paul had been taken from Catherine when he was an infant. He never had the chance to develop a relationship with his mother. He showed no grief at her passing. Two days after her death, Paul ordered his father exhumed, had him loaded in an elaborate sarcophagus and placed beside his mother as she lay in state. Peter III and Catherine II, sovereigns so at odds in life, received a joint burial, with a period of mourning for them both to last one year.

Paul I's ascension came at a critical time in European history. That same year, Napoleon Bonaparte became Commander-in-Chief of French forces in Italy. From then until his defeat at Waterloo two decades later, the European continent was knee-deep in blood.

Paul pursued a domestic and foreign policy that made him numerous enemies. He imposed a petty tyranny on his subjects, issuing decrees on every aspect of their lives. He terrorized the nobility with violent fits of rage. He turned against the British, declaring them the greatest menace to peace in Europe. He collaborated with the French on an ill-advised expedition against British holdings in India. At one point, he announced that he admired Napoleon.

Some army officers, upset not only at the way he treated them but also at the idea of having such an unsteady hand at the empire's helm, plotted Paul's assassination. They entered the Czar's recently built and well-fortified palace on the night of March 23, 1801. The assassins broke down the door, finding Paul cowering behind a screen. One conspirator hit the Czar on the head with a snuffbox, a second intruder strangled him.

Paul's son and heir,[51] Alexander, knew of the conspiracy but apparently believed his father would be imprisoned, not killed. Alexander was in his room across the courtyard from his father's quarters on the night of the assassination. Alexander's strange behavior in later years often suggested that he was haunted by the memory of that dreadful night and the muffled sounds that he hardly could have avoided hearing.

Like his grandmother, Catherine II, Alexander I dreamed of the day when Byzantium would again be in Orthodox hands. However, sharing a fate with many European rulers of the time, he was forced to defer his dreams while he dealt with Napoleon.

3 SUPPING WITH THE DEVIL

The Napoleonic Wars[1] permanently changed the balance of power in Europe. The Austrian defeat at Austerlitz in 1805 was to have severe consequences for the Habsburgs, leading eventually to the monarchy's loss of its power base in Germany. The Prussian humiliation at Tilsit, where the French Emperor attempted to exclude King Friedrich Wilhelm III from negotiations involving his nation, was compounded by a treaty reducing the proud kingdom to a beggar state.

Czar Alexander I, for his part, emerged after his army's victory over Napoleon in 1812 as the strongest – and, in the eyes of some, the most dangerous – ruler on the continent.

In 1805, Bonaparte's Grande Armée seemed invincible. In October, Napoleon's soldiers defeated the Austrians at Ulm in Bavaria; then they headed for Vienna, 300 miles down the Danube. Habsburg Emperor Franz II (later I) remained in the capital, waiting nervously for Alexander I. He and the Czar, allies in a coalition against the French,[2] had agreed to work together on a battle plan before engaging the Corsican's army. Emperor Franz, recognizing his personal limitations as a warrior, and overestimating the abilities of the Russian Czar, expected Alexander I to take charge of the coalition forces. Weeks passed before the Czar finally joined the Emperor at coalition headquarters. Alexander I's irresponsible behavior would be a major cause of the allies' defeat at Austerlitz. Alexander I had left St. Petersburg on a slow Progress westward in late September 1805. Adam Czartoryski, a nobleman of Lithuanian descent who was the Russian ruler's confidante and adviser, was among those who accompanied the Czar. Czartoryski wrote in his memoirs that "The time had come for the Emperor Alexander to approach the theatre of events. But as the hour of action drew near I perceived that his resolution grew weaker."[3] The Czar's entourage stopped off at the estate of Adam Czartoryski's parents at Puławy in Poland, lingering there for a fortnight. A courier kept the travelers informed about the French army's advance, but the Czar seemed oblivious to the urgency of the situation. Arriving on Berlin on October 25, Alexander tried to persuade the pathologically indecisive King Friedrich Wilhelm III to join the Third Coalition. At Potsdam the Czar and the King took an oath of eternal friendship on the tomb of Frederick the Great. The two rulers signed a treaty in which Friedrich Wilhelm III agreed that, unless Napoleon gave up his claims to Holland, Switzerland and Naples by December 15, Prussia would join the coalition against Napoleon's forces, with one month allowed for preparation for war.

Meanwhile, the French forces were heading down the Danube to Vienna. On November 13 they reached the gates of the Austrian capital. The Habsburg army, unable to defend the city, fell back to Olmütz (Olomouc), a heavily fortified town in Moravia. Emperor Franz II (I), still unclear as to the Czar's whereabouts, left Vienna to join his troops. Napoleon entered the Habsburg capital two days later at the head of his army. The French officers made themselves at home, taking advantage of the city's cultural attractions.

Some of the officers even attended the premier performance of Beethoven's opera, *Fidelio*, with the composer conducting the orchestra.

From Berlin, Alexander proceeded to Weimar, where his sister lived. During his visit, he enjoyed the company of literary lions, including German poet and dramatist Wolfgang von Goethe. Napoleon, in the meantime, left Schönbrunn, the Habsburg residential palace on the outskirts of Vienna, where he had been spending a few days of respite. He headed for Brünn (Brno), a town some 40 miles from Olmütz, where after arriving he immediately put the final touches on plans for a military showdown with the Russians and Austrians.

On the evening of November 18, eight weeks after he had left St. Petersburg, Alexander I finally appeared in Olmütz, where the coalition forces were regrouping. General Mikhail Kutuzov and his army of 73,000 men staggered in from Bavaria. Alexander I had placed the general in command of a joint Russian-Austrian army whose mission was to block the French advance on Vienna. However, by the time Kutuzov's forces arrived in Bavaria, the French had defeated the Austrians at Ulm. The Russian troops retreated, dodging Napoleon's forces as they struggled to make their way to Moravia. Many of Kutuzov's soldiers arrived at army headquarters in no condition to fight. They had subsisted for weeks on frozen potatoes without salt. Their boots were worn out, their uniforms ragged.[4]

Kutuzov was adept at reading military tea leaves. He had spent years in the service of Empress Catherine II (the Great), playing key roles in three Russo-Turkish wars. (In 1773, during fighting in Crimea, he had lost his sight in one eye.) He then served in the army of Czar Paul.

Kutuzov's long experience with warfare should have been an asset to the Russians as they drew up plans for the coming confrontation with Napoleon. During initial strategy sessions involving the Czar and his advisers, the General warned against undue haste in engaging the Corsican's troops. Austrian reinforcements would soon be arriving from Italy, he said, and the Prussians also were expected to join the coalition. The additional forces, totaling well over 200,000, would give the allies a good chance of victory. Nobody listened to the General's advice. The Czar insisted on an immediate attack on the French. General Kutuzov, out of respect for royalty, said nothing. During the final planning session before what became known as the Battle of Austerlitz, he is said to have feigned sleep in order to avoid making statements that would offend the Czar.

Czar Alexander I had surrounded himself with fawning young aides-de-camp from aristocratic families. They swaggered about in tight new uniforms with colorful sashes, their chests ablaze with decorations. These brash royals bragged that they would make short shrift of Napoleon's army.[5] Alexander I, puffed up with anticipated glory, refused to heed saner voices urging him to leave the command to military professionals. He decided that he, himself, would lead his troops to battle. Having dallied for weeks, he now was in a hurry. He wanted war and he wanted it now.

By this time Napoleon had meticulously mapped out every aspect of the coming battle. He sent a spy, a General Savary, to Olmütz, ostensibly to talk peace but actually to evaluate the strength of the allies' forces. According to a French army bulletin, the general reported that those around the Czar were "conceited fops,"[6] and that the Russians involved in military planning were presumptuous, imprudent, and thoughtless.[7] The coalition troops would face a professionally led army whose commander, Napoleon, cared about his soldiers' well-being.

Napoleon decided to give battle at a location some 15 miles southeast of Brünn. At that spot, the Pratzen plateau stretched for several miles. It ended in rolling fields that spilled into a valley with ponds and marshes, offering their own hazards in a Central European winter. Three miles back from the main valley lay the Kaunitz estate with its small palace, Austerlitz (now Slavkov).

Alexander I chose as his main military adviser an Austrian general named Weyrother, with whom the Czar had become acquainted during his visit to Pulawy, the estate of Prince Czartoryski's parents. In his memoirs, the Prince noted with concern that Weyrother "had obtained much influence over Alexander's mind."[8] Weyrother was a practiced flatterer who habitually peppered his conversation with irrelevant details. Emperor Franz was surprised that Alexander put his faith in Weyrother, who was not respected among the monarchy's officer ranks. However, the Emperor did not protest. He deferred to what he believed was the superior judgment of the young Czar.

In preparation for the battle, coalition troops had taken up positions on the Pratzen plateau. The French army was encamped on the plain below. Weyrother persuaded those in command to abandon the heights, to descend to the plain, and to surround Napoleon's forces, with the goal of blocking the way to Vienna. Napoleon, on the other hand, intended to take the Pratzen heights, which he considered as key to his army's success.

Alexander I arose at dawn on December 2. He rode with a few of his aides to the Pratzen plateau to inspect the troops before they took positions against the enemy. The sun began to penetrate the heavy mist, but the movement of the French forces was not yet visible.[9] Alexander, suddenly losing his nerve, ordered General Kutuzov to take command. The Czar's about-face came too late to prevent disaster. Around eight in the morning, the allied army, acting on Weyrother's advice, abandoned the plateau. The coalition troops immediately came under attack.

The mist cleared. The sun rose, revealing the unfolding debacle. Kutuzov, aware of Weyrother's enormous mistake, tried to keep as many troops as possible on the heights to resist the French onslaught.[10] The French occupied the plateau and installed artillery on the heights. They bombarded the allies, who, an hour later, were in full flight. The battle lasted until late afternoon, but its outcome was evident much sooner. The Russians sustained the majority of the day's casualties. They blamed the Austrians for the catastrophe.

The Romanov pattern of expecting Habsburg rulers to further czarist interests rather than to act on behalf of the monarchy, already was evident at Austerlitz. These czarist expectations would lead to a breach between Nicholas I, Alexander I's successor and brother, and young Emperor Franz Joseph early in the Habsburg ruler's long reign (1848-1916). Franz Joseph's failure to join his imperial brother, Czar Nicholas, in a war of aggression against the Turks (later known as the Crimean War), left the Romanov ruler permanently embittered. Each of three succeeding Czars – Nicholas I's son, Alexander II; his grandson, Alexander III and his great-grandson, Nicholas II – found new reasons to hate the Habsburgs in general and Franz Joseph in particular. The almost biblical feud between the House of Romanov and the House of Habsburg was to last for 60 years before ending on the battlefields of World War I.

On the battlefield in Moravia, in 1805, snow fell and December's darkness descended on the day's carnage. Emperor Franz headed to the village of Czeitsch where he found lodging and soon went to sleep. Shells were still falling as Alexander I, grief stricken and humiliated, rode away from the battlefield. The Czar showed up at the little house where Emperor Franz was staying, and the two rulers had a brief, cold conversation. The Austrian Emperor saw no alternative except to make peace; the Czar wasn't ready to acknowledge defeat.

Napoleon waited at the nearby Austerlitz chateau, where the next day he received Emperor Franz's envoy, Prince Liechtenstein. A meeting between the French and Austrian rulers was arranged for December 4 at Göding beneath a burnt out windmill – this was Napoleon's attempt to humiliate the Austrian monarch. Franz mainly wanted to be back with his large family, whom he dearly loved. He agreed to an armistice. It included a provision requiring the Russian army to leave Austria.

Alexander headed for St. Petersburg. The Russian people, hundreds of miles away from the theater of operations, still had only a vague idea of the extent of the disaster. Although the Czar knew that what had happened was largely his fault, he didn't want to admit he was fallible.

Officially, the Austrians were blamed for everything, as a letter from the Czar's wife, Elizabeth, to her mother shows:

"Their infamous conduct, to which we owe this reversal, has caused me inexpressible indignation. There are no words to tell what one feels at the sight of an entire nation that is cowardly, treacherous, foolish, and has, in short, all the vilest qualities ... Despite their reverses and the betrayal all around them, our excellent troops have acquired a new glory even in the eyes of their enemies and inspire the liveliest enthusiasm in their compatriots. These soldiers are angels, martyrs, and heroes at the same time. They were dying of hunger, collapsing on the spot from starvation, and asked only to fight..."[11]

The Czar followed an adviser's suggestion that he stage an entertainment, a ball and supper, in the Hermitage theater, "so as to disarm any who did not share in the general rejoicing."[12] The public celebrated the supposed victory. Nikolai Novosiltsev, a confidante of Alexander I, wrote an acquaintance on January 6, 1806, that he and his friends had returned to St. Petersburg anxious at what they would find there. They were astonished to learn that St. Petersburg "was in seventh heaven over the distinguished way ... (the) army had conducted itself ... and asked for nothing better than to begin (fighting) again immediately after the battle."[13] That had not been possible, people said, because the Austrians had surreptitiously concluded an armistice. In short, wrote Novosiltsev, the public believed that the Austrians were "real traitors" who had "sold out to France."[14] Novosiltsev then told what happened as the troops started staggering in with tales of the real reason for the Russians' defeat. The population, learning the truth, turned against the Czar, accusing him, "and him alone" of causing the fiasco.[15]

The Romanov family never acknowledged the truth. They continued to blame the Habsburgs for the disastrous outcome of the battle. As Emperor Franz Joseph was to learn later, the Romanovs were practiced in the art of self-deception.

The House of Habsburg never fully recovered from the defeat at Austerlitz. Capitalizing on his victory, Napoleon persuaded the German princelings of southern and western Germany to break away from the Holy Roman Empire, long a symbol of Habsburg authority and prestige, and to join his Confederation of the Rhine. The Germans' mass defection made inevitable the demise of the Holy Roman Empire, which dated back to AD 800, when Pope Leo III crowned Charlemagne King of the Romans. From 1453 on – except for a brief period following the death of Emperor Charles VI, who left no male heir – the Habsburgs had held the imperial crown and the title of Holy Roman Emperor. Over the centuries the Holy Roman Emperor had gradually lost some of his royal prerogatives, with a Reichstag (parliament) in Frankfurt, Germany taking charge of many day-to-day affairs. However, the Holy Roman Emperor continued to hold a privileged and powerful position. He had at his command an enormous household to help him fulfill his obligations. Among his prerogatives: He could propose, approve and veto laws; pardon and confer privileges, and found universities and legitimize children. In 1806, Franz II, bowing to the inevitable end of the institution over which he and his ancestors had presided, abdicated as Holy Roman Emperor, taking the far less impressive title of Franz I, Emperor of Austria. The monarchy's loss of influence in Germany, its traditional source of strength, put the Habsburg Empire on a downward trajectory.

The Habsburg Emperor temporarily sought comfort in the company of his family. Now another scene opened on the European stage, this one involving King Friedrich Wilhelm III. The King's vacillation, as natural to him as breathing, caused his enemies to gather like vultures, eager to feast on the King's weakness. The giant among these vultures was, of course, Napoleon.

With French incursions into Prussia continuing, Alexander I in 1806 promised the King that Russia would guarantee his kingdom's territory and independence. Buoyed by his Russian benefactor's offer of support, the King sent Napoleon an ultimatum demanding that French soldiers leave Prussia immediately. As might be expected, Napoleon was furious. As always, when he was furious, he acted. He led his powerful army into Prussia, crushing King Friedrich Wilhelm's forces at Jena and Auserstadt, then entering Berlin. The frightened Prussian King and Queen Louise fled the capital, taking refuge in a desolate eastern region of their kingdom. Prussia's proud citizens, their imaginations still heady with remembered victories of the Great Frederick, were aghast.

Responding to a desperate call for help from the Prussian King, the Czar honored his obligations. Stirring his peasant subjects to fight on behalf of the Prussians, who were generally regarded with suspicion in Russia, wasn't easy. The Holy Synod in Russia did his part to help the Czar, focusing the public's attention on the evil French despot's despoiling of Europe. He required prelates to read an anathema following Sunday mass and on holy days, accusing Napoleon of being "a disturber of the sacred peace of the world, an enemy of Orthodox Christian religion, a shameless supporter of the Infidels, a convert to the cause of the Koran, a propagator of the cult of idols, and a builder of synagogues who wanted to gather the Jews together and declare himself their Messiah."[16]

It is, however, likely that many of the peasants, called from their smoky hovels to participate in the Czar's Prussian project, lacked enthusiasm for the fight. The Russians were defeated at Eylau (Bagrationovsk). In another battle on June 14, 1807, at Friedland (Pravdinsk), the czarist forces retreated after losing more than a third of their troops.

Although Alexander's troops had performed poorly, Napoleon didn't want the bother of fighting them while he was pursuing other European conquests. He consequently devised a scheme to divert the Czar's attention from the northern theater of war. Aware of the Romanovs' obsession with Constantinople and the Balkans, the French ruler decided to stir up trouble there. He sent an ambassador to the Porte with instructions to make an alliance between France, Turkey and Persia.[17] His emissary was to demand that the Porte close the Bosphorus to the Russians; forbid Greeks from sailing under the Russian flag; arm Turkish fortifications against the Russians, and reassert the Porte's absolute control over Moldavia and Wallachia, which remained in Russian hands. The timid Sultan, Selim III, rushed to comply with Napoleon's demands. He dismissed the pro-Russian hospodars in the Danubian Principalities. A few weeks later he closed the Straits to Russian warships.[18] As Napoleon anticipated, these developments got the Czar's attention. Alexander I threatened an immediate attack on the Bosphorus. The Sultan, apparently fearing the evil at hand more than he feared the distant Corsican conqueror, backed down. He even reinstated the pro-Russian hospodars, but his attempts to restore calm came too late. Fearing that the French would cross into Moldavia and Wallachia from Dalmatia, which Napoleon's forces had recently occupied, the Czar, in November 1806, sent 40,000 soldiers into the Principalities. On 16 December the Sublime Porte declared war on Russia.[19]

Faced with a Balkan conflict and stunned by the heavy losses incurred from his efforts to defend the Prussian monarch, Czar Alexander I sought an accommodation with the French conqueror. It was to include an understanding about the fate of Prussian lands. Although the Czar knew a respite in fighting would probably be temporary, it would give him time to regroup his forces. Napoleon agreed to talk.

The resulting meeting of the two Emperors was to leave a lasting scar on the German psyche. It took place on a hazy summer's day in June 25, 1807, at the River Neman, the boundary between Russia and the wide patch of European territory to the west that had recently been laid to waste by Napoleon. Alexander refused to set foot on soil under French domination. The Corsican, indulging in a penchant for theatrics, arranged for the meeting on a raft, placed precisely in the middle of the river. A pavilion, looking a little like an imperial doghouse, was installed on the floating structure. A door on the Russian entrance bore the insignia "A" and one on the other an "N." On the Russian side of the river, courtiers clustered around a dilapidated cottage where the Czar awaited the arrival of Europe's most infamous adversary.

The barrel shaped, stumpy-legged Corsican soon appeared on the river's opposite bank. As his waiting troops cheered, Napoleon dismounted his horse and climbed into a boat. The Russian Czar watched from the other bank. Then, he too stepped into a boat, where rowers were poised to ferry him to the raft. Napoleon Bonaparte, competitive as always, spurred his oarsmen on so that their craft arrived slightly ahead of that of the Czar. The Corsican pressed forward to greet the Russian Emperor, acting the gracious host.

King Friedrich Wilhelm III of Prussia, "uninvited,

remained in disgrace on the right bank of the Neman, his eyes fixed on the makeshift structure in which his fate was to be decided,"[20] writes Troyat. Urging his horse down the bank and into water up to the animal's flanks, the King sat without moving.[21]

The Emperors talked. Napoleon paced back and forth. Those present said the meeting seemed to go well. On the following day, at Alexander's urging, Friedrich Wilhelm III was permitted to join the talks, which continued later at nearby Tilsit. Napoleon made it clear that the King was an unwelcome joker in the political deck. Out of earshot of the King, Napoleon railed against the Prussian monarch, telling the Czar, "He's a contemptible King, it's a contemptible nation, a contemptible army, a country which has deceived everyone and does not deserve to exist. Everything [Prussia] is keeping, she owes to you."[22]

Prussia, as it turned out, wasn't keeping much. The treaty, signed on July 7, 1807, left the kingdom with huge debts, its population diminished, its army cut. "Tilsit had reduced Prussia to the status of a third-class Power,"[23] writes Harold Nicolson, a British diplomat and author.

Many Prussians reacted to the humiliation at Tilsit by determining that they, as the political and military heirs of Frederick the Great, never again would allow their people to be humiliated in such a fashion. Many influential thinkers contributed to a rising national consciousness. Later, in a united Germany, Otto von Bismarck and then Kaiser Wilhelm II preached a gospel of exceptionalism. Eventually many Germans came to view themselves as God's chosen representatives of culture on earth. German leaders, encouraged by the Kaiser himself, declared the empire's right to a "place in the sun" – taking care to do this loudly, so no one missed it.

Napoleon continued his European rampage. However, in February 1808, the Corsican surprised Alexander I by suggesting that the two monarchs meet to discuss ways to cooperate. Behind the French ruler's suggestion was his wish to shield against any Habsburg attempt to get revenge for their army's defeat at Austerlitz. Napoleon believed that, arm in arm with Russia, it would be possible to show the Habsburgs how insignificant they were in European affairs.[24]

Alexander I agreed to the meeting, to be held at the end of September of that year, at Erfurt, in central Germany. Like Napoleon, the Czar knew exactly what he wanted to achieve. In exchange for the security that Russian friendship would provide the French, he hoped to be allowed a free hand against the Ottomans. The last of the Romanov czars, Nicholas II, would engage in an alliance with the French prior to the First World War, for the same reason.

Napoleon swung into action, instructing court dignitaries to plan festivities presenting him as a second Charlemagne. Everyone of cultural or political eminence in Germany was invited to attend – unless they were Prussian or Austrian subjects. The King of Prussia and the Emperor of Austria were, of course, not on the guest list.

Napoleon rode out toward Weimar to greet Alexander I, meeting him in Mönchenholzhausen, a few miles from Erfurt. The Corsican provided the Czar with a horse from the French royal stables, which, in the Russian's honor, sported an ermine saddle. Bells pealed, guns roared, drums beat. In the days that followed, the two rulers went to the theater and attended concerts. Napoleon seemed to believe his overtures to the Czar were succeeding. Even Alexander's mother and sister suspected that the Czar was taken in by the devious Corsican. Alexander was playing the dupe, convincingly.

Finally, the conversation became serious. Napoleon proposed that France and Russia join forces to strike a final blow against Austria. Alexander I wouldn't hear of it. It seems that Charles Maurice de Talleyrand, the controversial French diplomat, had persuaded Alexander I to join Austria in restraining Napoleon, rather than to collude with the French Emperor in destroying what remained of Habsburg power in Europe.[25]

On October 14, the two Emperors rode out together toward Weimar. They dismounted at Mönchenholzhausen where they talked for a long time. There were no plans for Alexander to come to Paris or for Napoleon to visit St. Petersburg. Napoleon and Alexander never met again.

Napoleon's campaign of terror continued. Nothing stopped him, not even Emperor Franz I's sacrifice of his oldest and best loved daughter, Marie Louise, who in 1810 was married off to the Corsican in the hopes of settling him down. Marie Louise was as malleable as fine, wet clay, and Napoleon seems to have loved her, but not so much that he was willing to abandon his lust for conquest. He prepared for his most formidable challenge. He would fight the Russians on their own soil.

Anticipating a French invasion of Russia, Alexander I in May 1812 concluded a hasty but fruitful peace with the Porte. The Russians received the right to annex Bessarabia. Serbia was granted autonomy, which suited the Russians nicely since it gave them an opportunity to send in administrators to "help" the local populace. While the Sultan's authority was confirmed in the Danubian Principalities, that too favored the Russians, since the traditional hospodar administrations (purportedly pro-Russian) were to be reinstated.[26] The Russians hadn't forgotten that the road to Byzantium went through the Balkans.

Napoleon's campaign in Russia was one of the notable disasters in the history of warfare. The Russian defense strategy required huge sacrifices from the local populace, involving their trashing foodstuffs, destroying animals and even burning houses prior to the arrival of the French army. The French forces finally occupied Moscow, on September 14, 1812, expecting not only a fight but a source of badly needed provisions. They got neither. The Russians had torched the city and withdrawn. There was little left for the sacking, certainly few of the full larders and wine cellars they had anticipated. Still, the French troops pilfered what they could, departing Moscow bent over with paintings and gold vessels and other valuables that they soon had to abandon as they struggled through the whirling, deepening snow. Defeated and hungry, Napoleon's army limped into Paris having suffered 380,000 deaths, most of them due to the cruel Russian winter.

Napoleon's favorable star had dimmed, but conquest of Europe remained in his sights. On August 12, 1813, Emperor Franz reluctantly joined the Russians in yet another coalition against the French. The decision to send troops against Napoleon was for Franz a wrenching decision. The Corsican tyrant was, after all, the husband of Franz's favorite daughter, Marie Louise. Napoleon was also the father of the Emperor's adorable little grandson, Napoleon II, the blond-haired and intelligent child who was heir to the French throne. But the Austrian Emperor saw no alternative: Napoleon had to be stopped.

The allies succeeded, winning a decisive battle at Leipzig on October 18, 1813. Alexander took much of the credit. He now saw himself as an "instrument of divine retribution," and even – according to Metternich – threatened to blow up the Tuileries Palace.[27] Fortunately, the Czar didn't make good on his impulse. Looking much like a Greek god, the handsome Czar rode at the head of coalition forces as they made a glorious entry into Paris on March 31, 1814. Emperor Franz, not wanting to participate in a ceremony that would assure that his daughter, Empress Marie Louise, lost her throne, kept his distance in Dijon. Napoleon, for his part, was soon shipped off to the island of Elba where optimists expected him to spend the rest of his days.

Alexander I's army had vanquished Napoleon. The Czar

should have been the hero at the Congress of Vienna, which convened in the fall of 1814 to restore order to the continent following the European wars. But Alexander I was showing signs of instability. European leaders became worried about what he would do next.

4 POLITICS PLEASING TO GOD

The Congress of Vienna was intended to reorder the map of Europe, so dramatically disordered by the French Revolution and the Napoleonic Wars. Emperors and kings and archdukes and cardinals and ministers flocked to the Habsburg capital, where ceremonies began in October 1814. Czar Alexander I made an ostentatious entry into the city, flanked by a fawning King Friedrich Wilhelm III of Prussia. The Sultan sent a representative; so did the pope. Dignitaries representing some 200 states, principalities and independent cities came, along with 100,000 members of official delegations. Highborn ladies arrived in the Austrian capital, as did women about town and courtesans, dancers and adventurers, writers and speculators, spies, faux aristocrats and palm-readers, alchemists and pickpockets.

Habsburg Emperor Franz I played the convivial host, while grumbling privately about the costs of the extravaganza. Fourteen hundred well-shod horses waited every morning for guests interested in hunting or in riding in the Prater park. Social calendars overflowed with balls and skating parties and opera presentations and concerts. Royals and their friends, weary from years of war and worry, flirted and danced and raised their glasses in hopes of a better future. There had never been such a gathering. There would never again be such a gathering. Prince Klemens von Metternich assumed the lead role at the Congress as master of ceremonies and as a deal broker behind the scenes. Already at this stage the 42-year-old prince was on his way to becoming the most powerful statesman in Europe. Metternich came from an ancient family that possessed vast estates in Germany's Rhineland. As a university student he had been appalled by the bloody aftermath of the French Revolution. He was a dyed in the wool autocrat for whom social unrest was a cardinal sin. He sought to reestablish a balance of power on the continent and to create a mechanism for maintaining peace and stability. Metternich urged rulers and their plenipotentiaries to get on board with what came to be called the "continental coach." In other words, he wanted everyone to head in the same direction in the interest of European unity. Metternich expected to drive the coach. A key question was whether the Russian Czar would go along for the ride.

Czar Alexander I, flush from his army's victory over Napoleon in 1812 and proud of his soldiers' performance in the battle of Leipzig, was the center of attention at the Congress. Emperor Franz I treated the Czar as his honored guest, putting him and his entourage up in the Hofburg, providing them with an entire wing of the imperial palace, and seeing that they wanted for nothing. But the Czar soon wore out his welcome.

Alexander I seemed to believe that as a conquering hero he had the right to cause offense. His frequent public insults to Czarina Elisabeth, whom he had asked to accompany him, didn't go over well at the court. His nocturnal visits, sometimes to several women in one night, shocked even jaded royals. Far more importantly, his temper tantrums and political demands hampered the delegates from making progress in the daunting task of piecing together the shards of a broken Europe.

A clash between Alexander I and Metternich was inevitable. Both men were egoists, accustomed to being the center of attention. Both sought female conquests; sometimes they vied for the favors of the same woman. The Czar as an absolute ruler considered it his God-given right to be obeyed. Metternich, to whom Franz I had turned over the reins of foreign affairs, expected his opinions to be heard and his sage advice followed. He didn't hesitate to challenge the Czar when he thought the Russian ruler was overstepping reasonable bounds.

Metternich deeply mistrusted Alexander I's ideology. Early in his reign, the Czar had flirted with liberalism. He had even approached the British with a scheme for overthrowing Europe's feudal monarchies and installing republican governments in their place. In 1813, the Czar, having spent time with advocates of constitutional government in Switzerland, came away spouting what Metternich considered radical views. On one level Metternich realized that the Czar's opinions were hardly more than passing fancies – or what the Prince disparagingly called "evolutions of mind." Metternich nevertheless took the Russian ruler's utterances to heart.[1] For Metternich, constitutionalism was an anathema, liberalism a plague. In pursuing his campaign for European order, Metternich advocated a series of "reforms," including strict restrictions on press and academic freedom. In 1848, the Austrian minister would pay dearly for his attempts to turn the Habsburg monarchy into a police state, when revolutionists forced him to flee from Vienna fearing for his life. However, in the post-Napoleonic era most Europeans, rulers and citizens alike, welcomed the restoration of order.

At the Congress of Vienna Metternich and Alexander I had a serious quarrel over division of the spoils of war. The Czar had arrived in the Austrian capital expecting that, as

Napoleon's conqueror, he was entitled to parcel out territorial rewards as he saw fit. Metternich thought otherwise. The Austrian minister expected the Powers to decide on the terms of boundary settlements, taking their cues from his own vast experience and sagacity. Alexander I sought to deprive Saxony's King Frederick Augustus of his crown on the grounds that the monarch had only belatedly denounced Napoleon. The Czar demanded that Saxony go to Prussia. King Friedrich Wilhelm III, grateful for the Czar's role in protecting his kingdom against Napoleon, could be expected to behave as a docile Russian vassal. The Habsburgs would not hear of this arrangement. They believed, no doubt correctly, that if Austria were squeezed between a significantly enlarged Prussia and the Russian Empire, the monarchy's survival would be in doubt. Alexander I also insisted that Russia be awarded all of Poland, including territory the Habsburgs had received during previous partitions of that unhappy kingdom. Metternich informed the Czar that Austria would have no objection to the creation of a free Poland under European auspices. However, he said, Austria would never agree to a "puppet Poland" with its strings pulled by the Czar.[2] Alexander I went into a rage, telling Metternich he was "the only man in Austria who would dare speak to ... (him) in such rebellious terms."[3] The Czar is said to have unsheathed his sword, suggesting that he and the Austrian minister settle the issue with a duel. Czar Alexander's attitude toward Metternich foreshadowed the problem between the House of Romanov and the House of Habsburg that would lead to the First World War. Alexander I viewed Metternich as "nothing but a permanent obstacle to his intentions, a man relentlessly occupied with thwarting and outwitting him, in fact as a sworn enemy,"[4] wrote diarist Friedrich von Gents. The Czar demanded that Emperor Franz dismiss the Prince. The Austrian monarch refused. The Romanov ruler didn't speak to Metternich for three months afterwards.

With the Prussians threatening war if they didn't get Saxony and with the Russians ready to fight over Poland, a new conflict threatened to break loose at any minute. The British and French were as concerned about this possibility as the Austrians. Viscount Castlereagh, the principal British diplomat at the Congress of Vienna, wondered if the Czar intended to make Napoleon Bonaparte his role model.[5] In response to what the three Powers perceived as an imminent threat, on January 3, 1815, Austria, Britain and France signed a secret treaty promising to resist Russian expansion in Europe. Article V called for the appointment of a military commission to create joint plans for use in case Russian armies advanced on Vienna. The Russians, learning of the treaty, backed down. They were as tired of war as anyone in Europe, and decided to negotiate instead of again taking up arms.

The final peace agreement in Vienna, reached on February 11, 1815, allowed Austria and Prussia to retain the provinces of Galicia and Posen, respectively. Krakow, along with its environs, was to be a free city. The remaining part of what had been the Duchy of Warsaw, with a population of 3.2 million, was to become the kingdom of Poland, under the Russian Czar. Poland was declared independent; it was to have a constitution. But this was a sham. The constitution was to be granted as a favor from the Russian Czar. Foreign policy was to remain in Russian hands. Within a few years the Russians exerted their authority over Poland, leaving few vestiges of the rights the people supposedly had received.[6]

News reached Vienna on March 7 that Napoleon had escaped from the island of Elba and was heading for Paris. Nevertheless, the delegates continued with their work until they completed the final act of the Congress, which was signed on June 9, 1815. Napoleon's 100 days on the loose ended on June 18, 1815, at Waterloo. That October he was shipped off to St. Helena, a barren island in the South Atlantic, where he never again would ravage the continent.

Europeans felt they could breathe again.

Before the Congress disbanded, Metternich had sought renewal of the secret treaty of January 3 against Russia, but Castlereagh refused to agree to it on grounds that it would be too divisive. In its place, he proposed a warranty in which the signatory powers of the Congress would publicly declare their support for the peace treaty being drafted by the delegates in Vienna, with a promise to back it up with arms if necessary.[7] Castlereagh approached the Czar with a suggestion that the Ottoman Empire be included in this Treaty of Guarantee. Alexander I denounced the British foreign secretary's suggestion. The Czar made it clear that he would brook no military interference from any of the other Powers on issues between Russia and the Ottomans.

The Napoleonic Wars had interfered with the Romanovs' latest military adventure in the Balkans, leading the Czar to complete the Treaty of Bucharest with the Sultan in May 1812. However, now that the Corsican conqueror was out of the way, Alexander I intended to resume his campaign of aggression in the Balkans. The British seemed surprised to discover that the Czar harbored dreams of expansion in the Black Sea and beyond. Nicolson attributes what he seems to consider as newfound Russian interest in the Balkans to the Czar's failure to realize his ambitions in Poland.[8] However, these Russian dreams did not begin with the latest contretemps over Poland, nor were they to end any time soon.

European leaders reassembled in Paris in the summer of 1815 to tie up loose ends on the treaty agreements. The Czar was undergoing another evolution of mind. For some time a mystic named Baroness Julie von Krüdener had pursued Alexander from place to place, claiming she came as an intermediary from God, entrusted with bringing the Czar a special message. This strange envoy, a Latvian by birth, had acquired social status with an early marriage to a Russian diplomat. An admirer of Madame de Staël, but lacking the French writer's genius, the Baroness had attempted, unsuccessfully, to establish herself as a woman of letters. After a series of amatory adventures, she sought solace in religion, falling in with a medium who convinced her of the merits of charlatanism.[9]

Continuing to press herself on the Czar, the Baroness finally was granted an audience. "Although at 50 she was a faded creature with irregular features, a blotchy complexion, a pointed nose and a blond wig, Alexander was conquered as soon as he saw her,"[10] writes Henri Troyat. The Czar may have welcomed a respite from his nightly trysts. It is likely that she offered him a way to assuage, at least temporarily, his guilt for failing to intervene when conspirators had entered the nearby rooms of his father, Emperor Paul, and strangled him. Also, the Baroness encouraged him to pursue the Romanov dream of planting a banner at the Hagia Sophia in Constantinople.

Alexander I became the woman's disciple. When she arrived in Paris, he set her up at a hotel near the Élysée Palace. The Czar visited his mystical friend almost every evening. He and the Baroness immersed themselves in the Scripture. The two would "comment on the sweet teachings with tears in their eyes and talk about the best way to conduct politics in a manner pleasing to God,"[11] writes Troyat. On one occasion, the diplomat Chateaubriand joined the prayer vigil, coming away openmouthed: "Madame von Krüdener had invited me to one of these sessions of celestial sorcery ... Although I am a man of dreams and fancies, I hate unreason, abominate the nebulous, and despise charlatanism ... I could find nothing to say to God, and the Devil was tempting me to laugh."[12]

The Czar's obsession with the Baroness and her message, and his religious fixation - so extreme it amounted to self-flagellation – flabbergasted delegates at the Paris conference. But it was their realization that Alexander's religious mania had political undertones that set the other

rulers on edge. On September 11, the Czar tore himself
away from his spiritual séances long enough to dazzle, and
disturb, spectators with a display of Russian military force
on the plain of Vertus, some 80 miles east of Paris. The
spectacle, which involved 150,000 men and 96 generals, was
staged at the Catalaunian fields where in AD 451, the
Romans had put down the hordes of Attila the Hun.
Madame von Krüdener, prominently seated in a court
barouche, beamed at the statesmen gathered to witness the
carefully choreographed maneuvers.[13] At a place so replete
with historical significance and present implications, it was
hardly surprising that people became suspicious of this
strange ruler from a vast and faraway land.

During his stay in Paris, Alexander's religious exaltation
took another bizarre twist. He called on his brother
monarchs in Prussia and Austria to join him in what he
called a Holy Alliance, "a solemn declaration of international
fraternity and submission to the commandments of the
Bible." Its signatories were to pledge to take as their own
rule of conduct the precepts of justice, charity and peace.
The Czar was proud of this abstract and profoundly
meaningless document, which purported to unite sovereigns
of rival beliefs – Orthodox, Catholic and Protestant. The
king of Prussia, Friedrich Wilhelm III, readily agreed to such
a profession of faith. Emperor Franz was hesitant to launch
into mysticism but signed the agreement after Metternich
urged him to do so, seeing in it a chance to make a united
front against revolutionary plotters and other enemies of the
peace. The English, suspicious of Russian intentions,
refused to sign. The pope declined to sign because the
document did not make distinctions between the three
faiths. The Sultan wasn't about to sign, since the fraternity
was "formed under the sign of the cross."[14]

The Sultan had reason to suspect Alexander I and the
eccentric Baroness. Constantinople was the focal point of
her mystic vision. While the Czar eventually brushed off his

strange friend as a nuisance and a bore, her last message to him encouraged him to fulfill the Romanov destiny. Blaming her enemies for keeping her from the Czar, she wrote, "They are tormenting you, they have even separated me from my brother! (the Czar) May you rise again greater than ever before and follow the celestial Bridegroom under the banners of the Cross; may you see it placed above the Church of St. Sophia and worship Jesus Christ on the steps of the mosque, which will have become the temple of the living God."[15]

The Holy Alliance left a legacy of unease in Europe. While many of the continent's statesmen took it to mean that Russia, Prussia and Austria intended to dominate the continent, it was on Russia that they focused most attention.[16] British Whig politician Thomas Creevey spelled out common concerns: "We long-sighted old politicians see a fixed intention on the part of Russia to make Constantinople the seat of her power and to re-establish the Greek church upon the ruins of Mohammedanism. A new crusade, in short, by a new and enormous power, and brought into the field by our own selves and one that may put our existence at stake to drive out again."[17] The long-sighted prophecy was only partly correct. In 1914, instead of attempting to drive the Russians out of the Balkans, the British marched with them as they made their final attempt to realize Peter the Great's dream at Constantinople and the Straits.

During the years after the Congress of Vienna, Metternich held forth as high priest of European order. At five Congresses (known as the Concert of Europe) he exhorted the Powers to stand up for order and to stand fast against revolution. At the first Congress, at Aix-la-Chapelle in 1818, crowned heads and ministers outdid themselves in proclaiming moral solidarity. A reconciliation seemed to be under way between Metternich and the Czar. The Prince's daughter, Marie Esterhazy, even reported to her mother that she had seen her father and Alexander I walking arm in arm on one occasion.[18]

Later gatherings of the Concert were less harmonious. When Metternich provided the European Powers with details of his plan for repressing political unrest, the British and French drew back. By 1820 it became clear that revolutionists hadn't abandoned their efforts to rid Europe of the old order and to move toward constitutional government. Citizen unrest was reported in Spain, Portugal, Naples and Piedmont – places with a long Habsburg history.

That year the Concert of Europe reconvened at Troppau in Silesia, a dreary town with streets that became mired in mud as winter approached. Perhaps the lack of diversions gave the Czar time to reflect. At any rate, he summoned Metternich to an audience in which he made a confession. Alexander I told the Austrian minister that his understanding of European politics had been flawed. In 1813 while visiting Switzerland he had fallen under the spell of liberalism. The Czar said that, with revolutionaries now stirring up trouble in Naples and elsewhere, he realized the dangers of that ideology. "You have not changed but I have," the Czar told the startled Metternich. "Between 1813 and 1820, seven years have elapsed," he said, "but to me these seven years have been as long as a century ... You have nothing with which to reproach yourself, but I cannot say the same for myself."[19]

Alexander I's conversion brought its own complications. Like many people who experience a religious epiphany, the Czar now showed extraordinary zeal for the Metternichian gospel of order. Many in European court circles, already discomfited by the Holy Alliance, became even more concerned by the Czar's enthusiastic offers to intervene in European affairs. In the spring of 1822, after the Austrians ordered 80,000 troops to put down an uprising in the Piedmont region of Italy, Alexander I offered to assist by dispatching 90,000 troops to the Austrian border. Echoing the messianic tone of Baroness Krüdener, the Czar declared: "Now I understand why the Lord has kept me here until this moment. How much gratitude do I owe him, for so arranging things that I was still together with my allies."[20] Metternich was pleased by the Romanov gesture of European solidarity. Others in the Austrian government were strongly opposed to czarist intervention, as were the English and French. Fortunately, order was quickly restored in the restive Italian province, preventing a showdown with the European allies. At another gathering of the Concert of Europe in the fall of 1822, this time in Verona, talk turned to unrest in Spain and to the wisdom of sending troops to that nation. The Czar offered to provide 130,000 troops to stamp out the rebellion. Again, Metternich welcomed the Russian show of European unity but many statesmen in Vienna, including Count Johann Graf von Stadion, the finance minister, were vehemently opposed to a Russian troop presence in the heart of the continent. After the French also objected to the Russian offer, the Czar dropped the matter.

During this period, Metternich and the Czar remained on seemingly friendly terms. In a letter to his wife, Eleonore, Metternich wrote that the harmony between Vienna and St. Petersburg "verges on the miraculous."[21] What seemed too good to be true, was just that. Trouble in the Balkans was to cast new clouds over relations between the Habsburgs and the Romanovs.

An uprising in March 1821 by Greek patriots, who sought independence from the Ottomans, brought the Eastern Question again to the forefront, revealing the fragile scaffolding holding the Russians and the Austrians to their vows as members of the Holy Alliance. The revolt was the work of a revolutionary group known as the "Society of Friends," or Philike Hetairia, established by three Greek merchants in Odessa in 1814. The organization's supporters

4 Politics Pleasing to God

included a number of Phanariot officers in the Russian army.[22] In March 1821 one of these officers, General Aleksandr Ypsilanti, an aide-de-camp to Czar Alexander I, led a small group of Greek patriots over the Russian border into the Danubian Principalities (Wallachia and Moldavia). Ypsilanti expected the local Orthodox population to rush to join the uprising. He also thought he would receive the Czar's blessing.

Nothing went as the rebels expected. The Czar, now showing an almost monk-like devotion to Metternichian order, promptly disowned his aide-de-camp. The peasants of the Principalities remained unmoved by Ypsilanti's exhortations, seeing no advantage in exchanging the remote Ottoman sovereignty to which they were accustomed for hands-on Greek-Russian rule.

The forces of Sultan Mahmud II quickly put down the rebellion in the Danubian Principalities, but a war of independence then broke out in the Peloponnese region in southern Greece. The Sultan became convinced that his Orthodox Christian subjects, backed by the Russians, had declared a jihad, or holy war, against the Muslims. Rumors that the Archbishop of Patras had blessed the Christian rebellion against the Ottoman government created hysteria at the Porte. The Sultan brushed aside attempts by Ecumenical Patriarch Gregorius V to assure the Porte that Russia didn't support the uprising.

On Palm Sunday 1821, the Patriarch issued an anathema (a formal curse) bearing his signature and that of 21 other prelates formally condemning the Philike Hetairia and excommunicating Ypsilanti and his principal supporters. The Patriarch ordered prelates and priests to "concur with the church in opposing the rebellion under penalty of suspension, dispossession, and, ultimately, the fires of hell."[23] The anathema was printed and published that same Sunday. There was no convincing the Sultan of the Russians' innocence.

On the following Saturday afternoon, April 22, Ottoman soldiers stormed into the church in Constantinople as the Patriarch was officiating at the liturgy preceding the solemn Easter Vigil. The service was ending. The intruders seized the Patriarch and the officiating bishops and priests, all still in their robes, and threw ropes around their necks. They dragged Gregorius to the gate of the Phanar quarter, hanged him from a hook above the entrance, and left him to slowly choke to death. Three other bishops and two priests were hanged elsewhere in the city. The Patriarch's body remained suspended from the gate for three days. Then it was tied down with weights and thrown into the Golden Horn.[24]

Even in death Gregorius V continued to trouble the Ottomans, to infuriate the Orthodox – and to worry the Austrians. In Russia there were calls for revenge against the Turks, raising the specter of a religious war between the Orthodox Catholics and the Ottoman Muslims. The Patriarch's body failed to decompose. One evening during that same Easter Week, it floated to the surface, near a grain ship involved in trade with Russia. A refugee from the Patriarch's household who was aboard the vessel recognized the bloated corpse and the tattered remains of the Patriarch's vestments. To Orthodox believers, the reappearance of the Patriarch was a sign from the divinity. The Greek captain of the ship retrieved the body and took it to Odessa, where Gregorious received a martyr's funeral and burial. The Patriarch became a symbol of the Hellenic awakening which he had repeatedly denounced during the last weeks of his life.[25]

Czar Alexander I faced a painful situation. The Easter Sunday massacre was a dagger thrust into the heart of his sincere religious beliefs. The Holy Synod of the Russian Orthodox Church urged him to get revenge against the Turks for the assassinations. Nevertheless, the Czar clung to his newfound faith in Metternichian order. It took precedence over all else. He made it clear to everyone concerned, including the Sultan, that he opposed rebellion against any legitimate government, whether Christian or Muslim. The Turks continued their rampage against Orthodox believers. The Czar wrote Metternich in agony, saying that such constant provocation from the Turks was more than he should have to bear.

Metternich determined to do all he could to keep the Russians from war with the Ottomans. The Austrian minister correctly realized that a volatile element had been added to the Eastern Question. Previous Russo-Turkish conflicts had occurred mainly to satisfy czarist territorial ambitions. Now, strong religious outrage threatened to erupt in a conflict that was different in kind from previous wars. Metternich knew that a war motivated by revenge could well bring an end to Turkey in Europe. The Austrian minister's effort to keep the Russians from war with the Ottomans did not stem from any particular fondness for the Ottoman system of administration. Rather, Metternich considered Turkey indispensable as a bulwark against Russian intrusions in the Balkans. He was convinced that if the Ottoman Empire fell the Habsburg Empire would soon meet its end. In letter after letter to the Czar, Metternich warned Alexander against intervention in the Greek-Turkish matter. Emperor Franz I also pressured the Czar to stay out of the conflict.

Demonstrations by Greek revolutionaries in Odessa that summer reinforced the Sultan's belief that the Russians and the Greeks were conspiring against him. In response, he ordered a search of all vessels sailing through the Straits. He also issued an embargo on grain ships. Another Russo-Turkish conflict appeared inevitable. British and Austrian diplomatic pressure led the Sultan to back down, and war was averted.

The Greek uprising and its tragic aftermath had far-reaching consequences. By sanctioning the Patriarch's murder and the desecration of his body during one of the most sacred moments on the Orthodox Church calendar, the Sultan alienated his subjects who were of that faith – some one-fourth of the Ottoman population. In Russia, the massacre stirred sympathy for the sufferings of Orthodox believers living under Ottoman rule. Accounts of Turkish atrocities against people of the "true Orthodox faith" – some of them accurate, some not – would provide future Romanov czars with unimpeachable excuses for furthering their imperialistic ambitions in the Balkans – always with the aim of driving the Turks out of Europe and seizing the Straits and Constantinople.

Pressured by Metternich to abandon any notion of fighting the Turks, but still clinging to Peter the Great's dream, Alexander I now sought to use diplomacy to dismantle the Ottoman Empire peacefully. At the beginning of 1824 he invited the Great Powers to send representatives to St. Petersburg for a congress, aimed at nothing less than settling the Eastern Question once and for all. In a plan highly favorable to Russia, the Czar called for the creation of three autonomous Greek principalities, guaranteed by the other five Great Powers of Europe. The new principalities were to enjoy status similar to that of Moldavia, Wallachia and Serbia, where the Russians were extending their influence by providing administrative assistance. It was evident that the Czar intended to offer similar assistance to the proposed Greek principalities. The Habsburgs refused to support this latest Romanov attempt to make headway toward Constantinople at others' expense, and they weren't alone. None of the Powers, except the Russians, would tolerate this dramatic redrawing of the Balkan map. The Czar's proposal was stillborn.

Alexander I was disappointed but undaunted by his failure to gain support for a full congress in St. Petersburg. He next attempted to organize a series of ambassadorial meetings where he hoped to get authorization for vigorous action against the Turks. The Austrians again blocked the

Czar's path, saying they would never sanction forcible intervention against the Ottoman Empire. Alexander I was outraged. Perhaps he had heard his relatives talk of Peter the Great's complaint that his Austrian allies had treated him "like a dog," by making an untimely peace with the Turks, and thus spoiling Peter's chances of taking his new navy all the way to Byzantium. He may have remembered the scornful reaction of his grandmother, Catherine the Great, to the Austrians' refusal to participate in her Greek Project, which called for dismantling the Turkish Empire and dividing the spoils. Now there was fresh evidence that the Habsburgs were no friends of the Romanovs. Alexander I lashed out at Metternich, accusing him of treating Russian concerns "with casual neglect." The Czar complained that in the seven years since he and the Austrian statesman "had found one another again at (the Congress in) Aix, Metternich had never once favoured specifically Russian interests."[26] The time had come, the Czar said, to change Russian policy. He declared that, henceforth, his foreign minister, Karl Nesselrode, was to pursue exclusively the traditional objectives of the Russian state. With this pronouncement the Czar threw dirt on the grave of the already moribund Holy Alliance.

It would be left for Nicholas I, the Czar's successor, to pursue the Russian dream in the Balkans. Alexander I's hopes of imperial gains at the expense of Turkey never materialized. In his last years the Czar sank into despondency, nursing his mood with gloomy passages from the Old Testament. Alexander is said to have spent so much time praying that he developed large calluses on his knees.[27]

The Czar turned many of the empire's domestic affairs over to Aleksei Arakcheyev, a man who seems to confirm the Elizabethan belief that a man's outward appearance mirrors his soul. He looked "like a workman's tool," with stooped shoulders, a crewcut, and "a thick nose shaped like a shoe..." writes Troyat.[28] Arakcheyev merged the Russian

Ministry of Education with the Ministry of Ecclesiastical matters, in the belief that the Bible was the sole source of knowledge. He viewed himself as an instrument of divine retribution, Old Testament style.

With the approval of Czar Alexander, Arakcheyev executed a scheme for turning whole Russian regions into totally regimented "military colonies" occupied by Russian soldiers and their families. Soldiers training for the army were forced to double as farmers. Required to wear military uniforms at all times, they marched in step to the fields to the sound of drums, where they plowed and chopped weeds and did other farm work. Those who defied their tyrannical master could expect to be caned, to have their noses bitten, or to face other cruel punishments. Residents were required to report every detail of their lives, including the number of eggs their hens laid. Families lived in identical houses, painted either pink of blue, with identical trees and fence posts. Military authorities determined who was to marry whom. Often the choice was made by drawing lots. Coupling was obligatory. There was no private life.

Leaving the empire in the hands of Arakcheyev and other cruel taskmasters, Alexander I and his wife, Czarina Elisabeth, both in poor health, wandered off to Taganrog, the port that Peter the Great had built on the Azov Sea. The Czar died there on December 1, 1825. The Czarina died soon afterwards.

The Czar's repressive policies left a legacy of discontent in the empire. Russia was ripe for an uprising, perhaps another assassination.

5 *"VIVE LA FORCE!"*

The regime of Nicholas I of Russia began in blood and ended in blood. The new Czar, who succeeded Alexander I in December 1825, was cut from a different cloth than was his Bible-believing brother. Taller than most men by a head, with chiseled features and a well-shaped mouth, Nicholas I seemed, to a French travel writer, Marquis de Custine, "more Germanic than Slavic."[1] The Czar called himself "Commander." He intended to be obeyed.

Unlike Czar Alexander I, who often appeared lost in a maze of inner contradictions, Nicholas I never doubted who he was. He was an autocrat, as unyielding as a ramrod. His goals were the same as those of Peter the Great or of his grandmother, the great Catherine. Like his forebearers, he believed that Russia's hope for imperial glory lay in the sun-drenched south.

As a new ruler, Nicholas I's first task was to dispense with a so-called "Decembrist" uprising, led by military officers who challenged his right to succeed Alexander I to power.[2] The Czar's brutal methods were intended to strike terror into anyone who contemplated revolution. Five of those involved in the plot against Nicholas I were executed and many more were sent to Siberia. The Czar even had some of the accused Decembrists thrown live into the Gulf of Finland. Later, passersby could see their corpses floating between cracks in the ice.[3]

Having stifled opposition at home, Nicholas I turned his attention to the Balkans. The Czar intended to show Sultan Mahmud II that, unlike his brother, Czar Alexander I, he had no patience with diplomatic discussions that went nowhere. Tensions between St. Petersburg and the Porte had been high since the onset of the Greek uprising in 1821. The Sultan, convinced that the Russians wanted to destroy the Ottoman Empire, had sent troops into the Danubian Principalities as a defensive measure. He ignored Alexander's demand that he pull his soldiers out of the region.

On March 24, 1826, Nicholas I startled the Turks with an ultimatum giving them six weeks to evacuate the Principalities. The Sultan, taken aback by St. Petersburg's sudden change of tone, yielded to the Czar's demands. Negotiations between the Porte and St. Petersburg were scheduled for that autumn at Akkerman, a small town on the River Dniester near Odessa.[4]

The Russians had viewed the Principalities as part of their sphere of influence since the reign of Catherine II (the Great). In 1774 at Kuchuk Kainarji, a small town in northeastern Bulgaria, the Empress had signed an important treaty with Sultan Mustafa III providing for Russian representation in Constantinople on behalf of Moldavia and Wallachia. (The Sultan retained sovereignty over the Principalities.) As time passed, the Russians increasingly inserted themselves into the region. In the peace of Bucharest, concluded with Turkey in 1812, the Ottomans ceded to Russia a large section of eastern Moldavia, which became known as Bessarabia. The Russians treated Wallachia and Moldavia like conquered territory. As Karl Nesselrode, the Russian minister of foreign affairs, observed in 1822, no major change had occurred in the Principalities in the previous 50 years without Russian approval.[5] During the first eight years of his reign, Nicholas I was to force the Ottomans to the negotiating table three times – at Akkerman in 1826, at Adrianople in 1829, and at Unkiar Skelessi in 1833. The resulting treaties worked to the Russians' advantage. The Turkish "sick man" was being picked clean.

The Akkerman convention, completed on October 7, 1826, was a major victory for Czar Nicholas. Turkish troops were to withdraw from Moldavia and Wallachia. The treaty gave the Russians "nearly dictatorial power" over the hospodars (governors), the British consul wrote later.[6] The Turks recognized Serbian autonomy, opening new possibilities for the Russians to exert influence in that province. The Russians' ships received access to the Black Sea and the Danube. Their merchant vessels gained free passage through the Straits. The Russians were making headway in the Balkans merely by browbeating the Turks.

During negotiations with the Turks, Czar Nicholas I paid little heed to Austrian interests.

"It appears to be obvious ... that the young Czar ... feels a certain dislike towards me," grumbled Metternich in November 1826.[7] Although the Czar's highhanded behavior offended Metternich deeply, the Austrian chancellor determined to avoid tangling with the headstrong Romanov ruler. He would challenge Nicholas I if the Czar directly interfered with the monarchy's commercial interests or attempted to annex the Principalities. Otherwise, Metternich intended to remain at a disapproving distance as Nicholas I intentionally disrupted the status quo.

The Czar went to great lengths to expand his sphere of influence in the Balkans. In a move that almost certainly had a hidden motive, Nicholas I in July 1827 joined the British and French in a military show of strength intended to convince the Ottomans that their only alternative was to agree to Greek autonomy. Count Zichy, the Austrian ambassador to St. Petersburg, reported that the Russian ruler confessed that he "abhorred" the Greeks and believed that they did not deserve enfranchisement.[8] It appears that the Czar supported Greek autonomy because he thought it would weaken the Turkish "sick man," making it easier for Russia to run the Ottoman intruders out of Europe.

When, in October 1827, Great Britain, France and Russia brought their warships to the Dardanelles, the Ottomans refused to give in to this audacious exercise in intimidation. What followed was one of those episodes in military history that most people, even hardened warriors, would rather forget. An unanticipated consequence of what occurred was that Nicholas I would be left to fight his first Balkan war without allies.

In response to the Turkish intransigence, British Vice-Admiral Sir Edward Codrington led 24 British, French and Russian warships into Navarino Bay where 81 Turkish and Egyptian vessels lay at anchor. In the ensuing three-hour battle, two-thirds of the Ottoman-Egyptian fleet was sunk with 8,000 lives lost.[9] Explosions lit up the sky for hours as the commanders blew up their badly damaged ships. Nicholas I was said to have "approved completely of the battle."[10]

Metternich denounced the attack as "appalling."[11] The Austrian Chancellor expressed outrage at hearing that Russian Foreign Minister Nesselrode had written to Count Tatishchev, the Russian ambassador in Vienna: "*Vive la force!* It is might which rules the world nowadays." Metternich's reaction: "Only Russia ... (is) a real threat to peace in the Near East."[12]

As might be expected, the Sultan wasn't happy at the destruction of his fleet. He refused to fulfill the conditions agreed to at Akkerman regarding the Danubian Principalities. He also ordered the closure of the Straits to states involved in the attack at Navarino Bay.[13] And that wasn't all. On December 20, 1827, he called for a Holy War against Russia: "This war will not be ... a political struggle for territory and frontiers ..." he declared. "For us lies ahead a struggle for the faith and for our national existence. Each of us, whether rich or poor, great or small, must look upon this struggle as a sacred duty."[14] The rhetoric for war had a familiar sound. Both the Russians and the Turks used the language of faith to persuade their subjects to fight.

Ashamed at the carnage they had helped cause at Navarino, the British backed off from hostilities. In January 1828, the Duke of Wellington had become Prime Minister. The hero of Waterloo was not sympathetic to the attack at Navarino, calling it an "untoward event" which had robbed "an ancient ally of its fleet."[15] In other circumstances the British might actually have come to the aid of the Turks against the Russians; however, they could hardly justify this since the Czar's forces ostensibly were fighting for Greek independence. The French navy also withdrew from Constantinople. The Russians and the Turks were left to settle their differences by themselves.

Nicholas I put his army on a war footing, but did not immediately engage the Turks in battle. The perils of a Balkan winter argued against an immediate deployment of troops. Another reason for waiting was that czarist forces fighting the Persians in the Transcaucasus soon would be available, since a peace settlement in that conflict was imminent. Additionally, Nicholas I may have preferred to continue the diplomatic extortion, used so successfully by his agents in dealing with the Turks, instead of taking his troops into battle. The Sultan, however, showed no sign of rescinding his call for a Holy War.

Nicholas I, claiming Russia's economic interests were at risk, declared war on April 26, 1828. Twelve days later, the Czar's Second Army crossed the River Prut into the Danubian Principalities, setting off alarms in Vienna's military circles.[16] The self-proclaimed "liberation army" proceeded through Moldavia and Wallachia, with military leaders declaring that they came at the behest of the Czar to restore order and protect peoples' rights.[17] Local boyars (high ranking aristocrats) headed for the hills or frontiers.

At army headquarters near Braila the Russians were in a partying mood. Nicholas I himself left for the front, crossing the Prut on May 7 and joining his troops that night. The Czar had naively persuaded himself that a spring campaign in the Balkans would lead to a quick victory. He reported to his brother, Constantine, in early June: "Gaiety and good health are the order of the day."[18] Foreign Minister Nesselrode described the atmosphere at the front as festive, with excellent dinners and entertaining conversation, including witticisms and pranks.

The good times, however, quickly turned to gall. Expecting the Turks to capitulate before his forces reached the Danube, the Czar commanded too few troops. Supplies were short. Epidemics plagued the forces, and even Nicholas I, young and unusually vigorous, came down with a fierce case of diarrhea.

After grueling months of fighting, the Russian troops made it to Varna, on the Black Sea. The port was important, since it commanded one of the best roadsteads on the entire Black Sea coast. The Turkish forces greatly outnumbered those of the Russians. The Czar arrived from Odessa on September 8, 1828, and took charge of the military operation. It was, writes military historian John Daly, the Czar's first real participation in the "glorious business" of commanding troops in war. Nicholas "set about interfering in the siege with great relish," Daly writes.[19] Still, the Czar's presence undoubtedly boosted the troops' morale. On October 11 the Turks surrendered Varna.

By now many Europeans shared the Sultan's concerns that the Russians intended to overthrow the Ottoman regime. When challenged, Nicholas I offered unconvincing reassurances. On August 10, 1828, while still in Odessa, the

Czar had tried to explain himself during a long interview with the British ambassador, Lord William Heytesbury. "What can Russia gain by the destruction of the Ottoman throne?" Nicholas I had asked. The Czar insisted that all he wanted was to be judged by his conduct and "not to be the victim of suspicion." He then revealed perhaps more than he intended. If the Ottomans "continued their obstinate policies," Nicholas I declared, he would be driven to "more decisive measures." These included "blocking the Dardanelles and starving the Turks into submission." In the closing weeks of 1828, the Russians did, indeed, attempt a blockade of the Dardanelles, but it accomplished nothing. The Turks neither starved nor submitted. The war continued.

For the 1829 campaign, Nicholas sensibly turned the command of his army over to Field Marshal Count Ivan Dibich-Zabalkansky. The army marched through the eastern Balkan mountains heading for Adrianople. Under the Count's professional leadership, the military operation went more smoothly, even though the treacherous terrain presented the troops with formidable difficulties. As a doctor serving with the army described it, "The soldiers became exhausted under the weight of their accoutrements; they had to lug on their backs a haversack, a uniform, a heavy overcoat, a mess tin with water, and rations for 10 days, that is, 20 pounds of dried bread crusts."[20]

At last, however, the mists cleared. The czarist forces arrived in southern Bulgaria, a land of bread and honey, where watermelons and grapes ripened on the vines. Fortified by decent food, the army marched on. Turkish strongholds fell in quick succession. The troops took the port city of Burgas on July 12, reaching Adrianople (Edirne) in early August. The Turkish soldiers, many of them hardly more than children, were shocked and demoralized at seeing the Russian troops south of the Balkan mountain range, and less than 124 miles from Constantinople. The Sultan sued for peace.

Nicholas couldn't decide what to do. His army awaited orders. Constantinople and victory lay a few days' march away. Perhaps the Czar had a premonition of disaster. Heeding his better angels, he appointed a committee to give him advice. The panel, meeting in secret, urged caution. They concluded that Turkey's survival, with its wings clipped, was preferable to the Ottoman Empire's complete disintegration. Nesselrode explained the panel's thinking:

> *"The idea of chasing the Turks from Europe, of re-establishing at St. Sophia the cult of the True God, is certainly very beautiful and, if realized, it would have us all live in history, but what would it gain Russia? Glory, undoubtedly, but at the same time ... inevitable disputes with the principal European powers, with what would be their acceptance at the moment, and perhaps a general war at the end."[21]*

The British ambassador to Russia, Lord Heytesbury, who did not participate in the meeting, expressed similar views. If war broke out, he said, "the whole of Europe" would be drawn into the conflict. Under those circumstances, he said, making a conquest of Turkey would be "impossible."[22]

With what must have been a heavy heart, Nicholas took the panel's advice. He accepted the Sultan's peace offer. News that British and French naval forces were amassing at Smyrna (Izmir), a few days' sailing from Constantinople, undoubtedly added immediacy to the Czar's decision..

The Czar, in discussing his seeming acceptance of the survival of Turkey, albeit in a weakened state, carefully chose his words. He repeatedly declared that he "did not want a single inch of Turkish soil ... as long as no one else took any."[23] He would serve as a gendarme, making sure that no foreign power made itself too much at home in territory near the Turkish Straits. He would send troops to the Dardanelles if "unwanted guests" (the British or French) turned up there.

Nicholas I was a warrior czar. He had been brought up to believe that the most important function of a Romanov ruler was imperial aggrandizement. War was the currency of conquest. He would temporarily retire from battle but he would be back.

For the Russians, the fruits of victory in the Turkish war were sweet. Although Constantinople and the Straits remained beyond the Russians' reach, the Treaty of Adrianople, signed on September 14, 1829, offered satisfying rewards. The Turks recognized Russian claims to Georgia on the east coast of the Black Sea. Wallachia and Moldavia became Russian protectorates. Neutral ships received free access to the Black Sea and the Danube. The Sultan also promised autonomy for Greece.

The Russians gained a stranglehold over the three channels connecting the Danube River with the Black Sea, including the main Sulina outlet.[24] This caused lingering friction between Vienna and St. Petersburg. The Danube River was a major artery for Austrian commerce. Once the Russians took control of the estuaries, they charged stiff fines and tolls on foreign vessels using the waterway. They also imposed lengthy quarantines that the Austrians claimed weren't fully justified by the need to control disease.

The Russians had promised negotiators at Adrianople that they would keep the Danube channels in good order. They went back on their word. Sand and silt built up so that the outlets were hardly deep enough for safe navigation. The waterways became clogged with tree limbs, dead animals, and skeletons of wrecked vessels. The Russians' failure to maintain the estuaries led to the loss of several ships.

Austrian and British shippers voiced suspicions that the Russians were sabotaging foreign competitors by making it difficult for them to use the Danube waterway. Finally a Russian diplomat, Nikolai K. Giers, confirmed that the complaints were justified. Writing in memoirs in the 1870s, he admitted that the Russians had pretended to clean the Danube channels, while not actually doing so. "...It was not to our advantage to make this route easier for foreign trade with the Black Sea region to the detriment of Odessa (the Russian port), whose development was proceeding rapidly at that time," he said.

The situation was only resolved in 1856, during negotiations ending the Crimean War. The signatories stripped the Russians of their authority over the estuaries. They created a European commission to oversee the Danube outlets. From then on there were few problems with the channels.

In 1833, a strange turn of events brought the Russian army to Constantinople. Czarist forces took military control of the city for the first (and what would be the only) time in Romanov history. The Russians marched into the city without firing a shot. They came at the behest of Sultan Mahmud II. They would not depart empty-handed.

A power struggle between the Ottomans and the Egyptians provided the Russians with this unusual opportunity. In response to the Greek uprising of 1821 Mehemet Ali, the pasha of Egypt, and his son, Ibrahim, had brought troops into Ottoman territory to fight in the Sultan's defense. The Egyptians, unhappy at what they saw as the Porte's lack of gratitude for their sacrifices, threatened to overthrow the Ottoman government. The Sultan appealed to Great Britain and France for help against the Egyptians, but both governments excused themselves, citing domestic concerns as revolutionary tides churned up trouble in Western Europe.

Having learned of the Sultan's predicament, Nicholas I secretly sent him a message offering Russian help against the Egyptians. The Czar wanted to make sure that nothing interfered with his empire's commercial interests in the Black Sea. As a result of the Adrianople agreement, the port at Odessa was bustling. The Czar was worried that the

Egyptians might rescind the treaty and restrict traffic on the Black Sea if they took power.

On February 2, 1833, after initial hesitation, the desperate Sultan accepted his traditional enemy's offer of help. Nicholas I, protesting that he wasn't eager to assist the Ottomans – after all these were infidels – rushed to their assistance. The Czar's conversation with Count Karl Ludwig Ficquelmont, the Austrian ambassador, reveals the nuances of his thinking: "I have taken the engagement and shall keep my word. I do not conceal with you that it is a sacrifice that I make. It is too opposed to all our old relations with Turkey for Russia to behold it with pleasure; besides religious principle is opposed to it. However, I shall keep my word. But that is all that I can do. I have no power to give life to the dead."[25] Nor, one might add, did he wish to resuscitate the Turkish corpse, whose wake he was anticipating with greedy relish.

On February 20, Russian Admiral Mikhail Petrovich Lazarev's squadron arrived at the Bosphorus, where it was becalmed. A comic interlude followed. The pasha commanding the entrance forts wasn't expecting such visitors. He demanded to know why the Russians were there. Lazarev told him, through a translator, that the Sultan had asked for Russian aid. The pasha countered that he had no such information. He asked Lazarev to remain outside the Straits until authorization for entry was received. "Lazarev tartly pointed out," writes Daly, "that the freshening wind which had arisen might expose the pasha to risk if he did not hurry back to his fort. The pasha hesitated, whereupon Lazarev gave the order for the squadron to set sail and form line of Battle; the Russian ships then sailed into the Bosphorus."[26]

The Russian presence in Turkish territory caught the world's attention. It could hardly be overlooked. Virtually the Czar's entire Black Sea Fleet was moored in the Bosphorus. Additionally, 11,000 Russian troops set up camp at Hunkar Iskelesi near the Turkish capital.

Naturally, suspicions were raised that the Russians intended to take Constantinople. Russian officers were observed sailing around Dardanelles fortifications, taking endless measurements and preparing detailed maps. The officers measured the height and size of the forts' walls at the Bosphorus and the Dardanelles and surveyed the two lighthouses at the Bosphorus entrance.

The Turks took pains to make their traditional enemies – turned protectors – feel at home. The Sultan sent his "guests" 25,000 eggs for their Easter celebrations. The naval officers received wines and sweets, and the soldiers rum, ox meat and even money. The Czar's forces were allowed to visit a weapons museum in the fourth century Byzantine church of Hagia Irene, within the first courtyard of the Sultan's seraglio itself, an area that had been totally off limits to Europeans.

While the Austrians, like the British and French, thought the Russians were making themselves too much at home in Constantinople, Metternich continued to stay aloof in the effort to avoid tangling with the Czar. However, after Mehmet Ali negotiated a treaty in which the Egyptians received Syria/Lebanon and Adana from the Sultan, the British and French stepped in. They let the Czar know that they saw no reason for the Russian forces to remain in the city now that the Egyptian pasha had made peace. With the British navy lurking in nearby waters, the Russians would hardly have been foolish enough to try to overthrow the Sultan, whom they ostensibly had come to save. They agreed to leave, but they insisted on ample rewards for their services. Until they received what they felt was their due, thousands of Russian soldiers would remain encamped on the Asiatic shores of the Bosphorus.

The Czar sent Count Aleksei Orlov, his personal friend and a charming and clever plenipotentiary, to Constantinople with instructions to seek a lasting treaty with the Porte. Orlov knew how to get on the Turks' good side. His gave generous gifts to high ranking officials and handed out 24,000 medals, bearing the Czar's portrait, to rank and file Turkish soldiers. These were intended, as historian Alan Palmer writes, "to express his Imperial Master's admiration for the courage with which they would no doubt have fought had Ibrahim's army borne down upon them."[27]

A treaty between the Russians and the Ottomans, completed at Hunkar Iskelesi on July 8, 1833, called for the signatories to come to each other's aid during a conflict.[28] A secret clause in the treaty required the Turks to close the Dardanelles to non-Russian ships in time of war. The Russians then would be free to pursue military adventures in the Balkans without interference from outside powers. In the event that the Czar was in a war with a Great Power, he could send Russian warships through the Straits into the Mediterranean, then bring them back to the safety of the Black Sea whenever he wished. The Hunkar Iskelesi Treaty threatened British and Austrian shipping interests in the Balkans. One member of the opposition in the British Parliament put the situation aptly, describing the treaty as "a visible manifestation of the fact that Russia ... is slowly but steadily advancing on Constantinople, and determined at no distant day to take possession of the Dardanelles, when all her energy, enterprise and ambition will be directed to the extension of her maritime power ..."[29]

As years passed, Nicholas clung to his dream of military glory and Byzantium. Revolution came to Europe; finally, the tide of unrest ebbed. The Czar believed that the stars were now aligned for his army's grand thrust to the south. In 1848, a new ruler had come to the Habsburg throne. The Czar expected the young Emperor Franz Joseph to join him in running the Turks out of Europe. Nicholas misread the celestial signs, plunging Europe into a bloody Crimean conflict. The Czar died as the war raged on.

6 WHEN PARIS SNEEZES

Austrian Chancellor Metternich, enjoying a summer's holiday at Königswart, his chateau in Bohemia, was expecting news from Vienna. It was early August 1830, and Archduchess Sophie, the daughter-in-law of Emperor Franz I, was due to go into labor at any time. The stakes were high for the Habsburg dynasty. Intermarriage had depleted the blood lines of the monarchy and the Archduchess had suffered five miscarriages.

That day a messenger appeared at Königswart with news of a different sort, so shocking that when Metternich read it, he collapsed at his desk. A few days earlier a Paris mob had forced the abdication of French King Charles X (the Comte d'Artois), the handsome and charming youngest brother of the ill-fated Louis XVI, who – along with Queen Marie Antoinette – had been guillotined during the French Revolution. The streets of Paris again were covered with blood.

Since the Congress of Vienna in 1815, Metternich had been the self-appointed keeper of the monarchical principle in Europe. He had presided over a number of smaller congresses where he pushed European rulers to work together in the interests of order on the continent and for the survival of the traditional monarchies. Now the dynasties of Europe were in danger of being overthrown. "My whole life's work is destroyed!" Metternich is said to have muttered.[1]

Europe was in fact entering a period of social and political turmoil that would last more than two decades. As the saying went, "When Paris sneezes, Europe catches cold."

Charles X, coming to power in 1824 at the age of 67, had sought to rule as his ancestors had done, by divine right or as the Duke of Wellington put it, "by priests, through priests, for priests."[2] For many Frenchmen who wanted no part of absolutist monarchy or of religion, this was bad enough. The King went further, revoking constitutional rights. Angry Parisians took to the streets. The 1830 July Revolution, as it came to be called, lasted just three days. Charles X would be the last Bourbon to occupy the throne of France and the last of that nation's rulers to claim authority solely by divine right.

The French revolutionists knew that their actions in forcing Charles X into exile had touched a raw nerve in courts whose rulers, such as the Habsburgs and the Romanovs, continued to claim absolute power by God's grace. Warned that war might result if they took the bold move of proclaiming a French republic, the rebels compromised. They proclaimed Louis-Philippe, a member of the House of Orleans, as *"King of the French, by the grace of God and the will of the people."* He accepted the crown on August 9. The attempt by the French to reestablish stability didn't work. Riots continued in the streets of Paris. Although Louis-Philippe was of a different stamp than his Bourbon predecessor, from the start he had a shaky hold on power. In different times, he might have suited the French just fine. Unfortunately for him, his subjects weren't in the mood to be pleased. For advocates of aristocracy, the King was too bourgeois. Legitimists cast the monarch as a usurper, refusing to honor his rule since he was not the Bourbon heir but rather a member of the rival house of Orleans. The voices of the proletariat in France grew louder, demanding a role in national affairs. Communists and anarchists were among those who took to the streets.[3] Bellicose elements on the French left called for war – any war, it seemed – with Austria over Italy, with Russia over Poland, with Prussia, Holland and England over Belgium and the left bank of the Rhine.[4] From the royal perspective, liberty had gone amuck.

Metternich, having cut short his Bohemian vacation to rush back to Vienna, prepared to close the floodgates against the anticipated revolutionary tide. He paused, however, long enough to join the Habsburg court and the public in celebrating news from Schönbrunn, the imperial palace just outside the Habsburg capital. On August 18, 1830, Archduchess Sophie had given birth to a healthy son, named Franz Joseph. Everyone expected that little Franzi, as he was called, would one day take the throne.

The Habsburgs sorely needed new blood. Archduke Ferdinand, the oldest son of Emperor Franz I and the heir apparent, was a gentle and loving young man, but he had inherited many of the infirmities to which redundantly intermarried princes of the blood were prone. He had epilepsy, sometimes suffering a dozen seizures in a day. Unable to mount a horse without being scotched up, he had difficulty remaining seated on even the noblest of steeds. Some people considered Ferdinand an idiot, which wasn't quite true, but leaving his mental deficiencies aside, he was hardly the man to lead the Habsburg Empire at a time when the very future of monarchial power was in doubt. Franz Joseph's father, who was second in line to the throne, had neither the ability to rule nor the desire to do so. Tiny Franz Joseph was third in succession.

The revolution that had begun in France spread rapidly. On August 25, 1830, an uprising occurred in Brussels, resulting in the little nation's independence. By the end of September, rioting had spread to German states, including Saxony and Brunswick. In response to stirrings of unrest in Italy, Metternich sent troops into the Papal States, Parma, and Modena. The Austrians and their surrogates soon regained control of most of the Italian peninsula. But then the Hungarians threatened to rise. Hoping to calm the situation in that often restive part of the monarchy, and to confirm Habsburg legitimacy, Franz I on September 28 had Archduke Ferdinand, his ailing heir, crowned King of Hungary. In late November, insurgents rose in Congress Poland, which was governed by a viceroy of the Russian Czar. Although the rebellion was soon quashed, the Russians' hold on Poland remained tenuous.

Metternich understood that more was at stake than the future of Louis-Philippe, or the fate of any particular ruler. Monarchy as a form of government was in jeopardy, especially when it was founded on absolutist principles. Realizing that the best defense against revolution was a united front, in 1833 Austrian Chancellor Metternich arranged for Emperor Franz to meet with King Friedrich Wilhelm III of Prussia to discuss ways to keep insurgents from gaining an upper hand. Nicholas I, shaken by what had occurred in Congress Poland, sent word that he wanted to join his royal brothers, who were to meet at Teplitz (Teplice), in Bohemia.

This took Metternich by surprise. At that time, he and the Czar were on particularly bad terms. As was often the case, the friction between Nicholas I and the Austrian chancellor concerned the Russians' aggressive maneuvering in the Balkans. A few weeks earlier the chancellor, encountering Nesselrode at the Karlsbad spa town, had lashed out at the Russian foreign minister, accusing the czarist regime of feigning interest in Greek independence in order to foster revolution in the Ottoman Empire. Metternich told Nesselrode that he understood perfectly what the Russians wanted – an excuse for another war with the Turks.[5] Such forthright language had not gone down well in St. Petersburg.

Only a few days before the Czar's self-invitation arrived in Vienna, Metternich had found another reason for anger at the Russians. He learned that they had signed a treaty with the Turks at Hunkar Iskelesi, with secret clauses concerning the Russian navy's Black Sea access. As far as Metternich was concerned, Russian meddling in the Balkans was always a threat to European stability.

Nevertheless, the Chancellor and the Czar were so eager to stand together against the revolutionary threat that they tried to ignore their differences.[6] The Czar, in fact, temporarily suspended his Balkan intrigues while focusing on preventing the revolutionary epidemic from spreading to his empire.

By the time the Czar arrived at Teplitz (Teplice) on September 10, Friedrich Wilhelm III, flighty as always, had left, suddenly remembering he had to attend previously announced military maneuvers. Emperor Franz and Czar Nicholas I moved to Münchengrätz (Mnichovo Hradiste), some 45 miles northeast of Prague, where they hunted stags while Metternich and Nesselrode talked. There were the usual billiards and whist, the dinners and banquets, but in spite of these diversions, the Emperor and the Czar had an agreement ready for signing on September 18 that suited them both. The monarchs promised to assist any sovereign who explicitly asked for help in combating liberal insurgency. They vowed to do everything possible to preserve Poland as well as the Ottoman Empire. In case the Ottoman Empire collapsed, they were to consult on a course of action. On October 15 in Berlin, King Friedrich Wilhelm III signed on to the convention.

The Holy Alliance had been resuscitated, but it was not

to survive the Crimean War. At that time a quarrel between Czar Nicholas I and Emperor Franz Joseph would cast a permanent pall over the friendship between the Habsburgs and Romanovs.

The Habsburg monarchy entered a particularly turbulent period after Emperor Franz I died in 1835. As Emperor, the ailing Ferdinand exercised little more than a rubber stamp on imperial decisions. A vacuum at the top led to all sorts of ills. A committee, which included Metternich, was named to steer the monarchy through the difficult times. The members failed to speak with one voice, confusing the public and causing resentment.

This situation occurred at a time when strong, consistent leadership from the crown was particularly needed. The industrial revolution was bringing major changes to the monarchy. Peasants flocked to towns such as Vienna and Prague expecting jobs, often finding nothing but squalor, sometimes even starvation. Shop owners replaced workers with machines, leading to rioting by those who had lost their jobs. A middle class emerged, with teachers, doctors, bankers, architects, and industrialists demanding that their voices be heard. The Austrian government ran up a huge debt. Interest payments barely kept pace with revenues. There were poor harvests in 1845. The next year, cattle plague hit Hungary; a potato blight occurred in other areas of the monarchy. In Salzburg, people were reduced to eating bread that was mixed with clover.

As societal unrest increased, Metternich clamped down on people's freedoms, creating what amounted to a police state. The public increasingly viewed the Chancellor as the source of all the monarchy's ills. Later, as the Austrian public rose in revolt, Metternich was among those most likely to end up dangling from a lamppost.

In France, Louis-Philippe, who valued tolerance and respected human life, faced constant attacks on his character. There were assassination attempts, eight in all.

The King tried to clamp down on troublemakers. That didn't work. Laissez faire didn't work either. As Louis-Philippe's biographer, T.E.B. Howarth remarks, it became "obligatory to cry up the constitution in danger,"[7] blaming the King for failing to abide by the sacred document's tenets. In February 1848, after the frightened King banned a banquet that was to address workers' problems, tradesmen and bourgeoisie raged in the streets. A crowd broke into the royal palace, desecrating the King's bed and hacking his red and gold throne to pieces.[8] Louis-Philippe, like his predecessor, abdicated. He would be the last of the French kings.[9]

7 ROYAL BROTHERS' FEUD

After word spread that King Louis-Philippe had fled Paris with a mob at his heels, disaffected factory workers as well as members of the rising middle class across Europe decided the time had come to demand their rights.[1] In a matter of days uprisings broke out in Marseilles, Amiens, and Lille, then in Baden, Cologne, Naples, Venice and Madrid. The European public seemed inclined to reject monarchy as a form of government. This meant that crowned heads of traditional empires such as Austria, clinging to the belief that their authority came straight from God, were particularly vulnerable.

For a brief time during that spring of 1848, Vienna seemed to have been spared from the revolutionary winds that were threatening imperial edifices across the continent. Citizens, receiving the news from France during Fasching, went happily about their pleasures, "reveling in a continuous state of intoxication," as one Austrian writer, F. Schuselka, put it. "For them it was always Sunday, always Carnival."[2] The good times would not last.

By March 1848, few locations in the vast Habsburg monarchy remained untouched by revolution. Vienna was in an uproar. Demonstrators set up barricades, demanding academic freedom and an end to censorship. Communists and anarchists marched side by side with republicans. Rioters stormed a national guard storehouse and armed themselves. Workers set factories ablaze in the suburbs. A mob gathered outside Chancellor Metternich's quarters, calling for his resignation. The royal family reluctantly decided that the chancellor had to go.[3] On March 13, he was dismissed. He fled the Austrian capital, by one account disguised as a woman, eventually making his way to England.

Metternich's departure left the monarchy adrift. The physically and mentally challenged Emperor Ferdinand was not equipped to deal with an empire that was being battered by revolutionary winds. Ferdinand, in fact, thought the revolution was great fun. The Emperor enjoyed the parades, the pretty flags, the music, the gunshots – "like it was on his birthday," wrote Eugene Bagger, a biographer of Emperor Franz Joseph.[4] On March 15, Ferdinand I agreed to a constitution for the Austrian half of the monarchy,[5] although its contents remained unclear. In an attempt to placate the Magyars, the Emperor installed a moderate government in the Hungarian cabinet headed by Lajos Batthyany. Ferdinand went to Hungary on April 11, 1848, where he endorsed laws that had been passed by the new diet, establishing a liberal constitutional government.[6] Habsburg family members became increasingly concerned about what Ferdinand would do next. They feared that the goodhearted Emperor would sign away all their imperial prerogatives if citizens approached him and asked him to do so.

In mid-May, armed students and workers entered the Hofburg in Vienna and tried to force their way into Ferdinand's quarters. Acting against the Emperor's wishes, the frightened royal family took flight. They pretended they were heading for Schönbrunn, the Habsburg palace on the outskirts of Vienna. But instead of stopping there, they kept on going in a wild gallop – all the way to Innsbruck, where they remained for most of the summer.

In Prague, protesters convened a Slav Congress, sparking an uprising. The agitators, some of them from Russia, urged the monarchy's Slavs to form a nation independent of Austria. On June 12, the dissidents set up barricades in Prague's Old Town section. Prince Alfred Windisch-Graetz, the gaunt, craggy-faced commander of troops in Bohemia, bombarded the city. That same day a rebel's bullet killed Windisch-Graetz's young wife, who was leaning out of a window watching the fighting. Within a few days the Prince, perhaps spurred to fight harder by the tragedy, restored order in the city. He soon would be asked to take measures against insurgents in Vienna.

As always, the situation in Hungary was complicated. Lajos Kossuth, a golden-tongued orator who had won a large following as champion of liberal causes in the Hungarian Diet, saw opportunity in the latest unrest and seized it. Considered one of the handsomest men in all Hungary, with piercing blue eyes and regular features, he was also, as historian Macartney says, "one of the most persuasive men ever to be born."[7] He knew instinctively how to capitalize on his countrymen's resentment toward Vienna. On March 3, 1848, he had delivered what came to be called the "baptismal speech" of the Hungarian Revolution. Speaking to a rapt crowd in Pozsony (Pressburg) – present day Bratislava – Kossuth claimed that all Hungary's troubles, particularly her economic woes, emanated from the Austrian capital.[8] He drew cheers as he railed against the "pestilential air which breathes on us from the charnel-house in Vienna, an air which dulls our nerves and paralyzes our spirit."[9]

Emperor Ferdinand's conciliatory efforts in Hungary had little effect. Intent on persuading the Hungarians to break away from Austria altogether, Kossuth applied his oratorical gifts to undermining the Betthyany government. On September 22, 1848, Kossuth persuaded the Hungarian Diet to create an "Extraordinary Governmental Council" with him as chairman. He was given emergency powers, which, in effect, made him dictator.[10]

Kossuth ignited a civil war in Hungary, something he seems not to have anticipated. He failed to notice growing nationalistic sentiment among non-Magyar groups in that half of the monarchy, particularly among the nation's sizable Serbian and Croatian populations. He could see no reason for the various nationalities to object to Magyar being Hungary's official language, since the other groups were to be permitted to use their own tongue in internal affairs and in church matters. "The magic of liberty," he averred, "is stronger than nationality, faith, affinity of blood and friendship."[11] Kossuth was wrong.

Other ethnic groups in Hungary, including Croats and Serbs, mindful of past abuses at the hands of the Magyars, were not easily seduced by pretty words about liberty and constitutions. In September, Croats, led by a pro-Habsburg general named Josip Jellacic, marched against the Magyar rebels with the Serbs fighting by their side.

The Habsburgs, under pressure from supporters in Vienna who felt they had been deserted, returned to the capital in mid-August. They found that unrest in the city had, if anything, become worse. They made secret plans for the royal family to flee to Olomouc – a fortified town in Moravia that strongly supported the monarchy – if they felt their safety was threatened. Olomouc was a fortified town that strongly supported the monarchy. After hours of tense discussions family members finally reached a heartbreaking decision. The time had come for Emperor Ferdinand to relinquish the throne to his nephew, Franz Joseph, who had just turned 18. The unhappy task of broaching the subject of abdication with Ferdinand fell to his unfortunate wife, Empress Maria Anna.

In Vienna on October 6, Austrian Minister of War Theodor von Latour was lynched and his mangled body was displayed hanging from a lamppost. The Habsburgs realized they might be the next victims of the mob. They left Vienna for Moravia immediately, accompanied by 7,000 troops. Some 400 carriages crammed with aristocrats and government personages followed the royals. As the procession made its way through the countryside, villagers in colorful costumes appeared to wish the royal family well. Once Vienna was cleared of those connected with the court, Windisch-Graetz put the city under siege. By the end of October the uprising was more or less under control.

Emperor Ferdinand initially was reluctant to abdicate, but when the time came to do so he behaved with gracious dignity. On December 2, Franz Joseph, dressed in an Austrian general's uniform with a white tunic and red trousers, became Emperor in a solemn ceremony at the Prince-Bishop's palace in Olomouc. Ferdinand and his wife departed for Prague, where they were to remain at Hradcany castle for the rest of their lives.

Franz Joseph accepted the duties that came with his ascension, but understandably with some regrets. "Farewell to youth!" he said shortly after he became Emperor. He was in a sense grieving for what he had never had. For his entire life he had been confined to a golden cage with little opportunity to stretch his wings. His earliest memories surely made him aware that he was different from other children. While Franzi, as he was called, was still an infant, his grandfather, Emperor Franz I, provided him with his own carriage, drawn by six horses. Whenever his nurse took her diapered charge out for a ride in his pram, court guards were required to snap to attention. Franz Joseph's school assignments, intended to prepare him for his role as future monarch, were far more demanding than those of his peers. His tutors emphasized rote learning, stuffing the young archduke with so many facts that at age 13 he fell ill from nervous exhaustion. Franz Joseph was intelligent. He had a gift for languages, mastering his native German along with French, the parlance of diplomacy. He also learned Czech, Hungarian, Polish and Italian, the native tongues of large numbers of his subjects. His upbringing was not, however, conducive to developing the critical thinking and sweeping imagination that might have allowed him to mold a single nation from the fractious ethnic clay of his vast empire.

Franz Joseph would reign for 68 years. His life was to be marred by personal tragedy. His marriage to the beautiful Elisabeth of Bavaria (Sisi) was hardly the stuff of fairy tales. Franz Joseph remained deeply in love with his wife, but she never fully reciprocated his affection. After Prince Rudolf, the Habsburg heir and the couple's only son, died in a murder-suicide tragedy at Mayerling in 1889, Sisi spent almost no time in Vienna. In 1898 she was assassinated by an Italian anarchist in Geneva. Franz Joseph died in 1916 as the war that would destroy the Habsburg monarchy and reduce Europe to ashes and tears, raged on.

The sovereign titles heaped upon the 18-year-old Emperor at his accession suggest the burden with which Franz Joseph was encumbered. He was "King of Jerusalem,[12] Apostolic King of Hungary, King of Bohemia, Galicia, Lodomeria, Lombardy, Venetia, Illyria and Croatia, and Grand Duke, Duke, Margrave, Prince and Count of some 30 other territories in the huge Austrian Empire with its 35 million inhabitants."[13] The Habsburg tent should have been big enough to accommodate these peoples, numbering some 11 nationalities. But many of these groups were discovering their own national identities and hoping to set their own course in the world. Some were inspired by republican ideals. Others, convinced of their own ethnic exceptionalism, hoped to get out from under the hated monarchy's restrictive yoke, but only so they could place such a yoke on the necks of others.

Czar Nicholas I rejoiced at the news of the young

Habsburg archduke's accession. The Czar, 34 years older than Franz Joseph, remembered him as a lively, rosy-cheeked, blond-haired youngster. Nicholas recalled fondly a visit to the Vienna court in 1835 when he had put five-year-old Franzi through a military drill.[14]

The Czar hoped to open a new chapter in the traditionally difficult relationship between the House of Romanov and the House of Habsburg. From the days of Peter the Great the Romanovs had accused the Habsburgs of riding roughshod over their interests. Even recently the Czar's family had suffered what they saw as yet another insult from the Habsburgs. Nicholas I had wanted to marry off his daughter Olga to Habsburg Archduke Stephan only to have the proposed union rebuffed on religious grounds (Olga was Orthodox; Stephan was Roman Catholic).[15] Nicholas I, who more than once had referred to Metternich as "Satan's cohort," blamed the Austrian Chancellor for the humiliating rejection. But now Metternich had been run out of Austria. For the Czar, the future of the two ancient empires, with their rulers standing side by side against republicanism and unrest, looked bright.

The Russian ruler expected his young imperial brother to follow his wise lead in matters that he believed were of shared interest. The Czar's failure to understand a basic fact about Franz Joseph's personality – that he put the interests of the monarchy above personal or inter-dynastic considerations – was to cause both rulers monumental grief in the future.

Franz Joseph's immediate task as Emperor was to restore order in Hungary. He gave Prince Windisch-Graetz that assignment. The Prince belonged to a small circle of nobles close to the Habsburg family. He had pushed for Ferdinand's abdication and for the ascension of young Franz Joseph. As military commander the Prince had saved the Austrian half of the monarchy, defeating the rebels in Prague and Vienna.

Franz Joseph had faith that Windisch-Graetz would perform similar miracles in Hungary. However, from the start the relationship between the young Emperor and the Prince was difficult. Windisch-Graetz was convinced of the superiority of his own views. In dealing with Franz Joseph he acted like an overbearing uncle, always ready with unsolicited advice. Ignoring the fact that Franz Joseph was now the sovereign of a vast empire, Windisch-Graetz assumed that the young man was "a cipher," says Alan Palmer, the Emperor's biographer. The haughty Prince certainly never thought to ask Franz Joseph's advice before heading for Hungary and war.

Windisch-Graetz left Vienna on December 16, crossing the Hungarian border with more than 50,000 troops. The Prince encountered little resistance in his initial march to Buda,[16] where he took the city on January 5, 1849. The rebels were not in residence. They had simply pulled back behind the River Theiss, where they were encamped for the winter.

The Prince, who owned vast estates in Hungary, felt at home in that part of the Habsburg Empire. He was among friends, the so-called Old Conservatives, aristocrats who had long exercised power over the kingdom's minorities. These nobles assured Windisch-Graetz that the revolution had been the work of "a handful of Protestants who had seized power against the will of the people." Nothing would come of it, they assured him. Never deigning to talk to the common people, Windisch-Graetz accepted his friends' assessment of the situation.

The Prince settled down in the capital and busied himself with governmental affairs. Life in Buda resumed a sort of surreal normality. Officers took their morning horseback rides, then went to cafes for coffee. Bands played as troops were reviewed. Royals watched from palace windows. There were theater performances. The casinos continued to separate gullible players from their money. Traffic moved again on the mighty Danube.[17]

In the third week of January, Windisch-Graetz informed the Habsburg court that the revolution in Hungary had been put down. Franz Joseph approved an official announcement for publication in the *Wiener Zeitung*, declaring the conclusion of the military campaign. Soon afterwards, reports arrived that the rebels were advancing on Buda and Pest. Franz Joseph began to doubt that Windisch-Graetz was capable of filling his military mission. The Emperor worried that the Habsburgs would lose Hungary forever.

Franz Joseph had one important option. He could ask the Russians for help. At Münchengrätz in 1833 Czar Nicholas I had joined with Emperor Franz of Austria and King Friedrich Wilhelm III in pledging to present a united front against the revolutionary threat. Both the other signatories had died, but as far as the Russian Czar was concerned the Münchengrätz agreement remained in effect. The rulers had promised their allies that they would come to the aid of their fellow sovereigns against revolutionaries if they received a formal request to intervene.

Nicholas I had been outraged at how King Friedrich Wilhelm IV of Prussia – the Czar's brother-in-law and ally – had responded to arms-wielding republicans who had appeared outside his royal palace in Berlin. The king, shaken down to his royal shoes, had promised the rebels a legislature and a constitution. Later, he had even marched in a procession wearing the tricolor armband of the revolutionaries.

Worried that the Austrians also would give in to the insurgents' demands, Nicholas I several times offered to send troops to help put down the Hungarian revolt. Franz Joseph's most trusted adviser, Prime Minister Felix von Schwarzenberg, warned the young Emperor against accepting the Czar's offer, arguing, correctly, that Russian involvement would make the monarchy appear weak.

In the meantime, the Hungarian Diet repaired to

Debrecen, a Protestant stronghold 140 miles east of Buda (and Pest) where Kossuth busied himself with organizing a rebel army. The insurgents were fortunate in their military leader, Arthur Görgei, one of the most gifted military leaders in history. Görgei started his mission at a disadvantage, as he himself acknowledged. In contrast to the Austrian troops, who were highly disciplined and well-trained, Görgei's young peasant recruits tended to melt away under enemy fire. Even the simple business of keeping troops in formation was a constant challenge, Görgei wrote later, recalling one scene in which "three battalions strolled on ... like peasants to the festival of their church's dedication..."[18] Under Görgei's command, however, his raw young recruits quickly became a fighting force.

The Habsburg commanders soon realized that the rebel general was no ordinary opponent. He had an initial advantage. In the Zips region (now in Slovakia), where much of the fighting was occurring, Görgei "knew every hill and vale, every river and stream," writes military historian Joseph Alexander Helfert.[19] The general came from that region. But his triumphs in the field depended on far more than knowledge of topography. Görgei had the courage of his imagination and the ability to inspire men to near impossible feats of daring.

Like most of the Hungarian rebels, Görgei wanted to fix a flawed dynastic system, not turn his back on it. Kossuth, on the other hand, wanted to tear Hungary loose from Austria.

Kossuth received a boost to his ambitions from an unexpected source. On March 4, 1849, Franz Joseph, relying on the guidance of Prince Schwarzenberg, approved a constitution based on a single crown, that of the Austrian Empire. This in effect canceled the constitution that had been agreed to by Emperor Ferdinand the previous year. The new constitution granted the monarchy's citizens many rights, including equality under the law and freedom of religion. However, its real significance was its centralized character. The Hungarian Magyars were to be on equal footing with the other ethnic groups in the monarchy.[20] This made much sense on its face, but it caused a huge uproar in Hungary. As disciples of their own brand of Hungarian exceptionalism, the Magyars were convinced that their nation's ancient constitution made them chosen people, entitling them to more rights than anyone else.

Kossuth successfully played on public anger regarding the March 4 constitution in promoting his anti-dynastic argument. On April 14, 1849, the provisional Diet, meeting in the Protestant church in Debrecen, declared Hungary and its outlying annexes, including Transylvania and Croatia, independent of the monarchy. The proclamation deposed "the perjured House of Habsburg-Lorraine from its throne forever."[21] The Diet banned Emperor Franz Joseph from Hungarian soil.[22] Kossuth was named President Regent.

In a few weeks, the insurgents had won an impressive string of victories – at Szolnok, Hatvan, Tapiobicske, Isaszeg, Waizen, Nagy Sarlo and Komorn. The Austrians were forced to fall back from Buda. Hungary seemed almost entirely lost to the Habsburg Empire.[23]

Franz Joseph knew that Windisch-Graetz had failed in his Hungarian mission. On April 12, 1849, he dismissed him. This move was extremely painful for the young Emperor. True to character, Franz Joseph put personal considerations aside on behalf of what he viewed as the interests of the Habsburg monarchy. This character trait soon would earn him undying animosity from the Romanovs.

Franz Joseph's fears increased that the monarchy was doomed. Windisch-Graetz's replacement, General Ludwig Baron von Welden, upon arriving in Hungary, had wasted no time in demonstrating his incompetence.

Disregarding Schwarzenberg's advice, Franz Joseph turned to the Czar for help, sending the Russian ruler a formal request on May 1. With this move he triggered the Münchengrätz agreement – which came, as the young Emperor later found out, with strings attached.

Ironically, some evidence suggests that the Austrians could have defeated the Hungarian uprising without Russian assistance. Kossuth's political support, both in the military and in the population, was waning. He may have been a wonderful orator but he was no leader. (As an American saying goes, he was "all hat and no cattle.") He showed little talent for organizing a government or for bringing together the factions of Hungarian society. His decision to declare Hungarian independence wasn't popular with the public. A large segment of the military itself didn't support it.

In June, Franz Joseph relieved von Welden of his duties as commander of the monarchy's forces in Hungary, replacing him with General Julius Jacob von Haynau, who had a long history of service in the monarchy's army. He was a born brute who won battles.[24] Perhaps Haynau could have won the war without the Russian intervention if Franz Joseph had given him more time.

For Franz Joseph, however, it was too late for second thoughts. On May 21, 1849 he arrived in Warsaw where he met Nicholas I at the Lazienki Palace. The Habsburg Emperor approached the Czar with evident humility. A ritual enacted by the two rulers harked back to the days of feudal fealty. Hungarian historian András Geró describes what happened:

> *"The Russian host did everything he could not to overawe his young guest. The Czar had Francis Joseph stay in his own quarters, and passed before him with sword held down, saluting Francis Joseph as an inferior would his superior. Yet it could not be clearer who was indebted to whom. On the balcony of the Lazienki Palace, Francis Joseph kissed the hand of the Czar of All the Russias. In the feudal world order under which Francis Joseph had been brought up, a kiss on the hand*

signified much more than a mere courtesy. It was the middle of the supposedly enlightened 19th century, yet both Franz Joseph and Czar Nicholas I embodied the spirit of a bygone age. This is the explanation of the apparent selflessness of the ruler of the Russian Empire; in the same spirit, a kiss on the hand signified subordination to the other's superior might.'[25]

Franz Joseph had made a bargain with the Czar that he surely did not fully understand. In return for Russian help, Nicholas I expected unflinching loyalty from his young imperial brother. He was to be disappointed. Franz Joseph, for his part, learned that, for the Romanov dynasty, refusal to repay an incurred obligation was little short of treason – never to be forgiven or forgotten.

Nicholas I was, if anything, overly eager to intervene in the monarchy's internal affairs. By June 1849 the Russian troops were swarming into Hungary. Arriving through mountain passes under the command of Field Marshal Ivan Paskevich, Duke of Warsaw, Cossacks led the way. These lithe and fierce troops, astride their small horses, were followed by soldiers of other stripes. Soon the Hungarian insurgents were under attack on all sides. The rebels were outnumbered. Macartney gives troop figures at 280,000 on the Austrian side (176,000 Austrians and 104,000 Russians), compared with some 150,000 on the Hungarian side.[26]

Kossuth sent out calls for help to foreign government leaders whom he believed were sympathetic to the "liberal" cause. He had promised his supporters that these groups would rush to the rebels' side. British Foreign Secretary Lord Palmerston refused to consider intervention. In fact, the London foreign office regarded Austria as a "European necessity."[27] The French took much the same position. Naturally, the conservative European Powers weren't going to help Kossuth overthrow a legitimate government. The firebrand orator had created false hopes among his followers, who found themselves exposed, bleeding, helpless. Having recognized that the rebels' fight was lost, Kossuth deserted his followers. He took the Holy Crown of St. Stephen of Hungary, buried it under a willow tree outside a village in Transylvania, and fled Hungary for Turkey. Görgei understood that the odds greatly favored the enemy.[28] He decided to lay down his arms, but to the Russians instead of the Austrians. He did this on the grounds that Austria had "lost all honor" by bringing in foreign troops and because it was the Austrians and not the Russians who had, as he saw it, overthrown the Hungarian Constitution. The end came on August 13, 1849, at Vilagos, a picturesque village in Hungary's wine country.

In his memoirs Görgei wrote: "in the twilight ... General Count Rudiger, the commander of a Russian army corps, inspected the Hungarian troops under my command. But the cavalry was dismounted and had their swords hung on the pommels of their saddles; the muskets of the infantry were piled in pyramids; the artillery was drawn close together and unmanned; the flags and standards lay there unprotected before the disarmed ranks."[29] Görgei surrendered to Field Marshal Paskevich. The Russian campaign had lasted just eight weeks.

A few days later, Görgei received word that the Czar had pardoned him. Nicholas I sent his oldest son, the Grand Duke, to Vienna asking Franz Joseph to do the same. The Emperor was in Bad Ischl, his summer residence in the Salzkammergut. Schwarzenberg, representing the Emperor, denied the Czar's request[30] on grounds that Habsburg honor had been compromised. By giving himself up to Paskevich instead of Haynau, Görgei had insulted the Emperor, who was deprived of the satisfaction of accepting the surrender of the insurgent army. The capitulation to the Russians was a galling reminder that the Austrians owed their victory to a foreign power.[31] [32]

The words Paskevich used to inform the Czar of

Görgei's surrender undoubtedly poured salt in the Habsburg wound. Paskevich told the Czar, "You are the sole victor, Sire; Hungary is at your feet and the war is over."[33]

The war, and particularly the Russian intervention, left a trail of bitterness in the monarchy along with the tears. As Schwarzenberg had predicted, the House of Habsburg lost face by bringing the Russians in to save the monarchy. The Habsburg troops were humiliated by their having needed help from the Russians to put down the revolution. Many ordinary Hungarians longed to revenge themselves on the Russians for bringing bloodshed and mayhem to their homeland. The Hungarian rebels got nothing immediate for their troubles except for some martyrs. After issuing a proclamation declaring the rebellion had ended, Haynau proceeded swiftly with courts-martial, in which large numbers of rebels received death sentences. When Franz Joseph learned of this, he informed the general that the executions were to be carried out only with Vienna's express consent. Haynau argued for haste in carrying out the punishments, presumably thinking it would deter future unrest. Schwarzenberg, who hated the Hungarians, persuaded young Franz Joseph to allow the general to proceed without interference from Vienna.

On October 6, 13 imperial generals who had fought for the rebels were shot or hanged at Arad (now in Romania). According to Hungarian sources, before Franz Joseph put a halt to the proceedings on October 28, more than 500 death sentences were pronounced, with 114 of them carried out. Some 75 rebels who had fled the country were executed in effigy. Haynau's pathological brutality left a legacy of anger against the Habsburgs, whose control of the restive Hungarian nation remained tenuous. Haynau, for his part, appears not to have understood that his behavior had caused offense. After he retired he bought an estate in Hungary and was said to be surprised when his neighbors didn't invite him to their parties.[34]

For Nicholas I the defeat of the Hungarian uprising marked a high point. It was one of the few times that the unpopular Czar was lauded by his subjects. There was great excitement in Russia, where the public believed that their ruler had "conquered Europe."[35] As Ian Roberts puts it, the Czar was "drunk with success."[36] He seemed to think he was now arbiter of European policy.

Czar Nicholas I was careful to portray his efforts on behalf of the House of Habsburg as stemming from generosity of spirit toward his young brother – Franz Joseph. However, he didn't fail to remind the Emperor of the very real sacrifices his army had endured, the loss of treasure and blood. In the occupied towns there often had been no flour for bread and no fodder for horses. The summer's heat had taken its toll as men slaked their thirst in dirty streams. Cholera had swept through the ranks. The Russian losses included 708 killed and 2,320 wounded. There were 95,387 cases of sickness, and 10,885 deaths.[37]

These sacrifices notwithstanding, Nicholas I served his own interests by intervening in Hungary. He had faced insurrection after coming to power in 1825 and it had left him permanently afraid of losing control over his empire. Realizing that the unrest in Hungary could easily spill over into Russian territory, Nicholas chose to quell the revolution "over there" rather than face the need to take on the rebels at home (in Poland). The strategy worked. It wasn't until 1905 that revolution would threaten the very pillars of autocracy with which the Romanov rulers supported their house.

On the surface, the Russian intervention seemed a bargain for the Habsburgs. Nicholas I only asked for refunds of the cost of supplies, transportation and medical care. But Franz Joseph had incurred a huge debt to the Russian Czar. Only four years later, in the run-up to the Crimean War, Nicholas I would attempt to collect what he felt he was owed. He expected Franz Joseph to march by his side into the Balkans – helping the Czar realize the Romanov destiny in Constantinople. The Habsburg Emperor's refusal to join the Czar against the Turks led to a quarrel that changed the world.

8 THE TURKISH SICK MAN

"Prince, Metternich" asked the Czar at one moment, "What do you think of the Turk? ... Is he not a sick man?" Metternich understood the question immediately. "Is Your Majesty addressing the doctor or the heir?" the statesman parried."[1] – Münchengrätz, September 1833

In early 1853, Czar Nicholas I of Russia was about to embroil his empire in a conflict with Turkey that later became known as the Crimean War. It would be a terrible mistake. He would fight without allies; his army would suffer a humiliating defeat.

But in January 1853 the Russians' future seemed bright. The Czar looked forward to a second war with the Turks. He intended to avoid the mistakes he had made in the Russo-Turkish conflict of 1828-29, when he was forced to halt his army short of Constantinople for want of allies. This time he believed he had Queen Victoria's backing for his crusade against the Turkish "infidels." He was so certain of Franz Joseph's support he never thought to discuss the matter with the young Habsburg ruler. Franz Joseph had incurred a blood debt to the Romanovs after their army, in

119

1849, put down a revolution in Hungary. The Czar assumed that the Habsburg monarch would be delighted to show gratitude for this favor by helping the Russians drive the Turkish "Sick Man" back to the steppes of Asia.

Confident that he had allies, Nicholas waited for an excuse for war. It came from an unexpected source.

In France, a parvenu ruler named Louis Napoleon, the nephew of the great Bonaparte, needed to establish himself as a legitimate leader. He had emerged from exile, riding the revolutionary tide that had swept the last French King, Louis-Philippe, from power. He became President of the Second Republic of France in 1848; then on December 2, 1852, he assumed the title of Emperor Louis Napoleon III in a newly established French empire.

Louis Napoleon was painfully aware that his fellow monarchs considered him a pretender because he lacked the requisite stamp of approval from God known as "divine right." Czar Nicholas I was said to have scoffed, "An Emperor without divine right is not an Emperor." Ambitious and insecure, Louis Napoleon needed a cause, something to show his imperial "brothers" that he would not tolerate being pushed around.

Shortly after Louis Napoleon came to power, a dispute had erupted between Roman Catholic and Orthodox monks over rights to the holy places in Jerusalem and Bethlehem. Although the vast majority of Louis Napoleon's subjects were indifferent to religion and had no interest in the Holy Land, the upstart Emperor saw an opportunity for political self-aggrandizement. He ordered his representative in Constantinople to demand that the Porte allow Roman Catholics greater access to the holy sites. With this move the French newcomer stirred the rivalry over the sacred places, not only between Roman Catholic and Orthodox believers, but also between the ruling houses of France and Russia – traditionally the protectors of organized religion.

The altercation among the monks scarcely deserved

mention in a parochial archive. It was over who had custody of the keys to the great door of the Church of the Nativity in Bethlehem (which ordinarily wasn't locked); which religious order was to maintain the roof of the Church of the Holy Sepulchre in Jerusalem, and which star, Roman Catholic or Orthodox, was to adorn the Bethlehem cave.[2] The opposing monks often engaged in unseemly behavior, chanting each other down, hurling candlesticks or even resorting to fisticuffs on behalf of their supposed rights.

Initially, Sultan Abdulmejid I agreed to honor Roman Catholic claims to the holy places. Nicholas I ratcheted up the controversy with claims based on treaties naming Russia protector of certain Orthodox interests in the Ottoman Empire. The pathologically timid Sultan reneged on his promise to the French. Napoleon III responded by sending a 90-gun steam-powered battleship, the *Charlemagne*, into the Dardanelles – violating the London Convention of 1841, which kept the Straits closed to foreign warships. The Sultan bowed to the higher authority of French military might. In early December 1852 he decreed that the keys to the Church of the Nativity were to be handed over to the Roman Catholics and that the French-backed church was to have supreme authority over the holy places. On December 22 a new silver star arrived from Jaffa and the Latins were presented with the keys to the church door and to the manger.[3]

Nicholas now had a cause for war that would touch the heartstrings of Russian peasants. He felt certain that his devoutly religious subjects, many of them still angry about the massacre of the Eastern Patriarch on Easter Sunday 1821, would support an invasion of the Ottoman Empire in defense of Orthodox believers' rights in the Holy Land.

On January 7, 1853, the Czar secretly approved a plan for an attack on Constantinople. It would involve a naval expedition to the Bosphorus consisting of 28 warships and 32 transports. Some 16,000 men were to provide cavalry and artillery support. The entire force was to be assembled and held in readiness at the Russian ports of Odessa and Sevastopol on the Black Sea.[4]

Although military planners routinely draw up scenarios for wars they don't necessarily intend to fight, when the Czar did this it was to be taken seriously. As absolute monarch, Nicholas I had the power to carry out his fantasies.

The Czar, cordoned off from the real world by his royal position, lacked the ability to understand those whose opinions differed from his. Having concluded, falsely, that the British and the Austrians would join him in his war, he clung to the delusion that he had their support even when confronted with evidence to the contrary. When he finally realized how matters stood, he exploded in self-righteous fury.

Nicholas I based his faith in the British on what had occurred during a visit to London in the spring of 1844, when he had startled the royals by showing up on their doorstep unannounced. Meeting with Queen Victoria's representative, Nicholas I declared that the demise of Turkey in Europe was imminent. He implied that he wanted help in finishing off the ailing Ottoman Empire. He generously offered to divide the spoils with the British. But the Czar completely misread the British tea leaves. Although he received no encouragement in London for his scheme, he convinced himself that Queen Victoria supported him in his "holy cause" against the Turks.

In early January 1853, while Nicholas I was putting his war plans in place, he approached Sir Hamilton Seymour, the Queen's ambassador in St. Petersburg, seeking assurance that the British were, as he thought, amenable to his new Balkan adventure. His initial approach came in a casual "conversational aside" as the ambassador left a private concert. Seymour wrote that the Czar referred to the Ottoman Empire as the "sick man" and said, "'The country

[Turkey] is falling to pieces – who can say when?"[5]

During the next few weeks, Nicholas I summoned Seymour to an audience on four occasions. Ordinarily, the ambassador was lucky to see the Russian ruler once or twice a year. The ambassador's accounts of the meetings reveal a pattern – Nicholas I would begin by denying that he wanted to follow in his grandmother's (Catherine the Great's) footsteps, either by trying to conquer Constantinople or by creating a large Balkan empire under Russian control; and then the Czar would steer the conversation around to Turkey, confessing to less than honorable intentions toward that empire.[6]

The Czar's statements show a consistent lack of concern for Habsburg interests. According to Seymour, the Russian ruler said that Great Britain and Russia were the principal governments concerned with Turkey's destiny. The Czar called for the independence of Wallachia and Moldavia, provinces adjacent to the Habsburgs' southern border. These were to be under Russian protection. Serbia and Bulgaria were to have similar status. This would give the Russians a string of satellite states on the western shores of the Black Sea reaching all the way to Constantinople.

Some historians, including Palmer, dismiss the Czar's scheme as so much talk. "Inside the Winter Palace," says Palmer, "these remarks of the Czar seemed in accord with the setting – like Rastrelli's masterpiece[7] they were grandiose, overelaborate and artificial enough not to be taken seriously; but read dispassionately in Westminster in an ambassador's dispatch, they caused a stir."[8] These remarks should have caused a stir. The scheme was, indeed, grandiose, but the Czar took it seriously.

Nicholas I, ignoring Seymour's attempts to dissuade him otherwise, clung to his delusion that he had British support for his war. The Russian Foreign Minister, Karl Nesselrode, persevered in attempts to make Nicholas I realize that the British had no intention of stripping Turkey of its European possessions before the "sick man" died. When told this, the Czar exploded. He declared that if no agreement were reached with Great Britain, his troops might have to place Constantinople under temporary occupation.

Now genuinely alarmed at the refusal of Nicholas I to accept reality, Nesselrode and other advisers of the Czar warned him that the French and English were circling like sharks, ready to leave blood in the water if he attacked Constantinople. At his advisers' frantic urging, the Czar changed tactics. His troops would occupy the Danubian Principalities (Moldavia and Walachia) until the Porte agreed to his demands regarding the holy places. Under the treaty of Kuchuk Kainarji (1774), the Russians had the right to enter the Principalities if necessary to preserve order.[9] The Turks, however, retained nominal sovereignty over the provinces. They were likely to respond to a Russian military presence in the region by sending in troops. If a war ensued, the Russians could brand the Turks as aggressors for violating their treaty obligations.

In an effort apparently intended to provoke a Turkish military response, Nicholas I sent 66-year old Russian General Aleksandr Menschikov on a mission to Constantinople. In March, the fire-breathing general, an avowed Turkophobe, steamed into the Ottoman capital aboard the warship *Gromovnik* (Thunderer). The ostensible purpose of his trip was to convey the Czar's demand that the Turks allow the Russians to maintain exclusive privileges for the holy places sacred to Orthodox Christians, but the general was widely suspected of having a hidden agenda. Colonel Hugh Rose, the British chargé in Constantinople, voiced the concerns of many in the diplomatic community, declaring that he remained unconvinced that Menschikov had come to the Turkish capital "simply to discuss an architectural problem or the election of the Patriarch."[10] The general's lack of preparation for his supposed mission gave weight to the suspicions of Rose and others.

Menschikov had neglected to bring maps pointing to the holy places, supposedly at the heart of the controversy. The negotiations were delayed for several weeks while an underling was dispatched to Russia to fetch the critical documents.

Menschikov gradually revealed his intentions. They seemed designed to assure that the Turks would reject them. He demanded that the Porte conclude a treaty reasserting Orthodox privileges over the holy sites in Palestine. The Sultan was to acknowledge formally Russia's right to protect the 10-12 million Orthodox Christians who were Ottoman subjects. He also was to give the Russians complete control over the Orthodox Church hierarchy in Jerusalem and Constantinople. Additionally, Turkish troops were to withdraw immediately from Montenegro, where they were attempting to squelch a local uprising. Menschikov was instructed to threaten to destroy Constantinople and to occupy the Dardanelles if the Sultan refused to submit to the Czar's demands.[11] Two more Russian warships soon showed up in Constantinople to support the bullying effort, one of them bringing Vice Admiral Kornilov of the Black Sea Fleet.

It is at this point that cracks began to appear in the relationship between Franz Joseph and Nicholas I. Their letters, exchanged over the next 10 months, reflect the growing alienation of these former friends. Nicholas I came from a world where feudal loyalty was a cardinal virtue. For him, Franz Joseph's refusal to join him in his war of aggression against the Turks was an unforgivable breach of trust. The differences between these two sovereigns grew into a chasm than could never be spanned.

Early warnings of trouble between the two rulers appeared in early April 1853 when Franz Joseph canceled a visit to the Czar, planned for that summer. The Emperor's explanation, that he remained in poor health following a February assassination attempt, may have had some merit but was hardly the whole truth. A more likely reason was that Franz Joseph wished to express his disapproval of Menschikov's menacing behavior in Constantinople.[12]

Nicholas I accepted the young Emperor's excuse of ill health, expressing his concern in a letter to his "dear friend" on April 8, 1853. Then he turned to the subject of Turkey. He denied claims that he had "really aggressive intentions" toward Turkey and insisted that the survival of the Ottoman Empire was in the interest of Russia and Austria.[13] But then he added a caveat, declaring his intentions to defend Russian interests and honor. "If the Turkish government ... in her blindness doesn't see her injustice ... I will have to take up my weapons."[14]

After the Porte refused to grant the protectorate for the Orthodox Christians, demanded in the Russian ultimatum, Menschikov broke off negotiations. He departed Constantinople on May 21, 1853, "in high dudgeon," as historian A.J. Barker writes. The general headed for Odessa, accompanied by the entire Russian legation.[15]

Menschikov's mission had been meant to convey a message, and it did. The Czar was opening a new and important chapter in the Eastern Question.

A few days later Nicholas I ordered Prince M.D. Gorchakov, commander of the Russian 4th and 5th Corps, to cross the Prut, a river flowing slightly southeast and joining the Danube about 70 miles from the Black Sea. At that time the Prut marked the southern boundary of the Russian Empire. In early July 1853, a Russian "liberation army," with some 80,000 troops, marched into the Danubian Principalities on the right bank of the Prut.[16] The Czar's "dear friend" (Franz Joseph) was not consulted. "This disrespectful action offended the Emperor deeply," writes the Emperor's biographer, Joseph Redlich.[17]

While the decision of Nicholas I to send troops into Moldavia and Wallachia didn't necessarily mean war, the Western Powers as well as Austria viewed the move and the way it was handled as a likely indication of the Czar's hostile intentions. Already on June 14, English and French naval vessels had taken positions at Besika Bay at the entrance to the Dardanelles.

Franz Joseph was furious that Nicholas I would stir up trouble in that way. The Czar tried to calm fears in Vienna, with promises that he would not allow his troops to cross the Danube.

However, the Czar, responding to Franz Joseph's letter of July 2, 1853, struck a bellicose tone. Boasting that he wasn't intimidated by English and French fleets in the Dardanelles, Nicholas I vowed to persevere until he received satisfaction from the Turks. The Czar then focused on the suffering of Bulgarian Christians at the hands of the Turks. It was hardly by chance that he gave special attention to their plight. Now that his soldiers occupied the Principalities, Bulgaria was the last stepping stone on an overland route southward to Byzantium. "We will ... have to unite regarding our behavior in this matter," the Czar told his "dear friend."[18]

Nicholas I could take heart from the support he was receiving from his own people. Many of his subjects thought a rescue mission for their Orthodox brothers and sisters in the Balkans was long overdue. As the British ambassador in Petersburg reported, Russians were being "led to believe by the village priests and vagrant monks, that their religion ... (was) in danger, and that the Turks ... (were) massacring the Greeks in all directions."[19] There were reports of visions and apparitions portending victory. Grassroots sympathy in Russia for the suffering Balkan population against the Ottomans helped fuel the Czar's decision to plunge into the Crimean conflict. A similar dynamic would be at work in 1914, when ordinary Russians, full of pity for "poor little Serbia," helped convince Nicholas II to enter yet another war, the last one the Romanovs would ever wage.

Franz Joseph's letters to Nicholas I were becoming increasingly frank. On July 21, 1853,[20] he warned the Czar that the demise of the Turkish Empire would be a disaster, leading to "difficulties that could not be disentangled." In responding to the Czar's suggestion that Russia and Austria establish a common protectorate over Constantinople, Franz Joseph praised the Russian ruler for his "altruism" in suggesting that the two imperial houses cooperate in Constantinople; then he curtly dismissed the scheme. The Emperor told the Czar that his proposal raised so many doubts about its feasibility that he was "unwilling to recommend it to anyone or even to present it as a possibility." Franz Joseph said he was worried that such a move would "encourage democratic tendencies" similar to those that were arising in Switzerland. A South Slav revolution could easily spread into the Habsburg monarchy, the Emperor added.

As Redlich observes, this letter should have made it clear to the Czar that if he pursued his Balkan scheme he would face strong opposition from Austria.[21] The Czar, as usual, was tone deaf when told something he didn't want to hear. Replying six days later, Nicholas I proceeded as though nothing had changed. The Czar provided additional details for carving up Turkey. The Danubian Principalities were to be independent, with the hospodars (governors) recognized as hereditary princes. "It is very likely," the Czar wrote, "that this example will have an effect on the other Christian folk of the Turkish region, if they haven't already risen up ..." In other words, the Czar intended to destabilize the entire Balkan peninsula. This could not have set well with the Habsburg ruler. Although Nicholas I gave up his attempt to persuade Franz Joseph to agree to an Austrian-Russian protectorate over Constantinople, he now proposed that the Ottoman capital be established as a free city, with the Austrians controlling the Dardanelles and the Russians the Bosphorus.[22]

Franz Joseph was in a terrible position. The 23-year-old Emperor hadn't forgotten that the Czar had saved the Habsburg monarchy by intervening in the Hungarian uprising four years before. He wasn't thankless, as some of his critics claimed, but he was nonplussed by the Czar's aggressive scheme. In spite of the Emperor's attempts to dissuade him, the Czar continued to assume that the Austrian monarch was with him in what he now viewed as his "Orthodox crusade." As Egon Caesar Conte Corti observes, the truth was that Franz Joseph felt the need for assurances that Habsburg interests would not be harmed by that very crusade.[23] On the other hand, the Emperor wanted to avoid war with Russia.[24] Franz Joseph was about to be gored on the horns of a dilemma.

Backed by his cabinet, Franz Joseph made intensive attempts at mediation. The Austrian efforts led to a meeting of the Powers (Austria, Prussia, France and Britain) in Vienna, where their representatives produced the so-called "Vienna Note" in late July 1853. It bound Turkey to earlier treaties that were advantageous to the Romanovs. The Czar was prepared to accept the proposal. However, the Turks, objecting to certain Russian demands that infringed on their sovereignty, rejected the note.

As war loomed, the Emperor tried desperately to stop Nicholas I from marching toward disaster. The Emperor wrote the Czar on September 15, 1853, warning him of a looming "European conflagration."[25] Those wishing for a revolution were being filled with "jubilation and hope" at what was happening, Franz Joseph said. He had even heard that Kossuth, the Hungarian firebrand who inspired the 1848 revolution, was only waiting for Austria to be drawn into the conflict so he could stir up new trouble in the monarchy. The Emperor said that the thought of more bloodshed so soon after the Hungarian Revolution's end was "painful" – surely his Russian friend would understand that better than anyone.[26]

In responding to Franz Joseph's letter of September 15, the Czar didn't outright accuse his imperial brother of disloyalty, but his language seemed intended to make the Emperor ashamed of his failure to support fully the Russian scheme. Nicholas I portrayed himself as a lonely protector of Christendom. He was defending the true faith "against the fanaticism of ... the unhappy Turks," while the British and French were fighting infamously for the Half Moon (Turkey). "Is it to be believed that Russia ... in this holy matter ... will have no allies?"[27] the Czar wailed. The question suggests that the Czar saw Franz Joseph as a Judas, betraying the sacred crusade by refusing to join him in battle.

Aware that Franz Joseph wasn't moved by his flights of rhetoric, the Czar in September traveled to the Moravian town of Olomouc, where he met with the Emperor and pled his cause. The two rulers talked for hours but failed to resolve their differences. Franz Joseph refused to join the Czar in going against Turkey. He and Karl Ferdinand von Buol, his minister of foreign affairs, pushed the Russian ruler for guarantees that he would consider Austrian interests during his Balkan campaign. The Czar halfheartedly promised that he would not carve up Turkey. He denied intentions of going beyond the Danube. This issue was always of great importance to the Austrians, because this would put the Russians in a position to interfere with shipping on that vital waterway. In Vienna, there was widespread doubt that Nicholas I would keep his word.

Events rapidly reached a crescendo. On September 22, British and French fleets edged slowly through the Straits. On October 4, the Porte gave Russia two weeks to evacuate the Principalities. Nothing happened. On October 23, the Ottomans formally declared war.

Barker describes the scene in Constantinople as the Turks girded for the fight: "Above the Bosphorus an army began to assemble; the streets ... were thronged with ill-disciplined but colourful Bashi-Bazouks – cut throats, hastily recruited from the scum of towns as irregular Turkish infantry..." General Omar Pasha, the Austrian-born army defector, was in command. By the end of October the Turks had engaged the Russian army in Wallachia.[28]

The Russian fleet, anchored at the Crimean port of Sevastopol, dealt the Ottomans a powerful blow on November 30, 1853. The Czar's navy sailed south across the Black Sea to Sinope, a mere 100 miles across the waters, where the Turkish navy lay at anchor. The Russians destroyed all except one vessel in the Sultan's fleet and killed as many as 4,000 Turkish sailors. The English public, hearing of the "massacre of Sinope," was outraged. Anti-Russian sentiment boiled over, as citizens demanded that their government assure that the Black Sea was not "turned into a Russian lake." Early in January 1854, 10 British and nine French ships of the line had sailed through the Bosphorus, prepared to do battle. All-out war only awaited the spring thaw.

An exchange of views between the Russian and Austrian rulers early in 1854 revealed the widening chasm between the former friends. Franz Joseph had written Nicholas I on January 7 to inform him about a conference by the Powers held in Vienna on December 5 of the previous year in which participants agreed to ask Russia to pursue peace negotiations in a neutral city. The request came with a caveat: The Russians must evacuate the Danubian Principalities prior to the negotiations. Nicholas I was furious at this one-sided proposal. He countered with a demand that the Western Powers withdraw their fleets from waters close to Constantinople.

Franz Joseph was blunt. He informed his Russian brother that he would oppose him if he continued his policies in the Balkans. The Emperor's words surely stung: "As for the political relations of Turkey's European provinces," Franz Joseph wrote, his irritation seeping into his language, "you will remember, dear friend, that I have frequently explained to you both in writing and orally that the emancipation of these countries would affect both our interests .... I could never consent to it, for the reasons I have already given you."[29]

Franz Joseph promised neutrality in case the local war in the Balkans spread, but he made this neutrality contingent on the Czar's keeping earlier promises. Then the Emperor did the unthinkable. He insisted that the Czar repeat his earlier promises. The Emperor said the interests of the monarchy required him to demand "the most definite and solemn assurance" that Russian troops, when on the defensive, would not go beyond the Danube. If the war forced the Russians to cross the river, the Czar was to promise to honor his earlier declaration that he "would not seek territorial enlargement or mix in matters involving the Sultan and his subjects."[30] Franz Joseph then added a new demand. Nicholas I was to agree to maintain the political status quo between the Balkan provinces and Turkey in Europe. Franz Joseph said: "I must have these in my hands, in the interest of Austria – You will understand that." After avowing his friendly intentions, the Emperor added, surely ironically, that he was certain that, since the Czar had said he had no desire for conquests, "he wouldn't mind repeating those assurances."[31]

The Czar most certainly did not "understand that." What Franz Joseph was saying was for him unthinkable. In biographer Redlich's words: "That was language such as the Czar had never heard from any one of the European sovereigns," and which he least expected from his young friend in Vienna.[32]

The Czar's reply, on January 16, 1854, was full of wounded pride and fury, couched in the stiffest of terms. Franz Joseph had surprised him and left a painful feeling, the Czar said. "Can you believe," the Russian ruler asked, incredulously, "that an honorable man (meaning of course himself) would be double tongued or that he could take back what he once had declared was his intention: When that is established, is it then not a hateful superfluity to allow oneself to doubt his given word, or to ask, that he repeat it? While I have obligated myself to the world and to you, and what still means more, while I have said it to my nation, that we don't need conquests and don't seek them, is there anyone who should ... doubt that?"

The Czar refused to repeat his guarantees. "Are you really going to make the concerns of the Turks your own?" Nicholas I asked. "Apostolic Kaiser, does your conscience allow that of you? If that is so, good, then Russia alone will follow her holy destiny under the holy cross. If you should turn your strength against me toward the Half Moon, so I declare that this will lead to a parricidal war." He ended on a defiant note: "God will be our judge, but I will not turn back."[33]

Nicholas I, confused and stunned by Franz Joseph's apparent disloyalty, sent an envoy, Count Aleksei Orlov, to Vienna to assess the situation. He arrived at the court on January 29, 1854. The visit did nothing to reassure the Austrians. Orlov refused to confirm the Czar's earlier promise that Russian troops would not cross the Danube. He offered no guarantees that the Romanovs would honor the territorial integrity of the Ottoman Empire. In a gesture of arrogant generosity based on assumptions that the Romanovs would achieve their Balkan aims, Orlov declared that the Czar was willing to offer Austria a protectorate over some areas of Turkey that would be gaining their independence. Franz Joseph rejected the Romanov ruler's proposal for a shared protectorate over Ottoman territory and insisted on retention of the status quo in European Turkey.

For Nicholas I the veil of illusion had been swept aside. He was forced to confront the disappointing truth. Writing on February 29, 1854, the Czar lashed out at the Emperor for ignoring the obligation he incurred when he requested the assistance of Russian troops in putting down the Hungarian Revolution. Nicholas I said that, even if it cost him his friendship with the Habsburg ruler, he had no choice but to rescue the helpless Balkan Christians from "the cruel Turkish yoke." He then issued an eerie warning to his young imperial brother, telling him that his present course, contradicting the long-honored mores of the monarchy, was likely to bring "terrible disaster" on the House of Habsburg.[34]

The letters between the Emperor and the Czar revealed major differences in the two rulers' personalities and assumptions. Franz Joseph was rational regarding imperial matters. He couldn't understand why the Czar took to heart his lack of support for the Romanov military adventure in the Balkans. To him it seemed self-evident that a ruler should act in the interests of his nation. Personal diplomacy was meant to serve those interests.

For Nicholas I, as for all the Romanov rulers, personal diplomacy was intended to serve dynastic interests, which were not necessarily those of the people. The sacred bonds of friendship between monarchs were the key to successful foreign policy. Imperial brothers owed each other loyalty. Honor required that blood debts be repaid. This feudal code of conduct was the foundation on which the Romanovs had built their house.

The failure of personal diplomacy was to play a pivotal role in bringing on the First World War.

That spring, as Russia's frozen rivers and roads became passable, Nicholas I prepared for his armies to march. He ordered General Mikhail Gorchakov to cross the Danube along its entire length between Vidin and Silistra. The capture of these two fortresses, located in present-day Bulgaria, was a priority.

The British and French declared war on March 28, 1854.

By that time Gorchakov's army of 45,000 troops was beyond the Danube, overwhelming the Turks in the Dobrudscha, today a region of northern Bulgaria and southern Romania. The Russians also took Tultscha (Tulcea), a town that commanded the Danube and its three branches near the river's estuary at the Black Sea.

The Russian military operation had the potential to bring the monarchy's shipping operations to a halt. The Austrians responded with a massive buildup of troops – more than 250,000 men – on the frontiers of Moldavia and Wallachia.[35] Upon receiving news of the Habsburg mobilization, Russian Field Marshal Ivan Paskevich ordered Gorchakov to suspend the Danubian campaign. However, the general pressed on to Silistra, where he began a siege.

June was to be a bad month for the Russians. On June 3, the Austrian ambassador in St. Petersburg delivered an ultimatum from Franz Joseph to the Czar calling for the immediate withdrawal of Russian troops from the Principalities. The Emperor also demanded that Nicholas I give up his claims for the religious and political protectorate of Orthodox Christians in the Ottoman Empire.[36] When the ambassador presented the ultimatum to the Czar in a private audience, the ruler went into a rant. Nicholas I claimed that Franz Joseph had forgotten what Russia had done for him in Hungary. Now the Emperor had wrecked "his most beautiful political plans," the Czar told the envoy.[37] Nicholas I declared that "the confidence that had existed between the two empires was destroyed and that the former intimate relations would never again exist." His words were prescient. There would be later attempts at reconciliation between Franz Joseph and the three generations of Romanov czars who succeeded Nicholas I, sometimes with seeming success, but the deep divide that developed during the Crimean War remained.

An officer who saw the Czar when he arrived to inspect the Imperial Guards later that day, saw that Nicholas I had undergone a dramatic change. "He was unrecognizable," the officer recalled. "His face had a greenish pallor, his profile had lengthened, and his eyes had a fixed expression: only his step was firm."[38]

Everything had gone wrong for Nicholas I. The Russian military considered Silistra the key to the conquest of Constantinople. The siege against that vital stronghold continued for 40 days, with the Russians suffering heavy casualties. On June 23 the czarist army gave up the fight. The Czar's soldiers also suffered defeats against the British. This was a shameful embarrassment for the Romanovs. The Queen's troops were a disgrace. British officers showed up for battle in full dress complete with epaulettes. Meanwhile ordinary British soldiers lacked tents and dry socks.[39]

The Czar was running out of options. Engaging in bitter reflection he wrote:

"I can understand Silistra — the strongest may fail in a siege — but, that Turks — mere Turks — led on by a general of Sepoys[40] and six or seven English boys — that they should dare to cross the Danube in the face of my troops — that, daring to attempt this, they should do it, and hold fast their ground — that my troops should give way before them; and that this — that this should be the last act of the campaign which is ending with the retreat of my whole army, and the abandonment of the Principalities ... Heaven lays upon me more than I can bear."[41]

Faced with impossibilities wherever he turned, Nicholas I agreed to withdraw from the Principalities on condition that neither Britain nor France be allowed to occupy the region. He ordered the withdrawal on July 24, 1854. The Austrians then entered the Principalities.

The Prussian King at this juncture sought to be a peacemaker. Friedrich Wilhelm IV wrote the Czarina urging the Russians to make no objection to the Austrian presence in the Principalities, telling her that he knew "positively" that Franz Joseph would undertake the occupation with no trace of enmity toward Russia.[42] These assurances undoubtedly did little to dress the wounds the Russian ruling family felt they had received from the Habsburg Emperor. As far as they were concerned, Austria's perfidy was the chief cause of Russian's humiliation before the world.

The war now took another unfortunate turn for the Russians. The presence of Austria's neutral army in the Principalities prevented the British and French from pursuing Gorchakov's troops across the Danube. The best remaining recourse for the western allies seemed to lie in an attack on Russia's prize ports of Odessa or Sevastopol, where a quick victory might encourage the Austrians and Prussians to join the opposing coalition.

Franz Joseph was at a crossroads. Karl Ferdinand von Buol, his foreign minister, was among those urging him to join the Western Powers. The Emperor saw the difficulties in this. "Did you know," Franz Joseph responded to his foreign minister's prodding, "that there are here in Vienna only two men, who are not inclined toward the Russians? And those are you and I."[43] Also, the Emperor found it hard to imagine joining Louis Napoleon III, who – increasingly self-confident at French military successes in Crimea – was eying Habsburg holdings in Italy. What is more, while Franz Joseph viewed as despicable the Czar's continuing aggression in the Balkans, he knew that the Russians would still be Austria's neighbors after the fighting stopped.

For a time, encouraged by Buol, Franz Joseph gave unofficial support to the Western allies, contributing to their cause in the battles of Alma and Inkerman.[44] On October 21, he even ordered all-out mobilization against Russia. A month later, however, he required his troops to stand down. This wavering infuriated the French and English, who threatened to withdraw their ambassadors from Vienna.[45] By the time the war ended, Franz Joseph had managed to offend both sides.

The conflict, in the meantime, was taking its toll on Nicholas I. A.F. Tiutschva, a maid of honor at the Russian court, bewailed the events of those difficult days, serving as a kind of Greek chorus as she recounted the woes of the Czar and his empire. She wrote on October 1854 of Nicholas: "His tall figure is beginning to bend. He has a sort of lifeless stare, his face a leaden colour. His brow, haughty not long ago, each day is lined with new furrows."[46]

For the Czar, yet another blow came in December when he learned that Austria had joined an alliance with Great Britain and France. The alliance wasn't a heart and soul affair, for certain. It is fortunate that it never had to be honored thanks to events overrunning it. But when the Czar learned what Franz Joseph had done he exploded at the Emperor's perfidy. He turned his "dear friend's" portrait to the wall and scrawled on the back *"Der Undankbarer!"* (the ungrateful one!).[47] He is said to have given Franz Joseph's bust, which had graced an honored place on the Czar's desk, to his valet.[48] Nicholas I expressed his bitterness to Count Esterhazy, the Austrian ambassador in St. Petersburg: "The trust that existed between us both (rulers) for the well-being of our empires has been destroyed and it can never again be restored." He declared that he and Polish King Johann Sobieski were the "dumbest kings who had ever lived ..." Sobieski drove the Turkish army back from the gates of Vienna in 1683 but, according to the Czar, the Austrians, rather than showing gratitude for the Polish King's help, treated him "like a dog."[49] It is interesting that in his furor and sorrow the Czar used the same phrase that Peter the Great had used after the Austrians disappointed him by making a separate peace at Karlowicz, thus depriving him of taking his navy through the Straits of Kerch and all the way to Constantinople.

Nicholas took sick in early 1855 and died of an acute respiratory illness on March 2. It was said in St. Petersburg that Franz Joseph's ingratitude killed the Romanov ruler. The Czarina considered Franz Joseph hardly better than the assassin of her husband. She never forgave the Emperor. For most members of the House of Romanov, Russia was forever an enemy of Austria.

Czar Alexander II, upon succeeding his father in power, declared his intention to continue the war, saying he would "perish rather than surrender."

The port of Sevastopol was a crown jewel among the Romanovs' possessions, a project of Catherine the Great, a stunning edifice in a crucial location on the western edge of the Crimean Peninsula. When the port's magazines exploded under bombardment from the coalition forces, creating a great conflagration of structures and causing huge loss of life, Russia's hopes of victory were laid waste. The siege of Sevastopol ended in September 1855. Russia had lost the Crimean War. One of its major casualties was the relationship between the Romanovs and the Habsburgs.

The search for an honest broker to negotiate the peace treaty began, not without some snags. The United States would have been the Powers' first choice, had it not been for a diplomatic spat between Washington and London over American attempts to annex Cuba from the Spanish. The Americans wanted the island because it was a lucrative center of the slave trade. The British warned the U.S. government that they would "not stand idly" by if the Americans attempted to seize Cuba. The British, who had abolished slavery in 1833, refused to agree to American-led peace talks. They feared that Washington would side with the Russians in the negotiations in exchange for St. Petersburg's support of the U.S. annexation of Cuba. James Buchanan, the U.S. minister in London, for his part, simply couldn't understand "why England should object to ... (the U.S.) annexation..." After all, he said, the Americans had

139

"extended the English language, Christianity, liberty and law wherever ... (they) went on ... (their) own continent."[50]

The negotiators finally agreed for Austria to take the lead in brokering the peace. Naturally many Russians felt humiliated at having the Habsburgs in that role. As the talks proceeded there were Russian complaints that they were being forced into "a dishonest peace."[51] When the protocol to the treaty was signed in Vienna that February (1856), some Russian men cried in humiliation, believing the nation's honor had been compromised. This did not bode well for future relations between Austria and Russia.

The Austrians were also highly unpopular with others at the conference table. The Earl of Clarenden grumbled that Austria was playing the lead in the discussions although the Habsburgs "had not spent a shilling or spilt a drop of blood in the contest which more nearly concerns her than it does any other."[52] Making matters worse, Buol, the Austrian foreign minister, and Alexander Bach, the interior minister, had come down with what might be called the Balkan sickness. Like the advocates of a Greater Serbia, a Greater Bulgaria, a Greater Croatia, etc., the two ministers began campaigning for a Greater Austria, based on a permanent Habsburg occupation of the Danube Principalities. Bach persuaded himself that the goodhearted and God-fearing people of Moldavia and Wallachia would just love to be subjects of Austria, which would bring roads, railroads and commerce and the rule of law to the backward regions.[53] The Greater Austria movement soon collided with a solid wall of political reality. At the Paris Congress where the final peace negotiations were conducted, the one thing all the parties (except Austria) agreed on was that the monarchy was not to have Moldavia and Wallachia.

The Treaty of Paris, signed March 30, 1856, dealt serious blows to Russian ambitions in the Balkans. Along with warships of other nations, the Russian naval fleet was barred from the Black Sea. Alexander II was forced to relinquish his claims of special rights to the protection of Wallachia and Moldavia. The Principalities were granted semi-independent status while remaining under nominal Ottoman sovereignty. The Russians as well as the French agreed to abandon their claims to act as protectors of Christians in the Ottoman Empire. The territories of both Russia and Turkey were returned to their prewar status.

Napoleon III emerged in a solid position, having positioned himself on the winning side of the conflict. He soon would be preparing for a military confrontation with the Habsburgs in which he would succeed in 1859 in relieving the monarchy of much of its Italian territory.

As for the holy places, they received no mention in the Paris treaty.[54] When Easter arrived one year after the treaty was signed, "the efforts of all participants in the war seemed to be mocked," writes Trevor Royle. Fighting broke out among the pilgrims and priests in the Church of the Holy Sepulchre in Bethlehem during the annual "miracle of flight from heaven" service. According to those present, it was "as bad as anything witnessed before the war."[55]

9 PAN-SLAVS

In spite of the Russians' military debacle in the Crimean War, Alexander II clung to his family's centuries-old dream of taking Constantinople and the Straits. Forced by the Treaty of Paris at the end of the war to dismantle what was left of Russia's Black Sea Fleet, the Czar changed his strategy. He now sought to create Slav satellite states in the Balkans with the help of a network of secret agents, including Orthodox bishops and priests. He hoped to use these vassal states as staging grounds for Russian troops when the time came for further military action against the Ottomans. The three Balkan states with predominantly Orthodox Slav populations – Montenegro, Bulgaria and Serbia – were the Russians' likeliest partners in a future conflict with the Turks. The meddling of czarist agents in these nations caused continuous tension between St. Petersburg and Vienna.

The disastrous outcome of the Crimean War not only forced the members of the House of Romanov to revise their Balkan policy; it also led ordinary Russians to rethink their relationship with the outside world. The Russian people traditionally had followed the lead of xenophobic clerics, who encouraged their flocks to keep to themselves. But in the post-Crimean era, a movement known as Pan-Slavism caught the public's imagination. Its advocates urged Slav ethnic groups, with their shared linguistic and cultural histories, to work for the good of the large Slav community. Pan-Slavism, as originally conceived by Croatian, Slovak and Czech thinkers, was a utopian vision that could not survive in its pure form. The movement eventually collapsed under its own contradictions. Militant nationalists co-opted the field, using Pan-Slavism as a forum for their own propaganda.

By welcoming Pan-Slavists' help in a mercy mission for suffering Orthodox Christians in the Balkans, Czarina Marie, the pious wife of Alexander II, gave impetus to the movement. The Czarina was incensed that the Great Powers, at the end of the Crimean War, had refused to honor Russia's claim as protector of the Balkan Christians. One day, as she was sipping tea with three ladies-in-waiting, the Czarina told her companions that the time had come to stop complaining and to act. Princess Vasilisa Chikova, the wife of a well-known general; Countess Protasova, wife of the procurator of the Holy Synod, and Countess Antoinette Bludova, eagerly joined the Czarina in her new cause. The women collected large sums of money. Soon messengers were heading south with saddlebags bulging with cash intended for the suffering Orthodox Christians.

For the ladies at the Romanov court, nothing could have been more innocent than these charitable activities. But the Czarina and her friends, hoping to start an organization to assist the Balkan Slav Christians, failed to receive encouragement for their project from Russian officials. They then turned for help to Moscow intellectuals whose motives were far from benign. Michael Pogodin, a history professor who had tried unsuccessfully to persuade Nicholas I to seek allies among the foreign Slavs, responded to the ladies' request for assistance. So did Ivan Aksakov, a Slavophile publicist. These men were instrumental in the formation of the Moscow Slavic Benevolent Committee in 1858.[1] While it was ostensibly a charitable organization, it promoted a virulent brand of nationalism. Pogodin and Aksakov believed that the Crimean War had shown the West to be hostile to Slavdom. In response, they claimed, the Slavs of various nations needed to join forces against a common enemy.[2]

Alexander II, preoccupied with a young mistress whom he had given quarters in the royal palace, was glad his wife had found a cause into which she could channel her passions. The Czar was skeptical that the various Slav nations, many of them hereditary foes, would suddenly put aside their grievances and work together. However, to the extent that the movement helped form a solid bloc of Slav ethnic groups, in opposition to the German and Austrian Teutons and the Turks, Pan-Slavism suited the Czar just fine.

In the past, Russian Slavs had generally kept to themselves. Slavophilism, a melding of romanticism, mythology and messianism, was based on a belief that Orthodoxy was the only true religion. Local priests toiled for the church, sowing seeds of belief and superstition in the fertile soil of unlearned peasant psyches. By virtue of their attachment to the land, Russian peasants were seen as occupying a special place in the Slavophile cosmos. The simple people were encouraged to view their Czar as untouchable and deific. Some of the peasants were even led to believe that their ruler journeyed to heaven once a week to consult with the Almighty himself on matters concerning their personal welfare. Slavophile priests sought to shield Orthodox believers from Western influences – particularly from the Roman Catholic Church, which Orthodox leaders saw as the archenemy of the true faith.

In contrast, Pan-Slavism was an ideology which, in its purest form, was outward looking and inclusive. George

Krizanic, a 17th-century Croatian Catholic, is said to have been the earliest advocate of Pan-Slavism.[3] In the 19th century, two thinkers, a Slovak poet and Lutheran pastor named Jan Kollar, and Frantisek Palacky, a Moravian who played a key role in the Czech National Awakening, sought to give coherence to the Pan-Slav idea. Whereas Slavophilism involved a particularist way of looking at the world, Pan-Slavism emphasized what Slavs of various nationalities had in common. The various Slav groups were urged to think of themselves and their ethnic brothers as occupants of one big tent, celebrating their shared culture and language and working for the communal good. Later, after ultranationalists emerged as leaders of the Pan-Slavist movement, their Slav supporters began to set themselves apart from the Teutons, sometimes taking a kind of glee in the notion of the Germans being outside the big tent looking in.

Pan-Slavism suffered from internal contradictions that soon dashed purists' hopes for a real unity of purpose. In common with the Romantic movements of the early 19th century, Pan-Slavism glorified the individual. It was Wordsworthian in stressing the language and culture of ordinary people as central to a nation's identity. This presented a problem that would have required someone of Friedrich Hegel's philosophical genius to resolve. While the original proponents of Pan-Slavism had sought universality, the Slav ethnic groups quickly discovered that they had less in common than they imagined. Non-Russian Pan-Slavists particularly resented the behavior of their Russian brothers, who were correctly understood to be militant nationalists in Pan-Slavists' clothing.

Russian philosopher Vladimir Solovyov defines nationalism as "worship of one's own people as the preeminent bearer of universal truth."[4] This conviction of inherent superiority soon emerged as a core philosophical belief of Russian Pan-Slavism. The Russians thought it was only meet and right that their culture should be acknowledged by other Slavs as superior to theirs. As Alexander Pushkin put it, "The Slavic rivers should join the Russian sea."[5]

Nineteenth-century novelist Fyodor Dostoevsky was among those promoting Russian exceptionalism. He made it more palatable to the Russian public by couching it in religious terms, melding the message of Orthodoxy from Slavophilism with the more secular thrust of Pan-Slavism. He encouraged his fellow countrymen to see themselves as chosen people, which meant they were "superior to other Slavs."[6]

In Dostoevsky's *The Devils*, Ivan Shatov – considered by some critics as the writer's alter ego – goes further: "If a great people does not believe that truth resides in it alone ... if it does not believe that it alone is able and has chosen to rise up and save everybody by its own truth, it is ... (not) a great people. A truly great people can never reconcile itself to playing second fiddle in the affairs of humanity..."[7]

A key element in exceptionalism is narcissistic myopia, deluding leaders and their followers into believing that the inhabitants of a nation that is being overrun, imposed upon, occupied or annexed are going to bow joyfully to the invaders' superior culture and will remain eternally grateful for the good fortune that has been visited upon them. This was a component of Russian ambitions in the Balkans, where the czarists liked to imagine that they were doing the poor, suffering peoples of the region a favor by sending in their troops. Of course, sometimes they were.

Naturally, there were cynics who understood the Russian fallacy in expecting to be beloved by virtue of their superiority. Foreign Minister Aleksandr Gorchakov, for one, considered the claims of exceptionalism coming from the Russian Pan-Slavists ridiculous. "I find it difficult to believe," he declared, "in the sympathy of the Slav people for autocratic Russia."[8] A Czech journalist, Karel Havlicek, remarking on the insularity of the Russian Pan-Slavs that he had observed while visiting Moscow in 1846, declared, "The Russian Pan-Slavs believe that we and the Illyrians would like to be under their domination.... They now look forward with joy to their future vineyards in Dalmatia."[9] Havlicek, who had been an ardent Pan-Slavist, wrote that his experience in Moscow had cured him forever of his attraction to that ideology.

Belief in exceptionalism is, of course, by no means unique to Russia. It has often been used as an excuse to justify questionable or even unjustifiable conduct. Otto von Bismarck encouraged the Germans to think of themselves as possessing cultural superiority that obligated them to impose themselves on others.[10] The British defended their colonial forays by telling themselves that they had a duty to bring good government and enlightened religion to the poor heathens. The Serbs claimed a moral right to Kosovo on grounds that they were a more civilized people[11] than the Albanian inhabitants of the tiny region. The Austrians also toyed with the idea of a "civilizing mission" in the East.[12] As we shall see later on, the Habsburgs' experience following their occupation of Bosnia and Herzegovina in 1878 would prove that imposing "civilization" on peoples who don't necessarily want it comes with untold difficulties.

The Russian insistence on playing first fiddle helped derail a Pan-Slav congress held in Moscow in 1867. The Poles boycotted the congress on the suspicion, which was valid, that the Russians would try to dominate the meeting. The delegates who attended came like distant relatives, eager to get acquainted with kinfolk whose names they had heard but about whom they knew next to nothing. As is often the case in meetings of this kind, many of the representatives became disillusioned, finding that they had much less in common with their relatives than they expected. Starry-eyed dreamers, who had hoped to lay the groundwork for a confederation of Slavs, not only confronted age-old clefts separating Orthodox and Roman Catholic Slavs; they also had to grapple with unexpected linguistic difficulties. The majority of the delegates – including Ruthenians, Croats, Slovenians, Czechs – didn't speak French, which was the language used between European courts. When the representatives spoke their own languages, they often could barely make themselves understood by Slavs from other regions. The delegates refused to bow to the Russians' insistence that they use that language, even if they could speak and understand it. There seemed nothing left to do except resort to the language many of them violently disliked, the hated German. After several sessions producing little more than platitudes and fancy phrases, the delegates went home in a huff.[13]

While the Russian Pan-Slavs were disappointed by the failure of the Moscow Congress, they were bolstered by the continued support they were receiving from Czarina Marie as well as from the heir apparent (later Alexander III), who believed that the movement could help the Russians finally realize the Greek Project of Catherine the Great.

The propagandist Aksakov became increasingly active in the Pan-Slav cause. In 1859, he briefly published a newspaper, (Parus) The Sail, advocating an international Slavic union. He urged Russia to fulfill its divine mission by freeing its Orthodox brothers from Western influences, particularly from what he called "unbridled rationalism." One of his goals was to stir up dissension among Slavs in the Habsburg Empire. He opined that the monarchy's Slavs had nothing in common with the Germans in language, history or creed. He accused the Austrians of planning to incorporate 10 million more Slavs, from regions to the monarchy's east, into the Habsburg Empire.[14] This is a classic example of projection. It was the Russian nationalists who wanted a large union of Slavs. The Austrians had from time to time entertained the idea of a tripartite monarchy of Germans, Hungarians and Slavs, but had never seriously pursued it.

Foreign Minister Gorchakov, who at the time was seeking peaceful coexistence with the monarchy, denounced *The Sail's* anti-Habsburg tone, saying it was a "caustic disparagement" of Russian foreign policy. He ordered Aksakov to stop publication. This caused an uproar among passionate Pan-Slavists. These included the head of the Russian department that controlled Balkan affairs at the foreign office. He complained to Countess Antonina Bludova about Gorchakov's move. She, in turn, persuaded the Czarina to intercede with her husband regarding the cancelled newspaper.[15] Alexander II had no appetite for protecting from Pan-Slav attacks those he considered the enemies of the House of Romanov, most particularly the Austrians. Additionally, he did not want to quarrel with the Czarina, who had taken the Pan-Slav cause so much to heart. The Czar compromised, giving Aksakov permission to start a new paper as long as he did not meddle in politics.

Keeping Aksakov from meddling in politics did little to quell the Pan-Slav (and Pan-Russian) fever that swept the empire during the last years of Alexander II's reign. Pan-Slav advocates spoke in increasingly menacing tones. Their combative language was accompanied by a change in emphasis. They talked little about purity of religion, or about overcoming differences of language, or even about the mission of Russia as a civilizing force. They glorified war and preached that the Slav federation must be brought under the domination of Russia. They "stood out nakedly for the annihilation of the Habsburg and Ottoman Empires through the military might of Russia,"[16] writes historian B.H. Sumner.

Nikolai Danilevsky, a general's son, argued in a treatise that "a struggle with the West" was needed to cure Russia's cultural ills and to cause the Slav factions to rise above petty differences and unite. "The already ripening Eastern Question is making this struggle inevitable..."[17] Danilevsky wrote. He envisioned a confederation of 125 million Slavs. The Poles, Finns, Latvians, Estonians and Lithuanians would remain in the Russian Empire. A separate governmental structure would bring into the large Russian tent a Czech-Moravian-Slovak kingdom; a kingdom of the Serbs-Croats-Slovenes and the Bulgarian kingdom.[18] All these entities were to be dependent on Russia for defense and foreign policy. Russian, in the meantime, was to sate "her iniquitous lust for power ... by freeing Christians from Moslems, Slavs from Germans ... and by re-establishing Constantinople as the greatest city in Christendom."[19]

A work by a militant nationalist, Rostislav Andreievich Fadejev, appearing in 1869 and entitled *Opinion on the Eastern Question*, is generally considered the most influential Pan-Slav polemic of its time. It rapidly went into several editions and was translated into most European languages. The book radically departs from the relatively benign Pan-Slavism of those in Czarina Marie's circle. Fadejev showed "no interest in the past ... no feeling for the unique mission of the Orthodox Church and the civilization based upon it, no blind belief in the virtue of the Russian peasant," according to Sumner. The treatise, like Adolf Hitler's *Mein Kampf*, is a manifesto for war.[20] Fadejev claimed that the realization of Russia's "historic individuality" required expansion into the Slavic world. The Eastern Question could only be solved by brute force, Fadejev argued. Russia's chief enemy, Fadejev declared, was "the German race in its enormous pretensions."[21] Austria would have to be eliminated due to its strategic location, which interfered with the realization of the Russian dream. Prussia was an enemy since it was certain to support Austria in the coming conflict. In girding for the anticipated fight, Russia needed to establish herself as "the undisputed leader" of the Slavs, Fadejev wrote.

The keynote to the book came in a phrase, attributed to Ivan Paskevich, the Russian general who led the army that put down the Hungarian Revolution in 1849. He wrote,

"The way to Constantinople lies through Vienna."[22]

From the end of the Crimean War to the start of the First World War the Russians would attempt, with mixed success, to create vassal states in the Balkans. Greece and Romania tended to go their own way, in part because of language differences. Bosnia and Herzegovina presented complications with their mixed population of Orthodox Serbs, Albanian Muslims and Roman Catholics. That left Montenegro, Bulgaria and Serbia, all of which not only had a Slavic language but also a preponderance of Orthodox believers. Russian agents were continuously active in these provinces, seeking to establish them as future bases of operation. Orthodox bishops often secretly served the Russian cause.

Among the Balkan nations, Montenegro had the closest relationship with the Russians. These ties went back to 1711, when Peter the Great sent an envoy to Cetinje, the provincial capital, exhorting those people "of one blood and one faith with Russia" to fight the Turks and to join him at Constantinople.[23] Spurred by the high-flown rhetoric of the Russian Czar, the Montenegrins went wild. A big battle, known as "The Field of the Sultan's Felling," took place on high ground between Rijeka and the present capital of Podgorica. The Turks were entangled in thornbushes and slaughtered wholesale.[24] The Montenegrins and Russians were never to meet in Constantinople, but the relationship between the two peoples would have significance for both. In 1715 Danilo Petrovic, the Montenegrin ruler, visited St. Petersburg in a trip that brought long-term rewards. Peter the Great provided subsidies for the Petrovic family, establishing a precedent that helped assure Montenegrin friendship.

Austrian representatives also made their way up the mountains to Cetinje during that century, and their presence initiated a long diplomatic struggle between the Romanovs and Habsburgs for predominance in the remote province. In

1779 the Austrians responded to a Montenegrin call for help in fighting Muslim Serbs in neighboring Bosnia and Herzegovina. In February 1853, Franz Joseph was prepared to send troops into Montenegro, again at their request. The people were being massacred by the Turks. The Emperor averted war by persuading the Sultan to stop the fighting.

At first glance, Montenegro was little more than a flyspeck on the Balkan map, hardly worth the effort that the two empires, over time, expended there. When Prince Nikola Petrovic became ruler of his mountain aerie in 1860, Cetinje consisted of several dozen one-story houses lining a single street. Nikola's palace, which stood at the end of the street, was distinguished mainly by its being slightly larger than the other dwellings.

In 1870, Montenegro had a population of 200,000, mostly shepherds and mountaineers, fierce warrior-people who had been known to wear their enemies' heads on their belts as they continued in battle. Until the 1860s Montenegro had no dentist. An Albanian who worked as a blacksmith filled in with tooth duty when difficulties arose. A principal export was flea powder. Women did most of the work.[25] Montenegro had no police and no laws except those of the fierce mountain clans. Tribal leaders lived in imposing stone houses, which characteristically had holes in the walls through which firearms could be pointed.

Prince Nikola rapidly established himself as a force to be reckoned with, both within Montenegro and beyond her borders. In a region that traditionally produced improbable characters, Prince Nikola was in a class by himself – eccentric, dynamic, tilting one way and another, as someone said, like a sturdy branch of a pine tree in a mountain wind. He was, in the words of Edith Durham, who knew him well, "the last of the medieval chieftains of Europe."[26] He had a rough face verging on handsome, a sturdy build, grayish hair and eyes as sharp as an eagle's. Educated in the West, he loved poetry. He knew the family names of all his subjects.

Nikola wheeled and dealed, holding audiences with local headsmen squatting under an oak tree in front of his palace. Little Montenegro caused a disproportionate amount of trouble. The province's geography made it easy for the inhabitants to cultivate an independent streak. The Ottomans never quite got Montenegro under control. Fighting the native warriors in the barren mountain passes and on the peaks was too much trouble. The Montenegrins intentionally neglected to build roads which might tempt invaders. Visitors to the capital had to make their way up steep, boulder-strewn trails, barely passable for donkeys.

The Habsburgs considered strategically situated Montenegro as key to the balance of power in the Balkans. Their main goal was to prevent Montenegro from joining with Serbia to create a large Slav state. They feared that this might induce restive Slavs in the monarchy to try to break away. It was therefore necessary for Austria to treat Nikola gingerly, even when he behaved outrageously, as was more often than not the case.

One redeeming factor in the situation, from the Habsburgs' point of view, was that Nikola had a compelling reason not to join the Serbs. He was infused with ambition. He yearned to reconstruct the Great Serbian Empire with his own Petrovic family as the reigning dynasty.[27] This put him at odds with the Serbs, who over the years had been ruled by either the Obrenovic or the Karageorgevic dynasty, one replacing the other, sometimes because the rival ruler or heir had been assassinated.

In Montenegro, the Russians enjoyed a natural advantage over the Habsburgs. Spiritually and culturally the Montenegrins and the Russians were close. In some ways Montenegro was a miniature version of Russia. The kingdom boasted an extraordinary number of churches, proportionally even more than Holy Russia. Since everything in Montenegro was measured by the Russian standard, the churches were a matter of pride to the ruler.[28]

The Austrians were generous with subsidies, but money went only so far in a bidding war where the stakes were always being raised. Alexander II gladly provided Nikola with weapons, which the Montenegrin ruler graciously accepted. Nikola gladly received subsidies for roads from the Austrians, whom he feared and hated. Taking care to be evenhanded, he also partook of monetary handouts from the Sultan.

The Russians had close cultural and mythical ties to the Bulgarians. Geography, religion and a common heritage drew the peoples together. After the Crimean War, the Russians cultivated Bulgaria as a vassal state, although the Bulgarians proved less tractable than the Russians hoped. In fact, the Bulgarians soon showed what was, for the Russians, a disturbing tendency to think for themselves. Most of the 3 to 4 million Bulgarians were illiterate, hardworking and relatively prosperous, living in large ethnic blocs north of the Balkan range and in some solidly Bulgar areas south of the mountain chain. Other neighborhoods had a mix of ethnic groups, with Bulgarians living alongside Greeks, Serbs and Turks.[29] The small Bulgarian middle class was strongly influenced by Hellenism. Those who could write did so in Greek, or in Bulgarian, using the Greek script.[30] In the neighboring Albanian region, teachers were said to have told children "that it was useless to pray in Albanian, for Christ was a Greek and did not understand other languages."[31] Of necessity the Bulgarian intellectual and cultural rebirth involved rebellion not only against the Turks but also against the Greeks. The Russians were initially glad to assist the Bulgarians in their efforts to rise up. However, the Bulgarians later set out on an autonomous political path.

Serbia in the late 19th century had not enjoyed the fruits of the industrial revolution. The country was landlocked, with no railroads and few roads. It consisted mostly of forests, dotted with pig farms. As in Bulgaria, most of the people were peasants. The literacy rate in 1874 was 6.7 percent. The nation had no native aristocracy. Belgrade had a small merchant class, but little in the way of culture.[32]

The Serbs were among the Sultan's most rebellious subjects. In 1804, a pig dealer named Karadjordje Petrovic started a revolt that lasted for nine years. The Turks regained full control of Serbia in 1813, but the rebels rose again in 1815. With Napoleon permanently relieved of his hopes at Waterloo, the Russians turned their attention southward, willingly intervening on behalf of the Serbs, pressing the Ottomans for concessions. In 1817, following several victories over the Turks, the Serbian ruler Milos Obrenovic had Petrovic assassinated. He sent his rival's head to the Sultan, who perhaps got the message that Obrenovic was a man with whom it would be wise to do business. In 1830, Serbia became a hereditary principality with complete domestic autonomy, although it remained a Turkish vassal.[33]

The Serbs' ties with the Russians were solid, but their primary concern was their own aggrandizement. They sought their roots in a mythic past, manifesting an unparalleled genius for manipulating history on behalf of their own territorial aims. The Serbs laid claim to much of the Balkans based on the existence of a great Nemanjic Dynasty, which rose to splendor under Czar Stefan Dusan. A national myth arose around a battle at Kosovo, where in 1389 the Serbs claimed that the Turks destroyed their flourishing kingdom in a single day. Researchers say that the Serbs' version of their glorious history is greatly exaggerated. Dusan, the towering figure in Serbian accounts of their history, is said to have presided over the nation's golden age. Yet his reign lasted only 20 years. After his death in 1355, according to Balkan historian Noel Malcolm, the kingdom disintegrated almost immediately and was in the throes of decline by the time of the battle.[34]

To the extent that advocates of a Greater Serbia had

access to scholarship that debunked their claims of past dynastic glory, they chose to ignore it. They convinced themselves that the greater part of the Balkan Peninsula was their birthright. The Serbian reality in the 19th century offered little to suggest that a flourishing civilization had once existed in that land. In the Balkans, however, myth often clashes with reality. When villagers, gathering evening after evening around the fireside, are regaled with tales of heroic deeds accompanied by the twang of the guzla, myth easily wins.

10 INCITEMENT TO RIOT

Emperor Franz Joseph stepped warily out of his train car in Berlin, immediately assuming a ramrod posture, as though that would serve as a brace against unpleasant contingencies. The Emperor's aides trundled along behind him with trunks containing not only the Austrian monarch's usual military outfits but also a German and a Russian uniform. It was customary for a monarch to pay tribute to another ruler by appearing before him in the uniform of that ruler's state. On this occasion, in early September 1872, Franz Joseph was to meet not only Kaiser Wilhelm I[1] of Germany, but also Czar Alexander II of Russia. Although Franz Joseph went through the obligatory gestures of imperial civility with no show of emotion, he surely felt apprehensive. He was not on friendly terms with either monarch.

Sixteen years earlier the Paris Peace Treaty had ended the Crimean War. Franz Joseph had neither apologized for his refusal to participate in the Russian invasion of the Ottoman Empire nor did he intend to do so. Alexander II continued to blame the Emperor for the Russian army's defeat and for causing the premature death of his father, Nicholas I.

Franz Joseph's rift with Kaiser Wilhelm I was recent and

painful. Six years before, in June 1866, the Prussian army had attacked the Austrians without provocation. The conflict, which lasted only seven weeks, ended in defeat for the Habsburg army at Königgrätz (now Hradec Kralove in the Czech Republic). The Habsburg monarchy had been dealt a near fatal blow.

Otto von Bismarck had arranged for Franz Joseph to meet with Wilhelm I in Berlin in hopes that the German and Austrian rulers would reconcile. Ironically, Bismarck, a heavy-set Junker with a gluttonous appetite for power as well as food, had been the devious puppetmaster behind the monarchs' estrangement. As part of a grand scheme for cobbling together a unified Germany from the region's princedoms and fiefdoms, Bismarck had persuaded the reluctant Prussian King Wilhelm I to wage three wars of aggression. All these conflicts were victorious – against Denmark in 1864, two years later against the Austrians, and finally, in 1870, against the French. In 1871, at the Hall of Mirrors at Versailles, Bismarck had looked on proudly as his King had been elevated to Kaiser of a united Germany. The Habsburgs had lost forever their position as the leading German power.

Having rearranged the balance of European power in favor of the new German Empire, Bismarck set out to stage-manage the peace, hence the invitation to Franz Joseph. Czar Alexander II had not been asked to attend the meeting. Upon learning that the Austrian Emperor and the German Kaiser were getting together, the Czar had invited himself to join his imperial brothers. August Fournier, in a book published in 1909, suggests that something other than a desire for reconciliation with the Habsburgs had prompted Alexander II to rush to Berlin. It is likely, writes Fournier, that the Czar came because he "didn't want Wilhelm I and Franz Joseph to be alone together."[2] The Russian ruler was worried about what his brother sovereigns would do behind his back.

Bismarck was pleased to have Alexander II join the other rulers. The chancellor believed that a united front by the three big northern empires would increase the chances for a lasting European peace. Bismarck hoped to reduce the temptation of the French for revenge against the Germans, who had claimed Alsace and Lorraine as part of their war bounty in 1871. He also wanted the Northern Powers to adopt a common policy toward the Balkans, a region increasingly racked by unrest.

Bismarck turned his talents to creating an impression of harmony among the three sovereigns. He encouraged the three rulers to be silent during public appearances, serving as living – but mute – symbols of peace. The ritual of friendship required dressing the part. Franz Joseph, surveying himself in the mirror after donning a Prussian uniform for a meeting with the German Kaiser, is said to have muttered: "It occurs to me that I am putting on (this uniform) against myself in the field."[3] Twenty minutes later he hastily donned the Russian uniform in preparation for a visit to the Czar, who received him in a Hungarian uniform. "To you this must all appear comic," wrote General Hans Lothar von Schweinitz to his fiancée, but then he added an afterword, quoting Friedrich von Schiller: "Deep meaning often lies in childish games."[4]

Soon the monarchs appeared in a cheerful frame of mind. Wilhelm I and Franz Joseph quickly came to an understanding about matters of common interest. Alexander II and Franz Joseph seemed to be getting along. The Austrian and the Russian ministers, Gyula Andrassy and Aleksandr Gorchakov, settled down to substantive talks.[5] Among other matters, they agreed that changes in relationships should occur only gradually, and that there was to be no mixing in "the inner affairs of Turkey."[6]

The following year, there were more signs of a thaw in the relationship between Franz Joseph and Alexander II. Czar Alexander II and his family were among scores of royals who trekked to Vienna to attend the 1873 World Exhibition. Franz Joseph took great pains to honor his Russian guests. Even Empress Elisabeth (Sisi), whose aversion to representative duties was well known, was called into service in entertaining the Romanov visitors. The Habsburgs staged a magnificent parade to the accompaniment of the Russian hymn. At a large military dinner in the Rittersaal (Hall of Knights), attended by 150 high-ranking guests, Franz Joseph raised a toast to the Russian army. Count Crenneville, the Emperor's Adjutant General, remarked, "The poor gentleman is untiringly kind – may it bear fruit in relation to the false Muscovites."[7]

Perhaps if the Empress had turned her full charm on Alexander II this might have overcome the years of ill feelings between the houses of Romanov and Habsburg. Sisi, with her slender figure and long, dark hair, was one of the most beautiful women in Europe. When she appeared before the Shah of Iran, radiant in a silvery garment, her hair sparkling with diamonds and amethysts, "he was," in Corti's words, "so taken with her beauty that he took out his golden eyeglass and stared transfixedly, then circled around her as though he were admiring a priceless statue ..."[8] Alexander II was hardly immune to female beauty and is said to have softened a bit when in Sisi's presence, but the Empress and the Czar never became friends.

Court watchers were generally skeptical that the Romanovs' visit to Vienna would make them friendlier toward the Habsburgs. One eyewitness observed that Alexander II sat stone-faced during the various events. The Italian ambassador reported that the Czar "seemed to be holding himself coldly at a distance; and the ... heir apparent (the future Alexander III) was even colder."[9] The Swiss ambassador noted that the relationship between Franz Joseph and Alexander II seemed cordial at official gatherings, but he agreed with what a German duke had said to him: "In their hearts they remain as of old."[10]

The two imperial ministers, Andrassy and Gorchakov, did, however, put finishing touches on what became known as the Schönbrunn Convention, following up on matters discussed the previous year in Berlin. The Austrians and Russians promised to consult on issues in which their interests diverged. Of major significance were Russian and Austrian pledges to cooperate in the Balkans. The Germans joined the agreement on October 22, bringing into being the "League of the Three Emperors."[11] The league would soon collapse under the weight of developments in the Balkans.

In 1874, Franz Joseph paid his first visit ever to the Russian capital. Arriving in St. Petersburg in February, during a raging snowstorm, he received only a smattering of applause from those who had bothered to come out to greet him. The Emperor laid a wreath on the sarcophagus of Nicholas I, honoring the man who in 1849 had saved the Habsburg monarchy. This gesture, meant to pour balm on Romanov resentment of the Emperor's refusal to support his imperial brother in the Russians ill-fated Crimean adventure, was well received. However, a gesture of reconciliation could not overcome accretions of acrimony between the great ruling houses built up over the centuries.

The Czar pointedly invited Franz Joseph to visit his father's rooms, which had been preserved as they were when Nicholas I had died. Undoubtedly this was a painful moment for Franz Joseph. It must have seemed to the Habsburg Emperor that the mausoleum-like setting not only honored the memory of the Czar in perpetuity but also served as a shrine to the carefully preserved resentment felt by the Russian imperial family for the Habsburgs in general and for him in particular.

The Russian royal family put on a sparkling display of hospitality. The festivities included a ball, where the room was lit by 12,000 candles, followed by a meal of 250 dishes served on golden platters, in a dining hall turned into a tropical garden replete with palm trees and orchids.

Countess Marie Festetics, lady in waiting to Habsburg Empress Elisabeth, so often trenchant in her observations, recorded in her diary her impressions of what she had been told about the visit to the Romanov court. After mentioning the incredible display of wealth and beauty, the women's costumes and diamonds, intended to dazzle the Austrian guests, the Countess wrote that she did not quite trust the Russians: "They are not quick to forget an insult."[12] Franz Joseph's failure to support Nicholas I in the Crimean conflict was an insult that the Romanovs were not prepared to forget.

Hopes of real reconciliation between the Habsburg and the Romanov rulers were dashed after a controversy erupted between the two imperial houses over a trip by Franz Joseph to Dalmatia. The Emperor's visit to the southernmost reaches of the monarchy in the spring of 1876 was prompted by reports of increasing unrest on the Habsburg border with Bosnia and Herzegovina. Since the 1860s robber bands from the two Turkish provinces had made regular incursions into the monarchy's territory. The Austrian border guards regularly marched into Bosnia to restore peace. Refugees from Bosnia and Herzegovina arrived in increasing numbers at the Habsburg border claiming they had been persecuted by their Turkish overlords. In June 1873 the government in Vienna, responding to the increasing unrest along the monarchy's frontier, began publishing an official *Red Book* recording pertinent developments in the border area. This amounted to an implicit acknowledgment that the region was about to explode.

Prompted by such reports, Franz Joseph traveled to Dalmatia in the spring of 1875 to assess the situation for himself. Although the Emperor was on what today would be called a fact-finding tour, his trip caused an uproar. There were claims that he was attempting to "incite" the beleaguered peasants in the two provinces to rise against their masters. Rumors swirled that the Emperor intended to annex the twin provinces. The fact that Franz Joseph traveled to Dalmatia at the urging of Gavrilo Rodic, the governor of Dalmatia, was partly to blame for fueling speculation about the Emperor's intentions. Rodic supported the insurgency against the local Turkish authorities (the Begs), which was occurring near the monarchy's borders. The Russians, whose strategy for taking Constantinople depended on establishing vassal states in the Balkans, viewed Franz Joseph's every move in the region with suspicion. The Emperor also upset advocates of Greater Serbia, who claimed parts of Bosnia and Herzegovina as their birthright.

There was nothing unusual about Franz Joseph's trip. Since coming to power in 1848 at the age of 18 the Emperor had visited far-flung corners of the monarchy, including Istria, Carinthia, Carniola, Bohemia, Silesia and Transylvania. Dalmatia, with an Adriatic coastline that extended from a point north of Zadar southward to Kotor and Budva, was of vital importance to the monarchy. Its location also caused Austria's military planners sleepless nights. These experts repeatedly warned that a blockade of the Dalmatian coast might leave the monarchy's garrisons in the region stranded. An overland retreat might be impossible, they said, if the neighboring provinces of Bosnia and Herzegovina fell into unfriendly hands (i.e. Russia or Serbia).

Franz Joseph's visit lasted 31 days. He stopped in Trieste and Venice, then continued to Dalmatia. Arriving on April 10 at the ancient port city of Zadar on board the warship *Miramar*, the Emperor headed southward through the coastal province all the way to Budva. The Emperor's letters to Empress Elisabeth during the Balkan trip suggest that he was engaging in what is quaintly called a Progress, stopping at some 50 towns, villages and markets, making more than 100 speeches, holding thousands of audiences, being toasted and feted by townspeople, welcomed by children bearing blossoms, and entertained by folk dancers in colorful costumes. Some places the Emperor visited were accessible only by horseback. As always when Franz Joseph traveled, he was approached by petitioners. Simple folk pushed forward, sometimes in tears, with requests or pleas stubbed out on small pieces of paper, handing them to the Emperor or his aides.[13]

Franz Joseph met with Franciscans and local dignitaries who urged him to get involved on behalf of Christians in those troubled regions. At Dubrovnik, where the Emperor arrived on April 28, there was a demonstration on behalf of Christians who were being persecuted in Bosnia and Herzegovina. The Emperor listened carefully to what was being said during these discussions but made no promises of intervention.

Prince Nikola of Montenegro, hoping to take advantage of any uprising that occurred to acquire some of Bosnia's meadows, descended from the rocky fastnesses of his province to meet the Emperor. He was accompanied by Petar Vukotic, a fierce-looking tribesman who was Nikola's advisor and father-in-law. Vukotic told General Friedrich Beck, the Austrian chief of staff, "We live up there in a rocky desert and look down upon the green plains of Herzegovina. We want to acquire enough pasture land to nourish our stock."[14] While these blatant territorial ambitions on the part of the Montenegrin ruler undoubtedly displeased the Emperor, on May 3 at the Gulf of Kotor, Franz Joseph received Prince Nikola. The two discussed solutions to problems in the twin provinces (not annexation). The Habsburg Emperor showed his friendship toward the Montenegrin ruler by riding with him up the treacherous slopes of Mount Lovcen and crossing the frontier into the prince's isolated aerie. Montenegro was the key to maintaining a balance of power necessary for stability in the Balkans. For the Emperor, stability was what mattered most. Franz Joseph wanted to head off attempts to unite Serbia and Montenegro. Such a union might tempt some of the monarchy's Serbs to break off and join an enlarged and powerful Slav state.

A number of historians have overplayed the significance of Franz Joseph's visit to Dalmatia or have misread his motives. Sumner argues, for example, that the Emperor was engaging in an "inciting" trip, intended to help the military achieve its goal of annexation of Bosnia and Herzegovina.[15] In reaching this conclusion, he fails to consider sufficiently the Emperor's personality, in which "incitement" was a most unlikely component. He also ignores Franz Joseph's later statements on his Balkan policy, which make it clear that annexation was to be imposed only if the situation in the twin provinces became unmanageable. Such a chaotic situation occurred in 1908 – at least that is what the Habsburgs thought at the time.

Alan Palmer, for his part, sees grandiose portents in the Dalmatian trip, deeming it "a historic turning point in Habsburg policy ..." From the time Franz Joseph landed at Zadar, Palmer opines, and "for the last 40 years of his reign, he looked determinedly to the East, partly across the Carpathians and toward the mouth of the Danube, but even more to the Balkans and, beyond the mountain ranges, to the two largest Ottoman cities in Europe, Salonika and Constantinople."[16]

While Franz Joseph would have liked to acquire territory to compensate for Italian lands lost to the monarchy through war in 1859, it is an exaggeration to suggest that he "looked determinedly to the East," in the serious belief in the possibility of expanding the monarchy to Salonika and beyond. He and Andrassy talked about exerting a "moral influence" in the Balkans but this is far removed from the grand Russian-style scheme of conquest suggested by Palmer. The Habsburg monarchy, with its multiethnic and political nature, was like a nerve-damaged octopus with its tentacles constantly moving at odds with the body imperial. Dynastic ambitions in such a situation could hardly take hold and flourish even if the Emperor had suffered from megalomania, which this almost overly rational ruler did not. What Franz Joseph's visit to Dalmatia actually did do was to give hope to the Christians of Herzegovina and Bosnia who were suffering under Turkish rule. However, the Emperor was at the time committed to the promises of nonintervention in the Balkans, as agreed to by the League of the Three Emperors two years earlier; thus he wasn't in a position to offer these people direct help. Of course, the beleaguered souls who confronted him with petitions could hardly know that. For many of these simple peasants an Emperor was next to God, capable of impossibilities.

Shortly after Franz Joseph left Dalmatia, non-Muslims in Herzegovina rose up, for reasons of their own. The rebellion stemmed from basic inequality in the social structure. Muslims, including Slavs who had converted to Islam following the Ottoman conquest, were the majority landowners. Non-Muslims, most of whom were peasants, had few rights and many grievances. Harvest failures and unfair taxation had pushed much of the region's population to desperation. Herzegovina's peasants had to wait until tax officials visited before harvesting crops. Often grain and other produce rotted in the fields before the arrival of the dreaded hired guns of the Sultan. Not only were the taxes exorbitant; sometimes the peasants were even required to pay taxes on animals that had long since died. Christians also did not receive justice in the courts. Only believers in the Koran were allowed to testify. The uprising in Herzegovina soon spread next door to Bosnia. As many as 100,000 victims of the conflict fled into Habsburg territory in Croatia, most of them arriving with first-hand accounts of torture.[17]

In an audience with Count Alexander von Hubner, an Austrian diplomat and historian, Franz Joseph explained where he stood regarding Bosnia and Herzegovina. He declared that he was "in no way thinking of an annexation" of the two provinces,[18] and only hoped that the difficulties in the region could be resolved peacefully. However, he repeated earlier statements that he would never consent to Bosnia and Herzegovina becoming independent states like Montenegro and Serbia. Based on past history, Franz Joseph declared, Russia would quickly exert her influence over any independent Balkan state. And even if the Russians failed to meddle in the affairs of these newly created states, the Emperor added, there would likely be an upsurge in problems from local Pan-Slavists, eager to persuade Habsburg subjects to break away from the monarchy. The Emperor didn't want a training camp for Pan-Slavists on the empire's southern doorstep.

Franz Joseph clarified his position, stating on July 20, 1875, that he would not allow the provinces to "fall into hands other than ours." Franz Joseph made it clear that his remarks were aimed not only at Russia and Serbia, but also were intended for Montenegro. Prince Nikola was becoming increasingly aggressive. On August 20, the Montenegrin ruler met with a Herzegovinian chieftain and promised his support. Nikola quickly took control of the uprising, claiming that he couldn't control his tribesmen. What he didn't try to control was himself. The green plains of Herzegovina were too tempting. The Serbians, by now open in their demands for a Greater Serbia, began secretly supplying the insurgents with arms and volunteers. Since their grand scheme depended on the acquisition of Bosnia and most of Herzegovina, future clashes between the Serbs and the Habsburgs were inevitable.

By the end of 1875 the rebellion was out of hand. The insurgents attacked Turkish guard stations, slashing and burning their victims. William Holmes, the British consul in Bosnia, visited the village of Nevesink, where the uprising had begun, finding "a Turkish boy's head blackening in the sun and a Turkish girl still breathing with her throat cut."[19] The Turkish authorities seemed unable to decide what action to take. There has been much speculation on why the Austrians didn't seize that moment and annex Bosnia and Herzegovina. Habsburg troops could have occupied the twin provinces with the legitimate excuse that the action was needed to secure Austria's borders. At that time Austria had the clout to deal with Turkey and Russia. The problem was, however, that within the monarchy there was no agreement about what course to take. In Hungary, the Magyars supported Turkey passionately and – remembering cruelties of the Czar's troops in putting down the uprising in 1849 – wanted war with Russia. In Austria, German liberals insisted that no more Slavs be added to the empire. The Slavs, for their part, wanted Austria to fight the Turks. Many in the military wanted conquests, but no war with Russia. Franz Joseph, who had the final authority to act or not to act, considered war a last resort.

On the other hand many Pan-Slavs, in Russia and in the Balkans, blaming Austria for the troubles in Herzegovina, viewed war as a desirable first resort. When Alexander of Hesse visited the capital in January 1876, he declared that he was astonished at the bellicose mood prevailing in St. Petersburg society. He wrote that "the hawks urged a Holy Crusade, which this time, they said, would witness the birth of a Russian-Slav empire with its capital in Constantinople...."[20]

Czar Alexander II did not want war – yet. He threatened to abandon the Serbs if they attacked the Porte. However, he and his family secretly supported the insurgents. Russians in key foreign posts hinted that the Serbs could look forward to the day in the not too distant future when Russia would join them in throwing off not only the Turkish yoke but the Austrian yoke. E.P. Novikov, the Russian ambassador in Vienna, worried that Serbian nationalists were fueling the insurrection, urged Belgrade to be patient:

"Until Russia can unite the Slavs as Bismarck had the Germans ... an insurrection is premature." In Paris, a Russian diplomat named Vlangali echoed that sentiment, telling a leader of the Serb conservatives that the time was "not yet propitious (for war) and when one harvests the fruit before it matures, one runs the risk of getting none."[21] On the other hand, Count N.P. Ignatiev, the powerful Russian minister in Constantinople, advocated going to war at once. The Balkan Christians "found more and more encouragement in extreme action from his embassy on the Bosphorus,"[22] observes Sumner.

With such divergent – and inciting – messages coming from the Russians, it is hardly surprising that the Serbs heard what they wanted to hear and ignored the rest. In December, Jovan Marinovic, a Serbian politician who opposed a war, wrote Andrassy that – "in Serbia, emotion ... (has) overcome logic; the public ... (believes) Russia would rescue the country from an unsuccessful struggle."[23] By secretly encouraging Serbian expectations for a rescue in the future, the Russians had started down a dangerous road. The time would come when they felt honor bound to make good on their promises.

11 CROSSING THE RUBICON

By the spring of 1876 Turkey's European provinces were out of control. The revolt in Bosnia and Herzegovina, begun the previous year, continued. In April a rebellion erupted in the Rhodope Mountains in Bulgaria, a region with a large Christian population. The victims' stories had a common theme. After years of oppression by their Turkish overlords, the oppressed population rose up, demanding reforms. They were tortured instead. As Sir Edwin Pears, a British barrister with first-hand knowledge of Ottoman politics put it, the Turkish government's only answer to its subjects' discontent was to massacre them.[1]

Those at the Romanov court who longed for an end to Ottoman rule in Europe had reason for hope. The Turkish "sick man" was undergoing convulsions suggesting the empire's demise. The Porte was near bankruptcy. Sultan Abdulaziz continued to spend wildly on palaces and harem girls. When faced with the consequences of his extravagance, he erupted in violent outbursts. On May 30 a group of Turkish military leaders confronted the Sultan in his palace. He appeared on the stairs brandishing a sword, but soon surrendered. He was imprisoned. A few days later he was found dead, his wrists slashed. The new Sultan, Murad V, proved no better able than his unhappy predecessor to rule his troubled empire. Abdul Hamid II, his successor, placated his enemies with promises of reforms that he never carried out.

Serbian ultranationalists, emboldened by the rot at the center of Ottoman power, called for the Balkan Slavs to join them in war against the Turks. Implicit in the Pan-Serbs' attempt to rally their ethnic brothers was a hope of uniting them under the banner of a Greater Serbia. The Serbs had been behind the uprising in Herzegovina and Bosnia the previous year. They continued to incite unrest in the twin provinces, expecting to claim large swaths of that picturesque region as victors in the coming conflict. This development was viewed with extreme unease in Vienna. Franz Joseph had declared that he would never allow Bosnia and Herzegovina to fall into unfriendly hands – and he meant it.

The Serbs acquired a powerful backer for their cause in the person of Russian General M.G. Cherniaev, the editor of a Pan-Slav newspaper in St. Petersburg. The general was a bushy-browed original whose mustache extended to the sides and ended in sharp points, conveying a certain fierceness. In 1865 he had won fame as the conqueror of Tashkent.[2] Now he decided to go to Serbia to spearhead the rebellion.

Alexander II sympathized with the Balkan insurgents, but he wanted to wage his dynasty's next Turkish war on his own terms. He didn't want a renegade general to seize control of the military initiative. He forbade Cherniaev to travel to Serbia and ordered the Russian intelligence service to put him under surveillance. Cherniaev didn't flinch. At Tashkent he had ridden to victory by flouting orders. The hardheaded general repeated his performance. Slipping away from his Russian minders, he bribed passport officials, showing up in Belgrade on April 28, 1876. The Serbs proclaimed him a citizen and made him commander of their eastern armies. One of his first acts was to ask the Russian Slav committees to lend Serbia 500,000 rubles.[3] Although the committees refused the request, claiming a lack of funds, they secretly channeled weapons to the Balkan insurgents. The Russian government tolerated the committees' activities as "the affair of private persons."[4]

At Fiume (now Rijeka, in Croatia) on June 16, Serbia and Montenegro entered an alliance, pledging to attack the Ottomans within 10 days of ratification. The parties agreed on the spoils of victory: Serbia would acquire Bosnia while Montenegro received Herzegovina. The war began in early July, with the armies of the two provinces soon going their separate ways. The poorly trained and equipped Serbian armies, led by Prince Milan, the ruler, and Cherniaev, stumbled from one defeat to another. Under Prince Nikola's direction the Montenegrin forces performed splendidly, allowing him later to extract important concessions from the Turks.

That summer the Russian public was swept up in a wave of war hysteria. Pan-Slavism caught the popular imagination as nothing ever had. For Russian peasants, sending money to Serbia became a moral cause. Black-kerchiefed little old ladies, their palsied hands quivering, parted with precious kopecks to save the poor Serbs from the Turkish tyrants. Even children joined in, amusing themselves with a new game called the Eastern Question.

Russians who doubted the wisdom of supporting Balkan insurgents failed to be heard above the shouting. An anonymous writer in the *Golos*, a widely circulated newspaper, remarked that people talked constantly about the "poor Slavs," but when asked who these Slavs were, the proponents would "stare goggle-eyed."[5] While many Russians claimed that the empire's role was to "liberate" the poor Balkan Slavs, not to conquer them, others, including writers for the ultranationalistic newspaper *Novoe Vremia*, repeated a familiar refrain: "Russia's future lies in the south ... only when Constantinople is in Slav (i.e. Russian) hands can Russia become a 'true world power.' "[6]

Even if Czar Alexander II had wanted to avoid a conflict, he hardly could avoid being moved by the impassioned calls for war coming from the Russian public. Additionally, he faced serious pressure from the Romanov heir (the future Alexander III) and from Czarina Marie to intervene on behalf of the Balkan Christians. The Czar, mindful of what seemed an opportunity to put the Russian humiliation in the Crimean War behind him, made a tentative decision to open a new conflict.

Before putting troops in the field Alexander II faced a disagreeable task. He had to determine how Austria and Germany, his allies in the League of the Three Emperors, stood on the matter. The treaty required the signatories to consult with their allies before taking action that would disturb the territorial status quo in the Balkans. An understanding with Vienna was particularly important; otherwise, the Russian army's right flank would be exposed during its thrust to the south.

The Czar's efforts to sound out the Habsburgs on a new Turkish war led to another of those misunderstandings that plagued the relationship between the two imperial houses. In early July 1876, the Czar had traveled to Bohemia, where he met Franz Joseph at the imperial chateau of Reichstadt, some 56 miles north of Prague. The two foreign ministers, Andrassy and Gorchakov, were also present. The discussions failed to result in any document bearing the signatures of both parties. The negotiators produced only a vague protocol involving cooperation in the Balkans. This left room for serious disagreements regarding promises made at the meeting.

Franz Joseph's later statements show that he thought the terms agreed to at Reichstadt would apply only after the European Powers concluded that the Ottoman Empire was no longer viable. Otherwise, as the Emperor understood it, the status quo was to remain. Like his father, Nicholas I, Czar Alexander II tended to hear only what he wanted to hear. The Czar seems to have left the meeting convinced that Franz Joseph would join him in war against Turkey without waiting for that empire's death certificate from the Powers. Another contentious matter of major significance concerned the creation of a Slavic state on the Balkan peninsula. Franz Joseph was certain that Alexander II had promised not to create such a state. The Czar claimed later that he had only agreed not to create a large state.

The Austrian and Russian foreign ministers differed widely in their accounts regarding the future of Bosnia and Herzegovina in case of a Turkish defeat. In Andrassy's account, Austria was to receive the greater part of both provinces, with Serbia and Montenegro making only small territorial gains. Gorchakov's version awarded all of Herzegovina to Montenegro, with Serbia receiving a large portion of Bosnia.[7] Given Franz Joseph's previous statements on the subject, it is most unlikely that the Habsburgs agreed to this.

Initially, both the Austrians and the Russians expressed satisfaction at the outcome of the Reichstadt negotiations. Andrassy, in fact, seemed to think he had scored a major diplomatic victory. Bernard Fürst von Bülow, the German statesman, recorded in his memoirs an encounter with Andrassy during an early morning horseback ride in the Prater (park) in Vienna, shortly after the Austrian foreign minister returned from Reichstadt. From the account, it is clear that Andrassy believed that the Russians had agreed for the Habsburgs to acquire Bosnia and Herzegovina if the Turks were defeated. According to von Bülow, Andrassy said the acquisition of the twin provinces offered "political, economic and strategic" advantages. "Bosnia is a magnificent land, very ripe for development, with a beautifully situated capital, Sarajevo,"[8] the foreign minister said.

Alexander II's initial optimism about the Reichstadt agreements seems to have turned to doubt once he was back in St. Petersburg. The more the Czar reflected on what had occurred at the meeting – and the more he listened to the Pan-Slavs and the Czarina – the more he appears to have suspected that Franz Joseph had played him false. He asked himself: Was he being forced to pay for permission to have the Austrians sit on the sidelines while Romanov forces shed their blood for the "holy cause"? The Czar would have to wait until October to find out.

The Serbian campaign against the Turks quickly lost steam, prompting Russian Pan-Slavs to rush to their ethnic brothers' rescue. The Russian sympathizers collected funds for their Balkan friends and sent recruits southward to fight in their behalf, but the effort at collaboration ran into snags. While Moscow and St. Petersburg committee representatives tried to screen volunteer applicants, the recruitment was haphazard. Even in Moscow, recruiters signed up flotsam, including petty criminals and drunkards. In Odessa, Pan-Slav organizers sent as volunteers "most of the city's wastrels,"[9] writes MacKenzie. All told, Slav committees reported that they had signed up 4,303 volunteers. Others traveled independently. Close to half of the recruits appear never to have reached the front, preferring to spend allowance money, provided them by the committees, in Russia or to enjoy life in Serbian or Romanian cafes.

If the Russians and the Serbs, caught up in their illusions of Pan-Slav brotherhood, expected that their ethnic ties would make them good fighting companions, they were to be disappointed. By the fall of 1876 serious friction had developed between the Russian volunteers and the Serbs they had come to save. General Cherniaev alienated much of the Serbian population with his take-charge tactics, although he stayed on good terms with the Russian Pan-Slav committees by doctoring the news they received to suggest the fighting was going splendidly.

The Russians and Serbs not only clashed regarding the conduct of the war; they also discovered disconcerting cultural differences. The Serbs complained that their Russian comrades were drunk and out of control. They accused Russian officers of ignoring Serbian law and showing scant interest in the little Balkan nation's culture. N.V. Maksimov, a volunteer Russian officer, acknowledged that the Russians, "from generals to sergeants were little Pompadours, adopted the role of dictators, and did not hesitate to dominate the Serbs and reproach them simultaneously for accepting money and clothing from Russia. It was only natural that Serbian pride was injured."[10]

On the other hand, Maksimov said he had discovered that he had nothing in common with Serbian soldiers. "All these assurances of our brotherhood with the Slavs, all this nonsense about our blood relationship ... is fine in the mouth of a politician or historian, but it is purely fiction in the sense of natural human feelings .... Serbia is for me a land of different views, manners, habits, convictions, education, and direction." He said he had found to his surprise "that the poor country of our oppressed brethren was a place where the peasants drink wine and live off the fat of the land."[11]

The Russians claimed that "many Serbian soldiers inflicted slight wounds upon themselves to escape action." Following a Turkish victory at Djunis (in Bulgaria), the Russians accused the Serbs of "cowering in the cornfields" while the volunteers fought. The Serbs blamed the Russians for the defeat. "Before the war," wrote a Russian major, "the Serbs did not know us and loved us; now having become acquainted, they hate us."[12]

Even though initial collaboration of the Russians with the Pan-Slavs in Serbia and Bulgaria was to end in acrimony, it established an important precedent. In the future the

Russians would use their Balkan vassals, particularly Serbia, in intrigues against their common enemies: the Ottomans, and increasingly, the Habsburgs. The assassination of Archduke Franz Ferdinand, the Habsburg heir apparent, by Bosnian Serbs at Sarajevo in 1914, was no isolated incident. Rather, it was part of a decade-long effort by Serbs and other Balkan ultranationalists, encouraged by the Russians, to undermine the monarchy. Over time, these subversive activities had a cumulative effect.

The British, in the meantime, kept a nervous eye on the rising crisis in the Balkans. Queen Victoria realized that a Russian takeover of Constantinople and the Straits remained a possibility, the czarist defeat in the Crimean War notwithstanding. Reports of Turkish atrocities in Bulgaria prompted the British government to dispatch a commission to investigate. The British delegation reported grisly details of Turkish reprisals that followed the revolt in the Plovdiv region of Bulgaria. Turkish volunteers called bashi-bazouks had gone on a rampage. A British agent named Macgahan, dispatched by the royal government to confirm earlier reports of the atrocities, described what he found in Batak, some 30 miles from Tartar Bazarjik. Once a thriving town, it had been reduced to a charnel house. He had seen "dogs feeding on human remains, heaps of human skulls, skeletons nearly entire, rotten clothing, human hair, and flesh putrid and lying in one foul heap." Many of the skeletons and skulls were small, suggesting that they belonged to women and children. The town, which had 9,000 inhabitants before the carnage, was essentially empty. Some 60 villages suffered a similar fate.[13]

Always happy to marshal piety on behalf of politics, William Gladstone, temporarily retired as British Prime Minister, leapt from the bed, to which he had been confined by gout, to write *The Bulgarian Horrors*, a pamphlet appearing in September that caused a sensation in Britain. Gladstone wanted the Turks driven out of Europe. He called for

Britain to assume the role of protector of Christians in Turkey, a role that the Russians had forfeited by bringing on the Crimean War.[14] As it turned out, Gladstone's intervention, which generated sympathy among the English for the Balkan Christians, would give the Russians an advantage they had not enjoyed during the Crimean War. It guaranteed that this time, if war broke out, the British would not intervene on behalf of Turkey.

In September, the Czar and his family as well as members of the Russian court and government, moved to Livadia, the royal residence in Crimea for an extended vacation. Livadia was a fairy-tale sort of place, with its spacious palace, set in the midst of olive trees and orangeries and vineyards, against a backdrop of mountains and overlooking the sun-splashed Black Sea. It was 50 miles from the nearest railroad, a world away from Great Power politics, but close to the Balkan states and their insistent demands.

Everybody in Russia who mattered politically was present in Livadia that fall. The Czarina was in residence, pushing the Pan-Slav cause, as were leaders of the ultra-Orthodox circles in St. Petersburg. D.A. Milyutin, the war minister, was present, as was General Nikolai Obruchev. Foreign Minister Gorchakov also was in attendance. By mid-October the heir apparent had arrived, as had Grand Duke Nikolai Nikolaevich, the Czar's brother.

By all accounts the mood of the gathering was militant. Reports of Serbian reverses suggested a need for immediate action on their behalf. Count Ignatiev, the Pan-Slav Russian ambassador in Constantinople – about whom we shall hear more later – played a prominent role in the discussions. Sumner, citing Ignatiev's memoirs as evidence, writes that the Russian ambassador used "all his skill ... to bring home the necessity of coercive measures .... Throughout his schemes ran two guiding threads, the need of force or the threat of force, and enmity towards Austria-Hungary."[15]

By this time, Alexander II was eager to get on with his war, but first he needed to be certain on how the Germans and Austrians stood on the matter. Relying on personal diplomacy, the traditional method of conducting foreign policy in the conservative old European empires, the Czar had inquiries dispatched to his uncle, Kaiser Wilhelm I, and to Emperor Franz Joseph.

General von Werder, the German military representative in St. Petersburg, who was in Livadia, dispatched two telegrams to Kaiser Wilhelm I, one on September 25, the other on October 1. Clearly, the Russian ruler was willing to go behind his Habsburg ally's back if it was to his advantage in the coming Turkish campaign. Alexander II attempted, among other things, to get the German ruler to promise that he would take steps to prevent the Austrians from attacking Russian troops in case Russia went to war unilaterally. The Czar reminded the Kaiser that in 1870 he had promised Prussia that he would send 300,000 troops to the Austrian border if the Habsburgs interfered in Prussia's war against France.[16] The Czar expected to be repaid in kind.

Through a bureaucratic blunder, however, the telegrams intended for Kaiser Wilhelm I wound up on Bismarck's desk. The chancellor took umbrage at the Czar's willingness to undercut Austria, Russia's own ally – and Germany's – in the League of the Three Emperors. Bismarck fumed for three weeks before taking it upon himself to reply. The German response would be verbal rather than written.

A few days before Werder sent the telegrams to Berlin, Alexander II dispatched Count Sumarokow-Elston, his aide-de-camp, to Vienna, where on September 27 he delivered a handwritten note to Franz Joseph. Using the familiar Romanov claim that Turkey was about to expire, the Czar urged the Emperor to join him in the coming war, in order to avoid "complications." The Russian ruler proposed that the Habsburgs occupy Bosnia and Herzegovina at the same time that Russia occupied Bulgaria.[17] Indulging in the soaring rhetoric typically employed by Romanov czars when they were contemplating an advance on the Balkans, Alexander II declared that this was "one of those moments which could determine the fate of both (our) lands for many generations to come."[18] Would Franz Joseph care to collaborate with him in taking down Turkey? Alexander II asked. The Czar demanded an immediate answer.

In replying to the Czar on October 3, 1876, Franz Joseph struck much the same unbending tone that he had used in warning Nicholas I, the Czar's father, against embarking on what had become the Crimean War almost a quarter of a century earlier. Franz Joseph told Alexander II that his proposal was dangerous. The Emperor said such a move against Turkey would "awaken the mistrust of all Europe." Franz Joseph, softening his refusal with an explanation, added that he lacked the power to go to war unilaterally. A decision of that kind, he said, would require the assent of representatives to whom he himself had given that authority.[19] Franz Joseph also rejected the idea of occupation, whether of Bosnia, Herzegovina or Bulgaria, saying a temporary occupation would be disastrous and a permanent occupation impossible.[20]

Alexander II, like his father Nicholas I, was tone deaf when confronted with what he chose not to hear. The Czar's response, on October 10, to Franz Joseph's letter caused disbelief and consternation in Vienna. Alexander II had misunderstood what the Emperor had said. The Czar assumed that Russia and Austria would be going to war together the following spring. He said he didn't expect Turkey to reform; assuming he was correct, it would trigger the Reichstadt agreements. The Czar suggested that the two empires conduct secret negotiations leading to a detailed treaty spelling out a strategy for collaboration.[21]

Writing the Czar on October 23, Franz Joseph sought to rid his Romanov brother of any notion that the Habsburgs would engage in a military adventure intended to hasten the dissolution of the Ottoman Empire. The Emperor declared that any action by Vienna against the Turks was to be contingent on European consensus that Ottoman rule no longer was viable.[22] In an important concession intended to calm Russian suspicions, Franz Joseph promised to negotiate a secret treaty with the Russians that would define the terms of Austrian neutrality during the conflict. The Emperor told Austrian historian Alexander von Hübner that he wanted to work with Russia as long as he could. However, he said he wondered if the Czar was "really in control" of those around him who were agitating for war.

The Czar's response[23] shows that he finally understood what the Emperor was telling him. Alexander II declared his intention to proceed alone, if need be. Striking an accusatory tone, he wrote, "I regret that you will not deal with me openly ..." The Swiss ambassador in St. Petersburg, Tschudi, reported that the Russians were furious at Franz Joseph's refusal to cooperate in their latest Turkish war. The diplomat said that the consensus among politicians and diplomats in the capital was that the Russians would avenge themselves against the Austrians as soon as they were in a position to do so.[24]

There was anger on the Austrian side as well. Some Hungarians responded to rising tensions between St. Petersburg and Vienna, calling for war against Russia, in revenge for the czarist army's cruelties during the uprising of 1848-49. Franz Joseph, however, was not in favor of war, and without his consent there would be no war involving the monarchy.

A.G. Jomini, a senior counselor in the Russian foreign ministry, writing from Livadia to N.K. Giers in the foreign office[25] on October 17, leaves no doubt about where the Russians were heading: "The Rubicon will be crossed. Ignatiev leaves (for Constantinople) tonight. He will present our claims, then an ultimatum, then break relations! ... (with Turkey) I only fear that Europe ... will come forward with mediation proposals. There is no more time to lose. If we wait beyond the end of November,[26] the opportunity to crush Turkey will be lost."[27]

General von Schweinitz, the German ambassador to St. Petersburg, who was highly regarded by the Czar, showed up on October 31 with Bismarck's verbal response to the Czar's inquiries – intended for the Kaiser – that had accidentally landed on the chancellor's desk. Bismarck's reply is a masterpiece of evasion. Schweinitz said the German chancellor told him: "In the event of an Austro-Russian war Germany could not bind herself to a course of action which should have no regard to the circumstances of the war; the attitude of other powers, and the consideration that it was not in Germany's interest that either Russia or Austria-Hungary should be essentially weakened." The Czar and Gorchakov, disappointed at this equivocal answer, gave General Schweinitz a difficult time. "We expected (greater) things from you," Gorchakov told him.[28] The Germans' reluctance to support czarist war aims in Constantinople would eventually lead the Romanovs to view the Germans along with the Austrians as enemies that must be destroyed if they ever were to achieve their imperialist ambitions in the south.

The British, alarmed by rumors of a Russian plot, sent Lord Augustus Loftus, their ambassador to St. Petersburg, to Livadia to assess the situation. The envoy's visit did nothing to calm fears in London. Loftus arrived on October 27, but was kept waiting for an audience with the Czar until the afternoon of November 2.[29] Alexander II, having finally condescended to see the British envoy, attempted to convince him that the Russians could be trusted. The Czar told Loftus that he had "not the slightest wish" to possess Constantinople. He even "gave his word of honor that he had no intention of acquiring it." His assurances were, however, carefully hedged. The Czar would not rule out a temporary occupation of the Turkish capital. Russia might have to occupy a portion of Bulgaria, he allowed, adding that Russian troops would remain there "only until peace was guaranteed and the Christians safeguarded." The Czar went on to say that if the Turks continued to defy the demands of the Powers, and "if the other Powers would not act with resolution," Russia would take unilateral action. The British had no need to read between the lines to realize that the Russians were heading for war.

Meanwhile, the Serbs were losing their fight with the Turks. On October 27 the Sultan's forces defeated the Serbian army at Djunis. Two days later they trounced the Serbs at Krushevatz. The Turks now had control of the main highway to Belgrade.[30] Their army headed for the Serbian capital in a victory march. Although Alexander II was angry at the Serbs for starting a war they could not finish, he saved them from being crushed. The Czar sent an ultimatum to Sultan Abdul Hamid II, giving him 48 hours to agree to an armistice.[31] The Russian agenda at the conference was intended to provoke war rather than to encourage peace.

The Czar had begun mobilizing his troops.

On November 7, Alexander II left Livadia for St. Petersburg and Moscow. On the train he drafted a speech that he would deliver in Moscow to an audience of nobles and government officials. The speech, on November 11, received a wild ovation. The Czar meted out praise and condemnation when he thought they were due and ended in a call to arms:

> "You know already that Turkey has complied with my demand for the immediate conclusion of an armistice to put an end to useless carnage Serbia and Montenegro. The Montenegrins have shown themselves, as always, true heroes in this unequal struggle. Unfortunately it is impossible to say the same of the Serbs, despite the presence in their ranks of our volunteers, many of whom have paid with their blood for the cause of

Slavdom. I know that all Russia joins with me in taking the deepest interest in the sufferings of our brothers by faith and by origin; but for me the true interests of Russia are dearer than everything... " [32]

The Czar reiterated earlier statements that he would act independently if the Porte failed to comply with his demands. He was certain, he said, that if the empire's honor demanded it, all Russia would answer the call to arms. He said in closing: "May God help us fulfill our sacred mission." [33]

Alexander II, having linked the Orthodox faith with the Pan-Slav cause, was now ready to send his army on a "sacred mission" to Byzantium. Aksakov, the Pan-Slav leader, was ecstatic. Commenting later, he hailed the Czar as "the glorious successor of Ivan the Great, Peter the Great, and Catherine the Great." [34]

12 ON THE WAY TO TSARIGRAD

Representatives of the European Powers gathered in Constantinople for a conference in late December 1876 aiming, as one diplomat said, "to bring the Turks to their senses." The delegates sought to force wide-ranging reforms on the Ottomans, whose cruelties toward Balkan Christians, vividly depicted in William Gladstone's *Bulgarian Horrors*, had caused an international uproar. Turkish representatives were excluded from the initial proceedings. The meetings were held at the Russian Embassy, hardly a neutral ground from the Ottomans' point of view.

The Constantinople conference was doomed from the start.

The European Powers[1], after months of wrangling, had finally agreed on reforms they would demand from the Turks. The delegates arrived in Constantinople expecting their démarche to proceed smoothly – and quickly. They were in for a surprise. The Russian ambassador to the Porte, Nikolai Ignatiev, insisted that Russia be allowed an indefinite occupation of Bulgaria. The other delegates knew that the Turks would never agree to this blatant attempt at imperial aggrandizement. Realizing that the Sultan might respond by declaring war, the diplomats met behind closed doors, hoping to convince the incalcitrant Ignatiev to soften his language. Between December 11 and 22, the diplomats held nine sessions before Ignatiev finally gave in, agreeing to ask only for Bulgarian autonomy.

The Turks suspected a conspiracy. They weren't in the mood to cooperate with foreign intruders who, flouting Ottoman sovereignty, had descended on the Sultan's capital intending to tell them what to do. They already were furious at the Russians for demanding an armistice with the Balkan insurgents at a time when the Sultan's army was preparing to take Belgrade.

The Constantinople conference finally convened on December 23, with Ignatiev assuming the lead role. The Russian diplomat was widely considered the most talented liar in Constantinople, beating out formidable rivals for the dubious honor. He came to the diplomatic table with a hidden agenda. While pretending to work for peace, Ignatiev set out to sabotage the negotiations. His goal was to neutralize opposition by the Western Powers to a Russian war against the Turks.

Ignatiev used an extensive network of agents and spies, cultivated over many years, to produce "facts" that were supposed to prove that the Ottomans were unspeakable villains. He wanted to make fighting the Turks a moral imperative. This was an increasing challenge, particularly with the British. While they had been at white heat for action against the Ottomans in the weeks following Gladstone's exposé of the Bulgarian atrocities, officials in London had begun to realize that the Balkan insurgents were as brutish toward their enemies as were the Turks.

Countess Ignatiev, a woman of intelligence and practiced charm, provided her husband with able assistance in sabotaging the peace conference. This formidable pair used mockery to diminish the Turks in the foreign delegates' eyes. They worked the crowd, using wit and flattery that disarmed almost everyone except their reluctant hosts, who remained, needless to say, unamused. The Turks, pushed into recalcitrance by Ignatiev's bullying, unwittingly played into the Russian envoy's hands.

Czar Alexander II had returned to Moscow from Livadia, where those present were in a martial mood, eager to get on with the war. Two days after his Kremlin speech he ordered mobilization of six army corps, along with some reserves. These forces were to take positions near Ottoman territory in the south. Then, however, the Czar confronted disturbing domestic realities that had been easy to ignore in his Crimean paradise. Reports of revolutionary plots arrived regularly at government headquarters.[2] The Czar's abolition of serfdom in 1861 had left widespread dissatisfaction not only among the nobility but also among the freed peasants themselves. Additionally, the empire's coffers were virtually empty. Deeply troubled by the situation on the home front, the Czar ordered Ignatiev to make a settlement with the Porte if possible. The ambassador, ardent Pan-Slavist that he was, took pains to see that such a settlement was not possible.

Ignatiev continued to promote his scheme for Russian occupation of Greater Bulgaria. He gained supporters in St. Petersburg. Government officials named Prince Vladimir Cherkasky governor of the future Russian colony. The Prince, known for his burning ambition and tyrannical personality, openly recruited staff for the Bulgarian vassal state. In developing his plans, he relied heavily on Aksakov and other Pan-Slavs.[3]

In mid-December two advocates of Bulgarian autonomy, who were touring Europe to plead their cause, arrived in Russia. During an audience with the Bulgarian visitors on December 23 – the same day the conference opened in Constantinople – the Czar told them that although he wanted peace, he would not be satisfied with hollow promises for Ottoman reforms. "If the other Powers content themselves with mere words," he declared, "we shall call God to our help and move forward and fulfill our duty: tell this to those who sent you."[4]

The Czar had a point. Midhat Pasha, the Grand Vizier of the Ottoman Empire, had startled delegates during the opening moments of the Constantinople Conference with booming cannons and the proclamation of a constitution. The document also called for a bicameral legislature with an elected lower house. This dramatic gesture was intended to convey a message to representatives of the six Powers[5] that their meddling in Ottoman matters was unnecessary. The constitution, the Turkish plenipotentiaries said, would allow the Porte to conduct its own reforms. The conference delegates, as well as the Czar, justifiably had no faith in an Ottoman conversion to republicanism. Abdul Hamid II, who had come to power on August 31, 1876, was weak and incapable of carrying out serious reforms. He flirted briefly with liberalism, then reverted to the absolutism of his royal forebearers. The constitution languished in a rarely opened drawer until 1908. Its revival at that time would bring Austria and Russia to the brink of war, as we shall see later.

While European eyes were fixed on Constantinople, Russia and Austria held secret talks concerning the Russians' conduct of the coming war. The negotiations had commenced before the Powers had gathered for the Constantinople Conference. Andrassy and Gorchakov took the lead in the talks. Mutual distrust informed the discussions. The Austrians were impatient at being forced to repeat what they thought they had made perfectly clear: Austria had no desire to declare Turkey moribund until all parties agreed that was the case. As Andrassy put it, "Dissolution of a state is like baldness – it's not clear when it begins."[6]

The negotiating parties had serious differences of opinion. Andrassy insisted that the Reichstadt agreement called for the monarchy to acquire most of Bosnia and

Herzegovina when and if the Turkish "Sick Man" actually died. Gorchakov claimed that in such a case Montenegro had been promised Herzegovina, with Serbia receiving part of Bosnia. Andrassy refused to budge. The Russian foreign minister complained that the Austrian price for benevolent neutrality bordered on extortion. Russia was to sacrifice blood and treasure for the war, Gorchakov said, while Austria then "swept up the pickings."[7]

The negotiators also sparred over what was decided at Reichstadt. Did the Russians promise not to create a large Slav state? The Austrians thought so. The Russians now claimed they only promised not to create a large Serbian state. Franz Joseph and Alexander II later were to have a falling out over this matter, further harming the already damaged relationship between the Habsburgs and the Romanovs.

At the conference in Constantinople, Ignatiev brought forward his plan for creation of a greater Bulgaria under Russian auspices. Ignatiev apparently was testing the political waters to see whether his scheme would float. This caused an uproar. The Turks saw no reason to renounce sovereignty over a vast portion of their empire just because the Russians demanded it. The Greeks were angry since they had claims to areas the Russians were eying. The Serbs were incensed at the Russians for failing to represent Belgrade's interests in Constantinople (including claims to some of the disputed territory). The Serbs complained that the Russians were treating them like poor relations. The Austrians were livid at Ignatiev for pushing his wily scheme for Russian expansion in the Balkans. They surmised, correctly, that the Czar intended to renege on his promise, at least as Franz Joseph and Andrassy understood it, not to create a large Slav state in the region. When it became clear that the conferees had no intention of handing over vast portions of Bulgaria to the Russians, Ignatiev temporarily laid aside his scheme, but he in no sense abandoned it.

By early January 1877, the Turks, full of offended pride, were refusing to cooperate with the conference. They rejected each of the representative's proposals in turn. The delegates watered down their demands. The Turks also rejected these, repeating their assertion that with a constitution in place they could carry out reforms without foreign interference.

The conferees packed for home. The delegates had unanimously declared that if the Porte refused their latest list of demands they would leave Constantinople *en masse*. The conference ended on January 20 but, as Sumner writes, "even the prearranged collective departure ... was ruined by an inconvenient storm which deterred all but Salisbury (the British delegate) by the prospective pangs of seasickness."[8]

A second conference was set for London in the spring. Since it was to cover much the same ground, it was unlikely that the Turks would be in a better mood to accept it. Already by January, some 190,000 Russian troops were poised to invade Turkey in Europe.

On January 15, 1877, Russia and Austria signed the first of two Budapest conventions. The Russians got what they wanted most from the negotiations – cover for their right flank as the czarist forces marched into the Balkans. The Austrians promised to be benevolently neutral in the coming war. They allowed their railway to be used for hospital trains and for shipping of materials but not for troops. If the Russians needed to cross the Danube to protect themselves from Turkish gunboats they could do so, but only temporarily. Russian and Austrian troops were forbidden to enter Serbia, Novi Pazar[9] or Montenegro.

Austria received the right to choose the moment and the mode of occupation of both Bosnia and Herzegovina. A subsequent political convention (of March 18, 1877, backdated to January 15), expressly used the word "annexation" in reference to the twin provinces.[10] Franz Joseph used this document, among others, to justify the monarchy's 1908 annexation of Bosnia and Herzegovina.

The Budapest conventions not only forced Gorchakov to yield on Herzegovina; they also loosened political ties between Serbia and Russia, since the Czar's troops were forbidden to enter the Balkan province. It is not clear how much this mattered. Many Russians felt that "poor little Serbia" had abandoned the "Slav idea." They also blamed the Serbs for rushing into a war with the Turks that they couldn't expect to win and then counting on the Russians to do their fighting for them.

For a while, the Russians singled out the Bulgarians for praise due to their perceived loyalty to Slavic Orthodoxy. However, the Bulgarians soon also disappointed their Russian "brothers." Like the Serbs and the Montenegrins, the Bulgarians were more interested in self-aggrandizement than in subservience to Mother Russia.

With the military convention with Austria signed and the political treaty near completion, war became inevitable. Speaking to Mikhail Reutern, his finance minister, the Czar declared, "There are moments in the life of states, as of individuals, when it is necessary to forget everything save the defense of honor."[11] The world would hear such high-flown language again as the Russians prepared to declare war on Austria and Germany in 1914.

Ignatiev, in the meantime, set out on a diplomatic offensive, visiting European capitals to drum up support for a Russian-inspired protocol, to be presented to the Turks at the London Conference in March. He achieved a major victory by persuading the British to collaborate on the protocol, which restated and expanded on earlier demands directed at the Turks. His ploy virtually guaranteed that the British would not object when the Russians enforced through war the mandate that they had helped draft. Predictably, the Turks rejected the protocol. The Powers received their answer on April 12, 1877. The next day the Russians issued a war manifesto.

Russia's first face-to-face conflict in the century, was to last 10 and a half months. Alexander II, in declaring war, called for Russia to march for "Orthodoxy and Slavdom." The Pan Slav periodical, *Ostov*, was ecstatic: "We live, and shall live, in a single great family which has a single Slav policy.... The great historic Slav idea hastens to its fulfillment. Czar Alexander, with the aid of the Slav God, will free twelve million slaves as he freed the serfs in Russia."[12] And there was yet another articulation of the theme, this one at the historical heart of all Russian efforts in the Balkans. As the periodical, *Zastava*, declared, "With its declaration of war Russia redeems the Czar's words in the Kremlin and reaffirms her mission as a great Slav state. The heirs of Peter and Catherine ... have not forgotten the way to Tsarigrad."[13]

The war got off to a vigorous start. The Russian troops crossed the River Prut. They went beyond the Danube, moving to the foot of the Balkan mountain range and driving the Turks out of large portions of Bulgaria. On July 19, General Josif Gurko captured the strategic Shipka Pass.

The string of initial successes caused anxiety in London and Vienna. The British thought the Russians sounded cagey about their intentions toward Constantinople, since they refused to say unconditionally that they would refrain from occupying the city. Lord Loftus, the British envoy to St. Petersburg, undoubtedly basing his conclusions on his experience at Livadia the previous fall, allowed that the Romanovs aimed for nothing less than "the subjection of Turkey to Russian domination and the reduction of the Ottoman Empire to a Russian province."[14] Loftus even advocated British occupation of Constantinople and the Dardanelles as the surest way to bring the Russians to heel. The British sent a ship to Basilka Bay as a reminder that there were limits to what they would tolerate in Russian behavior.

Although the Habsburgs also were nervous about the

rapid Russian advance, Andrassy was willing to give the Russians substantial leeway in the Balkans. The Austrians would not intervene, he said, unless they were certain that Russia threatened the monarchy's interests. Andrassy took no stand on a temporary Russian occupation of Constantinople, which so worried the British, or on changes in regulations regarding the Straits. His main aim was to prevent the Russians from occupying or establishing a protectorate over Bulgaria.

After early successes, the Russian troops were forced to give up much of the ground they had gained. The Czar joined his army on June 2 and would remain with the troops until December 22. He often got in the officers' way. Grand Duke Nikolai Nikolaevich, Alexander II's older brother, was ostensibly in charge of the military operation, but he felt obliged to confer with the Czar before making major decisions. This slowed operations significantly. The heir apparent (the future Alexander III) also was present. He was put in charge of an army and performed his duties satisfactorily, but other military officers had to take special pains to keep him out of danger since he was heir to the throne.

Finding themselves face-to-face with the people they had come to liberate, the Russian soldiers soon were cured of the desire to shed blood on behalf of the poor Bulgarians, repeating their earlier disillusionment with their Serbian kinfolk. "The Russians had been fed with stories regarding their Orthodox brothers in Bulgaria, harried or massacred by the Turks, awaiting with despairing eagerness the day when they would greet triumphantly the victorious legions of the Czar and rise like one man to free their country," wrote Sumner. "In sober fact (the Russians) found themselves in a foreign land among a close-fisted peasantry who, in most cases, seemed to show little spontaneous joy at their liberation."[15] The Russians had expected the Bulgars to be downtrodden, miserable people. In fact, they seemed more prosperous than the average Russian peasant. The Czar's troops were in northern Bulgaria where they saw no signs of the massacres they had anticipated; these were occurring in other regions of the country. Worse still, the Bulgarians weren't eager to join their Slav brothers in war, although some ultimately reported for duty. "The Russians disliked the Bulgars, (and) the Bulgars disliked the Russians,"[16] but, as Sumner says, these two peoples had deep historical ties. The Bulgarians who hoped for liberation believed that only the Russians could deliver them. To the extent that they realized that their benefactors from the north were interested mainly in their own national aggrandizement, they seemed willing to overlook it.

The Russians underestimated the Turkish determination to defend their homeland. The Ottomans brought in troops by sea, driving the Russians back beyond the Balkan range. For a time it seemed that even the Shipka Pass would be recaptured by Turkey. The real challenge came, however, at Plevna, a small fortified town where General Osman Pasha, the new Turkish army commander on the Danube, dug himself in. Plevna was on the right flank of the main Russian army and in the rear of the Russian forces that had advanced into the Balkans. The Turkish commander repulsed the Russian attack on Plevna on July 20 and repeated his performance with a near massacre 10 days later. A third Russian attempt to take Plevna failed on September 11-12.

The Plevna defeats didn't sit well with the Russian public. Scapegoating became a national pastime. The grand dukes were faulted for their military impotence. The Pan-Slavs were criticized for pushing the Czar into an unnecessary war. Aksakov, the Pan-Slav activist, blamed foreign influences for the Russians' failures in war. He railed against the English and that "monstrous political compound of German-Jewish culture and Magyar-Bazi-Bazouk savagery which goes by the name of Austria-Hungary."[17]

Aksakov called for a common Orthodox front against these enemies of the Russian national idea.

Desperate to put an end to their string of military losses, the Russians sought help from the Romanians, who had already generously allowed the Russian army to move through their province as the troops headed southward. The combined forces imposed a successful blockade and siege on Plevna. On December 10, a wounded Osman Pasha marched his half-starved troops through the Russian lines and surrendered. From there on the Czar's army met little resistance. The Russians were on their way to the city that was then known as Tsarigrad, but that many still recognized as Byzantium.

Alexander Hübner, the Austrian minister, recalled in his diary that in 1876, after leaving an audience with Franz Joseph, he had asked himself: What did the Russians really want? Now, Hübner wrote, he believed he knew the answer: Alexander II not only wanted revenge for what he considered Franz Joseph's betrayal of his father during the Crimean War; he also wanted to persevere in the Russian quest for the fabled lands to the south. "In the main," wrote Hübner, "the politics of both these czars is basically nothing other than the desire for territorial expansion of Russia from the time of Peter the Great to the present. With his (Alexander II's) despotic principal of unity his goal is to use force to establish a world empire."[18]

Franz Joseph almost certainly was of a similar mind with Hübner after receiving from Alexander II, in December 1877, an advance copy of the Czar's "peace conditions" for the Balkans. These were to be presented to the Porte. The Czar's newly drafted map not only presaged an end of Turkey in Europe; it amounted to what historian Viktor Bibl terms "Russification of the Balkans."[19] The Czar intended to preside over the birth of a huge, independent Bulgaria, covering more than half of the Balkan peninsula, with frontiers reaching from the Danube to the Aegean. The peace plan called for a two-year Russian occupation of the fledgling Balkan state. The Czar also demanded the return of parts of Bessarabia that had been ceded to Romania at the end of the Crimean War.

The Russian grab for hegemony in the Balkans created a huge stir in Vienna. As far as Franz Joseph was concerned, the Czar had violated the letter and the spirit of the Reichstadt agreement (1876) and the January Budapest conventions (1877). Sometime earlier Franz Joseph had told Hübner that although he believed Alexander II was honest and honorable, he suspected that some of the people around him were troublemakers. Now Franz Joseph's faith in the Czar himself was shattered. The Emperor considered the Czar's peace plan a personal insult. The Russian ruler had ignored Austrian interests in the Balkans. With Bulgaria as a Russian satellite and Bessarabia again in Romanov hands, Russia would control a good part of the western shore of the Black Sea. This would give the Czar's minions the ability to obstruct Austrian shipping on the Danube.

Writing to Alexander II on January 8, 1878, Franz Joseph chided the Czar for his peace plan in language similar to what he, as a young Emperor, had used to scold Nicholas I as that ruler careened toward what became known as the Crimean War. Franz Joseph reminded Alexander II that he had advised him not to rush unilaterally into war with Turkey, but rather to wait for the Ottoman Empire to expire naturally. The Emperor emphasized that he had not agreed to any disturbance of the status quo in the Balkans, such as the Czar now intended.[20]

As an absolute ruler, Alexander II was accustomed to hearing varnished pleasantries rather than unpolished truths, even from fellow monarchs. The Czar took offense at the substance and the tone of Franz Joseph's letter. The Czar seemed to believe that it was his divine right to pursue whatever Balkan policy he chose, even if that meant going back on his word. In characteristic Romanov fashion,

Alexander II considered anything less than total loyalty to czarist adventurism in the Balkans as perfidy. *"Je suis outré"* (I find that detestable) the Russian autocrat sputtered.[21]

In his answer of January 16, 1878, Alexander II dredged up resentments against the Habsburg monarch from the Crimean War. Well over two decades had passed since the end of that unhappy conflict, but the Czar had kept his anger alive as he remembered what he viewed as Franz Joseph's betrayal. The Czar declared that Count Karl Ferdinand von Buol, the Habsburg foreign minister during the Crimean War period, must have persuaded Franz Joseph to "overcome his scruples" by supporting the cession of parts of Bessarabia to Romania instead of leaving that territory in Russian hands. Alexander II said he felt sure that Franz Joseph was "anxious to abolish this memory that was incompatible with the friendly relationship" between the two imperial houses. However, the Russian ruler added coldly, "the effects have remained."[22] The Czar offered Franz Joseph a proposition that would have future significance: The Russians would acknowledge the Habsburgs' freedom to occupy Bosnia and Herzegovina in exchange for the monarchy's allowing Russia temporary occupation of Bulgaria. The Czar wrote that Franz Joseph would be free "to transform the temporary occupation into an annexation" if the Emperor considered it necessary. The Czar's statement would bolster Franz Joseph's claim to legitimacy when the Austrians, in 1908, finally annexed the twin provinces. However, while the Emperor welcomed this news regarding the two provinces, on the issue of a large Slav state in the Balkans, Franz Joseph refused to back down.

In the effort to resolve the resulting impasse, the Czar turned to Wilhelm I of Germany, the other member of the League of the Three Emperors. Czar Alexander felt absolutely certain that his uncle, the Kaiser, would take his side in the dispute. Instead, Wilhelm I, responding on

January 23, 1878, offered to mediate in the feud between his two allies. According to a diary entry by Prince Alexander of Hesse, the Kaiser's missive was handed to the Romanov ruler on January 26, while the Czar and he were at the theater. The Czar "expected something more" from his uncle, Prince Alexander of Hesse wrote. The Russian ruler felt the response to be "non-committal, chilly, and inspired by Bismarck,"[23] which it almost certainly was. Later that year, at the Congress of Berlin, Alexander II again took offense at Bismarck for playing the honest broker during those negotiations. The Romanovs, smarting from the damage to their image and interests sustained during the Congress, began to view the Germans and Austrians as a single enemy. This helps explain why, in 1914, the Russians had no battle plan for a military conflict solely with Austria.

13 OUTSIDE BYZANTIUM

Grand Duke Nikolai Nikolaevich, the brother of Czar Alexander II, was one of those men who, from childhood, had felt destined for military glory. The Grand Duke's nephew described him as "warlike." Even at the table, it was said, "he sat tall, as if he expected ... (someone) to play the national anthem at any moment."[1] During the Russian military campaign of 1877, he fulfilled his duties as Romanov commander brilliantly, leading his army from victory to victory over the Turks. After the fortress at Plevna fell, following a five-month siege, the Grand Duke took his army southward through the Balkans. The Russians captured Adrianople on January 21, 1878, and marched toward Constantinople, once known as Byzantium.

On the night of February 23, 1878, the Grand Duke moved his military headquarters to a villa in San Stefano, a picturesque village on the Sea of Marmara. The walls of Constantinople rose six miles in the distance.

The next day, Alexander of Battenberg, the nephew of Czarina Marie, accompanied the Grand Duke on horseback to the heights of the village. The morning mist had cleared. Byzantium, the fabled city of Russian dreams, with its Hagia

Sophia and its many minarets, lay at their feet. Battenberg captured the exultation of the moment. He wrote, "Tears stood in the Grand Duke's eyes. What satisfaction to stand with his army at the gates of Constantinople!"[2]

Viewed from the heights of San Stefano, the ultimate prize must have seemed within the Grand Duke's grasp. Perhaps he really believed that he was destined to realize the dream of Peter the Great and every Romanov czar since. But as every warrior knows, destiny can be a fickle mistress. When the time came to seize glory, the Grand Duke hesitated and missed his chance. The golden city; although tantalizingly close, was not to belong to the Romanovs, not at that moment, not ever.

There was widespread disbelief and anger in Russia when the news arrived of the Grand Duke's failure to seize Byzantium, the mythical prize that lay virtually at his feet. However, as with many aspects of human behavior, the Grand Duke's hesitation at San Stefano involved a muddle of difficulties: physical, psychological and tactical. Grand Duke Nikolai and his troops were exhausted from their recent effort. The Russian army had braved drifting snows and treacherous passes as the troops pressed through the Balkan ranges. The soldiers' boots had holes and their ammunition had run short.

The strain of this ordeal had taken its toll on the Grand Duke. By the time he led his army into Adrianople some of those around him hinted that he had become unhinged. He had previously urged St. Petersburg to make peace with the Ottomans. Now, he telegraphed the Czar using the messianic language that the Romanovs espoused when they were about to do something reckless: "It is necessary to go to the center, to Tsarigrad,[3] and there finish the holy cause you have assumed."[4] A few days later, he sent another message declaring, "With God's help I shall advance."[5] But then Nikolai Nikolaevich lapsed into lassitude.

One of the Grand Duke's problems was that, while he

ostensibly had absolute authority to make decisions and issue commands, he customarily deferred to his brother, the Czar, on important matters. However, communications between St. Petersburg and military headquarters were patchy. Messages sometimes were delayed for several days, making them meaningless in light of developments in the field.

Worse still, and perhaps most significantly, directives from Alexander II had become inconsistent. The Czar himself wasn't sure which path to take. Dmitry Milyutin, the war minister, pushed for a quickly arranged peace with the Turks. Count Ignatiev, who as Russian ambassador to the Ottoman Empire had done so much to bring on the war, wanted the Russian army to occupy the heights above Constantinople, then rapidly take the city and the Straits. At one point the Czar sent his brother an order, then remanded it later that same day.

The Czar's decision on military action hinged in large part on where Vienna stood. In going against Constantinople, the Russians now expected to face not only the Turks but also the British. Alexander II wanted absolute certainty that Franz Joseph would remain neutral, as he had promised. In light of the continuing quarrel between the Emperor and the Czar over stipulations in the Russians' preliminary peace with the Turks, those assurances were far from guaranteed.[6]

Events moved quickly. On January 30, the Turks, having fallen into a panic, accepted the Russians' preliminary peace terms. The Ottomans told the Russians abjectly, "Your arms are victorious; your ambition is satisfied; but Turkey is lost. We accept all that you desire."[7]

On the face of it, the unconditional surrender by the Turks offered the Grand Duke a marvelous opportunity to seize Constantinople and the Straits. But the hour of possibility had passed. While the Czar waited to learn Vienna's position regarding neutrality, the British fleet had shown its flag. By the time the Turks surrendered, the Royal Navy was lying at anchor at the Isle of Princes in the Sea of Marmara – in plain view of officers at Russian army headquarters in San Stefano. The British intended to demonstrate unequivocally that they would protect their interests in the Middle East and the Suez Canal. That meant assuring free access to Constantinople and the Straits.

On March 3, 1878, at San Stefano, the Turks concluded a preliminary peace with the Russians. The czarist victory would prove as ephemeral as the quest for Byzantium itself, but for the time being the Russians celebrated the conditions for peace. The Turks agreed to the redrawing of the Balkan map according to the Czar's specifications. That meant creation of a Greater Bulgaria, which was supposed to be autonomous, but which actually was intended to be a Russian vassal state. The Bulgarians were thrilled at their vastly expanded nation, although their jubilation and the vast expansion were to be short-lived. Montenegro not only got its independence; it also received a threefold increase in territory, including major acquisitions in Herzegovina. The Serbs, as was their wont, felt cheated. While they, too, gained independence, they received only a small part of the territory they had demanded. They had claimed the entire vilayet (province) of Kosovo, but were given only four counties, with the rest going to Bulgaria. They also had expected to acquire some or all of Bosnia. The Romanians were disgusted. They had saved the Russian's military campaign from disaster by joining the czarist forces in the siege of Plevna. In return for their sacrifice, territory in Bessarabia, which they had received in a peace settlement after the Crimean War, was handed to Russia.

Prince Alexander of Hesse, who was in Vienna in March 1878 for the funeral of Franz Joseph's father, had two long audiences with the Emperor. The Prince reported that Franz Joseph told him that it was "quite impossible for Austria-Hungary to agree to the Treaty of San Stefano ... ."[8] The

Emperor said he did not want war with Russia but indicated that he wasn't going to let the Czar push him around either. According to Prince Alexander of Hesse, Franz Joseph said the Russians had made fools of the Austrians (by ignoring solemn agreements between the empires). The Prince wrote that Franz Joseph seemed to be losing his belief that the two imperial houses could ever work together in the Balkans.

The Russians had arrived at that conclusion long since.

Czarina Marie, fearful that the Romanovs would be deprived of their winnings in the war, hit back at those she considered Russia's enemies. In a letter to Prince Alexander of Hesse on March 4, she expressed amusement at his telling her that the Prince of Wales had asked "whether it was really true that the Russians were so angry with the English." The Czarina replied, "Furious, you should have told him and that we hate the English as much as we do the Austrians."[9]

In spite of the Habsburg Emperor's determination to avoid a conflict with Russia, a war party emerged, mainly among Hungarians who wanted to get even with the Russians for their cruelty during the 1848 revolution. Habsburg Foreign Minister Andrassy argued for a conflict on grounds that the Russians had played Austria false. Speaking at a ministerial conference on February 7, Andrassy declared, "We must see to it that the Russians go home." Franz Joseph pointed to difficulties in seeing that the Russians went home. The Austrians weren't mobilized and the Russians were. "It's rare," said the Emperor, "for a war to occur in which one state has already mobilized and the other, however, first has to ask its parliament."[10] Franz Joseph told Count Richard Belcredi, who also was urging military action, "Regardless of what anyone in Vienna or Pest says, I will never let myself be led into a war with Russia."[11] While it was true that Franz Joseph had to confer with his parliament before going to war, he didn't have to ask anybody for permission not to go to war. And that was the path he chose.

The typical view of European governments concerning the peace of San Stefano was that the Czar, in his drive for hegemony in the Balkans, had far exceeded the boundaries of acceptable behavior. Lord Derby's successor as British foreign secretary, Lord Salisbury, demanded that the treaty be rescinded. Prince Alexander of Hesse, stopping in Dresden for tea with the king and queen of Saxony, found the king "openly anti-Russian." The Prince reported that the monarch "expressed regret that the Turks had not made more of their victory at Plevna at the beginning of September, where the Russian officers went into battle drunk or weeping."[12]

The Russian public turned on the Grand Duke, making him a scapegoat for failing to take Constantinople. Alexander II also was upset at his brother's failure to seize the golden city, although he surely understood that what happened wasn't all the Grand Duke's fault. The Czar sent Count Eduard Totleben, who had directed the siege at Plevna, to replace his brother at the end of April. The Czar ordered the Grand Duke to return to St. Petersburg, where he was to receive a grand marshal's baton as a consolation prize. When his train arrived the Grand Duke received an unexpected honor. "The Czar in person had driven to the station to welcome the generalissimo who had captured Plevna, Sofia, the Shipka, Philippopolis, Adrianople – but not Constantinople," writes Sumner. Alexander is said to have dryly explained that he had … (honored his brother in that fashion) so he would not be hissed at by the crowd.[13]

With the Russian army and the British navy near sword's point just outside Constantinople, war between those two Great Powers remained a threat. When rumors circulated that the Habsburgs were tilting toward England, the Czar became desperate, knowing his army would stand little chance against a coalition of England, Austria and Turkey. In the effort to smooth over differences with Austria, Alexander II sent a most improbable envoy on a peace mission to Vienna. Giving the Austrians little advance warning, Nikolai Ignatiev, known in diplomatic circles as "the father of lies," showed up on March 26. Although Andrassy and Ignatiev detested each other, they resolved some important issues. The Austrians promised to remain with Russia and Germany in the League of the Three Emperors. The monarchy was to remain benevolently neutral if Russia and Britain went to war. The Russian envoy agreed that Austria could occupy Bosnia and Herzegovina. On May 2, Ignatiev went further, informing Vienna that Russia agreed to a Habsburg annexation of the provinces. Franz Joseph would use these statements by the Russians, along with others, in justifying the monarchy's annexation of the twin provinces in 1908.

When the discussion turned to San Stefano and the creation of a large Slav state, Andrassy and Ignatiev came close to fisticuffs. Ignatiev had not participated in the July Reichstadt[14] agreements or the January 15 conventions, where the foreign ministers had laid out conditions for the coming war. Ignatiev had denounced the terms as treasonous when he heard about them. The San Stefano peace treaty, which bore Ignatiev's imprimatur, had been a flagrant attempt to override the agreements by calling for a large Slav state in Bulgaria.

In crafting his argument with Andrassy in favor of the large Slav state, Ignatiev showed a genius for polished sophistry, parsing the language of the Austro-Russian convention of January 15 to suit his purpose. Ignatiev interpreted the agreement to mean that the prohibition against the large Slav state applied only to Serbia and Montenegro. Andrassy, who had been involved in the negotiations, insisted that the Russians had promised not to create *any* large Slav state in the Balkans. With no resolution of the verbal battle in sight, Ignatiev surprised the Austrians on March 31 with a sudden departure from Vienna.[15]

After the furor over the San Stefano peace with the Ottomans showed no sign of abating, the European Powers convened, in June 1878, what became known as the Congress of Berlin. The continent's preeminent statesmen came prepared to consider the fate of the partly eviscerated Turkey; to hear complaints from other parties – and to redraft the Balkan map, so boldly redrawn by the Czar for the San Stefano treaty.

The leaders who gathered in the ballroom of the Radziwill Palace in the German capital were a colorful lot:

Imperial Chancellor Otto von Bismarck, donning the mantle of genial *Hausherr* (host), presided over alcoholic punch and cookies. The chancellor, given to biting comments during contests with opponents, attempted – not always successfully – to keep his sharp tongue sheathed. He tried to see that his guests comported themselves in a manner that would lead to a quick resolution of the issues on the table. He pushed the conferees to finish their work, begun on June 13, in three days. They finished on July 13.

The 80-year-old Russian state chancellor, Aleksandr Gorchakov, who was tall, skinny, unable to climb stairs without help, lacking basic knowledge of Balkan geography but quick with a bon mot, peered at fellow attendees through large glasses.[16]

Andrassy, a cynosure of eyes in his Hungarian uniform of cardinal red, set off with blazing decorations of gold, strutted about, looking, as Eduard von Wertheimer, Andrassy's biographer says, more like a "bold cavalry general" than a diplomat. A lock of very dark hair gave the former Hungarian insurgent a slightly rakish look.[17]

British Prime Minister Benjamin Disraeli, 73, bent and wrinkled, his face like yellow parchment, rather deaf, held forth as eloquently as ever, but only in English. The other representatives used French.

Turkey's representatives, characterized by Bismarck as "a Greek, a renegade and an imbecile."[18] The renegade, said to be a Turk from Magdeburg, Germany, whose original name was Karl Detroit, had converted to Islam while in Constantinople. Bismarck, offended by the gentleman's change of religion, departing from his recently assumed role of genial guest pleaser, mocked the Turkish delegate, wrote Bernhard Fürst von Bülow, who was present.[19]

Kaiser Wilhelm I, having survived two attempted assassinations in just over a month, did not attend. He still suffered from a wound in the neck. His absence reminded those present of the turbulence of the times.

Addressing the conference, Gorchakov declared that Russia had gone to war only for "Christianity and civilization." Now he merely wanted to change the Russian "laurels of victory for palms of peace." The hall became very quiet. Bismarck, again abandoning his role as host, "laughed sarcastically," wrote Fürst von Bülow.[20]

The Congress expected Austria to ask for annexation of Bosnia and Herzegovina. This required the approval of the Great Powers. Most delegates were thought likely to support the request. Franz Joseph had instructed his Foreign Minister to push for permission to annex. However, in a move that would have devastating long-term consequences for the Habsburg monarchy, Andrassy on June 28 surprised delegates with a long memo making the case for military occupation and administration – rather than annexation – of the twin provinces.

Andrassy's about-face seems to have surprised even Franz Joseph. At the very least the Emperor hadn't been fully informed about his minister's change of direction. However, as the diary of Countess Marie Festetics, the lady-in-waiting of Habsburg Empress Elisabeth, shows, Andrassy had been considering occupation for at least a month. In an entry dated May 25, 1878, Festetics wrote that "Andrassy wants to occupy Bosnia and Herzegovina ... the others (presumably his colleagues) want to annex." Andrassy thought occupation would be "of equal value and cheaper,"[21] she wrote.

Just three days before he presented his memo to the Congress, Andrassy telegraphed Franz Joseph, laying out three reasons for occupation instead of annexation (italics added):

1.   *Occupation would avoid the difficult question of whether and how the lands were to be incorporated in the monarchy.* Andrassy's Magyar supporters strongly opposed adding more Slavs to Hungary. That would have been a likely result of annexation, since Hungary was nearer the provinces than Austria. When it came to choosing between his Emperor and Andrassy's Hungarian constituency, the foreign minister stood with the latter. However, even his support of occupation landed him in political quicksand.[22]

2.   *The Porte was more likely to consent to occupation than to annexation. If the Austrians decided to annex, the Turks might feel compelled to defend their territory.* Here we see Andrassy characteristically opting for an easy way out. His assessment, however, had some merit. As Wertheimer notes, the Turkish Padishah, for religious reasons, forbade turning over a region to a foreign power except when it had been lost through war.[23] Ironically, it is unlikely that the Turks, still reeling after their recent war with Russia, would have intervened even if Austria had gone forward with annexation. Andrassy's attempt to avoid war failed. When the Habsburgs occupied the provinces later in 1878, the monarchy's mission was not easily accomplished. The Austrian troops met strong resistance from local Ottoman loyalists.

3. *The monarchy could still achieve its goal of acquisition of the provinces.*[24] Apparently Franz Joseph doubted this, prompting Andrassy to quickly fire off another telegram. Don't worry, the Foreign Minister telegraphed the worried monarch: "The annexation will take care of itself with time." When the monarchy finally annexed the provinces in 1908, the annexation hardly "took care of itself." Rather, it had consequences that led directly to the First World War.

The decision to occupy, rather than annex, the provinces was pivotal in Habsburg history. Andrassy had presented his Emperor with a poisoned chalice. Some of Andrassy's enemies in the monarchy considered his behavior that of a Judas, as might have been expected of a man who had betrayed the monarchy by siding with the rebels in the 1848 Hungarian Revolution, and, who, they thought, should have been hanged in actuality at that time rather than in effigy. They were upset that Franz Joseph had ever allowed a traitor like Andrassy inside the imperial tent.

And Andrassy hadn't finished doing damage to the Habsburgs' prospects for success. The Ottoman representatives at the Congress had twisted and suffered as the other delegates spent hours arguing, as Prince von Bülow puts it, over "which of their limbs could still be amputated."[25] Now, emboldened by Andrassy's apparent willingness to settle for half measures, they sprang to life. The Turks announced that they had been instructed to sign the Congress' act only if the provisional character of the occupation was made clear and if the Sultan's basic sovereign rights were upheld.[26]

On July 13, Andrassy responded to the Ottomans' demand by signing a secret agreement with Turkey which acknowledged the formal sovereignty of the Sultan.[27] The Habsburg minister even hinted that the monarchy might eventually return the provinces to the Ottomans.

Franz Joseph was angry when he learned what Andrassy had done. His minister had created a situation in which the Austro-Hungarian Empire faced all the problems it would have had with annexation, without full power to make basic legal changes in the lives of the empire's new and needy subjects. Andrassy had overstepped his authority but by the time the Emperor found out about it the deed had been done.[28] This move on the part of Andrassy undoubtedly contributed to Franz Joseph's decision, in October 1879, to dismiss the minister.

The Congress of Berlin left what Italian historian Luigi Albertini terms "a disastrous heritage of discontent."[29] Turkey lost a large hunk of her European territory. Bulgaria was hacked up into three parts. The Serbs didn't get as much territory as they thought they deserved. The Romanians felt cheated. They had helped the Russians win the war only to lose Bessarabia, which was handed to Russia. The Montenegrins fared relatively well. The Austrians agreed for them to acquire the strategically located Adriatic port of Bar on condition that it remained neutral. A limit was placed on the number of ships Montenegro could anchor there; Austria was to patrol the coastline. The Austrians had reasons for their requirements: they wanted to be sure that the Russians didn't take advantage of their close friendship with Montenegro and secretly set up an Adriatic naval base, but these restrictions inevitably led to friction between Montenegro and Austria.

Inexperienced mapmakers, charged by the Congress of Berlin with redrawing the Balkan maps, bungled the job badly. Lacking adequate knowledge of the Balkan terrain, they created maps that lacked clear borders. Worst still, the mapmakers failed to consider sufficiently ethnic sensibilities when they redrew the borders. The Balkans became a cauldron of discontent.

On its face, the Austrians scored a diplomatic triumph at

the Congress of Berlin, gaining substantive territory at seemingly little cost, without war or other sacrifice. But it was a Pyrrhic victory. The monarchy had become co-owner of two large and relatively ungovernable provinces. Within the monarchy the occupation remained exceedingly unpopular; many of the Germans and most of the Magyars opposed adding Slavs to the empire.

Anatol Murad, a biographer of Franz Joseph who is no friend of the Habsburgs, strikes a note of sympathy when he considers what the monarchy had gotten into with the occupation. He likens the situation to adding two more quarreling families to an apartment house of already dissatisfied tenants.[30]

The Russians left the Congress with little to show for their sacrifice of blood and treasure. They felt bitter, disgraced and humiliated before the whole world. Their efforts to create a vassal state in a greatly enlarged Bulgaria had failed. Constantinople remained a mirage, fading in the distance as they approached it. Alexander II and the two Romanov czars who succeeded him – his son, Alexander III, and his grandson, Nicholas II, the last Czar – would nurture a deep and abiding antipathy toward Franz Joseph, the disloyal "brother" who had laid waste to Romanov aspirations in the Balkans and beyond, first in the Crimean War and then in 1878.

The Romanovs had lost their latest battle in the Balkans, but they remained undaunted. The official Russian statement issued shortly after the ratification of the Treaty of Berlin was a bugle call for future war. The Congress of Berlin, the announcement declared, was only a "breathing space" on the "difficult path" to a final settlement of the Eastern Question.[31]

14 MASTER JUGGLER

The Congress of Berlin permanently damaged the relationship between the Romanovs and Habsburgs. But it was the unexpected appearance of a crack in the previously solid friendship between the Romanovs and the German Hohenzollerns that raised new doubts about a sustainable European peace.

Czar Alexander II was furious with his uncle, Kaiser Wilhelm I, for failing to require Bismarck to defend Romanov interests during negotiations in Berlin. In late 1878, in an apparent effort to demonstrate his anger, the Czar stationed a large force of cavalry near the German border.

The Czar nursed his anger and kept it warm. In August of the following year, the Czar sent his royal uncle a blistering letter, scolding him for interfering with Russian ambitions in the Balkans. He accused the Germans of supporting the Austrians, who were, the Kaiser claimed, "systematically hostile to Russia."[1] The Czar warned, prophetically, that the tensions between the two imperial houses could lead to the downfall of both empires.[2]

Chancellor Bismarck took offense at the brazen attempt

by Alexander II to bully his [the Czar's] uncle Wilhelm I into supporting Russia's aggressive Balkan policy at the expense of Austria. In a letter to the king of Bavaria, dated September 10, 1879, the chancellor confided that as early as 1876 the Russians had barraged him with inquiries as to whether the Germans would remain neutral if the Romanovs went to war with the Habsburgs. Bismarck wrote that in the aftermath of the Congress of Berlin, the mood at the Romanov court appeared more militant than ever. Pan-Slavist extremists were, he said, gaining influence with the Czar. Bismarck accused Russian war minister Dmitry Milyutin of organizing an arms buildup at a time when Russia faced no threat. "These war preparations can only be intended for use against Austria or Germany," Bismarck warned.[3]

In response to what he viewed as a Russian attempt to challenge German autonomy, Bismarck made a move that permanently shifted the alignment of the European Powers. Correctly assuming that the Austrians and the Russians were never to be friends, Bismarck concluded that Germany had to choose between her two allies, based on who would be more compatible with Berlin's interests. For Bismarck, Austria was the obvious choice.

Realizing that tensions in Europe were rapidly spinning out of control, Bismarck set about putting diplomatic balls in the air. The Chancellor's first step was to bring Austria and Germany into an alliance. The treaty was to stipulate that if either signatory were attacked by Russia, the other party would come to that nation's aid. If either nation were attacked by another Power, such as France, the remaining ally would be benevolently neutral. Bismarck insisted on the alliance in spite of strong opposition from Kaiser Wilhelm I. The 83-year-old German ruler's family ties with the Romanovs, including his nephew, the Czar, were deep-seated. "Prince Bismarck ... himself states in his communication that I shall find it difficult to ratify this treaty," wrote Wilhelm I. "Not simply difficult, but impossible: it would go against my conscience, my character and my honor to conclude behind the back of my friend – my personal, my family, my political friend – a hostile alliance directed against him."[4] Bismarck, using his full repertoire of powers of persuasion, including pleading, bullying and threatening to resign, eventually convinced the Kaiser that the treaty was necessary.

Franz Joseph, although still resentful about Prussia's unprovoked attack on Austria in 1866, welcomed Bismarck's plan for a defensive alliance against the Russians. The Germans and Austrians signed the treaty for the Dual Alliance on October 7, 1879. Three years later the Italians joined the coalition, which then became the Triple Alliance. The Italians eventually proved themselves fickle allies. The Habsburgs and Hohenzollerns remained loyal until both empires disappeared in the fog of the Great War.

Bismarck's next step was to resuscitate the League of the Three Emperors. The alliance, between Germany, Austria and Russia, had been formed in 1873. It had collapsed two years later after Russia and Austria fell out over Russia's support of Pan-Slav agitators in the Balkans. The alliance offered significant political advantages for each of the imperial courts. It stipulated that in case one of the signatories to the treaty went to war with a fourth Great Power the other parties in the alliance were to remain benevolently neutral. The parties also were to consult with their allies before attempting changes in the territory of Turkey in Europe. Bismarck wanted to protect the recently stitched together German nation from attack by the French, who yearned to revenge the loss to Germany in 1871 of Alsace-Lorraine. For the Austrians, closer ties with St. Petersburg offered hopes of reducing anti-Habsburg agitation, encouraged by Russian agents, in regions near the monarchy's southern border and within the empire itself.

The Romanovs desperately needed outside life support.

Their setback at the Congress of Berlin had seriously damaged the imperial family's domestic prestige. Revolutionaries lurked in public places. A plague of dissatisfaction infected normally peaceful segments of the population. Many members of the Russian old guard were angry at the Czar for liberating the peasants. The serfs themselves, once emancipated, found that the freedom for which they had so yearned came at a high price. They learned to their dismay that they now had to pay a poll tax. They also had lost their access to manorial forests. Not knowing how to cope independently, many of these former serfs supported revolutionary causes. Radical groups, including communists and nihilists, faulted the Czar for failing to do enough for the suffering masses. The efforts of Count Dmitry Tolstoy,[5] a tyrannical education minister, to purge the universities of troublemakers added to the public anger. So did attempts at Russification, requiring the empire's citizens to return home from abroad. Alexander II made the situation worse by arresting more and more rebels.

On June 24, 1879, the executive committee of a revolutionary group meeting in Varonezh, pronounced a death sentence on the Czar,[6] declaring that the ruler's assassination was to be carried out as soon as possible. Later that year, while Alexander II was on holiday in the Crimea, the terrorists laid mines on the train tracks between Crimea and St. Petersburg. On December 2 of that same year, as the Czar returned from Livadia, the train behind him, a baggage car filled with fruit from the region, was bombed.[7] By chance Alexander II and his entourage were safe in the front train. A revolutionary group, the "Will of the People," claimed responsibility for the attack and made demands.

Always the autocrat, Alexander II sought to punish the terrorists rather than listen to their complaints. He became increasingly fearful. He had bulletproof wadding sewn into his uniforms. His sled and carriage were lined with steel sheets. A small army of police and secret agents accompanied him everywhere. Nothing was to save him.

Several months later revolutionaries smuggled dynamite into the Romanov palace bit by bit. Fearing they were about to be discovered, the conspirators touched off a blast before they were ready to do so, killing 11 people and wounding 44 others.[8] "We must break the enemy," declared the badly frightened Czar. The problem was he had no idea who the enemy was.

In 1881, the Will of the People began selling cheese at a shop at Malaya Sadovaya 9 as a pretext, while members of the terrorist group dug a tunnel under the street that Alexander II usually used in going from the Winter Palace to the Kazan Cathedral. On March 13, the Czar, following his Sunday routine, traveled along the Catherine Canal embankment to review the imperial guards at the Michael Riding School. The conspirators waited by the roadside.

Testifying later, one of the terrorists, Nikolai Rysakov, admitted to throwing one bomb at the imperial sled as it approached. It killed a Cossack guard and wounded a child. The Emperor, who was not injured, rushed to assist those who were hurt. Another bomber, Ignoti Grinevitsky, hurled a grenade disguised as a snowball. The bomb tore the Czar's left eye from its socket. Both his legs were blown off below his knees. Attendants took the Czar to the Winter Palace, their route marked with large splotches of blood. They carried him up the marble stairs and through the corridor leading to his study. The awkward youth who was about to become Alexander III rushed to his father's side and asked the attending physician how long the Czar would live. The doctor said, "Up to 15 minutes."

Edvard Radzinsky, a biographer of Alexander II, describes the poignant scene: "A boy in a sailor suit was led up the marble steps. It was the heir apparent, 13-year-old Nicky, who as the last Romanov ruler would perish with his family at the hands of the Bolsheviks in 1918. The boy tried to avoid stepping in his grandfather's blood, but that was hard. The blood of Alexander II was everywhere. Nicky became the heir in blood. And in blood, he would cease being czar."[9]

Alexander III was a coarsened version of his Romanov predecessors. The new Czar was built like a bison. He stood six feet, three inches tall, an unusual height in Russia at the time. His jaw was square, his eyes small and dull. He had broad shoulders and the arms of a fighter. His strength later became legendary after tales circulated that he once singlehandedly lifted the ceiling of a wrecked railway car to allow his family to escape from the twisted metal.

Unfortunately, the Czar's mental abilities fell far short of his physical prowess. He was sluggish intellectually and lacking in manners. Even as a youth, he generally made an unfavorable impression. He was described as "uncomely, uncouth and bad-tempered ... all too keen to fight ..." with a "poor knowledge of languages." He was, as somebody said, a "null." Even his friend, Konstantin Pobedonostsev, acknowledged as much, characterizing him as one who "had been ... badly misused by nature who sent him into the world with the shabbiest of intellectual outfits."[10]

Bismarck, back at work on Wilhelmstrasse in Berlin following a serious illness, became nearly hysterical when he learned of Alexander II's assassination. Aware of the new Czar's anti-German proclivities, Bismarck wondered whether his efforts to revive the League of the Three Emperors were now futile. Although members of the Romanov family traditionally made marriages with German royalty, the new ruler, Alexander III, had acquired prejudices against the Germans and Austrians at his Danish mother's knee. Czarina Marie was understandably hostile toward the Germans for wresting the duchies of Schleswig and Holstein from Denmark in a war that Bismarck had provoked. The Czarina also held a permanent grudge against Franz Joseph for what she considered his disloyalty toward the Romanovs during the Crimean conflict.

Bismarck's worries about the new Czar's attitude toward his allies in the Emperors' League were justified but premature. Undoubtedly motivated by fear for his own safety following his father's death, Alexander III signaled his willingness to form an alliance with the other two Northern Powers.

A new treaty was approved by the Three Emperor's League on June 18, 1881. In a highly significant separate protocol, the Austrians reserved the right to annex Bosnia and Herzegovina whenever they chose. While the language of the protocol on this issue was clear, the loosely crafted agreement was ambiguous regarding the Balkans. Bismarck interpreted the agreement to mean that the Russians and Austrians would settle into an amicable division of spheres of influence in the region. The western part of the Balkan peninsula, including Bosnia, Serbia and Macedonia, would fall under Austrian auspices, while the eastern part, including Bulgaria and Rumelia, would be in the Russian domain. Italian historian Luigi Albertini points out the problems in this arrangement: The division of spheres of influence was not stipulated in the treaty. The Austrians were unwilling to allow Russia unfettered authority over Bulgaria.[11] The attempt by Alexander II at San Stefano to create a large vassal state in Bulgaria, under Russian auspices, was too fresh in Franz Joseph's mind to make such accommodations to czarist ambitions thinkable.

The emperors' treaty was renewed again in 1884, but shortly thereafter it foundered in a controversy between Austria and Russia over Bulgaria. The Austrians objected to the Russians' continuing military presence in the province. The Russians, viewing Bulgaria as central to their quest for Constantinople and the Straits, refused to order key military commanders to pull out of the region. Bismarck tried to persuade the Austrians to acknowledge the Russians' right to include Bulgaria in their sphere of influence. The Austrians would not hear of it.

The conclusions seemed inevitable: Austria and Russia were close to war.

It was Bismarck, on his last legs physically and politically, who imposed his large self between the two angry parties and prevented them from getting into a fight. Bismarck was genuinely worried that Alexander III would be carried away by those in the military urging him to invade Austria and settle the Eastern Question once and for all.[12] He also was concerned about Austria's recalcitrance. The Austrians and the Russians are "acting like snarling dogs," the chancellor grumbled. In a speech to the German Reichstag on January 11, 1887, he declared, "We shall allow no one to put a leading rope around our necks and embroil us in difficulties with Russia."[13] Having put the monarchy on notice that his support for Austria's Balkan policy was far from unconditional, Bismarck next dealt with the Russians. He presented Russian Ambassador Paul Shuvalov with the full text of the secret treaty of 1879 (the Dual Alliance) between Austria and Germany, in which Germany promised to support Austria should she be attacked by Russia. This was to be the stick that would persuade Russia to keep the peace.

Bismarck had then offered the Russians a rather flaccid carrot, a "Reinsurance Treaty," in which Germany promised neutrality toward Russia unless Russia attacked Austria, and Russia promised Germany neutrality unless Germany attacked France.[14] The treaty, completed on June 18, 1887, had limited value for the Russians. It gave them a free hand in Constantinople and the Straits, but prevented them from attacking the Austrians, who were viewed in St. Petersburg as standing between them and Byzantium.[15] In spite of its limitations, however, the Reinsurance Treaty improved relations between Germany and Russia – while it lasted.

Bismarck's juggling act required consummate skill to keep it going. Once the chancellor left office, in March 1890, the German Empire's diplomacy fell into far less capable hands.

Franz Joseph had hoped that his relationship with the Romanovs would improve with Alexander III in power. That did not occur. Alexander III did not renew the three emperors' agreement in 1887. Never again would the Habsburgs and Romanovs be allies.[16] Corti's remarks on the assassination of Alexander II are cogent: "Alexander II sinks into the grave, but Emperor Franz Joseph lives and continues to reign."[17] The poisonous heirloom of hatred toward Franz Joseph, woven and enlarged by memories of the monarch's every perceived and real slight, was to be passed down in the Romanov family from generation to generation, until the quarrel was fatally settled on the battlefields of Europe in 1914.

World War I did not start with the assassinations at Sarajevo. It did not start with the 1908 annexation of Bosnia and Herzegovina. As Corti writes, "the evolution of the catastrophe was in no way...rapid." It came about "over many decades."[18] Actually, Corti might have said, "over centuries."

Germany entered a turbulent period following the death in 1888 of Wilhelm I. His son, Friedrich III, whom Bismarck despised for his republican leanings, died of throat cancer after reigning for only 99 days. The new Kaiser, Wilhelm II, was a world-class provocateur, stirring up controversy wherever he went. Always a busybody, he was masterful at getting on people's nerves. It wasn't so much that he behaved badly as it was that he raised concerns about how he might behave. On home territory, he let few occasions pass without honoring his subjects with his presence. At monument unveilings, ship christenings, church dedications and parades, Wilhelm was there. Upon occasion he held forth with scripture and a sermon. He interfered with Greek lessons at the local high school and designed his wife's outlandish hats.

Wilhelm was also a master poseur. With his substantial

mustache, pointed upward at a 90 degree angle, and his theatrical costumes, he was a natural for a role in a third-rate farce. A favorite pose was that of a warrior king. In a portrait by Max Kroner, painted in 1890, the Kaiser wears high, shiny black Prussian-style boots; his head is thrust back at a fierce angle; he wields a cudgel in his right hand. Something in the portrait disturbed those who saw it. As one French general is said to have declared, "That is no portrait, but a declaration of war."

The Kaiser, a man who sought to dominate every situation, was unwilling to share the political stage with the imposing presence of Otto von Bismarck. Wilhelm II dismissed Bismarck on March 13, 1890, installing in his place Count Leo von Caprivi, a military man who was ignorant about foreign affairs and understood little about creating or maintaining alliances. When Russia, that same year, asked to renew the Reinsurance Treaty, Wilhelm II refused the request, saying he personally would deal with Alexander III if problems arose. Insulted by this rebuff, the Russians turned toward France. In July 1891, a French naval squadron paid an official visit to Kronstadt. Czar Alexander III, whose hatred of republicanism was well-known, went on board, where he stood bareheaded as the French national anthem, the *Marseillaise*, was played. On August 27, France and Russia agreed to a draft military convention. By January 1894 it had been officially confirmed by both states. The agreement was directed against Germany.

Czar Alexander III became seriously ill with kidney disease during the summer of 1894. He and his family moved to Livadia, the Romanovs' Crimean palace on the Black Sea, in hopes that the sun and fresh air would restore the ruler's health. That was not to be. He died on November 1.

That evening, in a ceremony on the palace lawn, Nicholas, his 26-year-old son and heir, became ruler of all the Russias. The reign of Nicholas II was to be a disaster for

Russia, Europe and the world. He would be the last of the Romanov czars.

Two years prior to the death of Alexander III, Vladimir Lamsdorf, a foreign ministry official, wrote that the heir apparent presented "... a strange appearance, half child, half man, small in stature, slender, insignificant."[19] Nicholas II failed to grow in the role fate thrust upon him. The young Czar was intelligent and charming – he enjoyed dancing, skating and the opera. He was, by nature, a dilettante.

Alexander III undoubtedly never expected to be taken at such a young age (only 49). He spent little time instructing his heir in his future duties – not that the crass autocrat would have been much of a role model for his sensitive son. Making matters worse, Nicholas' mother, Czarina Marie, encouraged her son to remain dependent on her.

Nicholas II commanded little respect. As General Peter S. Vannovsky, the Russian minister of war, later put it, Nicholas "takes counsel from everyone...grandparents, aunts, mummy and anyone else; he is young and accedes to the view of the last person to whom he talks."[20] He had no inner compass that might have led him to make sensible decisions. Nicholas II lacked the capacity to benefit from experience.

In 1910, as the clouds of war gathered over Europe, Austrian Count Leopold Berchtold, who was leaving his post as Habsburg ambassador to St. Petersburg to become the monarchy's foreign minister, wrote that the Czar was pious and peaceable, and sincerely wanted a good relationship with Austria. Berchtold added, however, that Nicholas had been miscast as a czar. Lacking the talent and training needed to govern, he "suddenly found himself as the unrestrained, unlimited ruler of the mighty Russian Empire. The fate of the whole world lay in the hands of this weak man."[21]

Those around the new Czar, aware of a vacuum at the center of power, rushed into the breach. Among them was

Alix of Hesse, young Nicholas's future bride. She had hastened to Lavidia to be with her fiancé after learning that his father was dying. Alix, the porcelain complexioned granddaughter of Queen Victoria of England, had good intentions, but she had inherited none of her venerable relative's common sense. Soon realizing that Nicholas' opinions were being ignored, she urged him to insist on being heard. Throughout the couple's long and happy marriage, Alix pressed her husband to live up to his God-given obligations as absolute monarch. "Be Peter the Great," she admonished her hapless "boysey," as she called him. When her admonishments failed, Czarina Alix increasingly blamed the Romanov relations for her husband's missteps as a ruler. The Czarina's awkward manners and her cold personality – which actually resulted from shyness – alienated those at the court who might have helped her husband succeed. After the couple's child, Aleksei, the heir apparent, was diagnosed with hemophilia, Alix tried to hide the terrible secret from the world. She encouraged her husband to avoid the public as much as possible – just when he most needed the people's support. The Czarina's trust in Grigory Rasputin, a dissolute "Man of God" who seemingly had the power to stop Aleksei's bleeding, did much to undermine public confidence in the House of Romanov.

Nicholas II had four uncles, brothers of his father. One was too young to interfere in czarist decisions, but the three older Grand Dukes engaged in a bullying campaign that made the young ruler's life miserable. When ministers or other officials were present with the Czar they said little. Once the visitors left, the uncles pounded the table and demanded that their nephew clamp down on dissenters and otherwise act as the autocrat that God, and his Romanov relatives, expected him to be.

Wilhelm II, who realized belatedly that he had erred in refusing to renew Bismarck's Reinsurance Treaty, saw an opportunity to draw closer to Russia once Nicholas became Czar. He regularly sent his cousin Nicky, who was nine years his junior, long letters full of unsolicited advice. One of Wilhelm II's goals was to persuade the Czar to abandon Russia's recently formed alliance with France and to renew the traditional Romanov ties with Germany. In a letter to the Czar on September 26, 1895, the Kaiser predicted that Russia's entanglements with France would end in disaster. He warned Nicholas II that if he continued to tilt toward France he could find himself "embroiled in the most horrible ... war Europe ever saw." The Kaiser added that the masses and history might well blame Russia for causing the conflagration. Wilhelm's predictions were apt but premature.

For the better part of a century, Wilhelm II and the Germans received most of the blame for causing the war. Historians, like hunting dogs following a false scent, turned out thousands of books on German war guilt without arriving at a satisfactory explanation of the origins of World War I. Only now is Russia's culpability for the conflict beginning to be recognized.

If Bismarck had been allowed to continue his diplomatic balancing act he might have preserved European peace. But the chancellor, dismissed from his post, had retired to his country estate where he died in 1898. Left to his own devices, Wilhelm was his own worst enemy. The Kaiser never seemed to realize that he himself was partly responsible for causing others to suspect his motives. In 1898 Wilhelm II made a pilgrimage to Palestine, arranged by travel agent Thomas Cook. The Kaiser's stated purpose of the visit was to be present at the consecration of a new Lutheran church in the Holy City. As usual, however, the Kaiser's behavior caused speculation about his intentions.[22] Upon arriving at the Jerusalem Gate, he made a triumphal entry into Jerusalem on a war horse, dressed in a white military uniform, and wearing a helmet ornamented with a gold eagle – looking, some said, like a Crusader. His entourage included a battalion of clerics as well as 1,300 horses and mules, 100 carriages, 12 wagons with 230 tents, 600 beaters (for hunting), 10 guides, 12 cooks and 60 waiters. The visitors made themselves at home, setting up a huge tent city just outside the city.[23]

Like many of Wilhelm II's theatrical gestures, his visit to the Holy Land was meant to impress rather than terrify, but to the English, the French and also the Russians, it had an unsettling effect. No Christian ruler had visited Jerusalem since Holy Roman Emperor Frederick II had conquered the city in the 13th Century. Now the Protestant German Kaiser had set up camp near the sacred places. Wilhelm II rushed to inform his friend Nicky about his triumph, not realizing that the devoutly religious Orthodox Czar could hardly have been pleased that his friend, Willy, the leader of a people belonging to a rival branch of Christianity, seemed to be staking out a claim in the Holy Land. The Kaiser's success, several months later, in winning Turkish concessions for a railway terminal as well as for a harbor on the eastern side of the Bosphorus also caused great anxiety in Russia as well as in England. Wilhelm's fellow monarchs were left wondering what the erratic Kaiser would do next.

Wilhelm II had a lifelong resentment of the English, stemming from a botched delivery that left him with a withered left arm, some six inches shorter than the other and virtually useless. He blamed his mother, Queen Victoria's oldest daughter, and her English doctor, for his handicap. It was particularly troubling for a monarch in an era when dashing horsemanship and hunting ability were requisites for royalty. It is true that Willy, as he was called by his English relatives, showered his grandmother with affection. He literally got between her and her children when she was dying, holding her in his arms as she passed away. But his fondness for his grandmother was an exception. He particularly detested his uncle, King Edward

VII, whom he blamed for Germany's troubles. The Kaiser convinced himself, correctly, that he was being "encircled" by what became known as the Triple Entente (France, England and Russia).

A devotee of ships from the time he received his first small boat when he was two-and-a-half, Wilhelm II set out to create a Navy that would guarantee Germany – in a phrase immortalized by Prince Bernhard von Bülow – "a place in the sun." The Kaiser, indulging in his usual verbal strutting, declared that there would come a time when "no great decision" would be made in the world without the participation of Germany and her ruler. The English, and to an extent the French, responded to the Kaiser's provocations by engaging in an arms race and by tightening their alliances to ward off what they viewed as a German threat.

The Kaiser's visit to Tangier, in Morocco, on March 31, 1905, provided more drama than even the attention-loving Wilhelm II bartered for. There were problems getting ashore. The Kaiser's chartered passenger ship, the *Hamburg*, was too large to enter the harbor, forcing the monarch to come ashore in an open boat. French, Spanish and Italian anarchists welcomed the Kaiser as he landed. His aide, forgetting Wilhelm's withered arm, arranged to have him ride horseback through the narrow streets into the city.[24] His high-strung Arabian racehorse, unimpressed by the high honor of escorting royalty on his back, threatened to rid himself of his burden at any minute. For a German ruler, falling off a horse among a gawking throng was just not done. Somehow, Wilhelm II reached his destination still astride. He dismounted, pale and furious, but unfortunately not speechless. He declared that all nations should have equal rights in Morocco, and that this could be realized only if the Sultan had full sovereignty and Morocco were fully independent. Wilhelm II's words caused an uproar. The French were furious at the Germans for meddling in

Morocco, which they considered part of their sphere of influence.

Hearing of the incident in Morocco, King Edward VII branded his nephew a "political enfant terrible." An international conference, at Germany's request, convening at Algeciras, added to the political polarization that was to influence decisions leading up to the Great War. The French, who had shown signs of forgetting about Germany's seizure of Alsace and Lorraine in the war of 1870-71, now began to relive that national trauma and consequently moved closer to England and Russia. In an era when personal politics still mattered, the Moroccan crisis would play a significant part in sides chosen in the war of 1914.

Wilhelm II also upset the opposing powers with his pursuit of German commercial interests in the Near East. By 1900, Germany was the largest investor in Anatolia.[25] The Berlin to Baghdad railway project, involving cooperation between Germany and the Ottomans, stirred jealousy among Germany's rivals. The Russians, in particular, worried that Wilhelm II would beat them in the race for control of Constantinople and the Straits.

Wilhelm II, concerned that Nicholas II would side with England and France in a future conflict with Germany, devised a ploy to divert his Russian cousin's attention. The Kaiser, playing on the Czar's insecurity, used flattery to persuade Nicholas II to engage in expansionist adventurism in East Asia. Signing his letters as the "Admiral of the Atlantic," he referred to his friend Nicky as the "Admiral of the Pacific." The Kaiser's encouragement was partly responsible for the Czar's decision to plunge into an ill-fated war with Japan that ended in Russia's defeat in 1905. The conflict drained the Russian treasury and inflamed revolutionaries on the home front.

On July 24, 1905, the Kaiser's yacht, *Hohenzollern*, pulled alongside his friend Nicky's yacht, the *Polarstar*, which was anchored off the Finnish island of Björkö. The two rulers greeted each other warmly. Nicky invited his cousin Willy to have breakfast on board his yacht. What happened later that morning might have set Europe on a course for peace – if Nicky had listened to his instincts instead of being swayed by those close to the Romanov throne who wanted a military reckoning with Germany.

Wilhelm produced a draft of a defensive treaty between Russia and Germany that called upon the signatories to come to each other's aid in case of an attack by a third European power. The treaty was primarily aimed at England; however, it also offered protection from an attack by France. The Kaiser later said the treaty was like a "mutual fire insurance" agreement against incendiaries.[26]

The Kaiser later told Bernard von Bülow, the German chancellor, that Nicholas read the treaty once, twice, three times. Then he said, "That is quite excellent. I agree to it completely." Wilhelm asked, "Would you like to sign? It would be a lovely souvenir of our meeting." The Czar hesitated briefly then agreed. Wilhelm II opened the ink stand and handed his cousin a pen. The Czar wrote with a firm hand, "Nicholas." Wilhelm then signed. The two rulers stood and embraced.

Nicholas said, "I thank God and I thank you…. You are Russia's single true friend in the entire world. I felt that during the entire war [with Japan] and I know it."[27]

In a letter to Nicholas II on July 27, 1905, Wilhelm wrote that "…by God's grace the morning of the 24th of July has witnessed a turning point in the history of Europe." He pointed to benefits from the treaty for both participants. The prospects of peace would restore calm in Russia and encourage foreign financiers to invest in projects that would open up Russia's still untouched resources. As for Germany, Wilhelm wrote, "a great load has been lifted from my Fatherland, which has finally escaped the terrible Gallo-Russian pincers."[28] Wilhelm was so excited about the treaty that he dashed off a telegram to U.S. President Theodore Roosevelt, informing him of the news. The telegram was never sent.

The treaty, which had been concluded in the absence of the German and Russian foreign ministers, caused a furor in Moscow and Berlin. Bernhard von Bülow, the German chancellor, threatened to resign, saying the treaty was too limited to offer his country much protection. However, the real pushback came from the Russians. Vladimir Lamsdorf, Nicholas' foreign minister, claimed that the treaty was at cross-purposes with the agreements Alexander III had negotiated with France. Wilhelm responded that, if the Russo-French treaties were only defensive, neither party need worry about the Björkö agreement. But French loans to Russia were at stake.

The Russians spread rumors that Wilhelm II had surprised the Czar by suddenly producing the treaty at Björkö, and had bullied him into signing it. There is, however, evidence, based on the Kaiser's letters to the Czar, found in a trunk by the Soviets after the Romanovs were executed, that Wilhelm talked about such a treaty with Nicholas on several occasions.[29] The Czar's interest in the proposed alliance was based in part on his belief that the English had secretly sided with the Japanese during the war.

While the Hohenzollern and Romanov sovereigns had lost much of their power by 1905, Wilhelm II and Nicholas II retained authority over their governments' foreign affairs. Both rulers had the ability to dismiss their foreign ministers at will. No one could have forced them to abandon the Björkö treaty if they had insisted on it. Furthermore, the two old northern monarchies had historically cooperated on matters of mutual concern. But Nicholas II lacked the courage to exercise his authority. He sent his cousin Willy word that he would need to consult with France before he could proceed with the treaty.

Wilhelm's move at Björkö was Bismarckian in its

conception. Perhaps the master juggler could have found ways to lure Russia away from the French. But Wilhelm II was no Bismarck, just as Nicholas II was no Peter the Great.

Wilhelm's comments on the Czar's decision to back out of the treaty were prophetic: "The Czar is not treacherous, but he is weak. Weakness is not treachery, but it fulfills all its functions."[30] That would prove true in late July 1914.

15 BATTENBERG

Prince Alexander of Battenberg, chosen by the European Powers as ruler of a newly autonomous Bulgaria, arrived in Sofia in July 1879, expecting to assume the authority ordinarily enjoyed by a crowned head. Battenberg, also called Sandro, was the handsome, agreeable 22-year-old nephew of Czarina Maria, who was married to Alexander II. The Romanovs considered Sandro family. But he also was the son of a German general who was known for his devotion to Austria. Additionally, his Hessian family was related to the British royals. Sandro was to find himself caught in a maelstrom of conflicting loyalties and expectations that required far more maturity than he had at his command.

The Prince, arriving in Sofia, was shocked to find the Bulgarian capital working alive with Russian military officers, who appeared none too glad to see him. A deadline, set by the Congress of Berlin for withdrawal of the Czar's troops from Bulgaria, had come and gone. Russian agents, most of them military, remained in control of the newly minted state. Battenberg soon realized they didn't intend to leave and weren't going to allow him to govern as

231

he saw fit. "The scum of Russia has set up its headquarters here and has infected the whole land," the Prince wrote home.[1] What Battenberg didn't realize was that the "scum" had at least the nominal blessing of his uncle, Alexander II.

The Czar had joined other European states in supporting the elevation of his wife's nephew to be the Prince of Bulgaria. However, the Czar's ambitions for Battenberg were different from those of Austria and Great Britain, the other powers with interests in the region. As the young Prince would learn through experience, Alexander II intended for him to be a puppet, whose strings were pulled from St. Petersburg. The Czar expected Sandro to further the Russians' immediate aim of establishing Bulgaria as a vassal state. The strategically located nation was to serve later as a convenient base for the Russian army as it pushed for a final solution to the Eastern Question in Constantinople.

Alexander II had good reason to think that Battenberg would support the Romanov agenda in Bulgaria. The young man had proven his mettle during the 1877 invasions of Turkey. Holding the rank of general in the Russian army, he had been among the first to lead the Czar's troops across the Danube and to take them to the very gates of Constantinople.

The Prince respected Alexander II and wanted to please him. On the other hand, he was appalled by the behavior of the Russians that he encountered in Bulgaria. In a letter to his father, he said, "The Russian spoils system is ... sanctioned and daily I find myself in the sad situation of having to sign on to the most unashamed demands or to be accused in Petersburg of betrayal and the injury of the holy feelings of the Bulgarians."[2] Writing again a few days later, he said, "Whenever anything bad happens, the hand of this nation (Russia) is clearly behind it." He complained that the Russians had trashed the palace, making it hardly fit for habitation. "In three rooms and in a passage the ceilings *fell in with a crash ...*" he said. "In consequence a scaffolding has been put up over my bed in case I should be flattened out one night."[3] The Prince felt surrounded by spies. "I must always be on guard to protect my skin without injuring Czar Alexander," he wrote.[4]

Battenberg, attempting to assert his authority over the Russian generals, made many enemies. Although the military men had the ear of the Czar, in deference to his ailing wife's feelings, Alexander II overlooked many of what he considered Battenberg's missteps as Bulgarian ruler. But in early 1881 Battenberg's uncle, Alexander II, died a bloody death at the hands of assassins.

The new Czar, Alexander III, and the Prince clashed immediately. Alexander III was Sandro's older cousin. They had known each other all their lives. The Czar took offense at Sandro for failing to pay sufficient heed to his elevated station. He was now ruler of all the Russias and not simply a childhood friend. The Prince failed in some letters to use the form of address required by protocol to show the respect Alexander III thought he deserved.[5] For the Czar, these lapses in royal etiquette came to symbolize Battenberg's disregard for him in every respect.

Czar Alexander III was an experienced hater. He despised Habsburg Emperor Franz Joseph and couldn't stand Queen Victoria of England. He viewed the Germans as Russia's natural enemies. Battenberg managed to give offense on all those fronts. Not only was he a German Prince; he also was on friendly terms with the Habsburgs.

The Czar became particularly upset when he heard that Battenberg hoped to marry Princess Victoria of Germany, the English Queen's granddaughter. Bismarck stepped in at that point, seeing an opportunity to draw closer to the Russians, who were still angry at what they considered his unfriendly behavior at the Congress of Berlin. He sent young Vicky's brother, the future Kaiser Wilhelm II, to St. Petersburg to let the Czar know that he would stand with him in blocking the union. Bismarck's effort succeeded, leaving Princess Vicky to mourn her lost Prince.

Battenberg, having come to despise Alexander III, no longer saw a need to defer to St. Petersburg. He consequently set out to establish himself as an independent ruler. In a sort of coup d'état, on July 13, 1881, the Prince induced a newly elected Sobranie (National Assembly) to give him wide powers, essentially allowing him to take over the government. His initial aim was to purge the Bulgarian army of Russian influence. He faced a task worthy of Sisyphus.

The Russians in Bulgaria were quick to pick up on the dissension between the Czar and the Prince. They, of course, had no ambiguity about where their loyalties lay. One telling incident occurred in early 1882 at an official dinner, when a toast was being offered to the Bulgarian sovereign. A Russian colonel named Timmler, who headed the Bulgarian war ministry, declined to drink the toast, shoving his glass haughtily away and glaring at the Prince. After the meal Battenberg told the colonel he had 48 hours to get out of the country; otherwise he would be sent before a court martial tribunal. The colonel laughed in Battenberg's face and said, "From you, my Prince, to be hounded away, is in Russia the best recommendation."[6]

Alexander III complied with Battenberg's pressing request to put the insubordinate officer on one year's leave, but shortly after the period was up the Czar named Timmler assistant to the chief of the Russian general staff. The message to Sandro was clear.[7] The Czar was biding his time, waiting to get rid of his unfaithful servant.

International tensions, with the Europeans increasingly dividing into opposing camps, formed the backdrop for Battenberg's difficulties. During a visit to St. Petersburg in May 1882, Battenberg wrote his father that he was struck by the growing animosity among the Russians toward Austria. Ignatiev, the Pan-Slav former ambassador to

Constantinople, was now minister of the interior. Sandro reported that a Russian general named Soboleff was making after dinner speeches expressing sympathy for the South Slavs, whom he claimed were being oppressed by Austria. The general expressed his hope that Russia and France would join forces to settle the Eastern Question once and for all.[8] The general would get his wish in 1914, although the results would hardly be what he desired.

Battenberg's attempts to purge the Bulgarian military of Russian influence kept running into barricades, but the Prince refused to back down. In one instance two Russian generals, Kaulbars and Soboleff, had been sent by the Czar to serve as Bulgarian ministers of war and interior.[9] Acting as regents while Battenberg was away attending Alexander III's coronation, they attempted to undermine the Prince's authority. They even spoke openly of another candidate for the Bulgarian throne.[10] When Battenberg returned to Sofia, he dismissed them. The Czar was furious at what he considered the Prince's insubordination in firing the generals. On a separate occasion, a Russian agent in Sofia refused to allow a certain officer, who was friendly to the Prince, to take the post of minister of war. When Battenberg protested, the agent mockingly replied: "Leave things alone. I have full power to bring about a breach. And it is not we who need fear anything if that happens."[11]

The Prince's efforts to rid the military of Russian influence weren't the only things that angered the Czar. Alexander III also was extremely upset at the Prince for approving an Austrian extension of a railway into Bulgaria, while refusing the Russians similar rights. "While Battenberg was being praised by Austria-Hungary for being firm and fair, he was putting the final touch to the quarrel with Russia,"[12] Corti wrote.

"A deep gulf now yawns between the Czar and myself, and I suppose it will never be bridged," Battenberg wrote his father. "Hatred and contempt are the feelings which animate this crowned fool, who is too cowardly to live in St. Petersburg, hides at Gatshina [his country estate], (and) imagines that he can impress his people by stirring up revolution among his neighbors ..."[13]

Battenberg continued to have faith that he would prevail in his attempts to eliminate Russian influence in Bulgaria. However, a report by Archduke Rudolf, the Austrian Crown Prince who visited Bulgaria in the spring of 1884, showed that the Prince's efforts were not succeeding. As Archduke Rudolf noted, the army remained under strict Russian control. All the generals, the staff officers, and the company commanders were Russian, the Austrian Archduke reported. The army and language of command were Russian. Even the uniforms had a Russian cut.[14]

Matters in Bulgaria came to a head on September 18, 1885, when Battenberg learned that the people of Eastern Rumelia (today part of southern Bulgaria) – separated from their ethnic kinfolk in Bulgaria by the Congress of Berlin – had rebelled and called for a union with Northern Bulgaria. They declared that they wanted Battenberg as ruler of their loosely joined state. Ironically, this union would have gone a long way toward establishing the Greater Bulgaria that the Russians had tried to create at San Stefano. But this was to be a Bulgaria led by a man who was defying his Russian handler at every turn.

On November 5, 1885, the Czar registered his disapproval of events in Bulgaria with the dramatic step of removing Battenberg's name from the Russian army list. This was a humiliating blow to the Prince's prestige. The Prince's days in power clearly were numbered. The only question was when and how the end would come.

The Serbs, never bereft of dreams for greater glory, provided Alexander III with what he hoped was an opportunity to force Battenberg to step down – without the Czar's lifting a hand.

The Serbs were angry at the Bulgarians' move toward

unification. In spite of five centuries of Turkish rule in the Balkans, the Serbs and Bulgars had clung to their hereditary hatred of each other. Claims over rights to Macedonia were central to that ancient quarrel. The Congress of Berlin had failed to clearly define Macedonia's borders, and the region was now in danger of being swallowed by a new, unified Bulgarian state. Determined not to stand for this, the Serbs on November 14, 1885, declared war on Bulgaria. It was widely believed that the Serbs would quickly defeat the Bulgarians and claim much of the principality's territory for themselves. If that happened there would be no place for a Bulgarian prince in a vastly expanded Serbian state. The Czar hoped by this development to be rid of Sandro forever.

However, expectations of a Bulgarian defeat turned out to be a figment of military prognostication.[15] Shortly before the war broke out, the Czar, misreading the situation in Bulgaria entirely and thinking to weaken Battenberg's hold on Bulgaria, ordered the Russian military to leave the principality. The Bulgarian recruits who rushed to replace the Russians were eager to confront their traditional enemy. After quickly defeating the Serbs near Slivnitza, by November 27 they headed deep into Serbian territory.

Franz Joseph had been favorably inclined toward Battenberg. However, in this case, the Emperor, a strong believer in the principle of legitimacy in matters of state, rose to the defense of Serbia. He was displeased that Battenberg had challenged his Balkan neighbor's sovereignty in violation of the Treaty of Berlin. Franz Joseph also had personal reasons for not wanting to see Serbia destroyed. King Milan, the Serbian ruler, had tilted toward Austria after being slighted, or so he thought, by a Russian delegate, at the Congress of Berlin. Milan complained that the Czar's representative had shown him no respect while Franz Joseph had treated him like a friend. In 1881, King Milan had signed a 10-year secret treaty with Austria, agreeing to suppress anti-Austrian conspiracies in his realm. He had even promised not to sign any treaties without Austria's approval. This was one of the few periods in Franz Joseph's reign that he didn't have to worry about Serbian dissidents threatening the Austrian monarchy.

Franz Joseph sent word to the Serbs and the Bulgarians that the fighting had to stop; otherwise, he would take action. Faced with an Austrian intervention, the warring parties agreed to an armistice.

Alexander III, whose hatred of Franz Joseph was already central to his foreign policy, viewed the Emperor's intervention in the Bulgarian-Serbian contretemps as an unwarranted intrusion into Russia's Balkan sphere of interest. Worse still, the Czar had been deprived of his opportunity to see Battenberg driven from power by a victorious Serbian army – with no effort on the part of the Russians.

Many Russians thought the Habsburgs' meddling in their sphere of influence was too much to bear. Count Paul Schuwalow, the Russian ambassador in Berlin, while in his cups, spoke for many of his countrymen. He put a proposal to Herbert Bismarck, the chancellor's son, who was state secretary in the Foreign Ministry, urging Germany to desert Austria and form a lasting alliance with Russia. "It is absolutely necessary," the ambassador declared, "that Russia and Germany let that Habsburg Empire disappear from the map of Europe. The German Empire should annex the German provinces of Austria-Hungary, and nothing then will ever again be able to separate the two remaining empires."[16] Presumably the Habsburgs' large Slav population was to become part of the Russian sphere.

Meanwhile, there were new developments in the Balkans. On April 6, 1886, Eastern Rumelia and Bulgaria entered into a personal union,[17] choosing Battenberg as general governor for a five-year term.[18] Hoping to separate Battenberg from his subjects, the Czar spread the word that if the Bulgarians forced Battenberg out of office, he would grant full recognition to the new union. When it turned out that the Bulgarians weren't eager to oust their popular Prince, the Czar took steps. On the night of August 20-21, 1886, his agents seized Battenberg and took him down the Danube by steamer to a Russian gendarmerie in Reni. Communication lines between Bulgaria and the rest of the world were cut. In Sofia, a Russia-friendly government was quickly installed. Throngs of Battenberg supporters took to the streets, calling for the Prince's return. Queen Victoria lent her voice to those denouncing the work of "the Russian devil," calling the behavior of Alexander III "monstrous," and declaring that his "barbaric, Asiatic, and tyrannical" rule was without parallel in modern history.[19]

On August 25 word came that Battenberg had been released from the gendarmerie and was on his way to Breslau. The new government in Sofia fell, and there were renewed calls for Battenberg's return. He arrived on August 29 in Rustschuk depressed and shaken so completely that not even a crowd of cheering supporters seemed to revive his spirits. A Russian consul who was among those meeting the Prince tricked him into believing that two-thirds of the populace as well as the Bulgarian officers had taken part in the conspiracy against him. The consul advised the Prince to write a conciliatory letter to the Czar and Battenberg followed the consul's advice. Unwisely, however, he included this statement: "Russia has given me my crown, I am ready to return it to the Czar."[20] The Russian ruler immediately seized the opportunity the Prince had unwittingly offered. He published Battenberg's letter along with a response saying he would not condone the Prince's return to Bulgaria. Battenberg saw no alternative but to step down. He later received a command post in the Austrian army.

The actions of Alexander III in Bulgaria made it clear to the whole world that the Russian ruler was thumbing his nose at the Powers. Defying their decisions at the Congress of Berlin, he intended to pursue his goal of establishing Bulgaria as a vassal state. In the Habsburg monarchy, a war party emerged, calling for a military response to the Russians' latest aggression. Andrassy, still active in politics although he was no longer foreign minister, thought the time had come to settle accounts with the Russians. Crown Prince Rudolf also favored war. Even Franz Joseph, ordinarily stalwart in his insistence on peace, showed signs that his patience with the Russians was waning. The Emperor was reportedly considering a preventive war, being advocated by some members of the Habsburg military, to forestall a Russian attack.[21] This pessimistic turn in the Emperor's thinking about the monarchy's ability to coexist with the Russians would become pronounced in the critical period before the First World War.

It was at this point that Bismarck stepped in, presenting the Russians with the text of the previously secret Triple Alliance and proposing the Reinsurance Treaty. The chancellor's deft maneuver prevented the contretemps between Austria and Russia from escalating.

In July 1887 the Bulgarians elected Prince Ferdinand as their new ruler. Like Prince Albert, Queen Victoria's consort, Ferdinand was a member of the German house of Coburg. A wasp-waisted Prince with a huge nose, a high-pitched voice and a penchant for pink nighties and violets, Ferdinand was hardly the Russians' ideal vassal Prince, particularly after he made it clear that he too was averse to taking orders from St. Petersburg. The Russians tried to have Ferdinand removed from power. However, they ran into such fierce opposition from Austria and England that they finally yielded to the others' demands. Ferdinand turned out to be a far more adept politician than his predecessor. He pirouetted between the Austrian and the Russian courts, managing to keep in fairly good standing with both. In 1894 a formal reconciliation occurred between

Ferdinand and the Czar, who was pleased that the Bulgarian ruler, a Roman Catholic, had baptized his son, Boris, in the Orthodox faith.

Much later, when Ferdinand, like the Romanovs, began dreaming of sitting on the throne at Constantinople – and even was said to have acquired ceremonial robes for a triumphal entry into the city – the Russians quickly put the upstart ruler in his place by threatening to use force if he dared try any such move. But for the time being, Bulgaria faded into the background as a pressure point in the Balkans.

16 BOSNIA AND HERZEGOVINA

Armed with the authority of the Congress of Berlin, the Austrians occupied Bosnia and Herzegovina in the fall of 1878. The occupation was to be a 30-year headache for the monarchy. The twin provinces were wilder and more backward than any other part of the Ottoman Empire in Europe, except perhaps for some areas in high Albania. Nature had blessed the region with emerald green rivers, verdant meadows, abundant wildlife and flowering plants, but the local inhabitants lived in primitive squalor, eking out a subsistence living with stone-age tools.

The Habsburgs would improve the lives of the inhabitants in numerous ways. They created a justice system, improved the residents' health and opened schools, but they never could bring lasting stability to the region. Ethnic divisions between Muslims, Roman Catholic Croats and Orthodox Serbs ran as deep as ravines and were as difficult to bridge. The Serbs, accounting for 47 percent of the region's population, were the most restive and ambitious of the region's inhabitants. They never became reconciled to the Habsburg presence on territory that they claimed, without basis in fact, as their hereditary birthright.

The Habsburg occupation was difficult from the start. The invasion of the twin provinces was a military fiasco. In planning for the Austrian entry into Bosnia and Herzegovina, Foreign Minister Andrassy assumed that the oppressed Balkan population would welcome the monarchy's troops as liberators. He is said to have boasted that the Austrians could take control of the provinces with only "a platoon headed by a military band." While this remark is apocryphal, there is no doubt that the foreign minister grossly underestimated the extent of resistance that Habsburg troops would encounter once they entered the provinces.

After the Berlin negotiators approved the occupation, more than a fortnight passed before the Habsburg commanders issued marching orders. This gave the monarchy's opponents time to organize their opposition. The Austrian soldiers, who numbered only 75,000, were ill-prepared for a mountain war. Worse still, they were sent in without basic provisions, lacking even enough food and water, because Andrassy wanted to avoid the appearance of an invasion. The terrain, with its steep hills and rocky inclines, provided ideal hiding places for the insurgents. The local Muslims, whose reputation as bloody combatants was well-earned, were determined not to relinquish their power to the Habsburg forces. Fighters from elsewhere in the Balkans also joined the local resistance. The Austrians eventually were forced to raise their troop strength to 250,000. By the time they had taken Sarajevo and subdued the two provinces following some 12 weeks of fighting, they had suffered, by official count, 5,198 casualties. It is likely that the damage was substantially higher than that.

This far-flung corner of the Balkans had largely been ignored by the Ottomans, mainly because of its geography. The region lacked basic services and infrastructure that most residents of Western Europe in the latter decades of the 19th century had come to expect. Roads built by the great sultans of Turkey had been allowed to go to ruin.[1] Bosnia was without a single train. At the time of Austrian occupation, the lone piece of railroad had grass growing between its tracks.[2] Mules and asses provided most of the region's transportation. Only four percent of the population in Bosnia and Herzegovina could read, and there were few schools. Doctors were nonexistent. Plague, cholera and syphilis were common. Agriculture in the twin provinces had hardly changed in a thousand years. Women cultivated crops with wooden plows. Pigs and sheep pastured on rocky hills or in the forests that covered much of the region. Although the forests were nominally owned by the government, they actually were a no-man's-land where anyone could plunder at will.

Except for Sarajevo and Mostar, the towns were hamlets. Peasant handicrafts were the main industry. Barter was the chief means of trade. Those lucky enough to have money hid it under their mattresses. Thieving was an established and almost honorable profession.

Feudal families imposed their own law and order, to the extent it existed at all. From time to time reforms had been enacted by the Porte but the governors in Sarajevo either couldn't enforce the new rules or collaborated with the local Muslims in sabotaging them. The landlords who had converted to Islam following the Turkish conquest had been allowed to retain their estates. Most peasants who were Muslims were considered "free" men. In 1878 there were some 77,000 free-peasant holdings, mainly owned by Muslims. Most of the Christian peasants – approximately 80,000 Orthodox families and 23,000 Catholics – were "kmets" (serfs), living and working on the estates of Muslim Agas (Begs). Kmets usually paid their landlord one-third of their crops of fruits, vegetables and grains, and one-half of their hay.[3]

The Habsburgs, treating their only colony much as well-meaning parents might cater to a recently adopted child, lavished attention on their new charge. Benjamin Kallay, who was from an ancient Hungarian family, took over as administrator of the twin provinces in July 1882. Having spent time as Austrian representative in Belgrade, he knew the Balkans and liked the people. He had written a sympathetic history of Serbia, even though he, ironically, banned the work for distribution in Bosnia and Herzegovina after he arrived. Presumably he feared that the Serbian tendency toward insurgency, described in his work, would inspire similar unrest in the occupied provinces.

Kallay arrived at his new post with lofty goals. He sought to transform the justice system, establish schools and introduce modern farming methods. He faced enormous challenges. Among his problems was a lack of the backup staff he needed for the job. Experienced Austrian officials did not sign up willingly for remote spots, which were lonely and unhealthy, and where the pay was low. Even the Czechs, whom Macartney calls "the only Slavs in the monarchy who were natural bureaucrats," were reluctant to help their brothers in such a backward region. Local service jobs generally were held by Croats, Slovenes and Poles, most of whom had little experience in administration.[4]

Adding to the complications was the fact the Hungarian Magyars, during the monarchy's deliberations regarding the annexation, had insisted that Bosnia and Herzegovina be self-sustaining. To that end, taxes were increased some fivefold during Kallay's tenure.[5] William Miller, a British expert on the Balkans and an admirer of the monarchy's accomplishments in the two provinces, points out that it isn't fair to compare tax collections under the Austrians with those of Turkish times, because the Turks "did practically nothing" for the residents of the two provinces. "Those who prefer the irregular collection of taxes, the lack of law and order, the blood feud, and all the other delights of the Middle Ages have but to go beyond the Austrian military posts in the Sandzak and they will find what they seek,"

Miller wrote.[6] A number of the peasants of the two provinces actually might have preferred to do just that. The fact that much of the tax money was supposed to go for education didn't always sit well with the local residents, some of whom saw little value in being able to read and write.

According to Macartney, one of the first things the monarchy's agents did was to tighten security in the provinces. Within a few years the Habsburgs had ended "the reign of anarchy which four centuries of Turkish rule had failed wholly to quell," he wrote. Macartney reported that "brigandage was stamped out" and the incidence of crimes of violence had become the lowest in the monarchy.[7] Miller, basing his account on observations during three trips to the Balkans in the 1890s, wrote that in contrast to Serbia, Bosnia and Herzegovina were "perfectly safe." He said he never carried a revolver in the twin provinces.[8]

Miller was aware of ethnic tensions, but he wrote that "at least in Sarajevo" in the 1890s Balkanization had not yet created a divided society.[9] At the time, he said, Sarajevo had a large majority of Muslims. He recalled that the town was alive with the voices of hawkers in the bazaars, with the whirr of dancing dervishes, with calls to prayer from the mosques, and with Spanish Jews praying. For Miller, such diversity added to the town's charm. He remembered attending a ball in Sarajevo where a leading Muslim (Sorgevo) danced the Hungarian Csirdas and the Kolo and the chief rabbi of the Spanish Jews sipped coffee among Catholics, Orthodox and Muslims.[10]

There was less unity in remote areas, Miller's account indicated. He said that in Travnik, Roman Catholic women sported tattoos, a custom which had begun centuries earlier as a way for Catholic priests to keep females in their flocks from defecting to Turk conquerors, as apparently they often did. Old women typically did the tattooing.[11] Muslim women generally kept to themselves, wrote Miller. Muslim mothers strongly objected to their daughters going to school with Christian girls. Veiling was practiced more in Bosnia than elsewhere in the region, more so than even in Constantinople, Miller reported. He said the Habsburgs made every effort to respect such customs.

Under the Habsburgs, justice was even-handed and accessible to all, according to Macartney. He wrote that the three local religions "were placed on a footing of complete and scrupulously maintained equality ..."[12] Muslim jurists attended a college erected by the monarchy, where they learned Sharia law and Arabic, Miller wrote. Muslims who made pilgrimages to Mecca were assured of their jobs when they returned, he said. Orthodox ecclesiastical appointments, which previously had been bought, with the bishops recouping their outlay at the expense of their unfortunate dioceses, were no longer for sale. After 1879, Bosnian Orthodox bishoprics were approved by the Austrian Emperor.[13] Roman Catholics had equal rights, as did Protestants, who comprised only .23 percent of the population. In Sarajevo, Habsburg officials even granted a "good site" and made "a substantial contribution" toward construction of a Protestant church.[14]

Under the occupation, medical and veterinary services were dramatically improved. Smallpox was brought under control. Sarajevo got a badly needed drainage system, important in preventing such diseases as cholera and malaria. While in Turkish times there had been only confessional schools, there were now state schools – 228 with 17,540 pupils in 1892, reported Joseph Baernreither, an Austrian statesman who was well-versed in Balkan affairs.[15] In Sarajevo, public government-operated schools were open to all faiths, with free tuition and free books, Miller wrote. There were also religious schools, partly supported by the state. Parents could choose their children's schools.[16]

Visitors to the provinces previously had been forced to bed down in caravanserai, used by traders from the East who came with exotic wares, Miller said. These fortress-like buildings provided housing not only for the merchants but also for their camels. Vermin and heat were regular accoutrements of these accommodations. The Austrians, however, set up a string of hotels, which Miller calls a "novel experiment in state socialism." There were strict rules for cleaning (twice a day), rules for fire prevention, and lighted stairs. There were also noise regulations. Dogs weren't permitted in private rooms. "Immoral behavior" also wasn't allowed.[17] Miller, who stayed in one such hotel in Mostar, the Herzegovinian capital, described an idyllic visit to the town. "There were blossoms everywhere, fish were darting to and fro in the Buna, the emerald green river that cuts through Mostar .... Even the dogs were friendly," he wrote.[18]

The Habsburgs sought to bring modern agricultural practices to the backward region. They created a model farm; they opened a dairy and a stud facility. They promoted modern methods of beekeeping and established a program to improve winemaking. There were programs for teaching farmers to improve the raising of livestock. However, persuading the peasants to adopt more modern methods ran into snags. They often preferred their old ways. Getting them to abandon their wooden plows for metal ones presented a formidable challenge.[19]

The Austrians were more culpable in their failure to accomplish extensive land reforms, despite a pressing need. Under Ottoman law, only Muslims were allowed to own land. Many of the landholders were Slavs who had converted to Islam in the years following the Turkish conquest of the region. These Begs clung ferociously to their rights, for which many of their ancestors had sacrificed their very consciences. Since Turkey had retained nominal sovereignty over the two provinces, the Begs could make a strong case for their continued preeminence.

The Austrian officials' hesitation to push reforms

resulted in part because Turkey remained nominal sovereign of the provinces. The officials believed that taking land from the mostly Muslim ruling classes would risk a backlash of instability directed at the Austrian "occupiers." Kallay had an additional incentive for allowing the Muslim community to retain its rights. Of the three populations, they were the ones who most strongly supported the Habsburg regime.[20]

Most of Bosnia-Herzegovina's Orthodox Serbs and Roman Catholics were serfs. They were naturally disappointed that the Austrians failed to move forward with land reform. The existing law, with all its inequalities, remained in effect.

Roman Catholics had other reasons for unhappiness with the Habsburg regime, wrote Macartney. The authorities had bent over backwards to see that no religious groups were favored. But Roman Catholic churches proliferated under the occupation, growing from 35 in 1878 to 135 in 1900. Some of the regions' Roman Catholics took umbrage at the Austrian occupiers for failing to give them special treatment as adherents of a common faith. These disgruntled believers expressed their discontent by remaining aloof from the larger community. By the end of the century, a number of these adherents of Rome began agitating for a Greater Croatia.[21]

The Serbs were the least satisfied of the three ethnic groups. Although they enjoyed religious freedom and equal justice under the law, Kallay barred them from the political process. He believed that if the Bosnian Serbs were allowed to participate in the government they would sabotage the Habsburgs' reform efforts in the interest of a Greater Serbia. The Serbs' exclusion from politics gave them all the more reason to strain under the weight of the Habsburg yoke.

The romantic yearning of the region's Serbs for a union with their mystical and mythical past blazed up during evenings around campfires. Baernreither described a scene at a village near Mostar, where a group gathered around a singer, who accompanied himself on a guzla, a long-necked stringed instrument that produces a plaintive, wailing sound. He sang old Serbian songs telling of bygone glory. Probably few of those in the group could read or write, but the national songs fed the listeners' fantasies of epic heroes who had successfully fought the Turks[22] and who would willingly fight the occupying power if they were alive.

It is unlikely that the Serbs ever would have settled happily under the wings of Mother Austria, regardless of what the monarchy did for them. Later, when the Serbs were granted more rights, ultranationalists in their ranks attempted to use their new privileges to subvert Habsburg efforts. "Unity has never been a feature of the southern Slavs, except at rare intervals, under the sublime influence of some great man," Miller wrote. He added, presciently, that "if the Austrians were not in Bosnia, the various creeds would be at each other's throats."[23]

17 SERBS, PIGS AND RUSSIANS

During the Congress of Berlin, Prince Milan Obrenovic[1] of Serbia approached a Russian delegate asking for assistance in putting down an insurgency that threatened his hold on power. Rebuffed by the Czar's representative, the Prince turned to Austria with the same request. Franz Joseph welcomed the chance to join Milan in clamping down on militants who were crossing from Serbia into Bosnia and Herzegovina and causing disturbances there. Many of the troublemakers had grandiose dreams of a Greater Serbia, encompassing large swaths of the Balkan Peninsula, including the twin provinces, and southern regions of the Habsburg monarchy.

It is hardly surprising that the Russians showed no interest in helping Milan remain in power. With their hopes quashed by the Congress of Berlin for a large Bulgarian state under their auspices, the Russians were seeking another Balkan vassal nation for use as a base during future military forays against the Turks. Serbia, with its strong Russophile contingent, was a logical choice. The Russians, hardly so naive as to imagine that the independent-minded Milan would be a willing puppet, were secretly, and sometimes openly, supporting his enemies.

Milan had come to power in 1868 after his cousin, Michael III, was assassinated. The Prince, not yet 14 years old, ruled under a regency that adopted a relatively liberal constitution and had pro-Austrian leanings. After Milan came of age in 1872, he remained on good terms with Vienna. This put him at odds with a powerful Pan-Serb faction in his nation that sought closer ties with the Russians. The Pan-Serbs and the Russians had a common goal. They both sought to rid the Balkans of the Habsburgs.

The relationship between Franz Joseph and Milan was beneficial for both sides. Both men understood the need for order in a volatile region where honor killings and blood feuds were commonplace. The two rulers joined forces against elements in the Balkans who preached republicanism but who actually were ultranationalists seeking dominance over other ethnic groups. Franz Joseph, hoping to help the Prince stabilize his country, supported Serbia's successful bid for full independence, which was granted by the Congress of Berlin.

Then, in June 1881, Franz Joseph and Milan negotiated a secret treaty in which the Prince promised to prevent anti-Habsburg elements from using Serbia as a base for "political, religious, or other intrigues" against Bosnia-Herzegovina.[2] The treaty also called for Serbia to reach an understanding with Austria before negotiating a political agreement with another government or allowing foreign troops on Serbian territory.[3] This stipulation was obviously directed toward Russia. In return, Austria promised to support Serbian efforts to expand their territory in the Vardar Valley, a wine-producing area in Macedonia. The Emperor also backed Milan when in 1882 he proclaimed himself King and made Serbia a kingdom.

The treaty between Austria and Serbia promised more than its authors could deliver. The King's ambitions for acquiring Macedonian territory were thwarted by the

Bulgarians and the Greeks, who asserted their own claims in the region. Milan's efforts to stamp out the Pan-Serb insurgency failed in the long run.

During the latter decades of the 19th century, Serbia became infamous as a "murder state." One study showed that between 1884 and 1895, 368 political murders occurred in the little kingdom. The Radical party was widely blamed for the killings, according to historian Viktor Bibl.[4] The party, originally a left-wing group with peasant roots, had been taken over by Pan-Serb extremists. In 1883, the Radicals organized a large peasant uprising against Milan in eastern Serbia, which the Prince successfully put down.

The Radical party's pro-Russian leader, Nikola Pasic, issued a manifesto in 1884 declaring that the Balkan peninsula was too small to accommodate both Austria and Serbia. He claimed that the Habsburgs, having lost their provinces in Italy and later their preeminence in Germany, had set their sights on expansion in the Near East. Pasic defended his party's ties with St. Petersburg on grounds that only Russia had the will and the ability to prevent Austria from enjoying "a free hand" in the Balkans. If the Austrians were to succeed in their aims, he wrote, "Serbia would disappear."[5]

There is every reason to believe that if the Serbians had been willing to stay in their own yard instead of attempting to scale the fence into territory for which they had no legitimate historical or political claims, they could have remained on good terms with the Habsburgs. Franz Joseph definitely had no interest in annexing Serbia. At one point King Milan, frustrated in his efforts to keep the peace in his nation, offered to sell, or even give, his kingdom to the monarchy. Franz Joseph declined the offer.

Milan ultimately fell from power not because he was pushed out by revolutionaries but because of his personal failings. He frequented the fleshpots of Europe. He had numerous affairs, including a liaison with Jennie Jerome, the wife of Lord Randolph Churchill and the mother of Winston Churchill. His womanizing was among the problems leading to his divorce from his wife, Queen Natalija. Also contributing to the breakup of the marriage was the fact that the Queen was a Russophile who actively undermined her husband's interests. Serbian law forbade a ruler who was divorced to remain in power. The King abdicated in 1889.

Once Milan stepped down, Serbia soon fell into the hands of the Habsburgs' enemies. King Milan's 13-year-old son, Alexander, became ruler. The young man's reign was to be brief, its end brutal.

Milan appointed three regents to run the government until Alexander turned 18. The regents followed Milan's tradition of friendship toward Austria, renewing the secret treaty with the monarchy. Alexander, however, showed no respect for his father's wishes. In 1893 Alexander, then 17, invited the regents to dinner, where he "arrested them at his own table,"[6] writes Harold William Temperley, the author of an early history of Serbia. The young man declared himself ruler; then he dissolved the Skuptchina (parliament) and abolished the constitution that his father had promulgated shortly before his abdication in 1889. Alexander turned his back on Austria, declaring that Russia was Serbia's natural ally. When Alexander and his Russophile supporters learned of Milan's secret treaty with Franz Joseph, they denounced it as treasonous. When it expired in 1895, Alexander refused to renew it.

Franz Joseph could not bring himself to grant the usual royal honors to Alexander as Serbia's new king. The Emperor was appalled at Alexander's lack of respect for his father, who, in the eyes of the Habsburg monarch, remained a king and deserved to be treated as one. The socially inept and physically unattractive King Alexander compounded his offense against the code of royal conduct to which Franz Joseph adhered when he became hopelessly infatuated with

Draga Mashin, a pig farmer's daughter with a shady reputation. Even Alexander's supporters were embarrassed by the misalliance. From the start, ugly rumors swirled around the unlikely couple. Draga, a handsome, seductive woman, was rumored to have bewitched Alexander with the help of a Gypsy who chopped Draga's hair and put it in the King's food. This according to Edith Durham, whose many years of experience in the Balkans during that period make her a unique source.[7]

The Russians, for their part, were not precious about codes of monarchical conduct. They rushed to insinuate themselves into the royal breach left by Franz Joseph's refusal to accord Alexander the honors that were customary between monarchs. In 1900, when Alexander announced plans to marry Draga, Nicholas II sent congratulations to the couple. The Czar then went further, dispatching a personal envoy to act as best man at the wedding.[8]

Political and personal scandal dogged the remaining days of Alexander, who would be the last member of the Obrenovic dynasty. Draga was much older than her husband and showed no signs of producing an heir. Rumors spread that the royal pair planned to leave the throne to one of Draga's ne'er-do-well brothers. Certainly, the ambitious Queen took advantage of her recently acquired status to assure that her relatives received prime positions in the government. The King's false move in choosing his marriage partner was bad enough. His political missteps, however, were his undoing. In 1903 he suspended a constitution that he had issued two years earlier. He turned on the Radicals, who now opposed him, and installed a military cabinet composed of his cronies. The King's enemies decided they had to get rid of this royal clown. As so often in Serbia, the sword became the instrument of change.

It was close to midnight on June 10, 1903, when assailants stormed the imperial palace in Belgrade where

King Alexander and his wife were sleeping. Using dynamite they blew open the bedroom door. The terrified royals cowered in a closet. After they were discovered the assailants attacked them and tossed them out of the second story window onto the square below. Draga died almost at once, apparently after being finished off with a hatchet. Alexander lived until 4 a.m. The assassins defiled their victims' bodies, carrying off parts of Draga's body to be dried and used for trophies.[9] Draga's two brothers and 17 others were killed later.

Alexander's successor, 70-year-old King Peter, was a member of the kingdom's rival Karageorgevic clan. The King's background suggests that, under other circumstances, he might have been an enlightened ruler. He had fought the Prussians on behalf of France in 1870 and had participated in the 1876 Balkan uprising against the Turks. He had translated John Stuart Mill's *On Liberty* into Serbian. He came to the throne proclaiming his intention of establishing a constitutional monarchy. But Peter was hostage to the criminals who assassinated Alexander and Draga, and brought him to power. The ringleaders in the brutal murders were Captain Dragutin Dimitrijevic and Second Lieutenant Voya Tankovic, military officers who in 1911 founded the secret ultranationalist association known as the Black Hand. Having been put in power by these terrorists, King Peter himself was, in the eyes of many, implicated in the assassinations of the former King and Queen.[10]

Dimitrijevic and Tankovic were the masterminds behind the plot to assassinate Archduke Franz Ferdinand and his wife, Sophie, in Sarajevo on June 28, 1914.

Although Franz Joseph was upset by the regicides in Serbia, he joined many other European sovereigns in recognizing King Peter, sending him a message wishing him well. The Austrian Foreign Ministry's publication, the *Fremdenblatt*, deplored the bloodshed, but added that the Balkans were "a bloody region."[11] The news item added that it didn't matter who reigned in Serbia as long as the regime remained on good terms with the monarchy.[12]

The Austrians' hopes for peaceful relations soon were dashed. In April 1904, King Peter wrenched himself free from the military junta to which he owed his office. He fled for protection to the Radical party. The king actively supported the attempt of Pasic and his supporters to rid the Balkans of the Habsburgs. He encouraged agitation in Bosnia, joining the Pan-Serbs in spreading propaganda intended to discredit the Habsburg government in the occupied provinces.[13] Worse still, from the monarchy's perspective, he declared support for Hungarian independence.

In Bosnia and Herzegovina the Serbian population was increasingly restive. In the summer of 1903 Baron Stefan Burian, who became administrator of the twin provinces after the death of his predecessor, Benjamin Kallay, concluded that it was impossible to continue to govern the provinces without giving the local Serbs cultural liberty and a role in the political process. Although the Serbs were not a majority of the population, they nevertheless constituted the numerically largest group. They also were the most active and vital element in the region. Burian took the optimistic view that if the Serbs' legitimate wishes were granted they would be satisfied with their situation. With that goal in mind, the Austrians in 1905 gave the Orthodox community in the twin provinces new freedoms, among them the right to administer their own schools and churches.

The liberalized policy made matters worse. It opened the flood gates for propagandists who now practiced hate speech with little fear of arrest. Numerous publications, most of them subsidized in Belgrade, preached an anti-Habsburg message, prompting censors to intervene, though with little effect. *Srbska Riječ*, a widely circulated newssheet published in Sarajevo, was confiscated in the twin provinces 70 times. "If what was not allowed to appear was worse than what did pass the censor, it must have been subversive indeed," writes Macartney. Serbian agitators roamed the provinces denouncing "Austria's bloody tyranny," and urging people to rise against the foreign rule. According to Bibl, in Bosnia a band of troublemakers ranted against Austria, urging their listeners to "beat ... (the occupiers) down like dogs and don't rest until the last little fiend has left Serbian Bosnia...."[14]

Austrian ministers closeted themselves away in council meetings trying to find a solution for the difficulties in which they found themselves. They considered returning the twin provinces to the Turks, but decided that would cause more, not less, unrest near the monarchy's southern border. They discussed putting down the insurgency by military force, but ruled that out. The Habsburgs had tried that in their Italian provinces and found it solved nothing. They finally decided that annexation, followed by providing the people with a parliament, a constitution, and major land reforms, was the only viable option. Having reached this conclusion, the Austrians waited for a favorable moment to act. It came in a surprise development in 1908 ... so they thought.

In the meantime, a contretemps which became known as the Pig War caused a serious rise in Serbian animosity toward the monarchy. In 1904 the leaders of the Serbian Radical party persuaded their Bulgarian neighbors to form an alliance under the slogan, "Balkans for the Balkan people." The following year the two nations established a Serbian-Bulgarian customs union. They were protesting against unfair practices by the Hungarians, who protected their own agrarian markets at the expense of their Balkan neighbors. The Serbs, for whom pigs and other livestock were fundamental to their livelihood, complained that Hungarian customs officials held up shipments of Serbian livestock until the animals lost so much weight that they sickened or died, or until shipments of meat had spoiled.

Yielding to Hungarian pressure, Vienna demanded that the Serbians modify the customs union. When Serbia balked, Austrian authorities closed the Hungarian frontier under a veterinary order. The trade conflict is known as the Pig War, although the border was closed not only to Serbian exports of pigs but also to cattle – dead or alive.

The Serbs found ways to limit the damage caused by the border restrictions. While Austria had been the main market for Serbian exports, the Serbs now obtained agreements to export livestock through Salonika (Thessalonica). They borrowed money abroad to construct their own slaughterhouses. The Serbs also prepared for an actual military confrontation with the monarchy, purchasing guns from France and ammunition from Germany. Austrian Foreign Minister Count Alois Lexa von Aehrenthal, forced into a corner, negotiated a new treaty so favorable to Serbia that both the Austrian and Hungarian parliaments rejected it.[15] The Austrians then sought to impose a complete boycott on Serbian goods. That also failed.

Edith Durham, who had gone into Serbia in the company of someone she described as "a wild, very black Gypsy," reported that she found the Serbs in high spirits. The government was spending large sums on the army. The boycott didn't appear to be hurting the people much. Durham, delayed at the Serbian border crossing at Visegrad, explained to the Austrian border guards the facts of life: "I told the officials their boycott was bound to fail, as you cannot starve out a people whose main assets are maize and pigs.... They will simply go on eating pigs till you are tired."[16] Edith Durham was right.[17]

18 EVE OF COMPLICATIONS

In the early years of the 20th century, as was the European custom, kings, counts, ministers and their wives converged on Carlsbad and Marienbad, popular watering holes in Bohemia, where they sipped the acrid waters, arranged children's marriages and talked politics. In the summer of 1908 Leopold Berchtold, the Austrian ambassador to Russia, was in attendance at Carlsbad, as was Aleksandr Izvolsky, the Russian foreign minister. The two men often encountered each other at dinners given by the high aristocracy. After Britain's King Edward VII arrived at nearby Marienbad, the center of social gravity shifted to that spa. At one of the gatherings, Nandine Berchtold, the ambassador's wife, invited Izvolsky to visit Buchlau (Buchlovice), the family estate in Moravia.

The ambassador, learning of this, arranged for Count von Aehrenthal also to be a house guest. This would give the two foreign ministers a chance to discuss, in an informal setting, a July 2 memo from Izvolsky that held promise for both the Habsburg and Romanov imperial houses. In the memo, Izvolsky had made Vienna an unequivocal offer: Russia would support the monarchy's annexation of Bosnia-

Herzegovina if Austria would support the opening of the Turkish Straits to Russian warships.

Izvolsky and Aehrenthal arrived at the Berchtolds' baroque chateau on the evening of September 15. The two men later would become antagonists, but these problems were for the future. The ministers settled in for what was undoubtedly a congenial evening, enjoying the region's fine Moravian wine and the excellent food grown on the estate. The next morning they headed out separately for constitutionals in the park, then, as now, a veritable Noah's ark of exotic trees brought from around the world. The two men met at the garden pond and returned together to the chateau. They chose for their negotiations a tiny corner room, decorated with antlers – the requisite wall adornments in aristocrats' dwellings – and just large enough for an overstuffed armchair on either side of the fireplace. No witnesses were present. The conversation that followed in that room set in motion a series of events that ended in war in 1914.

Photographs of the foreign ministers, appearing in W.M. Calgren's *Isvolsky and Aehrenthal*, suggest that the two came from different worlds. Izvolsky, a member of Russia's rural nobility, wears a wrinkled suit that appears to have been made of heavy, poor quality wool. He has a square forehead and an irregular nose. His eyes, narrowed into slits, hint at a regular habit of regarding the world with suspicion. Aehrenthal, on the other hand, exudes self-confidence. He is jaunty as a boulevardier, sporting an elegant cane and a bowler hat.[1]

Berchtold, the Austrian ambassador, writing in his journal, provides an account of what each minister told him about the negotiations. Aehrenthal said that Izvolsky spent the first hour-and-a-half of the meeting railing about an Austrian proposal for a railroad through the Balkans to Salonika (Thessaloniki). The Russian foreign minister appeared to consider the mere idea of such a project, announced by Aehrenthal in a January 1908 speech, an incursion in St. Petersburg's' sphere of influence. After the conversation finally got around to Izvolsky's July 2 memo, the two ministers quickly concurred with the Russian's Straits-annexation proposal. Aehrenthal also agreed to loosen restrictions, put in place following the 1878 Congress of Berlin, on Montenegro's use of the harbor at Antivari (present-day Bar).[2]

Berchtold describes the talks as becoming testy when Aehrenthal refused a proposal to allow Montenegro to build a naval base at the strategically located Adriatic port. The Austrians feared that if Antivari were open to an unlimited number of foreign warships, the Russians would take advantage of their Montenegrin vassal's hospitality and move in with their navy. That would jeopardize maritime freedom in the Adriatic Sea.[3]

Aehrenthal left Buchlau that night, stopping in Budapest where he met with Prince Ferdinand of Bulgaria. The visit sparked rumors, which were likely true, that the two plotted to have the prince declare Bulgaria's independence in close chronicity with an Austrian announcement of the annexation of Bosnia and Herzegovina. Perhaps the intention was to disperse international criticism rather than have it concentrated on either development.

Izvolsky remained at Buchlau, joining his host at the bridge table that evening. Before leaving the next day, the Russian foreign minister gave Berchtold his version of the negotiations, which his host later described as agreeing "almost word for word" with Aehrenthal's account.[4] Berchtold wrote that both ministers seemed satisfied with the talks. However, a controversy soon emerged that was never resolved. Izvolsky would later claim that he made it clear at Buchlau that the Straits proposal and the annexation had to be approved by the signatories of the 1878 Treaty of Berlin.[5] Berchtold, however, recounting his conversation with the Russian foreign minister the morning after the meeting, put a different slant on the matter, suggesting that Izvolsky was less forceful in insisting on a European conference after having heard Aehrenthal's arguments against it. Berchtold said Izvolsky merely told him that, while the basics of an agreement could be determined through negotiations between cabinets, a final conference "would be hard to avoid." Berchtold recalled that Izvolsky had at that point lapsed into French, telling his host, "You know, when something touches on the Treaty of Berlin, one cannot predict where it will end up."[6] That is precisely why Emperor Franz Joseph, usually so meticulous in adhering to international agreements, intended to bypass the Powers and proceed directly to annexation.

Franz Joseph knew quite well that Article 25 of the treaty authorized the Habsburgs to occupy and administer Bosnia and Herzegovina – and said nothing about annexation. But for the Emperor, the Russians' stance was what mattered most. Among the major Powers the only ones whose interests clashed over the twin provinces were Austria and Russia. Czar Alexander II, the grandfather of Nicholas II, had said that the Austrians could annex the provinces whenever they saw fit. For a monarch of the old school such as Franz Joseph, an agreement made by a ruler's ancestor was to be honored by succeeding generations until it was nullified. Additionally, Nicholas II, during a meeting with the Habsburg Emperor at St. Petersburg in 1897, had given his general consent to annexation. Franz Joseph welcomed Izvolsky's reaffirmation of the Russian position, arriving so unexpectedly at a critical time, but he did not base his decision on that alone.

For the Habsburgs the decision to annex the two provinces reflected a need to come to grips with growing unrest in the region. The population demanded reforms that the Austrians, as occupiers, could not legally provide. Pan-Serb agitators in increasing numbers were pouring into the Balkan provinces from neighboring Serbia. Eyewitnesses reported that Russian-made arms were being smuggled across the borders.[7] Several years earlier, the Habsburg council, after endless hours of mulling over alternatives, concluded that annexation was the monarchy's only viable move. The only question was when to make that move.

For the Romanovs, receiving permission for czarist warships to have exclusive access to the Straits would be a diplomatic as well as a military coup. Perhaps it would even help restore the public's faith in the dynasty, badly shaken by the Japanese defeat of the czarist forces in 1905. The war in the Far East had broken out after Russian troops occupied territory in Korea and Manchuria to which the Japanese had claims. The Japanese retaliated in February 8, 1904, with a surprise attack on the czarist navy at Port Arthur. By the time the conflict ended in August of the next year the Japanese had destroyed the Russians' Pacific and Baltic fleets. The Black Sea Fleet – one-third of the Russians' entire navy – had been bottled up in that body of water, unable to participate in the conflict due to strictures put in place by the Powers. Under the rules, only Ottoman warships were allowed egress from the Black Sea into the Mediterranean via the Straits.

Immediately upon being named foreign minister in March 1906, Izvolsky had set out to restore the Romanovs' reputation as a Great Power. Izvolsky was highly intelligent, obsessively ambitious and devious when necessary. Recognizing that the Czar's incompetence in foreign affairs left a vacuum of power at the top, Izvolsky had deftly stepped into that space. The Czar could be "handled," the foreign minister bragged. Izvolsky was on his way to becoming one of the most powerful men in Russia. He was not a man one would want to cross.

Izvolsky quickly shifted the axis of Romanov foreign policy back to the Balkans, reopening the always troublesome Eastern Question. Izvolsky was angry at the Germans for invading the Balkans with their Berlin to

Baghdad railway. Establishing himself as self-appointed gatekeeper for the region, Izvolsky was determined to block additional foreign incursions, particularly railroad projects, in what he considered the Romanov's private preserve. In a region like the Balkans, where donkey carts still rumbled along rutted dirt trails, railroads were symbols of power.

An immediate goal of Izvolsky was to assure that Russia would never again be deprived of her Black Sea Fleet for lack of egress to the Mediterranean Sea. During a visit to Vienna in September 1907 the Russian foreign minister had told Aehrenthal that he intended to "solve the Straits Question in the manner desired by Russia."[8] He hinted that Russia might support annexation of the monarchy's occupied provinces in exchange for a revision in the Straits regime that favored St. Petersburg.

Nothing had come of Izvolsky's suggestion at the time. In fact, the chances of any agreement between Vienna and St. Petersburg were nearly wrecked by a dispute in January 1908 over the Austrian announcement of plans for a railroad in the Balkans. The railroad proposed by Aehrenthal was to stretch from the Bosnian frontier to Mitrovica in Old Serbia and then connect with the Macedonian line. Never mind that the Treaty of Berlin sanctioned the Austrian railroad and the Sultan approved it. The Russian foreign minister denounced Aehrenthal's plan as "a bomb thrown between his legs."[9] The St. Petersburg press accused the Habsburgs of colluding with Berlin in an effort to make the Balkans "the Hinterland of Germany."

Izvolsky and Aehrenthal had exchanged secret memos in the effort to find a diplomatic solution to the contretemps. Izvolsky's anger at the railroad project cooled somewhat after the Austrians agreed to support plans for a Russian railroad from Romania across Serbia and Montenegro to the Adriatic. Neither project materialized, largely because imperial purses proved unequal to the construction costs involved in boring through mountains of rock. However, as tensions diminished in the railroad dispute, the two ministers began corresponding about other matters of interest to the two monarchies. In his memos, Izvolsky expressed general support for the annexation-Straits scheme.

In July 1908, a sudden turn of events in the Ottoman Empire convinced the Habsburgs to move quickly to annex Bosnia and Herzegovina. A Turkish major named Ahmed Niyazi and a handful of his supporters had staged an uprising in Macedonia, demanding that the Sultan restore certain political rights to his subjects, remanded in 1876. The insurgents, known as Young Turks, soon occupied large parts of the Macedonian provinces of Monastir and Salonika (Thessalonici). The Austrians became worried that the unhappy residents of the twin provinces, still nominal subjects of the Ottomans, would break away from the monarchy and cast their lot with the rebels.

On almost the same day that news arrived in Vienna that the Young Turks had taken Constantinople, Aehrenthal received a confidential memo from Izvolsky, dated July 2. In contrast to the Russian Foreign Minister's earlier memos, which had merely raised the general possibility of an understanding regarding the Straits and annexation, this one was specific: The Russians would agree to the Austrians' annexation of the occupied provinces if the Austrians would support Russia in revising the Straits regime. With Russian backing assured in writing, Franz Joseph felt free to proceed with the annexation. As Habsburg historian Macartney writes, "This offer must have come as a gift from heaven, for the situation in Bosnia itself … and … in the monarchy's relations with Serbia … had become genuinely intolerable."[10]

Meanwhile, the Turkish insurgents roamed from village to village in Albania and Macedonia, singing the Marseillaise and attracting an enthusiastic following by making promises they couldn't keep. They told Muslims that they would implement Sharia law; they offered non-Muslims hope of greater religious freedom; they assured Albanians that they could retain traditional privileges, including the right to bear arms – a matter of great import in a tribal society where men considered their weapons symbols of masculinity. The revolutionaries approached Sultan Abdul Hamid II with demands for representative government. The timid Sultan – known to his subjects as Abdul the Damned – appeared, looking confused and scared. He quickly agreed to restore the constitution and to revive the long-dormant legislature with its elective lower body. The Sultan's Balkan subjects, hearing that he had bowed to the revolutionaries' demands, went wild. Edith Durham, who was present at a celebration on August 2 in Shkodra (Scutari, in northwestern Albania), described the scene: "The Muslim band played outside the cathedral, and Christians and Muslims swore brotherhood on the Koran and a revolver. 'Ah! *La bella cosa, la liberta,*' cried a man... 'We are united. Albania is free.' "[11]

Bolstered by the July 2 memo and pushed into action by reports that the Young Turk revolution was gaining ground, Aehrenthal on August 19 sought and received the Habsburg ministerial council's approval for annexation of Bosnia-Herzegovina. Upon Aehrenthal's advice, the council agreed to return the Sandzak of Novi Pazar, a narrow strip of land separating Serbia and Montenegro, to Turkey as a consolation prize for the loss of the twin provinces. As long as the Habsburgs controlled the Sandzak, the Greater Serbia proponents were prevented from uniting with Montenegro in a powerful bloc opposed to Austrian interests. In defending his position for voluntarily abandoning that important region, Aehrenthal argued that holding that territory would require too much manpower and too many armaments to justify its strategic value.

The decision to relinquish the corridor would prove to be a strategic mistake.

Having left Buchlau on September 17, Izvolsky made a

leisurely journey across Europe. He reached Paris on October 4, 1908, where he planned to lay the groundwork for his Straits proposal. He then was to proceed to London for similar talks. Once the preliminary discussions were completed, the Russian foreign minister hoped to clinch his argument with the Western Powers by surprising them with the news that the Austrians supported his Straits proposal. It is not clear why Izvolsky thought that Britain and France would agree to give Russian war ships exclusive access to the Straits – the vital passageway connecting the Black Sea with the Mediterranean – regardless of where the Austrians stood on the matter.

Izvolsky's hopes for British support for his Straits proposal appear to have been raised at Reval (present-day Talinn) in May 1908 during a meeting between Czar Nicholas II and King Edward VII. At that time the Russians and the British were on the friendliest of terms. Izvolsky also concluded from recent conversations with French government officials in Paris that they might be willing to cooperate. The Russian dream, as was so often the case, bore little resemblance to reality.

In Paris, Izvolsky received a surprise – one that left him shaken and angry. On the day he arrived in the French capital, the Habsburgs announced the annexation of Bosnia and Herzegovina as a fait accompli. Izvolsky never imagined that Aehrenthal would make such a move behind his back. The Austrian Foreign Minister had promised to inform the Russians of the annexation "in good time." Izvolsky assumed this meant that he would receive notice before the Austrians acted. He had no reason to think the Habsburgs were in a hurry to annex the twin provinces, which had been under Austrian occupation for 30 years.

The Habsburgs' decision to rush to annexation was taken in response to news of more developments in Constantinople. The Young Turks were inviting provinces that remained under nominal Ottoman suzerainty –

including Bosnia and Herzegovina – to send delegates to their lower house of parliament. Now that the annexation was out of the way, the Austrians intended to provide their new subjects with constitutional rights comparable to those enjoyed in other parts of the monarchy.

Before plunging fecklessly ahead with annexation, the Habsburgs would have done well to seek the advice of Edith Durham, whose knowledge of the Balkans far exceeded that of the diplomats. She was in Scutari when she learned of the annexation. She encountered the Austrian attaché on the street. He was beaming.

"We have annexed Bosnia and the Herzegovina," he said. "Then you have done a dashed silly thing!" she told him.

"He was greatly surprised and promised to come to dinner with me to fight it out." Durham went from there to the Montenegrin Consulate where she found the consul, "with a red-hot proclamation of Prince Nikola's in his hands, calling on all Serbs ... to unite and denounce the breaking of the Berlin Treaty." The consul laid great stress, Durham wrote, "on the fact that all his ancestors were buried in ... Herzegovina, which was now seized by Austria." He believed "that war was inevitable; otherwise all the plans of the Serbs for Great Serbia were ruined."[12]

The Habsburgs needn't have panicked where the Young Turks were concerned. As Noel Malcolm, who has written extensively on Balkan history, points out, the expectations raised by the Young Turks were "grotesquely at variance from their real political program."[13] Ultranationalists soon took control of the revolutionary movement. They turned out to be Old Turks in Young Turks' clothing – and in some ways more cruel and autocratic than their predecessors. The Habsburgs, of course, had no way to predict this.

What happened to Izvolsky, on the other hand, was predictable. His chances of persuading the Powers to change the regime of the Straits were ruined by the Habsburgs' surprise rush to annexation.

Imperial Europe was in an uproar. Kings raged and ministers fumed. King Edward VII of England, who had visited Franz Joseph at Bad Ischl only a few weeks earlier, was said to have turned red to his ears when he learned what had transpired. The Emperor had not said one word about the annexation, the English King sputtered. Kaiser Wilhelm II declared himself "personally most deeply wounded" by not having been taken into confidence by his Austrian ally. He complained that he was always the last to know anything.

Ultranationalists in Russia and Serbia railed at what they considered the Habsburgs' brazen act of laying claim to the two provinces, with their large Slav populations. In Serbia, the clergy denounced the Austrians and declared that their little Balkan nation stood in danger of being swallowed up by the monarchy. Thousands of Serbs volunteered to fight to defend their homeland. Troops assembled on the Habsburg border. Russian agents operating in Belgrade encouraged the Serbs in the belief that they had been damaged by the annexation and urged them to seek compensation.

The Ottomans, as nominal sovereigns of the twin provinces, were justifiably aggrieved at Austria for violating her treaty agreements. The Porte responded with a boycott. The Turks refused to enter Austro-Hungarian shops; Austrian cargo in the ports was not unloaded; and depositors withdrew funds from Habsburg banks. The monarchy's economic losses from the boycott were significant.

Supporters of the Concert of Europe bemoaned the monarchy's defiance of international legitimacy. The consensus at most continental courts was that Vienna should have sought the approval of the other signatories of the 1878 Berlin Treaty before exceeding its mandate for occupation and administration of Bosnia-Herzegovina, as specified by Article 25 of the document.

Izvolsky received an icy reception in the French capital. In England, his welcome was more cordial, with both the King and Sir Edward Grey, the British foreign affairs secretary, honoring him with lavish banquets and flattery, but he did not get what he wanted. Edward VII might have gone along with the request for opening the Straits, but Grey had reservations about the proposal. Failing to understand what the Russians were about, he insisted that if the rules were to be changed, other nations should have the right to enter and leave the Dardanelles on equal terms with Russia. He should have known that there was no way that St. Petersburg would agree to that.

Izvolsky was embarrassed before the whole world. He blamed the Austrians, particularly Aehrenthal, for the fiasco. The Russian foreign minister was not one to forgive a slight. He would soon set out on a campaign of revenge that would end on the battlefields of World War I.

Full of self-justification and rage, Izvolsky returned home to more troubles. The foreign minister had conducted his negotiations with the Habsburgs behind the backs of his own government. The other ministers knew nothing about the memos Izvolsky had exchanged with Aehrenthal or about his meeting at Buchlau. When P.A. Stolypin, the Russian premier, learned what the foreign minister had done he threatened to resign. The Straits didn't interest him much; rather, it was Izvolsky's support of the annexation that raised his hackles. An ardent Pan-Slavist, Stolypin declared that he would never consent to annexation of a Slavic land by a German power (which, by then, had already happened). N.V. Charykov, assistant to the Russian foreign affairs Minister, joined Stolypin in lambasting Izvolsky's injudicious action. The Russian foreign minister could hardly acknowledge publicly that his own memos had provided the Austrians with their latest grounds for claiming that the Russians had no objections.

Izvolsky wasn't the only person in St. Petersburg with something to hide. Nicholas II, in a letter to his mother in October 1908, revealed what he called "most distressing" news. He wrote that the Russian envoy in Constantinople had recently sent him secret papers from the 1878 Congress of Berlin, showing that Russia had, at that time, consented to "a possible future annexation" of Bosnia and Herzegovina by the Habsburgs.

Making matters worse, Nicholas II told his mother he had received a letter from Franz Joseph reminding him that the monarchy had received consent for the annexation from his "Anpapa" – Alexander II, the present Czar's grandfather.[14] The letter from Franz Joseph had arrived two weeks before. He hadn't answered it yet. The Czar later begrudgingly acknowledged to the public the previous agreements between St. Petersburg and Vienna, but he never admitted Izvolsky's responsibility in the events leading to the annexation. The Czar denounced Aehrenthal for duping the Russian foreign minister.[15]

Izvolsky was not one to ignore an insult. The foreign minister launched a war of revenge, using the Serbs as proxies against the monarchy. He encouraged them in their belief that they had been severely wronged by the annexation. With his public outpourings of sympathy for Serbia, Izvolsky also hoped to ward off any suggestion by Russian Pan-Slavists that it was he who had delivered their Balkan brothers into the hands of the "German enemy." Izvolsky sent the Serbs a message wishing them "a swift and bloody revenge"[16] against the monarchy. Sounding like a fundamentalist Christian sermonizing on the second coming, the Russian foreign minister urged his Serbian friends to "hang on to their aspirations in preparation for the great day when Teutons and Slavs would confront each other in the ultimate showdown." Patience was needed for the time being, he added, because the ground "wasn't prepared for a conflict" just yet.[17] In the meantime, Izvolsky sent word to the Serbs that they should clamor "for compensation as loudly as possible."[18]

As the crisis worsened, Aehrenthal, also wanting revenge, began a campaign of intimidation against Izvolsky. He demanded that the Russian foreign minister immediately stop encouraging Serbian protests against Austria. Otherwise, Aehrenthal warned, the Austrians might be compelled to reveal Izvolsky's complicity in the annexation. Izvolsky twisted in agony, entangled by his guilty secret, despising the man with whom he had so recently supped.

Berchtold, back at his ministerial post in St. Petersburg, reported to Vienna that Nicholas II, on November 6, had informed Serbian minister and Radical party leader Nikola Pasic that the Bosnian question would be decided "only by war." However, the Czar made it clear that he did not want war yet. In the meantime, Serbian policy should involve "understanding with Turkey, a quiet attitude, military preparation and waiting." As Bernadotte Schmitt writes, with the Czar thus making his position clear, "the Serbs had good reason to be content."[19]

The Russians were being forced to face hard realities. The imperial treasury remained depleted by the 1904-05 war against the Japanese. The army was in disarray, the navy almost nonexistent. Revolutionaries were building bombs at home. In light of these difficulties, Nicholas II on November 18 joined Britain, France, Germany and Italy in presenting notes to the government in Belgrade asking the Serbs to withdraw their troops from the Austro-Serbian border. The Serbs made it appear that they had complied with the Powers' request. However, Count Forgach, the Austrian minister in Belgrade, wrote Aehrenthal that this was "just a pose." He reported that a general on active duty in Serbia was fitting out bands of mercenaries for future war against the Austrians.[20]

In the monarchy, as well as in Serbia, there were voices

raised for war. Aehrenthal was among those who lashed out, calling for "the complete destruction of the Serbian nest of revolutionaries for the benefit of Bulgaria and the Monarchy." Franz Ferdinand, who had opposed the annexation, wrote Aehrenthal on August 6, 1908, that steps should be taken to prevent war from breaking out with Serbia or Montenegro. "This, at the present moment would be a mistake," the Archduke said. "I shall shortly see (Field Marshall von Hötzendorf) Conrad in Vienna and will endeavour to restrain him and the war-mongers in his suite."[21] Franz Joseph let it be known that he disapproved of the warmongering.[22] By January 1909 Aehrenthal had changed his position, telling Conrad that "the absorption of Serbia was not practicable ... and that the monarchy would have found difficulty in digesting it."[23]

At several times during Franz Joseph's long reign, personal diplomacy had saved Austria and Russia from going to war. When problems arose, the Habsburg and the Romanov rulers exchanged letters or paid visits that resolved or at least smoothed over differences. During crises, the exchanges between the rulers of the two imperial houses tended to follow a pattern. The Russian ruler would launch a diatribe against his Austrian brother, claiming the monarch had betrayed him by not supporting him in the Balkans. Franz Joseph would defend himself, sometimes getting caught in a web of self-justification. The accretion of acrimony would be at times so heavy that the structures of imperial civility seemed about to implode. Nevertheless, in previous crises, the two monarchs had managed to salvage civility from the wreckage of their differences and ultimately to keep the peace. During the Crimean War period, Franz Joseph and Nicholas I had expressed their feelings in strong words, but by keeping communication lines open they managed to step back from war instead of lurching toward it. Personal diplomacy had helped avert a clash of the two empires during the turbulent period of the Russo-Turkish

War of 1877-78, and in the days following conclusion of the Peace of San Stefano.

During the crisis arising from the annexation of 1908 Franz Joseph and Nicholas II again tried personal diplomacy. But this time things were different. Remembered slights and felt wrongs dredged up by both parties cast a heavy weight on the very language used in these exchanges. At times the missives resembled Old Testament chronicles, with tribal references to past quarrels and unacknowledged favors.

The letters in the immediate aftermath of the annexation were the last series of substantive exchanges ever between Franz Joseph and Nicholas II. There would be one more abortive attempt by the Emperor to reach an understanding in 1912. By the summer of 1914, as the world careened toward Armageddon, the two rulers appear to have concluded that efforts to communicate were futile.

Franz Joseph's letter of December 7, 1908, to Nicholas II was in response to two letters from the Czar, one a pro forma greeting congratulating Franz Joseph on the 60th anniversary of his reign, the other chastising the Emperor for his "unilateral" action in annexing the twin provinces.

In his response, Franz Joseph ranged over the past, recounting policies pursued by his royal house and by the Czar's Romanov ancestors that had been beneficial to both empires. The Emperor pled for the Czar's understanding of Austria's situation in the Balkans, complaining that he wasn't getting the consideration he deserved. He declared it was his duty to take steps in Bosnia-Herzegovina necessary to buttress a vulnerable part of the monarchy. Franz Joseph said that following the traditions of Habsburg policy, he had sought to include the Russians in his plan in a way that would work to their advantage (by supporting the Straits project).

Franz Joseph went on to say that the annexation had been sanctioned not only by the Czar's predecessors but also, more recently, by Nicholas's own government. Declaring he was "pained" that the Russian ruler distrusted his plans, the Emperor accused the Czar of an attitude that seemed "more suitable to be invoked against an adversary than against a sincere friend." The Austrian monarch justified his decision to bypass the Powers regarding the annexation, saying if he had taken the matter before the Concert of Europe he would have encountered opposition from Turkey, from the small Slav states, and from the other Powers. He said that the very conflict that he was trying so hard to avoid would likely have resulted if he had brought the proposed annexation before the Powers.[24]

Franz Joseph was correct in assuming that a European conference on the annexation would have caused difficulties for the monarchy. Izvolsky's speech to the Duma on December 25, 1908, showed that this was precisely what the Russian foreign minister wanted. He acknowledged that the Romanovs had been bound by earlier promises to the Habsburgs. These gave the monarchy the right to proceed with the annexation. He went on to say, however, that if Austria insisted on changes in the Treaty of Berlin, Russia "had the moral duty" to point to other articles that the Balkan states and Turkey believed worked to their disadvantage.[25] In other words, if the annexation had come – or should come – before the Powers, the Berlin Treaty was to be hacked to pieces, with all interested parties making off with whatever they thought served their nationalistic interests.

Aehrenthal kept up his pressure on Izvolsky, hinting at blackmail. In late December, giving his archrival a foretaste of what was to come, the Austrian Foreign Minister released to the Viennese press several relatively innocuous documents on Balkan policy stemming from an 1897 meeting between Nicholas II and Franz Joseph in St. Petersburg. Izvolsky, proving fast on his patent leather shoes, quickly turned this effort at intimidation to his own ends, convincing the impressionable Czar that the dignity of his imperial person had been insulted by the document release.

Although Nicholas II honored tradition by sending New Year's greetings to his "brother" in Vienna, his message of December 30 was hardly intended to raise spirits at the Habsburg court. The Russian ruler commenced his letter by denying knowledge of the conclusions reached by Aehrenthal and Izvolsky at Buchlau. He said that any agreements between the two ministers required his approval before action could be taken. Aehrenthal, however, had announced the annexation as a fait accompli before waiting for an official Russian response. The Czar challenged Aehrenthal's claim that Austria's action was "in full agreement" with Russian wishes.

Nicholas II reserved his strongest words for the supposed insult to his royal person occasioned by Aehrenthal's release of the confidential documents. "I cannot conceal from you, my dear friend," he wrote Franz Joseph, "that I see a lack of consideration towards me in the procedure of your minister." The Czar stated that in response he had ordered Izvolsky to limit relations between the two foreign offices to "strictly official communications."[26] The Russian ruler ended his New Year's greeting on an ominous note: Expressing "deep regret" for what he was about to say, Nicholas II confessed to "acute apprehension for the future." He said that he wondered whether Aehrenthal intended to desist from the policy that had already caused so much trouble, or whether he planned to continue on that path. In the latter case, the Czar wrote, the Austrians and the Russians would find themselves "on the eve of complications" still more threatening to the general peace. A Balkan conflict, Nicholas II cautioned, would result in what he called a "great effervescence," not only in that region but also in Russia. The Czar closed by asking God's protection against "such an eventuality" which might bring on a general European war.[27] [28]

Nicholas II, convinced that the Austrians intended to start a Balkan war, appealed to Wilhelm II for help. Writing the Kaiser on December 28, the Czar characteristically blamed others for what was happening. He told his friend Willy, "If you can make them understand at Vienna that a war down there is *a danger to the peace of Europe* – then war will be avoided!"[29]

The last thing the 78-year-old Habsburg Emperor wanted was war. Franz Joseph had spent much of his long reign trying to avoid a Balkan conflict. But Franz Joseph was running out of patience with the diplomatic bungling of Nicholas II. In his January 28 reply to the Czar's letter of the previous month, the Habsburg Emperor launched what the Czar surely viewed as an attack on him personally. Franz Joseph pointed out that the Buchlau negotiations and the annexation stemmed from proposals Izvolsky himself had initiated in correspondence with Aehrenthal two months before the Russian foreign minister's visit to Moravia. That being the case, the Emperor said, it was hard to see how the Czar could claim that the annexation was a surprise.

Franz Joseph went on to say that Aehrenthal would never have engaged in discussions with Izvolsky without Franz Joseph's express consent. The monarch said that Aehrenthal had assumed that Izvolsky was likewise "armed with (the Czar's) authority" when he presented his views to the Austrian minister. Franz Joseph said that he could hardly hide his amazement that the proposals were not submitted for the Czar's previous approval, but instead had been brought to the Russian ruler's attention, "(as) ... belated and untimely revelations."[30] In other words, either Nicholas sanctioned the proposals and refused to admit he had done so, or his minister had conducted top-level diplomacy behind his master's back. The implication is that the Czar was either hopelessly incompetent or an outright liar – or both. The Emperor added that if the Straits proposal did not go over well in Paris and London, that wasn't his fault.

Franz Joseph wasn't finished. He went on to scold Nicholas II for failing to take the trouble to understand the situation faced by the monarchy in the Balkans and for blindly concluding that Austria's attitude toward Serbia and Montenegro was "aggressive."[31] Franz Joseph declared that he cherished "no designs of conquest" at the expense of either of these states. On the other hand, the Emperor said, he intended to "repel to the utmost" any aggression that the two Balkan nations might attempt in "pursuit of chimerical dreams which have been suggested to them from more than one side." (Franz Joseph clearly had in mind Pan-Slavist supporters in Russia and the Balkans). The Emperor declared that no Great Power should have to put up with constant harassment from its small neighbors.[32] In other words, although the Emperor had no desire to annex Serbia or Montenegro, he wasn't going to sit back and let Austria's ultranationalist neighbors run over the monarchy either.

The relationship between Franz Joseph and Nicholas II was beyond repair. The personal diplomacy, traditionally practiced between rulers, had failed. The Czar continued to expect Wilhelm II ("Willy") to serve as a go-between with the Habsburg Emperor, whom the Russian ruler never could understand. "Willy" tried but never succeeded in resolving the differences between the Emperor and the Czar.

On February 26, Austria settled its controversy with Turkey over the annexation by paying the Porte an indemnity of 2.2 million pounds. As far as Aehrenthal was concerned, this agreement entitled Austria to demand recognition of the annexation from Serbia, as well as from the Powers who were signatories of the Treaty of Berlin.[33] Since Turkey was the only party with a legitimate grievance, this should have ended the disagreement. But the Serbs continued to insist on compensation for alleged wrongs they had suffered.

European statesmen, working to end the controversy, began to realize that the Russians were behind the Serbian agitation. The English warned St. Petersburg that risking a war on behalf of Serbian claims to territory was out of proportion to the interests involved. Alfred von Kiderlen-Wachter, of the German foreign office, declared that it would be too silly if Europe "fell to fighting and hundreds of men were killed for the beaux yeux of those Serbian pigs."[34]

Aehrenthal, incensed at the Russians for failing to rein in their Serbian vassal, brandished his ultimate weapon: blackmail. The Habsburg Foreign Minister instructed Berchtold in St. Petersburg to present Izvolsky with a choice: he must either see to it that Belgrade recognized the Austro-Turkish agreement, or the Austrians would publish the memos exchanged by the Russian and Austrian foreign ministers prior to the annexation.[35] Berchtold surely cringed when he received those instructions from his superior. He was being asked to blackmail the man who had sat at his dinner table at Buchlau only a few months before. However, on March 8 he carried out his unpleasant assignment. Berchtold reported that Izvolsky, finally seeming to realize that he had overplayed his hand, appeared "utterly disconcerted."[36]

The Austrians, in the meantime, dispatched a note to Belgrade on March 5 offering the Serbian government significant economic concessions if it became "a peaceful and loyal neighbour."[37] Aehrenthal declared that what Austria wanted, most of all, was to be allowed to settle her quarrel with Serbia herself. Sir Fairfax Cartwright, the British envoy in Vienna, telegraphed Grey on March 6, 1909, that Aehrenthal had told him that the monarchy would never acknowledge what the Austrian foreign minister called Russia's "mad claim" to act as protectress of

Serbia.[38] Instead of responding to the Austrian note the Serbians, attempting to avoid direct negotiations with the Austrians, sent a note to the Powers on March 10. This caused great irritation in Vienna. The Austrians decided in a minister's council on March 13 to bring the 63 battalions already stationed in Dalmatia and Bosnia up to war strength, and to send 15 additional battalions into those provinces unless they received a satisfactory answer from Serbia by March 16 – that is, within three days.[39] War seemed imminent.

By this time, the Russian government was eager to resolve the crisis. At a secret session of the Duma on March 8, Aleksandr Guchkov, leader of the Octobrists,[40] had laid out the hard facts: Russia was in no position to intervene on behalf of Serbia even if the Austrians attacked the Romanov's Balkan vassal. Not only was the military ill-prepared for war, but there were also fears that with the Czar's troops away, terrorists might take advantage of the army's absence to stage an attack. On March 13, participants in a council of war at Tsarskoye Selo, the imperial residence outside St. Petersburg, agreed that war was out of the question.[41]

The Germans had been keeping their heads down as diplomatic notes flew back and forth between those involved in the dispute and those who were trying to prevent war from breaking out. Now, at Izvolsky's instigation, Berlin became involved in the crisis. Before the Germans were finished they had prejudiced much of the world against them. On March 14, the Russian ambassador in Berlin called on the German imperial chancellor, Bernhard von Bülow, with a personal appeal on behalf of a desperate Izvolsky. The envoy implored the chancellor to stop Aehrenthal from carrying out a threat, made a few days earlier, to publish compromising documents connected with the annexation. Prince von Bülow agreed on condition that the Russians would rein in Serbia. That would be easy enough once the Powers consented to the annexation.[42] On March 22, 1909, Nicholas II telegraphed his friend Willie, declaring himself "heartily glad" about Bülow's intervention. The Czar said he hoped that, with the Kaiser's "powerful help," war between the Habsburg monarchy and Serbia could be avoided. Nicholas went on to say that Austria would have nothing to gain from such a war. Even if it were localized, which he acknowledged wouldn't be easy, it "would put an end to every possibility of good understanding ... between Austria and Russia."[43]

Although the Russian reply to the German note left room for negotiation, Prince von Bülow, among others in Berlin, felt the response from the Czar's foreign office wasn't adequately self-effacing. The chancellor sent Izvolsky a message using bullying language: St. Petersburg was to provide an affirmative answer to the Austrian note and must "unreservedly" agree to the abrogation of Article 25 of the Treaty of Berlin dealing with the occupation of Bosnia and Herzegovina. Regardless of whether the chancellor's message was an ultimatum, its language was harsh: "Your Excellency will make clear that we expect a definite answer: Yes or No; any evasive, involved, or vague answer would have to be regarded by us as a refusal. We would then withdraw and let things take their course; the responsibility for all further eventualities would fall entirely on M. Izvolsky."[44]

Izvolsky understood what "things" would be taking their course if the Russians failed to comply with the German demand. If he had not feared his own unmasking through the release of the compromising documents, he could have answered the Germans with a resounding "no." But he was trapped. He saw no viable option except to accept the German demand. Appearing before the Russian cabinet, he argued that refusal to accept the note would leave Austria free to act against Serbia and might even put Russia in danger of an attack. This was, of course, nonsense, and

Izvolsky knew it. Neither Germany nor Austria had any intention of attacking Russia.

Ironically, Aehrenthal knew nothing about the so-called ultimatum Germany had sent to Russia.[45] The blame for the diplomatic fiasco lay with Berlin alone. The Russian cabinet, equally in the dark about Izvolsky's intrigues playing out behind the scenes, immediately agreed to the German demand.

In a last-minute effort to avert war, Sir Edward Grey came up with a brilliant solution. He and Aehrenthal prepared a note declaring that Britain and Austria had abrogated Article 25 of the Berlin Treaty. He then persuaded the other signatories, France, Russia, Italy and Germany, to agree to the abrogation. This left Serbia with no possibility of compensation, since her claim was based on the grounds that the Habsburgs had violated the Treaty. Franz Joseph was overjoyed. He immediately sent a message to the British ambassador expressing his "relief and gratitude at the prospect of a peaceful settlement." On March 30 the Russian, English, French and Italian ambassadors, joined at the last minute by the Germans, presented the Serbian government with the note agreed to by London and Vienna. The Serbs had nowhere to turn. The Russians had deserted them. The Powers were exerting their collective will. The Serbian note, identical to the wording agreed to by Aehrenthal and Grey, acknowledged that Serbia had not been injured by the fait accompli in Bosnia and Herzegovina. The Serbs agreed to accept the Powers' decision regarding Article 25 of the Berlin Treaty. Additionally, they promised to adopt "a footing of good neighborliness" toward the monarchy.[46]

Although Serbia accepted the note, her attitude toward Austria remained unchanged. As Macartney says, Serbian promises to be good neighbors of the Habsburgs were "not worth a piecrust."[47]

Peace may have been preserved but problems festered in

the annexation's aftermath. Many Russians were genuinely convinced that little Serbia was being victimized by her Habsburg neighbor rather than the other way around.

Two scandals in 1909 badly tarnished the Habsburgs' reputation, seeming to confirm what the monarchy's enemies claimed – that the Austrians couldn't be trusted. In March, 53 Serbs were put on trial in Zagreb for high treason. A group known as the Croats of the Pure Right accused the defendants of Pan-Slavist revolutionary activities against the monarchy. The Zagreb court sentenced 31 of the defendants to lengthy prison terms. However, an appeals court found that the charges were based on fraudulent evidence. The court ordered a retrial. The case was subsequently dropped. A second scandal, in December at the height of the annexation crisis, involved forged documents provided to the Foreign Ministry in Vienna by a Habsburg agent in the Balkans. These purported to offer proof that Serbian insurgents were pursuing intrigues against the monarchy in Bosnia. Those involved in the forgery hoped to provoke Austria into war with Serbia. Foreign Minister Aehrenthal, unaware that the documents were fraudulent, gave them to a respected Austrian history professor, Heinrich Friedjung, who used them in a newspaper article. In both cases Habsburg justice prevailed, in part due to the legal talents of Czech Professor Tomas Masaryk, who went on to become the first President of Czechoslovakia in November 1918. But these near miscarriages of justice caused justifiable outrage.[48]

The belief that Austria had grand designs on the Balkans became firmly implanted in the Russian psyche. The Russian Ambassador to Paris, Aleksandr Nelidov, urged Izvolsky to bring Russia closer to France and England "in continued resistance to further Austro-German penetration in the Balkans." The ambassador said Russia should "at the opportune moment compel Austria-Hungary to renounce her Balkan schemes and restore freedom of action to the now subjected Serbia."[49]

The annexation crisis marked the point of no return on the long road to the Great War. Personal diplomacy between the Habsburgs and the Romanovs failed. While Izvolsky's role in the annexation controversy became clear only much later, the whole world knew about Prince von Bülow's ultimatum. The Germans were seen in a most unflattering light. As Berchtold said, appearing relieved: "the lion's share in the crisis itself is now laid at the door of the German government. ... My German colleague, to whom it fell to take the step, has become overnight a terrifying and sinister Nibelung figure, the cruel Hagen of Tronje after he slew the unsuspecting Siegfried."[50] The German ambassador in St. Petersburg wrote Prince von Bülow on April 1 that "the legend that Germany threatened ... (Russia) with the 'mailed fist' finds credence in wide circles and has for the moment made feeling run high against us, even in circles usually well-disposed towards us."[51]

To the extent that the Young Turks ever intended to bring representative government to the Ottoman Empire, their movement soon self-immolated. Military officers who rode the revolution to power were ultranationalists, not democrats. The new government was as absolutist as the previous one. The leaders instigated a program of forced Ottomanization, attempting to make the Balkan nationalities forget their ethnic roots and to settle under one large Turkish tent. The constitution, which had been promised as a sort of elixir bringing the Balkan people together, changed nothing. As Edith Durham said, "Territorial aggrandizement" rather than unity was what the small Balkan nations wanted.

Durham writes of a conversation she had in Scutari with two Young Turk officers. They were excited about the constitution. They weren't sure what it was but they were certain it would make everything right. They were busy preparing to be photographed in their new uniforms, and "were childishly happy." She told them: "But you have the Bulgur question, the Greek, the Serb, and Albanian questions all to solve in Europe alone – surely those are more important than new uniforms." They replied, "These questions no longer exist. We have made a law. All are now Ottomans!"

Durham explained the facts of life to the Young Turk officers: "You may make a law that a cat is a dog, but it will remain a cat."[52]

19 THE POISON TREE

In the fall of 1909 Czar Nicholas II of Russia accompanied his foreign minister, Aleksandr Izvolsky, on a portentous journey to Italy. The Russians were to spend a few days with King Victor Emmanuel at his palace in Racconigi, south of Turin. The Czar and his entourage attracted widespread attention in the press by ostentatiously taking the long way round to Italy, adding some 3,000 kilometers to the trip. Nicholas II said publicly that he had avoided Habsburg territory to show his displeasure at the Austrians' conduct during the crisis of the previous year,[1] when Count Alois von Aehrenthal, the Austrian foreign minister, had surprised Europe by abruptly announcing the monarchy's annexation of Bosnia and Herzegovina. The Habsburgs' action had come just as Izvolsky was about to approach France and Britain with a proposal that Russian warships be granted exclusive access to the Bosphorus and Dardanelles Straits. Riled by the Austrians' audacity at announcing the annexation as a fait accompli, the Western Powers were in no mood to upset the Balkan status quo further by agreeing to changes in the Straits regime – even if they otherwise might have been amenable to the idea.

Izvolsky blamed the Habsburgs for the failure of his Straits proposal. The foreign minister was bent on revenge against the monarchy for the public humiliation he had suffered. He intended to enlist not only Italy but also the Balkan Slavs in his cause.

Shortly after arriving at Racconigi, Izvolsky handed Tommaso Tittoni, the Italian foreign minister, the draft of a treaty that he himself had prepared. It called for giving the Italians a free hand in Tripoli, where they had claims, although the territory remained under Turkish sovereignty. In exchange, the Italians were to agree not to interfere with Russian attempts to gain control of the Bosphorus and Dardanelles Straits.

As a member of the Triple Alliance, with Germany and Austria, Italy had pledged to support the status quo in the Balkans. The Russian proposal required Italy to violate this pledge. The Italians were pleased to collude with the Russians against the Habsburgs, with whom they had never gotten along well.

Izvolsky's diplomatic scheme had a clear logic. If the Ottomans were forced to defend their holdings in North Africa, their attention would be diverted to that war theater. That would leave Russian agents free to pursue intrigues in the Balkans. Izvolsky intended to use the small Balkan states as proxies in a scheme not only to weaken the Ottomans' grip on their European lands but also to undermine the Austrians in Bosnia and Herzegovina. The foreign minister was preparing the ground for the day when the Teutons and Slavs would meet in a final confrontation. In St. Petersburg as well as in the Balkan capitals, belief was widespread that a clash of empires was inevitable and imminent.

The negotiations at Racconigi, resulting in a treaty along the lines of Izvolsky's draft proposal, were so secret that Tittoni and Izvolsky wrote the documents themselves and exchanged them in private. The only other Russian besides Izvolsky to know about the treaty was the Czar, and he was to deny its existence, not only to England but also to his closest ally, France. Austria and Germany, Italy's allies, were told nothing about the Racconigi agreement.[2] The Russians put out the story that the Italian trip was intended to affirm the status quo in European affairs, as well as to pay a visit to royals connected to the Romanov family by marriage. The world only learned the truth about the treaty much later.

The Russians' choice of Racconigi for the visit, in Italy's Piedmont region, was guaranteed to resonate unpleasantly in Vienna. Early in Franz Joseph's reign, Piedmont had been a wellspring of irredentist activity directed against the Habsburgs. The nationalistic strivings inspired by Piedmont had led to a war in 1859 in which the Austrians forfeited most of their Italian holdings. Franz Joseph himself had for a time taken command of Habsburg troops in that conflict. The Emperor's experience on the battlefield gave him a lasting abhorrence of war – and hatred for the very word "Piedmont."

While he was at Racconigi, Izvolsky likely shared with the Italians his plans for a Balkan Alliance. In his annual Christmas speech to the Russian Duma in 1908, the foreign minister had mentioned a plan for a federation of Balkan states.[3] It was to serve as a bulwark against what Izvolsky insisted were Austria's vast schemes for expansion on the peninsula. These unsupported claims of Austrian ambitions formed the bedrock of Izvolsky's propaganda campaign against the Habsburgs. The foreign minister's Duma speech carried tremendous weight in Russia. Nicholas II, a ruler notably devoid of imperial certainty and lacking in will and purpose, was known to rely heavily on Izvolsky's advice in foreign affairs.

The Serbs were the first of the possible candidate nations to express an interest in joining the Balkan league. They harbored anger at the Powers for refusing them compensation for damages they claimed from the annexation of Bosnia and Herzegovina. They were furious that negotiators, eager to end the annexation crisis, had coerced them into signing the so-called "Treaty of Good Neighborliness" with the hated Habsburgs.

In April 1909, hardly before the ink was dry on the so-called good-neighbor treaty between Austria and Serbia, the Royal Serbian government sent a memorandum to the Serbian minister in Vienna "concerning the continuation of the Great(er) Serbia propaganda in Austria-Hungary." Serbian agents were advised to go underground while waiting for the time when they could realize Serbia's "legitimate interests in the Balkans and in the whole Slavic south." The government communiqué advised diplomatic staff to refrain from overt Serbian propaganda – for the time being. They were, however, to use money to influence the Austro-Hungarian press. The memo said "a new focus (of agitation) is being projected in the fraternal Czech kingdom, around which can rally all those who wish to seek, or must seek, the salvation of their national individualism in the triumph of the Pan-Slav idea." To the extent that revolutionary propaganda appeared necessary, the memo continued, it was "to be carried out by St. Petersburg and from golden Prague."[4]

The Serbians did have legitimate grievances against the Hungarians. A settlement of the tariff dispute, known as the "Pig War," was being worked out,[5] but the Serbians remained convinced that their livestock producers would never be treated fairly. This was particularly the case in regard to pigs, a major source of income for Serbia's mostly peasant population. The Hungarians, eager to protect their own agricultural interests, persisted in trying to squeeze the Serbians out of the market. Hungarian customs officials continued to turn porkers away at the border, claiming that the animals were diseased – an accusation that Serbian Prime Minister Milovan Milanovic dismissed as ludicrous and offensive. In a conversation with Joseph Baernreither, Milanovic ardently defended his nation's pig and cattle population. He declared that the local animals enjoyed fine living conditions. They breathed fresh mountain air. They did not live in stalls. If sick livestock was a problem, he said, it more than likely came from Hungary.[6]

Their grievances notwithstanding, the Serbs and the Habsburgs might have settled their differences had it not been for the Serbs' deep-seated belief in their own exceptionalism. They considered themselves the chosen people of the Balkans, which afforded them special rights. Their superior culture, based on an ancient civilization, as they thought, entitled them to expect their less advanced neighbors to join them gladly in a vastly expanded nation. The Serbs' ambitions for territorial acquisition included lands that had long been part of the Habsburg Empire.

The advocates of Greater Serbia were, as usual, encouraged by the revolutionary zeal of Russian Pan-Slavist groups. These organizations, in turn, got much of their inspiration from Izvolsky. The executive committee of one large organization in St. Petersburg sent a circular to likeminded groups in the Balkans telling them that the time was near when Russia would "take up energetically her historic mission as protectress of the Slav world."[7] Once the Russians finished organizing their army and government, the circular said, the Balkan Slavs could expect help in their struggle for liberation. The committee's circular outlined a strategy for the coming struggle: Serbia and Montenegro were to be ready to "complete their union" by occupying the Sandzak of Novi Pazar, the corridor separating the two small states. It had been garrisoned by Habsburg forces until 1908, when it was returned to Turkey as part of the annexation settlement with the Porte. Serbia and Montenegro also were to make plans for invading Bosnia and Herzegovina. Bulgaria was to prepare to seize the territories promised to her in the Treaty of San Stefano, extending herself to the gates of Constantinople. The Slav committee's communiqué assured the group's Balkan friends that the Young Turk regime would not last much longer. Once the Turks were trounced, the committee circular said, the Habsburgs would get what they deserved.[8]

On November 4, 1909, shortly after the meeting at Racconigi, Izvolsky sent instructions to the Russian ministers in Sofia, Belgrade and Cetinje repeating his call for the Balkan states to unite. The Racconigi meeting "favored these efforts," he wrote, saying that what transpired during the visit there would contribute to the development of Russian policy in the Near East. That policy, said Izvolsky, was to be summed up as "the Balkans for the Balkan States."[9]

Nicholas Hartwig, an Austrophobe and intriguer, arrived in Belgrade as Russian minister in the fall of 1909.[10] There he took the lead in recruiting the Serbs as well as the Bulgarians, Montenegrins and Greeks for the future Balkan league. Hartwig and other Russian agents, including Anatoly Nekliudov in Bulgaria, found this more challenging than anticipated. The Balkan neighbors were accustomed to feuding rather than cooperating. The Serbs, Bulgarians and Greeks were quarreling over territory in Macedonia. Also the rulers of Montenegro and Serbia were at odds over which imperial family would occupy the throne of a future Greater Serbia.

The Serbs needed no urging from Hartwig when it came to violating their good neighbor agreement with Austria. Among other things, the Serbs had promised that *Narodna odbrana* (National Defense), an organization founded in Belgrade by enemies of the Habsburgs immediately after the annexation of Bosnia-Herzegovina, would confine itself strictly to cultural activities. This was as absurd as requiring a tiger to become a lamb. The stated aim of *Narodna odbrana* was to organize, equip and instruct insurgents detailed "for fighting as independent units" and to create an action plan for the "defense of the Serbian people." The intention was "to strike terror into the enemy rear," meaning, of course, the Habsburgs. Volunteers were instructed in making bombs and explosives, which they could put together independently at the scene of battle. They received training in bomb throwing and in wrecking bridges and railways. These activities were to be carried out in Bosnia and Herzegovina.[11] A pamphlet appearing in Belgrade in 1911 declared that every Serb from childhood to old age must train as a sharpshooter. "Today demands quiet work, fanatical, indefatigable, and incessant, on the tasks and duties needful as preliminary preparations for the fight with rifles and heavy guns." Listed among the organization's "needful duties and tasks" was "pointing to Austria and the first and greatest enemy."[12]

With Hartwig's prompting, some 200 branches of the organization sprang up, in Serbia but also in Bosnia. The Russian minister knew full well that the participants weren't there to sip tea and socialize.

A later statement by Hartwig left no doubt about his policy in the Balkans. Writing to M. Neratov, at the foreign office in St. Petersburg on November 5, 1911, he set forth two main aims. The first was to make it easier for the Slav nations, who owed their independent existence to Russia, "to attain their 'sacred ideals' ... an amicable division among them of all Turkish possessions on the Balkan Peninsula." While Austria wasn't mentioned in the statement, Hartwig's long-range plan clearly included stripping the monarchy of Bosnia and Herzegovina. The second aim was to realize the Romanovs' century old dream of "planting a foot on the shores of the Bosphorus at the gates of the Russian lake."[13]

Although the news of Izvolsky's intrigues in Italy never leaked out, the minister was becoming increasingly unpopular in St. Petersburg. His conduct during the annexation crisis had offended a number of moderates at the Romanov court. They objected to his anti-Habsburg rhetoric and to his zeal in promoting the Greater Serbian cause. Nicholas II, finally yielding to demands that Izvolsky be relieved of his post, named him ambassador to France. He assumed his duties in Paris in September 1910. Izvolsky was to demonstrate a remarkable ability to land on his feet.

Many members of the diplomatic corps assigned to St. Petersburg were relieved at Izvolsky's departure and pleased with his replacement. S.D. Sazonov, the new Minister of Foreign Affairs, was an experienced diplomat, having been posted to Russian embassies in London, Washington and the Vatican. Sazonov, the brother-in-law of the well-regarded Russian Prime Minister, Pyotor Stolypin, was generally considered more conciliatory than Izvolsky. However, while the sickly, high-strung Sazonov may have initially seemed less revengeful than his predecessor, he had arrived at many of his views while sitting at the feet of Izvolsky, his superior at the foreign office. Sazonov shared Izvolsky's mistrust of Austria and Germany, as well as his ambitions for Constantinople and the Straits. By July 1914, Sazonov was as committed to Izvolsky's agenda as his predecessor ever had been.

In Paris, Izvolsky immediately plunged into a propaganda campaign to gain French support for Russia's anti-Habsburg policy in the Balkans. He was adept at seeming to be what he was not. Underneath his polished veneer of sophistication he was a man of peasant cunning, continuously weaving the web into which he planned one day to lure his enemies.

Izvolsky's exile in Paris actually added to his power. While carrying on his anti-Habsburg campaign in France, he also continued to exert influence on the foreign office in St. Petersburg, where he was actually the shadow minister. He made use of an established network of informants and operatives, cultivated during his days in the foreign office. With their help he regularly intervened in matters that did not directly concern him, most particularly those involving Austria, the Balkans and the Straits.

When Sazonov and Izvolsky clashed, Izvolsky, with his

overbearing personality, almost inevitably prevailed. The Czar, overwhelmed by worries about the health of the crown prince, who had hemophilia, and by revolutionary unrest in his empire, increasingly sequestered himself within the bosom of his family. Nicholas II chopped wood, took walks, played tennis, and faithfully recorded each day's events in a diary of monumental inanity. This left the two ministers, Sazanov and Izvolsky, to run the foreign affairs of the vast Russian Empire with few constraints.

Izvolsky found fertile soil in Paris for planting and tending the poison tree that would blossom into war in 1914. His grand scheme for the Balkans would take time, but it was falling into place. Cutting the Ottomans loose from their weak grip on Europe remained his first priority. He expected the Italians to do yeomen's work on that score. The Balkan league would be directed against Austria as well as Turkey. Germany still could block Russian ambitions, but Izvolsky intended to see to it that the French helped out on that front.

Izvolsky took pains to remind the French people of their grievances at the hands of the Germans, most particularly by the loss of Alsace-Lorraine in the Franco-Prussian war of 1870-71. Reporting to St. Petersburg soon after he arrived, Izvolsky complained that his campaign was more difficult than he expected. Although the French had a legitimate reason for hating the Germans, the Russian ambassador found that four decades after the Prussians' victorious war of aggression, the edges had worn off people's anger. A new generation had grown up in France. The Germans' brutal deeds, inspired by Bismarck, were moldering in the history books.[14] To the extent his finances allowed, Izvolsky paid French journalists to write stories reminding the nation's citizens of wrongs perpetrated by the Germans. He didn't forget Austria either, taking care that negative reports were planted regarding the Habsburgs' actions and intentions in the Balkans.

In the meantime, Izvolsky's carefully laid plans regarding Italy were generating unintended consequences. At Racconigi he and Nicholas II had given the Italians a blank check to go after the Turks in Tripoli. The Italians were happy to take on the task of routing the Ottomans – too happy, as it turned out.

Once unleashed, the Italians showed a ravenous appetite for conquest. On September 27, 1911, Italy, alleging mistreatment of her nationals and claiming Ottoman interference with her economic concerns, sent the Turks a 24-hour ultimatum demanding that they choose between Italian occupation and war. Although the Porte's reply was conciliatory, the Italians refused it. The war opened on September 29 and quickly spread. On October 3 the Italians bombarded the fortress of Tripoli. By mid-day, the Italian flag waved over the Sultan's fort. The Italians occupied Derna on October 18, Benghazi on October 20 and landed at Homs on October 21. They announced the annexation of Libya on November 5. They moved into the Aegean. They even threatened the Straits. The Russians hadn't bargained for that.

Habsburg Emperor Franz Joseph followed these events with great unease. His support of the Triple Alliance had been based on its value in maintaining the status quo in the Balkans. Now here were the Italians, in spite of Austria's reminding them of their promises, blatantly violating these agreements. Nevertheless, Franz Joseph, bowing to the Germans' determination to keep the Triple Alliance intact, felt obligated to abstain from public condemnation of his Italian ally.

On the other hand, Conrad von Hötzendorf, the hotheaded chief of the general staff of the Habsburg military, saw no need for minced words. Franz Joseph and Aehrenthal spoke softly regarding the Italian aggression. Conrad favored a big stick. He soon found himself in the Emperor's bad graces because of his warmongering.

Chief Conrad is one of those interesting creatures that history throws up on the beach from time to time. He wasn't your usual general. Conrad was a renaissance man, in many ways a throwback to a bygone age. He adored Mozart and Wagner. He was an avid reader in numerous languages, including Russian; he was fluent in French, Italian, Serbian, and German, and able to get along in Czech and Polish.[15] He was passionately in love with Gina von Reininghaus, a much younger woman, the married mother of six minor children. Their liaison prompted his detractors to claim that he was seeking military glory in the hopes of seducing Gina into leaving her husband and marrying him.

In actuality, Conrad seems never to have imagined a war he didn't want to fight. While he envisioned nests of enemies hidden in the branches of almost every neighboring tree, he focused his immediate attention on Serbia and Italy. He accused the Serbs, with justification, of unabashedly and "without scruples" aiming to acquire the monarchy's South Slav provinces. Conrad was out on a shakier limb where Italy was concerned. He claimed that the monarchy's ally intended to acquire territory in Italian-speaking coastal areas of the Balkans, and to take full control of the Adriatic Sea. Conrad's assessment of Italy's intentions had some truth to it, but it hardly demanded the preemptory military attack that the general began advocating in public. The Habsburg chief of staff's irresponsible utterances inspired press campaigns that were contrary to the empire's foreign policy.

Conrad and Aehrenthal soon found themselves in their own war, one over Austria's role in an increasingly troublesome Europe. The foreign minister's first line of defense in dealing with Italy involved diplomacy. He had no objection to that nation's acquiring Tripoli, as long as that did not disturb the status quo in the Balkans. He saw no advantage in gratuitously attacking the monarchy's admittedly eel-like ally. Thwarted in his demands for immediate military action against either Serbia or Italy,

Conrad lit into Aehrenthal, denouncing the ailing foreign minister as utopian for his attempts to "appease" Austria's enemies. After the two ministers almost came to blows over whether to go to war, Franz Joseph reined in his chief of staff. On October 17, 1911, the Emperor sent Conrad a memo informing him that in some of his public statements he had exceeded his authority. Franz Joseph told Conrad that Aehrenthal, in his post as foreign minister, "conducts affairs of his department according to the directives of *my* will."[16] Conrad, ignoring Franz Joseph's warning, kept up his verbal and written assaults on the foreign minister. This led to a stormy audience with Franz Joseph on November 15, 1911. The Emperor ordered Conrad to stop attacking Aehrenthal. "The ever-recurring reproaches on the question of Italy and the Balkans are directed at me," the Emperor said. "Policy – it is I who make it! ... and it is a policy of peace."[17] Conrad remained recalcitrant. On November 30 Franz Joseph relieved him of his post, naming him Inspector General of the army.[18]

The events here are significant in the debate as to whether, as many historians have asserted, Franz Joseph was pushed into war by "the generals" in 1914 or whether he made the decision according to his own conscience. The latter is likely the case.

Aehrenthal's peace party carried the day, but on February 17, 1912, he lost a battle with leukemia. Berchtold, who had been popular in St. Petersburg, where he served as Austria's ambassador, was named Minister of Foreign Affairs. Reluctant to take the job, Berchtold accepted the assignment out of loyalty to the Emperor. Berchtold had rather more ability than has been generally acknowledged. He struggled to save the old monarchy, but would be unable to prevent the convergence of events that swept it to destruction.

As for Conrad, he would be back.

Izvolsky, meanwhile, continued to wrap his tentacles around the idea of getting the Straits opened to Russian warships. He had unsuccessfully raised the issue during negotiations for an Anglo-Russian convention in 1907 and again in 1908 at Buchlau. Now, he would make a third and final effort to achieve his goal by peaceful means. His scheme involved undercutting the Italians, something that appears not to have given the Russian foreign minister qualms.

In September 1911, acting on information of the imminent Italian attack on Libya, Izvolsky telegraphed Neratov in the Russian foreign office advising him to take advantage of the Turco-Italian war and the weakness of a new Grand Vizier to try again to solve the Straits question to Russia's satisfaction. In a masterful exercise in double dealing, Russia was to pose as protector of Ottoman interests in Constantinople, against the Italians – whom they themselves had unleashed against the Turks. Neratov consequently dispatched a message to N.V. Charykov, the Russian ambassador in Constantinople, instructing him to offer Russian assistance to the Turks in protecting the Bosphorus and Dardanelles Straits as well as adjacent territory. In return for this help, the Ottoman government was to allow passage of Russian warships through the Straits, so long as those ships did not stop there without the Porte's permission. The Turks were given one week to reply.

Said Pasha, the Grand Vizier, recognized this proposal for what it was – a preposterous attempt to take advantage of the Turks while they were fighting Italy for their very lives. For the Grand Vizier, the clause referring to Russian support in the Straits and in the "territories adjacent" had an ominous sound. He put off replying for several weeks on grounds he had to consult other ministers.[19] The Young Turks had the last word on the subject, declaring that the Ottomans never would tolerate such an arrangement, which would "degrade the great and glorious Turkish Empire into a province standing under a Russian protectorate."[20]

Faced with the failure of the Russians' latest Straits

scheme, Sazonov responded to reports of those negotiations by denying that they ever took place. He implied that Charykov had acted independently of the Russian foreign office, which was, of course, untrue. In March 1912, Charykov, having failed in his mission, was relieved of his ambassadorial post. Izvolsky at this juncture abandoned hope of gaining control of the Straits by peaceful means. From that time on, American historian Sidney Fay writes, Izvolsky would work "persistently and consistently" for the grand conflict, so that he at last would be able to say, *"C'est ma guerre!"*[21]

The Italians continued to upset the other European Powers by expanding the war. In mid-April 1912 they sent a squadron of torpedo boats to the Dardanelles, intending to blow up the Turkish fleet. The Turks, catching sight of the boats, refused to come out and give battle. Shore batteries and the Italian forces exchanged fire for about two hours before each side abandoned its efforts. The Turks retaliated by temporarily closing the Dardanelles to all shipping, a development that naturally unnerved the Russians.

The Italians headed into the Southern Sporades, where they ignored their Austrian ally's wish that they limit their occupation to three islands – Rhodes, Scarpanto and Stampalia – that weren't clearly part of the Aegean.[22] The Italians quickly took those islands, along with Kasos, Episcopi, Nisyros, Kalymnos, Leros, Patmos, Kos, Symi and Khalki. By the end of May the Italians controlled all the Dodecanese. In mid-July a flotilla of torpedo boats actually entered the Dardanelles, but turned back after it was spotted and fired upon.

By this time European governments were holding emergency meetings, focusing on how to stop the Italians. However, the Turks themselves, worried about the growing threat to their holdings in the Balkans, were the ones who ended the hostilities. In a peace settlement, concluded in the fall, the Ottomans ceded Libya to the Italians, while requiring them to abandon the occupied Aegean islands.[23]

The Italian bombardment of Tripoli late in September 1911 had set in motion a chain of events that reordered the Balkan peninsula and eventually all of Europe.

The Balkan populations were a seething mass of discontent. The Young Turks had come to power in July 1908 promising liberal reforms, which they had failed to deliver. Behaving like conquerors instead of rulers, the Young Turks sought to force Ottomanization on their European subjects. The Young Turks' demands led to protests across the Balkans. Even many Albanians, traditionally loyal to the Sultan, turned against the new government after its Young Turk leaders stripped them of their firearms. Christians, in particular, suffered under the new regime. They had previously enjoyed immunity from service in the Turkish army, privileges that the Young Turks had promised to honor. Now, they were being ordered to fight for the Sultan, whom the Christian believers considered an infidel. Forced into negotiations by their outraged subjects, the Turks made new promises that they didn't keep. As one group of angry Christians told Edith Durham, "The Turk ... is, in one particular only, like the Lord God. As he was in the beginning, he is now, and ever will be. We don't believe in any of his reforms. They are only dust in the eyes of Europe."[24]

In April 1909, uprisings had broken out in Albanian strongholds, including Kosovo. Sporadic unrest continued in the region through 1910 and 1911. By the early summer of 1912 outbursts against the Young Turks had spread across Turkey in Europe. In Adrianople, the garrison mutinied; in Monastir there was a public proclamation against the Young Turk government; in parts of Albania an insurrection erupted. Following a battle between Turkish troops and Albanians, the latter took possession of the Sandzaks of İpek, Prizren and Pristina, and later occupied Uskubs (Skopje).[25] Albanian rebels, hating the Young Turks but remaining loyal to the old regime, won victory after victory. Finally, on August 18, 1912, they created a framework "for an Albanian quasi-state, within the Ottoman Empire."[26] The fight for a free Albania would soon serve as a fulcrum for conflict.

Russian agents in the meantime remained busy with their project for a Balkan league. The alliance involved a series of agreements negotiated by Serbia, Bulgaria, Greece and Montenegro, shepherded through by Russian agents in the Balkans – Hartwig in Serbia and Nekliudov in Bulgaria. As conceived by Izvolsky, the alliance was intended to impose a certain order on the chaos implicit in the Russian scheme for changing the political landscape in the Balkans. The region's Slavs were expected to band together to prevent the Austrians from stepping into the breach and claiming Turkish territory for themselves once the Ottomans were forced out of Europe. In constructing his scheme, Izvolsky attempted to guarantee that the Balkan participants would take orders from St. Petersburg. The Russians were to determine when the conflict between the Slavs and the Teutons was to commence, and how the battle lines would be drawn. Izvolsky would not get what he wanted. His plans fell prey to the irrational exuberance of the alliance members themselves.

In a treaty of March 13, 1912, Serbia and Bulgaria pledged to support each other if they were attacked by other states, or if a great Power (meaning Austria) sought to "annex, occupy, or even temporarily to invade" any Balkan territory under Turkish rule. A secret annex set forth rules to assure that the Russians kept control over their Balkan protégés. It stipulated that, if a difference of opinion arose between Serbia and Bulgaria involving the status quo in the Balkans, or if one of the states decided that military action was "indispensable," the two parties were to "take counsel." If the parties agreed on a particular action, they were to ask Russia's consent. If they failed to agree, the parties were to appeal to Russia, whose opinion would be binding.[27] The problem with this seemingly fail-proof agreement was that it was built on the fallacious assumption that the fiercely tribal Balkan ethnic groups would behave rationally once they got a scent of their traditional enemies' blood.

The Serbo-Bulgarian treaty was followed on June 12, 1912, by a defensive Greco-Bulgarian agreement. It contained no provision for sharing Turkish territory, probably because the Greeks and the Bulgarians both intended to press their claims for Salonika.[28]

Montenegro was the last Balkan nation to join the alliance. The eccentric and willful King Nicholas (Nikita) was in a surly mood, having been subjected to several plots against his throne and even an attempted assassination. He suspected that the Serbians were behind the treachery and said so, loudly. The Serbs, angered by the King's accusations, initially sought to exclude Montenegro from the federation. Bulgaria, however, welcomed the tiny Balkan nation as an ally. The agreement between Montenegro and Bulgaria followed the lines of the Serbo-Bulgarian treaty, but with one difference. It proposed initiating hostilities with Turkey earlier than previously had been intended.[29] Having decided to enter the race for territory to which he, along with the other Balkan Alliance members, had dubious claims, King Nikita was eager to get out of the gate. In September, Bulgaria and Montenegro completed a military convention providing for war against Turkey no later than September 28, 1912. By this time Montenegro and Serbia had settled their differences and had reached an agreement of their own.[30]

Neither Austria nor Germany knew the truth about the Balkan Alliance.[31] The official Russian line was that the alliance was solely a defensive treaty against Austrian territorial aggrandizement in the Balkans. In April of that year Franz Joseph, having probably gotten wind of the Balkan negotiations even if he didn't know their substance, sounded uncharacteristically pessimistic. He told Philippe Crozier, the French Ambassador to Vienna, during an audience just before the minister was to leave his post, that it might not be possible to keep the peace.

Czar Nicholas II had received copies of the agreement between Serbia and Bulgaria on May 7. He seems to have understood that Izvolsky and Sazonov, the ministers to whom he had, by default, entrusted the future of his empire, had created a ticking political time bomb. The Czar's response to the looming catastrophe was, however, flaccid. At the end of June, Nicholas II told the French ambassador that the Russians would do all they could to keep the peace but that it would "probably be a waste of breath." The Czar said that for the Balkan people the chance for war would "be too tempting."[32] He seemed not to realize that his ministers themselves were responsible for tempting the small Balkan nations with possibilities for conquest that they never would have imagined on their own.

An order, issued under the Czar's authority and sent to the Russian army on March 12, 1912, the day before the Serbo-Bulgarian treaty was completed, suggests that Nicholas II understood that Izvolsky's Balkan scheme might lead to a European war. The message to the military was ominous: "In accordance with His Majesty's decision, a telegraphic order for mobilization in the European military commands on account of political complications on the western frontiers *is to be interpreted as an order also for the commencement of hostilities against Austria and Germany.*"[33]

Izvolsky continued his attempts to recruit the French as Russia's allies in the future confrontation between the Teutons and the Slavs. His chances for winning support in Paris were tremendously enhanced by the elevation, on June 14, 1912, of Raymond Poincaré to Prime Minister and Minister of Foreign Affairs. A native of Lorraine and a hardened enemy of Germany, he yearned for revenge against the Prussians, who had driven his family from their home. He was 10 years old at the time, and his emotional scars had never healed. Poincaré wasn't immediately willing to support the Russians' Balkan policy. However, Izvolsky, the master persuader, playing on the French leader's painful childhood memories, gradually won him over.

Poincaré showed his animus toward the Germans in a gesture intended to convey a political message. In August 1912, the French prime minister, heading for a visit with the Czar, avoided a shorter and easier route through Germany, traveling to Russia by sea from Dunkirk.

Poincaré recorded details of the St. Petersburg visit in his journal. Upon arriving, he paid an obligatory visit to the Peter and Paul Fortress, with its mausoleum where 53 members of the Romanov family, from Peter the Great to Alexander III, lay in eternal rest. He took note of what must have been a curiosity for him and his entourage – the People's House, built by Czar Nicholas II in 1901 to protect Russian youth "from the dangers of alcohol." The French minister wrote that he saw several thousand young people in an enormous temperance restaurant partaking of a sober breakfast.[34]

Arriving at the Ministry of Foreign Affairs, he found Sazonov awaiting him in his cabinet, surrounded by official documents. Poincaré said Sazonov greeted him with "great warmth." The two commenced a long and intense discussion on international affairs.[35] The talk turned to the Balkan league, particularly the treaty between Bulgaria and Serbia. Poincaré wanted to know why the Russians had not told their French allies about the federation. Sazonov claimed he had no idea why France had been kept in the dark. (Surely he was dissembling. He and the Czar had sole authority to decide who was to be informed about the alliance). Sazonov assured his French visitor that the agreement was intended to guarantee the continuation of the status quo in the Balkans. Poincaré questioned this. The treaty called for dividing Turkish lands, he pointed out. That didn't exactly suggest fealty to the status quo. Finally, after being pinned down, Sazonov confessed that he hadn't been forthright in his description of the treaty. Pressed for the exact wording of the agreement, Sazonov translated the documents, which were in Russian, into French on the spot.

Poincaré was horrified at what the Russians were up to.[36] The status quo seemed to be mentioned "only as to how it could be disturbed," he wrote. Poincaré cited a host of flaws in the treaty that were certain to cause conflict between the Balkan allies. Boundaries in disputed territory were not defined. Bulgaria was to have the eastern zone of Macedonia and Serbia the western, but no border was stipulated for Bulgaria southward toward Salonika; likewise no boundary was specified for Serbia in the direction of Albania. Sazonov assured Poincaré that Russia would deal with those matters in due time.

Asked about a statement by the Russian agent in Sofia that the treaty was "an agreement for war," Sazonov replied that there was nothing to worry about. Under the treaty, Serbia and Bulgaria were not allowed to mobilize, much less go to war, without Russian consent. Poincaré surely realized that once the Balkan states were unleashed they would be hard to control. He responded that he believed the agreement contained "at the core not only a war with Turkey, but also a war with Austria."[37]

Before leaving St. Petersburg, Poincaré agreed that France would recognize the defensive aspects of the Bulgarian-Serbian alliance. He refused to support the Russians' latest attempts at hegemony in the Balkans. He said, however, that France would almost certainly have to become involved if Germany joined her Austrian ally in a war. Izvolsky surely was jubilant when he heard this. In order to win France's unqualified support for Russia's Balkan policy, he needed only to persuade the French prime minister that the Germans would inevitably support the Austrians in any serious conflict.

As the Balkan states engaged in frenetic preparations for war, Sazonov and Izvolsky began having second thoughts about the forces they had unleashed. They had expected their vassal states to behave like obedient children, taking orders from St. Petersburg. Now their Balkan charges were acting like free agents. The two plotters confronted a classical mythological conundrum. The younger Slavs, those in the Balkans, were threatening to overthrow their Russian elders and claim heaven for themselves. They were preparing to march.

Sazonov, who had been traveling around Europe, arrived in Paris from London on September 20, 1912, close to hysteria at the situation that was developing in the Balkans. Izvolsky at that point seemed to share the Russian foreign minister's anxiety. Poincaré, who met with them, was hardly sympathetic to their concerns, telling his Russian visitors that they were now "trying to put on the brakes" to something they themselves had started.[38]

Sazonov flitted from one point of view to another to like an inebriated hummingbird. He said he wanted to avoid war, but added that he feared it was inevitable, since Austria, hand in hand with Germany, was a mortal threat to Russian interests.

Izvolsky, on the other hand, seemed to take a perverse pleasure in the hounds of hell that he and Sazonov had unleashed. In the fall of 1912, when the Balkan states scored victories in several skirmishes with the Ottomans, he rhapsodized about the future. In a letter of October 23, 1912, Izvolsky wrote Sazonov that a decisive victory by the Balkan allies would "bring into the foreground in its future historic magnitude the question of the struggle of Slavdom not only with Islam but also with Teutonism." In that case, he continued, there would be "no hope of any palliative. It would be necessary to prepare for a great, decisive, universal European war."[39]

Izvolsky persisted in his efforts to gain the unequivocal

support of Poincaré for Russia's Balkan policy. He returned again and again to a simple message: Austria intended to expand her empire all the way to the Aegean Sea, joining Germany in a drive for world domination.

In a note to Sazonov on November 7, Izvolsky reported progress in his propaganda campaign. He wrote that on the question of Austrian territorial expansion in the Balkans, the French were beginning to show enlightenment. Previously, they had restricted themselves to diplomacy in matters affecting only the Balkans, ruling out active intervention. Now, however, Izvolsky wrote, they seemed to realize that Austrian territorial conquests would affect the balance of power in Europe, and therefore France's interests.[40] Finally, on November 17, Izvolsky jubilantly reported a breakthrough. Poincaré told him that if Russia went to war, France would do the same. The French prime minister declared that he now realized that in the resulting conflict, "Germany would stand at Austria's back."[41] France had provided Russia with a blank check.

20 HOLLOW CHIMES OF PEACE

Well-intentioned delegates at the (1878) Congress of Berlin drew maps of disputed areas in the Balkans without ever setting foot on the ground. These amateur cartographers failed to give adequate consideration to ethnographic issues – in the Balkans of all places, where ethnic origin so often defines people's lives. As Edith Durham wrote in 1914, "Solid Albanian districts, which hated all things Slav, were handed over to Montenegro, and solid Slav districts, which asked nothing better than to be Montenegrin or Serb, were handed over to the Turkish Empire. Worse, if possible, tribes and groups of tribes were divided, and this, in a tribal land, should be avoided at almost any price."[1] The mapmakers created frontiers that were, according to Durham, "so impossible that in many places they could not be defined, much less enforced. As the borderers themselves described it, 'The frontiers floated on blood.'"[2]

Izvolsky, crafty genius that he was, saw an opportunity in the unrest caused by the Powers' bungling in mapping the Balkans. While still foreign minister, he had come forward with a scheme for a Balkan federation whose allies would make common cause against the Ottomans. Once the Turks were routed, the Habsburgs were to be the Balkan allies' next targets, but only when St. Petersburg gave the signal for an expanded war. The Balkan Alliance finally materialized in 1912. Between March and October of that year, four Orthodox nations – Montenegro, Serbia, Bulgaria and Greece – signed a series of treaties drawn up by Russian agents. Serbia and Montenegro then engaged in a military free-for-all near the Habsburgs' southern border, more than once raising fears in Vienna of an imminent invasion. Franz Joseph's decision to go to war with Serbia in July 1914 should be seen in the context of events of the previous two years.

King Nicholas of Montenegro opened hostilities with Turkey on October 8, using as an excuse an incident involving an alleged incursion of Ottoman border guards into his kingdom. The other Balkan allies – Bulgaria, Serbia and Greece – followed suit, with war declarations 10 days later. The armies were off, sometimes cooperating, oftentimes competing for the same territory, based on ethnic claims owing more to mythology than to fact. Turkish sections of the Balkan peninsula, already the scene of forced Ottomanization, were turned into killing fields.

The conflict, later known as the First Balkan War, had three theaters of operations: in Thrace (mostly in present day Bulgaria), in Macedonia and on the Greco-Turkish frontier. The combined forces soon routed the Turks from most of Europe. The Bulgarians took Adrianople (Edirne). On October 24 they defeated the Turks at Kirk-Kilisse. The Bulgarian army pressed toward Constantinople, but failed to take the capital. The Serbs marched into Kosovo. Serbian and Montenegrin detachments occupied the Sandzak of Novi Pazar, the strategic corridor that the Habsburgs had unwisely turned over to the Turks as part of their 1909 annexation agreement.

Among the allies, King Nicholas was the one most eager for war. In 1910, the Montenegrin ruler had become worried that his hold on the throne, where he had ruled as Prince for

50 years, was slipping. Intending to bolster his prestige, he declared his mountain aerie a kingdom and proclaimed himself King. On a world map Montenegro was scarcely larger than a pinhead. It had a population of 250,000, less than the Habsburg city of Prague at that time. Cetinje, the capital, numbered hardly more than 5,000 souls. Having anointed himself King, Nicholas wanted a real kingdom, rather than a pile of rocks interspersed with a few desultory sprigs of grass. He had lusted after the verdant meadows of Herzegovina, only to have that land rudely snatched from him by the Habsburg annexation in 1908. Nicholas then turned his sights toward Albania to his south.

Nicholas portrayed himself as a friend to the Orthodox Catholic communities of Albania, who were suffering under the Young Turks' policy of forced Ottomanization.[3] However, charity was hardly what the Montenegrin King was about. The turmoil in the neighboring province pleased Nicholas because it helped him rally his subjects for an invasion of the region. As for the Muslims, Nicholas despised them, as they would soon find out.

During negotiations with Nicholas for the Balkan league treaty, the Russians specifically warned him against unilateral moves in Albania or Macedonia. Attempting to make sure that the Montenegrin King correctly understood the need to delay the gratification of conquest until the proper season, St. Petersburg resorted to a time-honored method for controlling its closest Balkan friend. As a Jubilee present for Nicholas, in 1910 the Russians promised him 600,000 rubles annually. The generous stipend, part of a military convention, came with knotty strings attached. The Montenegrin King was required to obtain Russian permission before engaging in any offensive alliance and he was to allow the Russians to use the small Montenegrin army whenever they wanted its help.[4] Nicholas bowed politely to the Russians' demands. For the Montenegrin King, however, such promises were like marks in a running stream.

The Montenegrin army's departure for war occasioned a national celebration. The little capital of Cetinje was decked out as for a festival. Headsmen of the Montenegrin clans and their kinsmen, fresh from their fortress-like stone houses in the mountain hollows, their weapons at the ready, gathered for goodbyes before marching off to fight. Bells rang; the crowd cheered. Babies looked on wide-eyed. Queen Milena and the princesses sobbed. The King's son fired the first shot. King Nicholas rushed off to Podgorica to join his troops.

The mood was feral. Shortly before the fighting started, Professor Kovachevitch, a teacher of French and German at the Gymnasium (high school) at Podgorica, told Edith Durham: "Soon you will see noses come in. We shall not leave many a Turk with a nose."

Durham was appalled. "If you do any such swinery," she warned, "you will rightly lose all European sympathy."

The Professor was adamant. "It is our national custom.... Of course we shall cut noses; we always have."[5]

Even though the Russians provided the Montenegrin army with a number of military officers, the troops' initial efforts went poorly. Hardly any planning had gone into the war. Lulled by a fatalistic belief that God was on their side, the Montenegrins had marched first and considered the consequences later. The country's tribesmen had the unsettling custom of attacking their enemies head on (some also followed tradition by attaching their victims' severed heads to their belts as they continued to fight). This savage style of warfare led to inordinate injuries. With only 150 hospital beds for the entire army, soon there were problems as to where to treat the writhing wounded. In spite of setbacks, however, the Montenegrins clamored for battle. Having grown to stature amid meadows edged in among piles of rock and surrounded by mountains of stone, these warriors were a particularly hardy lot. The tall, dark-haired clansmen soldiered on, aiming for Scutari, an ancient fortified Albanian town of 35,000 at the toe end of the lake by the same name.[6] The population was overwhelmingly Muslim.

The Serbs crossed the rugged mountains of northern Albania and headed for the Adriatic sea. By mid-November they had occupied Durazzo and San Giovanni de Medua on the coast.[7] This rattled nerves in Vienna, since these ports were near the monarchy's southernmost extremities. On November 25, Serbian Prime Minister Nikola Pasic declared that his nation must have about 50 kilometers of coastline between Alessio (Lezha) and Durazzo (Durres) in Albania. The British minister to Serbia, writing in November 1912, noted the Serbs' excessive exuberance. In his words, the Serbs were "quite off their heads, with visions of blue seas and Serbian ships in the offing bringing home the wealth of the Indies."[8]

In Vienna, near hysteria seized the public after news arrived that Serbian and Montenegrin troops had pitched their tents near the Habsburg Empire's southern borders. For a few weeks that fall a war party controlled the dialogue at the court. Two of the Habsburgs' most powerful army officers, Blasius Schemua, Chief of the General Staff, and Oskar Potiorek, Governor General of Bosnia-Herzegovina, clamored for military action. Potiorek, during a single four-week period, presented Franz Joseph with various mobilization options on 13 different occasions.[9]

The crisis, which came to a head in December 1912, was the first of three episodes in a matter of months in which the Austrians came close to war – twice with Serbia and once with Montenegro. Each time the Habsburg monarch chose peace. However, these crises left many of those within the empire's circle of power convinced that the only way to end the constant bullying of Austria by Serbia (and Montenegro) was to fight back. That might have been simple enough if it hadn't been for a threat of Russian intervention.

Franz Joseph took steps to shore up the monarchy's defenses; that was as far as he intended to go, unless pushed. On October 28, 1912, following a meeting of the monarchy's Common Ministerial Council, Franz Joseph approved a 50 percent increase in troops in Bosnia and Herzegovina. Then reports arrived that the Russians were mobilizing on the empire's Galician frontier. The Austrians countered by increasing armed strength along their northeastern border by 50 percent. Archduke Franz Ferdinand, usually firmly on the side of peace but now out of patience with Serbia's stubborn intractability, leaned toward war. At the Archduke's insistence, Franz Joseph reinstated Conrad as Chief of the General Staff and replaced dovish General Moritz von Auffenberg with hawkish General Alexander von Krobatin.

Berchtold and other civilian ministers who wanted a diplomatic solution to the crisis realized that their voices were being drowned out by the squawks of the militarists. The Austrian foreign minister arranged for a showdown at Schönbrunn on December 11 where the Emperor would have the opportunity to hear both sides of the argument. Berchtold saw to it that Conrad and Krobatin, the inveterate war hawks, were not invited. Franz Ferdinand gave his reasons for wanting to settle accounts with Serbia and Montenegro – among them his belief that the Russian military was not yet prepared for war. Berchtold urged that the Austrians wait for the outcome of a Powers' conference, set to start on December 16 in London. He added that he expected Germany to oppose a military solution. Franz Joseph sided with his foreign minister. The Emperor understood that an aggressive action against Serbia almost certainly would draw the Russians into the conflict, regardless of whether the czarist army was prepared to intervene. The recent troop movements in Galicia suggested this. Franz Ferdinand soon came around to the Emperor's way of thinking.[10]

In the interest of ending the crisis, Franz Joseph instructed Berchtold to pare down the monarchy's demands dramatically, adopting what American historian Williamson terms a "policy of containment." The Austrians would make only two demands. They were to insist on an independent Albania and they were to continue to refuse to agree to Serbia's having an Adriatic port.[11]

The Emperor had important reasons for wanting an independent Albania. He sought to save the Muslim population from extermination by the Serbian and Montenegrin armies, reports of whose atrocities continued to arrive regularly in Vienna. He also wanted to prevent the Serbians from engorging themselves on Albanian territory in their quest for national aggrandizement.

The Habsburgs had traditionally opposed an Adriatic port for Serbia on grounds that its proximity to southern regions of the monarchy would pose a security threat. They remained worried that the Russians would use their vassal's Adriatic port as a naval base. The Austrians now had additional concerns. They feared that if the Serbs gained control of a strategically located port such as Valona or Durazzo they might join with the increasingly nationalistic Italians, never loyal allies to the Habsburgs, in attempts to restrict or block Habsburg access to the Adriatic.

One would think that the Austrian shift toward a defensive policy would have calmed Russian fears about the monarchy's ambitions in the Balkans. Nothing of the sort happened. While it is possible that Sazonov and Izvolsky failed to understand what the Austrians' policy change meant, it is far more likely that they stuck to their propaganda about the Habsburgs' intentions in the Balkans because this served their own interests. Both men had invested political capital in the notion that the Habsburgs, in collusion with the Germans, entertained vast ambitions for hegemony in the Near East (depicted in the widely used expression Drang nach Osten) and beyond. Nicholas II, insecure and relying on the self-serving and distorted reports emanating from his foreign office, was convinced that the Habsburgs intended to crush what was being portrayed as "helpless little Serbia." The Czar believed that the Austrians then would stomp on whatever lay in their path as they pushed ahead, hand in hand with the Germans, intent on world domination.

Rumors of Austrian plans for conquering the Balkan peninsula and then extending the empire's reach far into the Orient had circulated since at least 1878, when the Habsburgs occupied Bosnia and Herzegovina. The monarchy's detractors repeatedly claimed that the Austrians were scheming to send their army down the Vardar River Valley – the arid corridor that stretches past Skopje and extends through the present Republic of North Macedonia – southward to Salonika in Greece. Even if the Austrians had previously given serious consideration to such schemes, which is unlikely, they definitely had no such intentions during the years prior to the outbreak of war in 1914. Aehrenthal had, after all, volunteered to return the Sandzak of Novi Pazar to Turkey as part of the 1909 annexation settlement.[12] Such a decision would have made no military sense if the monarchy had intended to send its army to Salonika. The Sandzak corridor was the logical route for any army heading through the Vardar River Valley to the south.

It is true that Franz Joseph from time to time expressed hopes of compensating for territory lost in Italy early in his reign with acquisitions in the East. However, Franz Joseph, like most of his Habsburg forebears, was no warrior.[13] The Emperor's interest in the two provinces had more to do with securing the empire's southern holdings, which snaked along the Adriatic coast with no natural barriers to protect them from attack, than with acquiring the twin provinces for their own sake.

Franz Ferdinand's views on the monarchy's Balkan

policy were generally misunderstood. Ultranationalists in Serbia and the annexed provinces believed that the Archduke was hatching diabolical schemes for Teutonic domination of the Balkans. In fact, Franz Ferdinand, showing a clear understanding of the difficulties of Habsburg involvement in the Balkans, had little or no interest in further adventures in the region. The Habsburg heir apparent spelled out his views in an important letter to Berchtold on February 1, 1913.[14] He said he had no doubt that Austria could quickly defeat Serbia in war. However, he said, that would only create more problems. "God spare us, that we should annex Serbia," he wrote, dismissing the little nation as a totally "indebted land" of "regicides and rogues." The Archduke said that, rather than attempting to add new territory to the monarchy, as Emperor he would try to put his own house, the House of Habsburg, in order. Conrad reported that Dr. Oberst von Bardolff, Franz Ferdinand's aide-de-camp, told him that the Archduke had said that he wasn't interested in "a single plum tree or sheep" from Austria's troublesome Balkan neighbor.[15]

Izvolsky, however, as well as Sazonov and various Pan-Slav agents, continued to see to it that a lethal fog of propaganda and paranoia obscured the far simpler imperial aims of the Austrians. The Czar's preoccupation with little Serbia unfortunately also helped blind him to the situation in Russia, where revolutionaries were preparing to overthrow his government. By leading Nicholas II to war, Izvolsky and Sazonov ultimately were to cause the Czar to collude willingly in his own destruction – and in that of the House of Romanov.

On December 3, 1912, the allies agreed to an armistice, ending the First Balkan War. The London Ambassadors' Conference, convened on December 17, 1912, intending to settle issues raised by the conflict. The gathering got off to a promising start, but the delegates soon encountered a welter of contradictions and opposing demands that made viable solutions to the Balkan problems well-nigh impossible. The representatives agreed to an independent Albania, with boundaries guaranteed by the Powers and drawn to include such assets as would "assure the new nation's economic survival,"[16] whatever that meant. Falling into the same rut as had the amateur cartographers at the Congress of Berlin, the representatives in London failed to settle the future nation's boundaries. Their decision to include Scutari and its environs in Albania angered the Montenegrins and Serbians, who coveted these regions for themselves. The Austrians had asked that Ipek, Djakova, Dibra and Prizren be included in Albania, but that request was denied. "This meant," wrote Fay, "according to Austria's contention, that something like half a million Albanians, forming a compact group within the watershed which constitutes the natural geographical boundary of Albania, were to be left to the mercy of Serbian and Montenegrin troops."[17] The Powers denied the Serbians' request for a port, but allowed them commercial access to the Adriatic through an Albanian free port. The Serbs were naturally displeased by this development.

Franz Joseph became convinced that a solution to the Balkan troubles, if it existed, lay with the Russian Czar. Since the 1908 annexation the relationship between Nicholas II and Franz Joseph had been icy. Nevertheless the Emperor, realizing that the future of the monarchy and indeed all of Europe was at stake, sent Prince Gottlieb zu Hohenlohe-Schillingsfürst to Russia on a peace mission. This would be the last time the Emperor tried to solve problems between the House of Habsburg and the House of Romanov with personal diplomacy. The Emperor's envoy carried with him a message from Franz Joseph to the Czar in the monarch's own hand. Hohenlohe arrived in St. Petersburg in early February 1913. He had spent five years as a military attaché at the Romanov court, where he was well regarded.

In his letter to Nicholas II, Franz Joseph declared his

"unbounded friendship" for the Russian Czar. He then went on to say, however, that he considered it his "heartfelt duty" to set straight a misunderstanding regarding Austrian intentions in the Balkans. The Emperor expressed hope that Russia and Austria would stay clear of the Balkan conflict and would work together in the interests of European peace.

Hohenlohe reported that initially the Czar was friendly enough, declaring that he "revered Franz Joseph as a father."[18] And, indeed, the Austrian envoy said he thought that Nicholas II and most of his government seriously wanted to avoid complications with the Habsburgs. Ominously, Hohenlohe could not disabuse the impressionable Czar of his conviction, so carefully and constantly nurtured by Izvolsky and Sazonov, that the Austrians were engaging in devious schemes in the Balkans

Hohenlohe's other impressions were generally negative. The envoy described Sazonov as suspicious and "thickheaded," unwilling to consider the Austrian point of view. Since Nicholas II followed the lead of Sazonov instead of the other way around, the foreign minister's attitude did not bode well for the peace mission – or for peace. Hohenlohe reported that a war party was in the ascendancy at the court.[19] On February 10, 1913, Sazonov wrote Izvolsky that nothing positive had come of the meeting.[20] Izvolsky surely was pleased with this outcome. One of his worst fears was that Nicholas II would reach rapprochement with one or both of the German Powers.

The Czar's reply to Franz Joseph's letter had an accusatory tone. Russia had agreed to the creation of Albania to please Austria, the Czar wrote, but the monarchy wasn't cooperating with the Powers' attempts to settle boundaries for the new state. Behind this criticism was the Russians' insistence that Scutari be awarded either to Serbia or Montenegro rather than to Albania. The Austrians knew that whoever possessed the town would have a strategic foothold less than 100 miles from the Habsburg border. In view of the aggressive behavior of both Serbia and Montenegro, actively being encouraged by Russia, it is hardly surprising that Franz Joseph objected to having either Balkan nation control that fortified town.

In his letter, Nicholas II also questioned why, if the Emperor wanted peace, Habsburg troops remained mobilized on the Galician border. The Czar seemed unaware that the Austrians' increased troop presence in the region came in response to reports of Russian war preparations in the area. Part of the Russian military's Balkan strategy was to tie up as many Austrian forces in Galicia as possible in order to compromise the monarchy's troop strength in the south.

Now, however, the Russians themselves needed their troops elsewhere. Bulgaria's flamboyant King Ferdinand had begun to fancy himself as Emperor of Byzantium. He had even procured a regal costume, said by some to have been purchased from a theatrical supply house, for his triumphal entry into Constantinople at the head of his army. The Czar decided that a Russian show of force was needed to make the cheeky Ferdinand understand that Byzantium was never to be his. To that end, Nicholas II proposed that both the Romanovs and the Habsburgs reduce troops in Galicia. The Emperor eagerly agreed to draw down forces in the region. The Russian and Austrian troop cuts were put in place in March 1913.

While the London ambassadors pondered alternatives, Serbian and Montenegrin forces rained terror on the Balkan countryside. Before heading into battle, the Montenegrins swore that once they controlled Albanian territory they would "stamp out the whole Muslim population."[21] The Serbs, in sending troops into Kosovo as well as Albania, had vowed to accomplish the same kind of ethnic annihilation. Both armies were making good on their intentions.

Edith Durham, who worked as a volunteer helping care

for the Montenegrin wounded, confirmed that the earlier boasts by the Podgorica language professor about taking noses were true. The troops were engaging in unspeakable acts. She wrote that "They all glorified in their bestiality, and related in detail their nose-cutting exploits, imitating the impaling of a Turk upon a bayonet, and the slicing off of his nose and upper lip, and the shouted advice to the still living man: 'Go home and show your wives how pretty you are!' All, with very few exceptions, had taken noses. An old man of 70 had taken only two, but excused himself on the grounds of having taken ill at the beginning."[22]

The Serbs practiced equally heinous cruelties. They buried people alive or, perhaps worse still, as people from one village told Durham, "they amused themselves by bleeding some of their defenseless victims to death. Not quickly, as you do sheep, but slowly. They made little cuts on the wrists and the elbows and on the necks, so that they should be 'a long time dying.'"[23] Not only the Muslims but also the Roman Catholics were tortured. The bishop of Prizren was reported to have witnessed an episode in which 400 Roman Catholic Albanians were forced to visit an Orthodox church, where they were treated brutally.[24] Franz Joseph, taking seriously the Habsburg family's historic role as protector of the Roman Catholic Albanians, urged the Powers to coordinate an effort to stop the violence in the region.

The Powers dallied. The Russians tended the boiling Balkan cauldron. On February 26, Conrad reported the appearance of 23 Russian officers in Durazzo and Antivari (Bar). Two days later, 49 additional Russian officers and 70 Russian junior officers in Russian uniform arrived by Greek ship, with saddles and riding equipment.[25] These were obviously intended as reinforcements for the Montenegrin army.

The London ambassadors "invited" the Serbs and Montenegrins to leave Albanian territory. The Balkan armies paid no heed to these politely phrased demands. In mid-March, Conrad reported that 60,000 troops were massed on the boundary with Austria, near Scutari.[26]

Even though the Montenegrins had help from the Serbs, taking Scutari proved difficult. The Turks had spent months fortifying the town, as the attackers were surprised to discover. The Montenegrins could easily have sent spies to report on such activity and to provide logistical information, but apparently they had not thought of that. However, the troops never lost their determination to take Scutari, a determination shared by King Nicholas, who vowed to "fight to the last goat and carriage" for the coveted territory.

Franz Joseph's reaction to the Scutari crisis is important in understanding his behavior during the crisis of July 1914. The Emperor was beginning to set limits to his politics of peace. He had turned to the Powers for help and gotten nowhere. He had tried personal diplomacy with the Czar. That had failed. He did not intend to allow the Montenegrins to establish a stronghold at Scutari.

A conversation between Berchtold and the Emperor in early March 1913, passed along by Conrad, shows the evolution in Franz Joseph's thinking. The Foreign Minister told Conrad that he had warned Franz Joseph that the Montenegrins might be unwilling to leave Scutari once they took it. "Then that means war," Franz Joseph told Berchtold. The Emperor added that he hoped the situation could be resolved peacefully, or at least with limited military involvement.[27] About two weeks later Berchtold had another audience with Franz Joseph. Again, according to Conrad, Berchtold told Franz Joseph that a peaceful blockade in the vicinity of Scutari was unlikely to have much effect. The Emperor replied: "Then there will have to be shooting." Berchtold responded that shooting from ships would not suffice. Troops on the ground would be required. For Franz Joseph that was a line he was not yet willing to cross: "That would mean war, which I do not want,"[28] he said.

The situation involving Scutari remained at an impasse. The London ambassadors, lacking the ability, or the will, to force events to a conclusion, merely ratcheted up their language. Previously the ambassadors had invited the Serbians and Montenegrins to leave Albania. Now they ordered them to do so. The Balkan generals ignored the mandate.

Frustrated by the continuing stalemate, Franz Joseph ordered a naval demonstration. On March 30, British and Italian ships joined the Austrians; so did the French and Germans a little later. The Russians refused to take part out of loyalty to their Balkan friends. Participants in the demonstration gathered in the Bay of Katar, under the shadow of Montenegro's Mount Lovcen, the towering mountain of rock that stands sentry over the rugged reaches of the nation's uplands. The Balkan troops, encamped a few miles to the southeast and beyond the range of naval fire, didn't blink.

During this second crisis, Franz Joseph moved closer to war; he hoped that if it came it would be only a local conflict. News came from Cetinje that the Montenegrins were mobilizing near the Bosnia-Herzegovinian border. On April 3, Conrad learned that a Russian ship, ignoring the Powers' naval demonstration, had landed at Antivari (Bar), some miles south of the Bay of Katar, bringing war materials for Montenegro.[29] The Serbs were reported to be landing additional troops at Shengjin, an Adriatic port near Scutari. There were now, by Austrian count, some 110,000 Serbs on Albanian soil.[30] The Serbs temporarily withdrew some of their troops in order to fight the Bulgarians, who were infringing on territory the Serbs had recently occupied, but they soon returned to Albania, continuing their ethnic cleansing. The Emperor ordered pack horses for Bosnia and Herzegovina and called up non-active military troops.

Defying not only the odds but also the international

community, King Nicholas of Montenegro on April 22, 1913, took Scutari from the Turks. "For the first time since 1405," says Treadway, "the ancient capital of Zeta was in Montenegrin hands."[31] The highly fortified town had not been conquered. Rather, the wily Nicholas had made a bargain with Essad Pasha, the Ottoman military commander, allowing him and his army of 20,000 men free passage out of the town and permitting them to take along rifles, field guns and other supplies. According to Treadway, Nicholas also offered the Turkish commander a bribe and a promise that he would be named King of Albania.[32] The next day Essad greeted Crown Prince Danilo at the entrance of the town and formally surrendered. Montenegrin flags flew defiantly over the town and its fortifications.

Two hours after midnight on April 23, 21 cannon shots were fired over Cetinje, jolting Edith Durham out of her bed, fearing that someone had bombed the palace. The loud salutes signaled that Scutari had fallen.[33] Despite the hour, the town celebrated. Men, women and children turned out, jumping in delight. Wounded soldiers limped joyfully down the streets. The demonstrations continued the following day. Drunken citizens shot guns into the air and called out, "Down with Austria! Down with Baron Giesl! (the Austrian ambassador to Montenegro) ... Down with all the Great Powers!" Later Gustav von Hubka, the Austrian military attaché in Cetinje, recalled that "a donkey attired in an old dresscoat was paraded around the streets, an anti-Austrian placard around its neck."[34]

The German ambassador to Vienna, Heinrich von Tschirschky, described the reaction in the Habsburg capital as one of "smothered rage." Berchtold got much of the blame for his perceived inaction.[35] Franz Joseph continued to press the Powers to engage in joint measures regarding Scutari. During a meeting with the Emperor on April 25, 1913, Berchtold told Franz Joseph that if the Ambassadors' Conference got no results, Austria might need to mobilize.

Franz Joseph agreed, but said not to mobilize against Serbia, only Montenegro.[36] What the Emperor wanted was a solution to the immediate problem of Scutari, not a wider war.

The London ambassadors, alarmed at the deteriorating situation, again flexed their flabby muscles. On April 27 they sent an envoy to Cetinje to deliver a démarche ordering Nicholas to evacuate Scutari. The envoy was informed that the King was not at home to visitors. Thumbing his nose at the Great Powers, Nicholas left word that he was busy with Easter celebrations and would get back to them later. Even the Russian minister was outraged at the King's behavior. On April 30 the Montenegrin government, still defiant, refused the démarche, voting unanimously to continue opposition to the Great Powers' demands.[37]

On May 2, Berchtold presided over a crucial meeting of the monarchy's Joint Ministerial Council. Scutari topped the agenda. The council eventually accepted Berchtold's proposal for the mobilization of Austrian forces against Montenegro at Scutari.

At this point, King Nicholas found himself abandoned by his friends and allies. The Russians, having already warned the Montenegrin ruler that they opposed his occupation of Scutari, now turned their back on their unruly vassal. The King's Balkan league cohorts then followed suit, refusing to support their Slav brother in a last stand for Scutari. With Austrian forces on his kingdom's border ready to strike, Nicholas decided that, as Treadway puts it, "the Montenegrin falcon, deserted by all its friends, was no match for the Habsburg eagle in physical combat." Instead of risking the loss of his gains east of Podgorica and in the Sandzak, the Montenegrin King declared himself willing to submit to the "will of Europe." He surrendered Scutari unconditionally.[38] On May 12, the Montenegrins departed Scutari, burning villages and taking noses as they went.

King Nicholas was furious at the Russians for failing to

support him against the other Powers. The King even wrote the dowager Empress (Czarina) Marie of Russia, asking her to close Cetinje's Russian Institute, a girls' school she had founded in 1869. The Russians were deeply insulted at this move by their Balkan vassal. Alexandr Giers, St. Petersburg's minister to Montenegro, went so far as to say that his government "doubted the sanity of the King."[39]

The Montenegrin estrangement from Russia did not, however, last long. The Black Mountain princesses, Nicholas's two daughters who were wives of Romanov archdukes and in residence at the Russian court, regularly practiced propaganda along with their embroidery. Now they stepped up their efforts, portraying Montenegro and Serbia as victims of the Austrians' evil intrigues in the Balkans. These young women were to play a significant role in persuading the gullible Czar and those in his immediate circle that Austria was an enemy that could only be put down by war.

The Treaty of London ending the First Balkan War was signed on May 30, 1913. But having gotten a taste of blood, the Balkan allies wanted more. Greece was already considering more mischief against Bulgaria. Serbia and Bulgaria were in a snarling mood. Serbia, having been deprived of what she considered her rightful due on the Adriatic, now demanded Macedonian territory south of the line from Mt. Golem to Lake Ohrid, which the Bulgarians claimed. The Bulgarians felt that the Serbians already had received more than their share of the spoils.

Sazonov, trying to manage the situation to Russia's advantage, sent a message to his minister in Belgrade, dated May 6, 1913, to be passed on to the Serbians. It adds to the mounting evidence that the Russians were encouraging their Balkan friends to engage in enemy acts against the Habsburg monarchy. The message said: "Serbia's promised land lies in the territory of the present Austria-Hungary and not there where she is now making efforts and where the Bulgarians stand in her way. Under these circumstances it is of vital interest to Serbia to maintain her alliance with Bulgaria on the one hand and, on the other, to accomplish with steady and patient work the necessary degree of preparedness for the inevitable struggle of the future. Time works on the side of Serbia and for the ruin of her enemies, who already show evident signs of decay. Explain all this to the Serbians."[40]

The Russians continued to worry that these restive nations would trigger a general war before the czarist troops were ready to take on the Austrians and Germans. Nicholas II sent personal telegrams to the kings of Serbia and Bulgaria reminding them that they had promised to let Russia mediate if they had disputes. The feuding neighbors agreed to come to the Russian table. Sazonov prepared for negotiations. Then word came that on the night of June 29-30, 1913, Bulgaria, in a quarrel over territory in Macedonia, had suddenly attacked the Serbian army at Bregalnica River. The onslaught caught the Serbians unaware. Since the Bulgarian and Serbian camps were adjacent, and because they were still pretending to be allies, most of the astounded soldiers were confused about whom they were fighting. Montenegrin forces, camped a few kilometers away and hearing the uproar, ran to the battlefield in their underwear.

The Second Balkan War ended almost as soon as it began. Romania and Turkey joined Greece and Serbia in fighting the Bulgarians, who were defeated in a few days.

On July 22-23, the Turks retook Adrianople (Edirne). It had been captured earlier by the Bulgarians after a long siege. For Izvolsky, who continued to have a heavy hand in Russia's Balkan policy – albeit from Paris – the loss of Adrianople was a serious blow. He had intended for the Russians to use the strategically located city as a base for an attack on Constantinople and the Straits, only 133 miles away.

Izvolsky, always swift on his feet, now came up with a new plan for realizing the Russian dream. It called for czarist forces to advance against the Ottomans in Asia, thus opening a backdoor route to Byzantium.[41] To that end, the Russian foreign office raised what is known as the Armenian question, demanding that the Turks instigate reforms in that unhappy region of the Ottoman Empire. The Porte, offended at the violation of the Sultan's sovereignty, refused. The Russians were now positioned to intervene as the Armenian Orthodox Christians' protector and to advance on Constantinople and the Straits from the east.

Izvolsky's scheme might have succeeded had it not come under fire from an unexpected source. The French strongly objected to Russian intervention in Ottoman Asia, claiming it would disrupt the lucrative business of French bankers in the region. This was true. But historian Friedrich Stieve, basing his statement on extensive archival research, suggests that something more significant was behind the French opposition to the Russian initiative. A hint emerges, Stieve says, in a report filed in February 1913 by Count Alexander Benckendorff, the Russian ambassador in London. "France is on her hind legs again,"[42] the Count wrote. Poincaré had become President of France the previous month. He and his supporters were salivating for a European war that would allow France to win back Alsace-Lorraine from the Germans. The French President apparently had hoped that Austria would attack Serbia during or after the First Balkan War, inevitably bringing Russia, and then Germany, into the conflict. The Austrians had persevered with their peace politics, leaving Poincaré and his war party with their tongues hanging out. The French President and his supporters were committed to the destruction of Germany, their hereditary enemy. They believed that this could only occur in a war between the Entente and Central Powers.[43] The last thing Poincaré and his friends wanted, Stieve suggests, was for the Russians to gain control of the Straits and Constantinople on their own, avoiding the European conflict that the war party in Paris so desperately desired.[44]

In deference to the French allies, Izvolsky abandoned his latest scheme for control of Constantinople and the Straits and returned to beating the drums for his European war.

The Treaty of Bucharest ended the Second Balkan War on August 10, 1913. "The chimes of peace ... have a hollow sound," wrote Berchtold, who had been present at the negotiations.[45] By delivering the weary inhabitants of whole areas into the hands of their hereditary enemies, the agreement prepared the ground for new atrocities.

The Bulgarians, soundly punished for their midnight attack on their erstwhile allies, lost territory to Rumania and were stripped of most of their gains from fighting the Ottomans. In a separate treaty, the Ottomans were awarded Adrianople and Kirk-Kilisse, previously occupied by Bulgaria.

The Serbians, having been attacked by the Bulgarians, were amply rewarded in the peace settlement. The Serbians received Kosovo, so important to the kingdom's national myth. Serbia's population grew from 3 million to almost 4.5 million. Most of the territory that nation acquired had a predominantly Bulgarian population. The jubilant Serbs intended to force the Bulgars to forget their ethnic background and enter happily into their new identity under the Greater Serbian umbrella. Montenegro grew by 3,185 square miles and roughly doubled her population – acquiring many Albanian Muslims in the process.[46] Serbia received part of Novi Pazar, gaining a common border with Montenegro. The unification of Serbia and Montenegro seemed likely. The Habsburgs could hardly be sanguine about this development.

While the Serbs had enjoyed enormous territorial gains, their appetite for expansion remained unsated. Prime Minister Pasic seemed swept up in megalomania as he imagined Serbia's brilliant future. Speaking to a Greek colleague, M. Politis, at the end of the Bucharest peace conference, he said: "The first round is won; now we must prepare for the second, against Austria."[47]

The Balkan Alliance had failed. Russia's grand experiment in political and geographical engineering had produced unintended consequences. The Turks had, indeed, been driven out of Europe, save for Constantinople and her immediate surroundings. But Russia's four vassal states had failed to wait for the command signaling the start of the epic confrontation of Teutons and Slavs. The Balkan allies fell to fighting among themselves, intent on settling ancient scores.

And in the autumn of 1913 the Habsburgs confronted a third crisis. The London ambassadors, having agreed at the end of the First Balkan War to an independent Albania, still hadn't fixed the borders of the newborn state. They established three commissions which were to assure that Albania was viable. One commission was to determine the southern frontier between Albania and Greece; another was to fix the northern boundary between Serbia and Montenegro; a third, the Commission of International Control, was to attempt to administer Albania until the Great Powers agreed on a ruler for the new state.

The commissioners dallied, dotting bureaucratic I's and crossing procedural t's before setting off on their Balkan mission. There were more delays as they attempted the rough mountainous terrain, over trails never intended for automobiles and hardly fit for horses. In the South, local Greek officials resorted to devious ploys to persuade the commission that the majority of inhabitants spoke Greek and were wildly eager to join Constantine's kingdom. The Greeks forced the Muslim population to stay indoors and remain silent, the commissioners wrote in a complaint to Athens. In the north, Serbian troops often stopped, or even arrested, members of the commission.[48]

The Serbs took advantage of the hiatus created by the Powers' ineptitude and occupied Albanian territory they only recently had been ordered to vacate. Reports reached Vienna that Serbian forces had even expanded into new areas.[49] The invading troops took over as many as 179 villages, running their inhabitants out, committing the usual atrocities.

The London ambassadors' failure to defend the nation that the Powers themselves had created disgusted the Austrians. Many people at the Viennese court were coming to the conclusion that the Habsburgs would have to depend on themselves in settling disputes that threatened the monarchy's interests. Berchtold began seriously considering a military confrontation to force the Serbs to decamp from Albania. A state visit by Pasic to Vienna on October 3, 1913, did nothing to change his mind. The prime minister refused to promise that the Serbs would respect Albanian boundaries. Meeting that same day, the monarchy's joint council pondered Austria's options. Count Stephen Tisza, who had joined the council after becoming Hungarian Prime Minister, came out on June 6 in favor of strong measures against Serbia. The opinion of this powerful Magyar carried weight. By the end of the session the council members unanimously endorsed a military solution if peaceful efforts failed. Franz Joseph was of a similar mind with the joint council.

The Austrian Foreign Minister sent the Serbs a message, requesting that they withdraw from Albanian territory. Sazonov, confronted with a war for which the Russians still were not prepared, urged Belgrade to back down. The Serbian prime minister ignored the Austrian request as well as Sazonov's admonition. On October 17, Berchtold sent the Serbs an ultimatum giving Belgrade eight days to remove their troops from Albanian lands. Reflecting their extreme frustration with the gaping incompetence of the London Conference, the Habsburg ministers acted without consulting the other Powers.[50]

Both Franz Joseph and Berchtold now believed that the survival of the monarchy lay in the balance. The Habsburg monarchy was being beaten into the ground. The Emperor was prepared to use force if the Serbs refused to evacuate. The public supported the move. The general feeling in Vienna was that "enough was enough from Belgrade."[51]

The Serbs pulled out of Albania on October 25, 1913, muttering and pillaging and killing as they went. As usual they complained bitterly, claiming that the ultimatum was unfair. The Austrians had taken away territory Serbia had acquired through conquest and blood and given it to the "half-wild Albanians." The Serbs regarded themselves as victims. This caught the attention of fellow Slavs in America. A Chicago expat newspaper, the *Srbobran*, announced on December 3, 1913, that Franz Ferdinand was planning a visit to Bosnia. Serbs were urged to grab whatever they could, "knives, bombs, dynamite," and to "take holy revenge." Early the following year several alienated young Bosnian Serbs began preparing to do just that.

21 DEATH IN SARAJEVO

When Serbian Colonel Dragutin Dimitrijevic learned that Austrian Archduke Franz Ferdinand planned to attend army maneuvers in Bosnia during the summer of 1914, he bristled with anticipation. He saw in the Archduke's visit an opportunity for holy revenge against the Habsburgs. By striking at the heart of the monarchy, Dimitrijevic, known as Apis (the "Holy Bull"), hoped to advance the Greater Serb cause. As ringleader in the ultranationalist society, the Black Hand, Dimitrijevic was experienced in the arts of terrorism. He had masterminded the brutal murders of Serbia's King Alexander and Queen Draga in 1903. He already had in place a network of patriotic advocates of Greater Serbia, stretching from Belgrade to Sarajevo. He immediately began organizing a plot to assassinate the Austrian heir apparent.

The last act of the long drama leading to the outbreak of World War I was about to begin. St. Petersburg traditionally had encouraged intrigues and even attacks against Austrian interests in the Balkans. But now Apis and other militant ultranationalists were about to ratchet up the campaign against the Habsburgs to a level no self-respecting power was likely to accept. The conspirators had reason to believe that they could count on Russian support for their daring assassination scheme, even if it led to war.

Theodor von Sosnosky, a biographer of Franz Ferdinand, provides details of the terrorist plot. They are based on his extensive research during the aftermath of the assassinations.

Apis spread rumors that the monarchy's maneuvers in Bosnia were a smokescreen. He claimed that the Austrian Archduke actually intended to invade and crush Serbia. Apis was a specialist in military tactics. He surely knew that Habsburg troops on maneuvers, lacking service units and munitions, were not equipped for actual combat.[1] What is more, the maneuvers were planned for Tarcin, 15 miles to the west of Sarajevo, a good distance from the Serbian border and a most unlikely place from which to launch an invasion of the neighboring state.[2] Apis didn't let such minutiae deter him. Like most master conspirators, he dealt in falsehoods rather than facts.

Dimitrijevic and his lieutenants, Voja Tankosic and Milan Ciganovic, had no trouble lining up young men full of romantic dreams of becoming heroes in defense of a Greater Serbia. The three volunteers chosen to lead the effort to assassinate the Habsburg heir were young Bosnians who had impressed the Black Hand with their devotion to the radical Serbian idea. These would-be martyrs had much in common with others who have shed their victims' blood on behalf of a misbegotten cause. They were drifters, more or less alienated from their families and society, and angry at a political system that had left them on the outside looking in.

Gavrilo Princip, a hollow-eyed, sickly young man, would take the lead in the assassination scheme. He came from a remote mountain area in western Bosnia near the Dalmatian border. Frustrated by his inability to get an education in Bosnia, he had made his way to Belgrade, where he was able to continue his studies. He fell in with a crowd of would-be terrorists. For perhaps the first time in his life he was part of a group in which he felt appreciated.

Nedjelko Cabrinovic was another conspirator at the center of the plot. He also had spent time in Belgrade, working in the Serbian government printing office. Returning home to Sarajevo with anarchist journals among his few belongings, he ran into trouble with his mother, who burned some of the treatises. Cabrinovic's father, who operated a small café in Sarajevo, was so concerned about his son's irredentist tendencies that on June 4 he reported the young man to the police. They failed to take seriously what the elder Cabrinovic told them, even though the youth had been arrested previously and banned from Sarajevo.

A third conspirator, Trifko Grabez, was the son of a Greek Orthodox village priest. He had been expelled from the Bosnian town of Tuzla in the fall of 1912 for striking a teacher in the face. He, too, had espoused revolutionary ideas in Belgrade.

The plotters trained for their terrorist assignment at a park in the Serbian capital. Apis's lieutenant, Cabrinovic, a firearms expert, instructed the young men in the use of their weapons. Toward the end of May 1914, the three youths left for Sarajevo on what they thought of as their holy mission. They carried six bombs and four guns. The bombs came from the state weapons depot; Dimitrijevic had bought the guns specifically for the occasion.

At every stage of their journey, not only in Serbia but also in Bosnia, sympathizers were on hand to help. A visiting card here, a letter of introduction there, a carton of Stefanie cigarettes in one instance, as a sign, opened doors for the conspirators.[3]

Fearing that three strangers traveling together might attract the attention of the local populace, the youths split up before heading into Bosnia.[4] Cabrinovic crossed the River Drina at Mali Zvornik. Arriving in Tuzla on May 31, he made his way to Sarajevo. Princip and Grabez went to

Ljesnica, where a farmer was to take them across the Drina into Bosnia. Failing to find him, they spent one night in the guardhouse, compliments of a friendly government official. The conspirators spent a second night on the river bank. The farmer finally arrived and the party left. They were accompanied by a customs official, who warned the youths to guard carefully the secret of what they were transporting, whatever it was; otherwise, he said, they might lose their heads.

The conspirators weren't always careful to conceal their weapons. They seemed convinced that those they met were silent sympathizers with their cause. When Princip and Grabez spent the night on the bank of the River Drina, they even got in some shooting practice. At Trnova Gornja, where they had a meal with a farmer, the youths laid aside their weapons, which they had strapped to their bodies. They borrowed two large containers in which they placed their bombs and firearms – while their host looked on quietly.

Princip and Grabez, worried that security might be tight in Sarajevo in anticipation of Franz Ferdinand's visit, persuaded a cinema director in Tuzla named Jovanovic to hide the weapons in his house. Another conspirator, Ilic, the son of a cobbler and a washerwoman who lived in Sarajevo, was to pick up the cache at a designated spot. The cinema director went there, carrying the bombs and revolvers in a pasteboard sugar box. Failing to find Ilic, Jovanovic left the explosives under his raincoat in the railway waiting room and later in a friend's shop in care of a child.[5] Finally, Ilic showed up and took the weapons to Sarajevo.

Upon arriving in the Bosnian capital, the conspirators staked out their positions along the route that the Habsburg entourage was expected to take. The youths waited, whiling away their days in out-of-the-way cafes.

Although Franz Ferdinand's trip to Bosnia attracted considerable attention, his visit was nothing extraordinary for Habsburg imperials. During his long reign, Franz Joseph had routinely traveled to far-flung locations in the empire to watch his army in action. Now, however, the aging Emperor could hardly sit on a horse, a requirement for attending maneuvers. It was time for his nephew, the heir to the throne, to show the flag. "Peasants like to see their princes," Oskar Potiorek, the Governor of Bosnia, had told the Archduke.[6]

As the date for the maneuvers neared, Franz Ferdinand became increasingly nervous about the trip. He undoubtedly knew of the Chicago newspaper's call for revenge, directed specifically at him. Assassination attempts in the two annexed provinces were nothing extraordinary. In 1910, a law student named Bogdan Zerajic had stalked Franz Joseph during the Emperor's visit to the region, but lost his nerve when the time came to shoot the monarch.[7] Three Austrian border officials had recently been murdered, with Serbian agents suspected. In early June, Franz Ferdinand sought the Emperor's advice about whether the trip to Sarajevo was a good idea. Perhaps the Archduke hoped that his uncle would tell him to cancel his trip. The Emperor said, "Do what you want."

Sophie Chotek, who had received the title of Countess of Hohenberg after her morganatic marriage to the Archduke, urged her husband to call off his visit to Bosnia. Terrorists weren't her concern. Rather, she was worried that the summer heat might cause a recurrence of the tuberculosis that had almost killed the Archduke in his youth.

However, it was partly for Sophie that her husband wanted to make the trip. His wife, lacking the requisite blood line for a royal union, was excluded by protocol from most court events in Vienna. In Bosnia, such rules would not apply. Franz Ferdinand wanted his wife to enjoy the honors he thought she deserved.

Plus he wanted to show the flag. Of course he would go.

Europe in the summer of 1914 was divided into two

camps, with the Triple Alliance (Austria, Germany and a reluctant Italy) on one side, and the Triple Entente (France, Russia and Britain) on the other. The incendiary potential of these alliances made every move by royals suspect.

Tongues wagged when on June 13 the impetuous Kaiser Wilhelm II of Germany roared up the tree-lined lane to Konopiste, Franz Ferdinand's castle near Prague, for a visit. There is no evidence that the Kaiser had anything sinister in mind. He had a habit of dropping in on fellow royals, whether or not he had an agenda. The Archduke's rose garden was famous and the German Kaiser wanted to see it (it failed to reach full bloom until several days after Wilhelm II had departed). Other guests also were present. The visitors piled into cars and toured the lovely surroundings, including the forest across from the castle's little lake. The trees, chosen by Franz Ferdinand himself so that their foliage formed variegated shades of green were, at least, in full leaf.

Franz Ferdinand and the Kaiser naturally talked about the worsening Balkan situation. Foreign Minister Berchtold, who arrived later, recalled that the conversation centered primarily on domestic issues. These included ways to prevent the Magyars in Hungary from persecuting the region's ethnic Romanians.[8]

Nevertheless, rumors swirled, spread by Wickham Steed, an English journalist whose articles tended to have an anti-Habsburg slant, as well as by French writers. Some press reports claimed that during the visit, Franz Ferdinand and Wilhelm II had plotted to redesign the map of Europe, with the ultimate intention of world domination.[9] This conspiracy theory increasingly took root in the minds of the many enemies of Germany and Austria.

A few days after the Kaiser's visit, Franz Ferdinand left Konopiste for Bosnia. Sophie was to travel separately, meeting her husband at Ilidze, a spa village known for its restorative waters, just outside Sarajevo. On June 24 the

Archduke arrived at Korcula, an island south of Split, in a 20,000-ton battleship, the *Virabes Unitis*. The sea voyage from Trieste to the little Adriatic island, thought to be the birthplace of Marco Polo, had taken 24 hours.[10]

Initially, the visit went well. On Korcula, Franz Ferdinand was officially greeted by General Oskar Potiorek, who then accompanied the Archduke and his entourage up the Narenta Valley to Mostar. The capital of Herzegovina is famous for its lovely 16th-century arched stone bridge, spanning a river of emerald green that cuts through the heart of the town. During much of Mostar's long and troubled history the bridge failed to unite the mostly Muslim families who lived on one side of the river, and the mostly Orthodox and Roman Catholics on the other. But the Habsburg heir apparent, pleased with the welcome he received, telegraphed to Vienna that the greeting was enthusiastic and included all faiths.

The maneuvers at Tarcin were directed at protecting the Ivan Pass, connecting Sarajevo with the Adriatic. Some 22,000 men participated in the exercises in high, treeless karst country. The war games, held on June 26, passed off smoothly.[11]

Sophie joined her husband at Ilidze, where windows of shops were decorated with pictures of Franz Ferdinand and with flags and flowers. The royal couple was in a happy mood. Once the maneuvers ended, Franz Ferdinand and Sophie planned to spend the day in Sarajevo, the Bosnian capital, a bustling town of 50,000 with winding streets, nestled in a narrow valley along the banks of the River Miljacka. There were to be official meetings, of course, but the royal couple also intended to go shopping. One attraction was an oriental-style bazaar where colorfully dressed hill people sold copper crafts, handwoven rugs and elaborate embroidered cloths. As usual, Franz Ferdinand would be looking for St. George's art, for which he had an insatiable appetite, regardless of its quality.

The Archduke had recently learned techniques for haggling and he wanted to practice them. Destiny decreed otherwise.

It was June 28, St. Vitus Day, a most unfortuitous choice for a visit by Habsburg royalty since on that day in 1389 the Serbs had been defeated by the Turks at Kosovo Polje. St. Vitus Day was an emotionally charged holiday for Serbs outside as well as inside that nation. Why Austrian officials chose that day, with its cultural sensitivities and potential for perceived affronts, remains a mystery.

On the morning of the royal visit the conspirators took up their posts on the quay along the banks of the river, anticipating that this was to be the route the royal procession would take. Due to the summer heat, the river was reduced to a trickle, its rocks protruding like dry bones. Four more terrorists joined the group. They too stationed themselves at points along the expected route.[12]

When Franz Joseph had visited Sarajevo four years before, 1,000 uniformed police, along with a plethora of plainclothesmen, had been on the streets. During Franz Ferdinand's visit only minimal security forces were on duty, reportedly at the Archduke's request. In visiting King Carol I of Romania in 1909, he had been annoyed at being cordoned off from the public.[13] Also, the authorities wanted to avoid anything giving the impression of a display of armed might.[14]

At around 10 a.m. the imperial couple reviewed troops, then headed for the town hall by automobile. The mayor and police chief were in the lead car. The royal couple's automobile, with its top rolled back, came second in the procession. The heir apparent was in full uniform, Sophie in a white dress and a large hat. General Potiorek sat facing them.[15]

Suddenly a bomb landed on the folded convertible cover of the car in which the royals were riding. It bounced off, hit the street and exploded, injuring two passengers in the car behind the royal couple.[16] The bomb thrower, later identified as Cabrinovic, sprang over the railing into the nearly dry river-bed, where the police caught him. Franz Ferdinand yelled, "Come on, the fellow is insane, gentlemen. Let us proceed with our program."

At city hall officials milled around in formal dress and fezzes, preparing to bestow the usual greetings on the arriving royals. A pale and angry Franz Ferdinand, his heavily pomaded moustache quivering, rushed in and confronted the officials. He lashed out: "I make you a visit and you receive me with a bomb!"[17] After the ceremonial greetings ended, Franz Ferdinand and Sophie decided to head to the hospital to see the wounded man. General Potiorek assured Franz Ferdinand that the streets were safe. The entourage started off. The driver of the first car apparently didn't understand instructions that he was to change his route. He turned at the Lateiner Bridge, as he had done previously, and the second car followed. As soon as the drivers realized their mistake they stopped their cars, preparing to turn around.

Gavrilo Princip, positioned on the right side of the vehicles, fired two shots. One bullet hit Franz Ferdinand and another hit his wife. For a minute both royals remained upright in their seats. Then the Countess fell into the lap of her husband, as if she were trying to protect him. Franz Ferdinand was shot in a carotid artery. A bullet had struck Sophie in her lower body, causing inner bleeding.[18] The Archduke's tight bodice, into which he was sewn, is said to have cost him his life. He said, "Soferl! Soferl! Don't die! Stay alive for our children!" and died. Sophie was already dead.

Princip was seized and beaten up. He tried to shoot himself, failed, took cyanide; that failed, too. He would be sent to Terezin, a prison not far from Prague later infamous as a Nazi prison camp for Jews. Princip died there in 1918 of tuberculosis of the bone. He never publicly repented of his crimes.

Most people, upon hearing that an obscure Archduke had been assassinated in faraway Sarajevo, probably gave the news little more than a passing thought. But on June 28, 1914, the death knell pealed for Old Europe.

That Saturday, Franz Joseph was at Schönbrunn, the Habsburg palace on the outskirts of Vienna. The Emperor, suffering from bronchial problems, planned to spend some weeks at Bad Ischl in hopes that the clear mountain air of the Salzkammergut would restore his health.

Count Eduard Graf von Paar, the Emperor's adjutant general, handed him the telegram with the news from Sarajevo. According to Albert Freiherr von Margutti, who was Paar's aide, Count Paar gave him this account: Franz Joseph, having begun to read the message, acted as though he had been struck. He closed his eyes, appearing deep in thought. Then, the story goes, the Emperor, breathing with difficulty, said, "This is horrible! ... The Almighty is not mocked! Order, which I was unable to maintain, has been restored by a higher will."[19] It is doubtful that these were Franz Joseph's exact words. When experiencing intense emotions, the Emperor tended toward understatement rather than melodrama. Nevertheless, for a fleeting moment Franz Joseph may have felt relieved that he no longer had to deal with his headstrong heir. Franz Ferdinand had staged ugly arguments with the Emperor on many occasions. The Archduke's defiance of Habsburg family laws by his morganatic marriage had added to the Emperor's distaste for his nephew. But for Franz Joseph, far more was at stake in Sarajevo than his personal feelings. The assassination was a regicide, a direct hit on the House of Habsburg. The murders seemed to confirm a dangerous truth: Serbia was a mortal threat to the monarchy. Something had to be done to save the empire, the Emperor realized. But what?

Franz Joseph was almost 84 years old. If there is a time for all things, as the Scripture says, 84 is not the time to start a war. What the Emperor wanted on that day in late June was rest. He had so looked forward to his time in Ischl, one of the few places where he had any private life. He told an aide, in a sad voice, that he never expected to see Ischl again. He did return to the quiet little village, but remained there only until the monarchy had broken off relations with Serbia.

Leopold Berchtold was relaxing at his country estate in Moravia when he got word of the tragedy. The Habsburg foreign minister took the news extremely hard. He and Franz Ferdinand had known each other since childhood and, although they had often disagreed, they had managed to have serious discussions about problems facing the monarchy.

As foreign minister, Berchtold would play a pivotal role in the monarchy's response to the assassinations. He caught the next train to Vienna where he found the foreign ministry offices in the Ballhausplatz swarming with distraught officials and agitated politicians. Emergency meetings went on well into the night and commenced again early the next day.

A foreign office memo, completed only a few days before the assassination, had sought to clarify Austrian policy concerning what was termed the "intolerable situation" created by the Russian-instigated Balkan wars and the Bucharest peace. The treaty, at the end of the Second Balkan War, had left Serbia stronger than ever and more of a threat to the monarchy. An underlying assumption in the report was that the Habsburgs' enemies would view failure to respond forcefully to the Serbian threat as weakness, prompting them to try to bring down the monarchy. Berchtold was under increasing pressure to act.

Conrad, as always the banner carrier for a military response, appeared at the foreign office in Vienna on the evening of June 29, puffed up with self-righteous certainty. He reminded everyone in earshot of what he had been drumming in people's ears for years: Serbia had to be put in her place. He saw no reason for further negotiations with that rogue nation. "If one has a poisonous viper at one's heel, one must step on its head and not wait for the deadly bite," Conrad declared. Finishing his spiel, he pivoted and marched out, his words, "War, War, War!" echoing in the halls of the Ballhausplatz.[20]

Berchtold, summoned to Schönbrunn for an audience with the Emperor on June 30, found Franz Joseph clearheaded and outwardly composed but shaken. "The old monarch came toward me," he wrote, "and reached me his hand, something he didn't ordinarily do"[21] during audiences. Franz Joseph and his foreign minister talked about the tragic end of Franz Ferdinand and his wife. "There were tears in his eyes," Berchtold recalled. The discussion turned to the political situation in the Balkans – the escalating unrest in Bosnia and Herzegovina and the hostility of Belgrade. The Emperor was "completely oriented" in these matters, Berchtold wrote. The foreign minister said Franz Joseph agreed with him that the monarchy's "politics of peace had been poorly rewarded" and that the empire's prestige had suffered major reverses.[22]

Those in Conrad's camp stepped up their rhetoric, insisting on the need to strike while the iron was hot. The iron was hot. This was true notwithstanding the fact that Franz Ferdinand had never been popular with the monarchy's subjects. People complained about the Archduke's stinginess, his arrogance and his sadistic killing of animals, many of whose heads continue to enjoy a gruesome immortality mounted on the walls of the long dark halls at Konopiste. But the ancient and venerable Habsburg monarchy, as well as the position of Franz Ferdinand as heir apparent to the throne, commanded widespread public respect.

The more everyday Austrians thought about what had happened in Sarajevo, the angrier they became – and the more they blamed the Russians. Heinrich von Tschirschky, the German ambassador to Austria, described what he witnessed in Vienna on July 2, just days after the assassination: "While I was writing this report – between 12 and 1 o'clock at night, I heard a howling and whistling of a great throng, who were staging a demonstration near the Russian Embassy. They were singing '*Gott erhalte*', the Austrian hymn, and the '*Wacht am Rhein*' " (a German patriotic anthem).[23]

The Russians were noticeably sparing in their condolences over the Archduke's death. The Russian Embassy in Rome was alone among the Great Powers in the city in failing to fly its flag at half-mast in memory of the Habsburg heir. Nicholas Hartwig, the Russian agent in Serbia who had inspired so much of the unrest in the Balkans, was said to have shown no regret at the Archduke's death. Rumors swirled that he had entertained a bridge party on the night of the assassination and that he had refused to lower his legation's flag to half-mast during a memorial service for the murdered Archduke. Hartwig finally went to the Austrian legation on July 10 where he denied both rumors. He and the Austrian minister, Baron Giesl von Gieslingen, had a brief conversation. Suddenly Hartwig slumped over on the sofa then fell to the floor. A doctor, arriving a few minutes later, pronounced him dead. His daughter rushed to the scene, accusing the Austrians of poisoning her father. While it is likely that the terribly overweight Hartwig died of a heart attack, the Serbian public remained convinced that he had been assassinated.[24]

A report by the Bulgarian minister in Belgrade, passed on to the Austrians, said that the Serbs considered the Archduke's murder as "a step towards realizing ... (their ideal) union of all Serbians." The minister reported that the editor of the *Balkan*, a Belgrade newspaper, told him that the Serbs' only regret was "that the shot had not also killed the old Emperor."[25]

Franz Joseph refused to be swayed by war hysteria. The assassination alone, he said, could not be considered an adequate cause for military action. The Emperor was aware that two recent scandals involving evidence that had been forged by Austrian agents in the Balkans and presented as proof of Serbian terrorist activities against the monarchy had shamed the House of Habsburg. The Austrian legal system had functioned brilliantly in exonerating those who were falsely accused, but the Habsburgs had lost credibility in the process.[26] The Emperor wanted to make sure that Vienna had adequate proof of the complicity of Serbian officials in the murders before he allowed further steps to be taken. He also wanted to gauge the extent to which Serbian officials would cooperate in investigating the assassinations.

Additionally, the Emperor wanted assurances of Germany's support in case Austria decided on an aggressive policy toward Serbia. Wilhelm II had kept a judicious distance during earlier quarrels between the Balkan nation and the monarchy. He had never been convinced that Serbia represented a serious threat to Austrian interests. The Habsburg Emperor wondered if the Sarajevo murders would lead the Kaiser to change his mind.

On the day of the assassination, Wilhelm II, yachting near Kiel, suddenly caught sight of a little launch heading straight toward the imperial craft. The Kaiser gestured to the captain to keep off. Admiral Müller, who was at the helm of the launch, signaled that he had a message. Holding up to view a piece of paper, he folded it into a cigarette case and threw it on board. A sailor picked it up and handed it to the Kaiser. Wilhelm II opened the case, took out the paper, and turned pale as he read the news from Sarajevo.[27] The assassination outraged Wilhelm II. Terrorists had murdered his friends, whose company he had enjoyed at Konopiste only a few days before. Also, like Franz Joseph, the Kaiser felt passionately about the sanctity of dynastic considerations. Wilhelm II, always impulsive, immediately declared that the revolutionaries responsible for the regicide must be taught a lesson.[28]

The Kaiser's stance, from the time he received the news of the assassinations until the Great War actually broke out at the end of July, has been subject to endless scrutiny. Some scholars have depicted Wilhelm II as the evil actor behind the Austrian decision for military action against Serbia. Some have even argued that the German ruler pushed Franz Joseph to go to war with Serbia in order to bring on a European conflagration.

The evidence does not support such a contention. These claims reflect a misunderstanding of the dynamics involved in the Austrian declaration of war. For Franz Joseph and for Berchtold, the decision for military action against Serbia was not made on the spur of the moment. It evolved over many months. It sprang from their conclusions that other options for dealing with Serbia had been exhausted. It seems quite possible that Franz Joseph would have declared war on that nation even if the Germans had failed to support a military effort.

Franz Joseph had hoped to discuss strategies for dealing with the crisis while Wilhelm II was in Vienna for Franz Ferdinand's funeral, but the Kaiser decided not to come after rumors spread that 12 terrorists were heading to the Austrian capital to assassinate him. The Emperor consequently dispatched Alexander Hoyos, Berchtold's hawkish chief of the cabinet, to Berlin late on July 4. Hoyos brought a letter from the Emperor for the Kaiser as well as the recently completed memorandum on Balkan policy from the foreign office.

Franz Joseph's letter to Wilhelm II, which was drafted by Berchtold, reflects a major departure from the usual Habsburg peace politics. The Emperor wrote that the attack on his "poor nephew" was the direct result of Russian and Serbian Pan-Slav agitation, intended to disrupt the empire. According to all indications, the Emperor said, the Sarajevo crime was not the work of one person, but was instead "a well-arranged plot whose threads reach(ed) to Belgrade."[29] After acknowledging that proving the complicity of the Serbian government would be almost impossible, Franz Joseph declared that without doubt the Serbian effort to unite all South Slavs under Belgrade encouraged such crimes. Franz Joseph wrote that it was necessary to isolate Serbia. Also, undoubtedly recalling that the Balkan nation had almost doubled in size in the agreement ending the Second Balkan War, the Emperor said Serbia should forfeit some of its territory. The Emperor then made a dramatic statement: A friendly settlement of Austria's differences with Serbia was "no longer to be thought of." It was necessary, said Franz Joseph, to eliminate Serbia "as a political factor in the Balkans."[30] This indicates that Franz Joseph had decided to take whatever steps were needed to make the little rogue nation understand that its reign of terror no longer was to be tolerated. This is not the language of someone who needs to be prodded into action against an adversary.

While it has become a commonplace that the Kaiser handed the Habsburgs a blank check for action against Serbia, that isn't quite the case. Wilhelm II promised to "back Vienna in any action that it took," but he made one important stipulation. Vienna should act quickly. The Kaiser, like the Emperor, was thinking of a punitive expedition to be begun and ended before the Russians could mobilize for a fight. Certainly Wilhelm II did not envision a full-scale war involving Germany. Berchtold, for his part, hoped that early and decisive German support would deter the Russians from becoming involved.

The road to the First World War was mined with miscalculations of this kind.

In a tension-filled four-hour session on July 7, the Habsburgs' Common Ministerial Council sought unsuccessfully to reach a consensus on the crisis with Serbia.

Berchtold argued for a hard line response to the assassinations. After all, he told his colleagues, three times in the previous 20 months the monarchy had been on the brink of war – twice with Serbia and once with Montenegro. Three times the Austrians had opted for peace. Three times their efforts had reaped new trouble. All the ministers who had participated in the grueling earlier sessions now came out in favor of "a diplomatic confrontation with Serbia that would risk war,"[31] writes Williamson. Stephan Tisza, the Hungarian minister president, who was new to the council, was the sole holdout. He said that he first wanted to give the Serbian government a chance to show its "loyalty." In the meantime, Tisza argued, Austria should pursue an alliance with Bulgaria, wooing Czar Ferdinand with visions of handsome expanses of territory in lovely Macedonia. The council could not afford to ignore the opinion of the powerful minister president. However, his failure to join the other council members in an immediate decision for military action was to have unfortunate consequences. The delay deprived the monarchy of the element of surprise, eliminating the possibility of a successful punitive expedition against Serbia. It is not far-fetched to say that the delay cost the Habsburgs their empire.

Ironically, although Russian intervention on behalf of Serbia came up at the council meeting, that possibility appears to have been mentioned only in passing. Berchtold, among others, apparently couldn't believe that Czar Nicholas II would support the government of Serbia, which was being intentionally blind to a regicide plotted on its own soil. The conviction that the Russians would stand on imperial principles rather than go to the aid of their Serbian vassal was yet another fatal miscalculation. The Austrians had no way of knowing that Sazonov and the generals in his inner circle had a specific reason for wanting Serbia's survival. As recent archival evidence has shown, the Russians expected their Balkan vassal to play a key role in the European war they were about to wage.

The Russian military initially had planned to open the epic confrontation between the Slavs and the Teutons in 1917. But their plans had changed. In response to developments in Constantinople, Foreign Minister Sazonov had put the schedule for the long-anticipated war on a fast track. When in late 1913 Sazonov learned that German General Liman von Sanders had taken command of Turkish defenses at the Straits, the Russian minister was so upset he nearly fainted. In a classic case of projection, Sazonov became convinced that German seizure of the Straits was imminent. He hastened to draw up a countervailing strategy against the perceived threat, knowing full well that it would bring on a European war.

General Liman von Sanders was actually in Constantinople at the invitation of the Porte. He had brought some 40 subordinate officers with him. The German officers were there to provide training for the Ottoman troops. A British admiral had been put in charge of the Ottoman navy with a similar training mission. The situation, however, led to a flurry of angry exchanges between St. Petersburg and Berlin. The Germans, hoping to ease the Russians' concerns, promoted Liman von Sanders to the post of inspector, where he had no command authority, but it did little to calm Sazonov's nerves.

The Russian foreign minister saw a dual menace in the developments at Constantinople. Not only was the German presence a continuing worry; additionally, the Germans and British were training the Turks in advanced warfare. The Porte, embarrassed by its military's abysmal performance during the Balkan Wars, was working hard to upgrade its defense capabilities. The Ottomans understood that the Russians remained a threat to their very existence. They knew from long experience that the Romanov rulers had never abandoned, and would never abandon, the dreams of Peter and Catherine the Great of taking control of

Constantinople and the Straits. As added insurance against the Russian menace, the Turks had ordered two dreadnought-class vessels from the British, with delivery expected in the spring of 1914. Military planners in St. Petersburg warned that once these battleships were in the hands of the Ottomans, the Russians' entire Black Sea Fleet would be obsolete.

Worried about losing what might be a final opportunity to realize the Romanovs' historic destiny in the south, Sazonov busied himself in preparing the political ground for the coming conflagration. An initial task was to make sure that the Czar was firmly on board. Sazonov had once declared that Nicholas II could be "handled." Now he set out to confirm his assertion.

A report by Sazonov, dated December 8, 1913, prepared for the Czar, reveals the foreign minister's manipulative genius. Sazanov's carefully crafted argument in favor of war plays to the Romanov ruler's vulnerabilities and predilections. It is a masterpiece in the art of persuasion.

Sazonov commences on familiar ground, raising the familiar wraith of the likely demise of the Turkish "Sick Man." He offers a rhetorical question as to what will happen once the Ottoman Empire is gone: "Can Russia afford to let anyone else control the Straits?" He provides a rhetorical answer, a resounding "No." Next, like Satan tempting Christ, Sazonov offers the Czar a vision of the vast dominions that he will control once the Straits are in Russian hands. That vital passageway, declares Sazonov, "is the key not only to the Black Sea and the Mediterranean, but to the penetration of Asia Minor and the overlordship of the Balkan countries."[32]

The crafty foreign minister next invokes the memory of the Czar's late father, Alexander III, whom Nicholas II greatly admired, and compared with whom his son had always felt inadequate. Sazonov recounts the late Czar's accomplishments, including rebuilding the Black Sea Fleet, and urges Nicholas to carry on his father's work by preparing for an advance on Constantinople. That means making the Black Sea Fleet superior to the Turkish fleet.

Now and again this adept psychologist pauses in his argument for war to reassure the Czar that he himself actually prefers the status quo to war. These asides seem intended to soothe a Czar whose wife urges him to "be Peter the Great," and who knows too well that he will never be Peter the Great and that, deep down, he would prefer to be outside on his estate chopping firewood rather than leading an army to Byzantium. As Stieve notes, these asides "do not diminish the strong impression that the conquest of the Dardanelles has been thought out to the last detail."[33]

Sazonov had appealed to the Czar's baroque vision of the Romanovs' grandiosity on the world stage. He had urged the hesitant Czar to make his late father proud by preparing to take Constantinople. Having convinced Nicholas II of the need for bold action, Sazonov confronts the Czar with an unsettling truth: The Straits question can "hardly be advanced a step except through European complications."[34]

Having primed the Czar for war, Sazonov's next step was to get the Russian military on board with his plan. On February 8, 1914, Sazonov presented his recommendations to a conference of ranking members of the Russian military as well as high level government officials. His language was more blunt than it had been in his memo to the Czar. The foreign minister urged immediate action to assure that Russia was prepared to force the Straits and to occupy them.[35] He told the conference that it could not be assumed that Russia could acquire the Straits without a general European war. Sazonov then brought up the subject of Serbia. Unlike Nicholas II, who appears to have genuinely believed that Austria was victimizing the small Balkan nation, Sazonov's sympathy for Serbia was as shallow as a saucer. Once war came, the Russian foreign minister said, it was to be assumed that *"Serbia would direct all her forces against Austria-Hungary".*[36] This would leave Russia free to go to war against Germany, now viewed as an even greater obstacle to seizing Constantinople and the Straits than Austria. In other words, Serbia was to be a designated handmaiden to Romanov destiny, as imagined by Peter the Great and Catherine, and by every Russian ruler since.

Nicholas II signed the conference report on March 23, 1914, attaching a handwritten note: "I entirely approve of the *resolutions* of the conference". This suggests a certain ambivalence. While Nicholas II "entirely approves" of the practical steps to be taken as the empire prepares for war – such as streamlining the Black Sea Fleet – he is not yet ready to endorse Sazonov's "European complications."[37] The Czar's 11th hour conversion to war is to come at the end of July, 1914, during an emotional confrontation with Sazonov as the empire's vast army is poised to march.

On July 9, Berchtold, accompanied by Hoyos, arrived at Ischl for talks with the Emperor. These lasted a good part of the day. Franz Joseph and his foreign minister agreed to use diplomacy for the short term, combined with specific demands to be made to Serbia.

In the meantime, the Emperor wanted more evidence. Even though the trail of terrorism pointed to Belgrade, it was soon apparent that the Serbian government had no intention of launching a genuine investigation into the Sarajevo crimes. On June 30, the Austrian charge d'affairs in Belgrade asked Serbian officials what their police had done to "follow up the clues to the crime which ... (were) partly to be found in Serbia." He was informed that "the matter had not yet engaged the attention of the Serbian police ... that up to the present nothing had been done, and that the matter did not concern the Serbian government."[38]

Instead of concerning himself with the assassination, Nikola Pasic, the Serbian prime minister, absented himself from Belgrade, claiming a need to campaign for an upcoming election. Before leaving town, he paused to issue a statement claiming the Habsburgs were victimizing the Serbians. He insisted that Serbian officials were trying to curb terrorists, adding that it was wrong to hold a "civilized government responsible for the excesses of immature and wild youths."[39] He added that tighter controls on weapons and explosives had been proposed but had not been considered by the National Assembly.

In Serbia, in addition to the official government, there was a shadow government under the auspices of the Black Hand. This militant organization of ultranationalists was far too powerful for Pasic and his supporters to challenge. King Peter owed his throne to the Black Hand. Apis and his collaborators, having carried out the murders of King Alexander and Queen Draga in 1903, had put King Peter in power. Anyone in the official government of Serbia daring to reveal the truth about the Sarajevo assassinations likely would have paid for his courage with his life.

Berchtold sent Dr. Friedrich von Wiesner, a legal counselor at the monarchy's foreign office, to Sarajevo on July 11 to look for evidence of conspiracy. He spent only two days in the Bosnian capital and failed to turn up hard proof of the Serbian government's complicity in the plot. It is not clear why anyone thought that two days of sifting through documents and conducting interviews in Sarajevo would have given any investigator, however talented or diligent, sufficient evidence to establish complicity in the assassinations.[40] The bulk of the evidence of Serbian government involvement in the murders lay in Belgrade, not in Sarajevo. Austrians investigators weren't welcome there, as they soon would find out.[41]

Wiesner's findings were at times misleading because he limited himself to evidence that he believed would be applicable in a court of law. He named Serbian officials Ciganovic and Tankosic as ringleaders in the plot, and said they should be prosecuted. He established that these men had provided the terrorists with bombs, firearms and ammunition. He found that the bombs had come from a military arsenal in Serbia. He determined that Ciganovic and the frontier captains at Shabats and Loznica had helped smuggle the three assassins into Bosnia. He asserted that the Austrian government was justified in demanding that the Serbs stop their official agencies from cooperating in smuggling persons and goods across the frontier.

While Wiesner reported that knowledgeable persons in Bosnia believed that the ringleaders in the conspiracy had been involved in spreading propaganda for a Greater Serbia "with the knowledge and approval of the Serbian government," he added that he had no evidence that the government had promoted the propaganda.[42] Wiesner stated that he "found no proof *to cause even suspicion*" that the Serbian government was aware of the plot or knew how the weapons were supplied. Furthermore, he said that there were indications that this was "to be regarded as out of the question."[43] There is no way Wiesner could assert unequivocally that such suspicions were out of the question. As any student of logic knows, a lack of evidence is insufficient as proof that no evidence exists.

American delegates at the Paris Peace Conference of 1919 cited these two logically tainted statements in Wiesner's report as evidence of Belgrade's innocence in igniting the Great War. "In stating that these two sentences were the 'the essential portion' of the Wiesner report they gave a totally misleading impression of its true character," writes Fay.[44] It is likely that the Americans, in reaching their conclusions, relied heavily on documents provided to them by the Serbian ambassador in Paris.

Those familiar with the situation inside Serbia at the time of the assassinations had strong reservations about Wiesner's report. General Potiorek, writing to Conrad, expressed certainty that somebody in the Serbian government knew about the plot.[45] Theodor von Sosnosky, a contemporary biographer of the Archduke, whose research on the assassination is invaluable, declared that the conspiracy could not have succeeded if the legitimate government hadn't "tolerated or even encouraged" it.[46]

The Russians, as one might expect, cried foul at these allegations. In his memoirs, Sazonov blamed the Austrian press for "an incessant campaign of persecution" of Serbia. In making his case for the Serbian governments' innocence in the assassination plot, Sazonov relied heavily on Wiesner's sketchy investigation of the murders. The former Russian foreign minister asserted that "the inquiry held at Sarajevo ... afforded no grounds whatever"[47] for assuming that the Serbian government had been involved in the assassination. Sazonov's reminiscences (*Fateful Years*) were published in 1928. By that time he surely knew that his claims had been thoroughly discounted.

Details of the Sarajevo murders emerged too late to sway public opinion during the run-up to the Great War. Two trials, one in 1914 after the war was under way, and another in 1917, revealed the extent and origin of the terrorist network involved in the assassinations and provided proof of the involvement of the Serbian government in the plot. During the trial of Princip and the other conspirators in the fall of 1914, it became clear that the assassinations were the work of a sophisticated terrorist organization whose participants included not only students and peasants, but also craftsmen, a merchant and local officials. The operation was shown to be the work of the Black Hand and National Defense (*Narodna odbrana*) organizations.

Evidence of Serbian government officials' collusion in the conspiracy came to light in 1917 in Salonika, during a trial in which Apis was charged with the attempted assassination of the Serbian crown prince. Ciganovic, whose role in the Sarajevo plot had been established and who was wanted by Austrian officials, was the chief witness against

Apis. Shortly after the Sarajevo murders, the Austrians had attempted to get the Serbians to extradite Ciganovic, but officials in Belgrade said he had been dismissed from his railroad post and was nowhere to be found. In fact, Serbian officials had spirited Ciganovic out of Belgrade to a remote region of their country. He had continued to work for the Belgrade government under an assumed name before being forced to come out of hiding to testify against his co-conspirator. Apis was executed on June 27, 1917, almost three years to the day from the Sarajevo crime he had plotted.[48] By some accounts, the Serbian government sent Ciganovic to the United States for the duration of the war.

While Habsburg ministers pondered their next move, civil war threatened in Bosnia and Herzegovina. Bosnian Serb nationalists clashed with supporters of the monarchy. Responding to the worsening situation, Tisza, on July 14, changed course. He said he now realized that the situation in the Balkans threatened the survival of the monarchy. The minister president explained his about-face to the Hungarian Diet, saying that while war should always be a last resort, "... every state, every nation, must be in a position to carry on war as an ultima ratio, if it is to continue as a state and as a nation."[49]

With Tisza on board, Berchtold quickly finished the ultimatum to Serbia. The ministerial council unanimously approved it on Sunday, July 19. The council agreed that before engaging in any conflict they would inform the Powers that they had no intention of annexing Serbia. They reserved the right to reduce Serbia's territory so that, as Berchtold said, "she would no longer be dangerous."[50] Serbia was to lose much or all of the territory she had acquired in the treaty ending the Second Balkan War. The other Balkan states were to be the beneficiaries of the territorial readjustment.

Berchtold's actions naturally drew criticism. He was accused of intentionally making the ultimatum so severe that no sovereign nation would have accepted it. That seems hardly to have been the case. Franz Joseph, at least, thought that Serbia actually might agree to the terms of the ultimatum. Belgrade had, after all, yielded to Austrian demands before – and then ignored them.

The Austrians were said to be unfair in setting a 48-hour limit for the Serbian response to the ultimatum. There were reasons for this stricture. The Austrians didn't want to give the Serbians time to make extensive war preparations while pretending to consider their reply to Vienna. They also hoped to head off Russian intervention by acting quickly.

The Austrians decided to wait to send the ultimatum to Serbia until July 23. That meant that the 48-hour time limit for a Serbian response would occur on July 25. The official reason for the latter date was that on July 25 many Habsburg troops, on leave to work in summer crops, would be returning to their posts. However, a more pressing reason for the delay concerned the coming visit of Raymond Poincaré, the President of France, to St. Petersburg. Berchtold wanted to make certain that the French ruler had left St. Petersburg and was back on the high seas before the Serbian answer to the Austrian ultimatum arrived in European foreign offices.

Berchtold explained himself in a July 14 report to Franz Joseph. The foreign minister said he thought it would be "unwise to threaten Belgrade while 'the peace-loving, hesitating Czar and the cautious Sazonov were subject to the immediate influence of the two instigators, Poincaré and Izvolsky;' then Russia, under the influence of the 'champagne-mood' of the warm Franco-Russian toasts and the chauvinism of the French President, Izvolsky, and the Grand Duke Nicholas, would be more likely to intervene with military action."[51]

The curtains were about to come down on Old Europe. But for many of those at the Romanov court, set apart from reality by the royal mote of privilege and caught up in the pleasures of the French President's visit, the future had hardly seemed brighter. War was coming – most everybody knew. Nobody expected it to last long. Constantinople and the Straits would finally belong to Russia. For the French the return of Alsace-Lorraine lay just ahead. Germany and Austria were finally to be "put in their place."

22 C'EST MA GUERRE!

July 20, 1914: A few days short of catastrophe.

A large battleship, *La France*, steams up the Baltic bringing
Raymond Poincaré to St. Petersburg. Czar Nicholas II,
dressed in an admiral's uniform, awaits the French President
on board the imperial yacht, *Alexandria*. Flanking the Czar
are Sazonov and Izvolsky, as well as General de Laguiche,
the French Military Attaché, and G.M. Paléologue, the
French ambassador to Russia. They have lingered over a
long lunch.

It is Izvolsky's moment. He is to accompany the French
President's entourage during a visit to the Russian capital.
The humiliation of his ill-fated meeting with Aehrenthal at
Buchlau in 1908 is a shadowy memory now. He has lured
the French into an alliance that has tightened a noose
around the necks of Austria and Germany. The British are
now aligned with France and Russia. The encirclement of
Austria and Germany, so feared by Kaiser Wilhelm II, is
nearly complete. Izvolsky now can look forward to the war
he has worked so hard to provoke.

In his memoirs, Paléologue offers a flowery description

of Poincaré's arrival in the Russian capital. The French ambassador's language, with its blend of romantic and martial imagery, captures the heady mood of the moment: "The Tsar (Czar) made me go up on the bridge with him .... In the quivering silvery light, the *France* slowly surged forward over the turquoise and emerald waves.... Then she stopped majestically. The mighty warship which had brought the head of the French state is well worthy of her name. She was indeed France coming to Russia."[1]

The French President's trip to St. Petersburg had been planned months earlier. By chance it coincided with a major European crisis. On June 28, 1914, Archduke Franz Ferdinand, the heir to the Austrian throne and his wife, Sophie, had been assassinated in Sarajevo. Preliminary evidence showed that the plot had been hatched in Belgrade. War loomed. The Habsburgs were known to be preparing an ultimatum to Serbia with demands, according to some, that could hardly be met.

Early in Berchtold's tenure as Austrian foreign minister, Franz Joseph had told him, "Do whatever you want; just don't get us in war with Russia." Now the Habsburg Emperor himself was leaning toward military action against Serbia, risking Russian intervention.

Franz Joseph had no way of knowing that Sazonov and a military coterie in St. Petersburg had stepped up the Russians' timetable for commencing a European war, hoping to ward off what they feared would be a successful effort by the Germans and the Ottomans to bar them permanently from Constantinople. What Sazonov lacked was a *cause d'guerre* that would convince Nicholas II that his only option was to set the gigantic Russian war machine in motion without delay. The Habsburg decision to use military measures against Serbia was to give Sazonov the ammunition he needed for persuading the Czar that he had to act.

President Poincaré had come to St. Petersburg on a

mission of his own. He sought assurances that the Czar's troops would join France in fighting the Germans on the Russians' western front. Perhaps nobody, except Izvolsky, wanted war more than the French President. His childhood memories of Bismarck's soldiers driving Poincaré family members off their estate had left a painful bruise on his soul. It could only be healed by victory over his nation's conquerors.

The French President received a lavish welcome at the Romanov court. On the first evening of his visit, the Czar welcomed his guest at a formal banquet. The setting was unrivaled in Europe for its opulence. The Romanov archdukes wore uniforms heavy with gold decorations. The women glittered with diamonds and rubies and emeralds. Czarina Alexandra, a vision in a low-cut brocade gown and a diamond tiara on her head, put in a rare appearance to show her support for the French cause.[2] Wearing a drab black coat, Poincaré lent a sober note to the redundant profusion of the occasion. His attire reflected his almost puritanical sense of purpose. Nicholas II listened carefully and sympathetically to the French President, whose forceful personality overshadowed that of his insecure host.

The next day the Czar and Poincaré spent hours behind closed doors. Details of what occurred during the talks remained secret. However, Paléologue said the President was finding the Austro-Serbian dispute "more worrying every day, owing to the arrogant and mysterious attitude of Austria."[3]

The two rulers probably knew at least the gist of what was to be included in the Austrian ultimatum to Serbia, because the Russians had broken the secret code used by the monarchy. Nicholas II and Poincaré undoubtedly planned to coordinate their reaction to the ultimatum once it was made public.

Paléologue provides an interesting glimpse of Poincaré's comportment as the French President mingled with the foreign diplomatic corps at the Romanov court. The French foreign minister writes that Poincaré was at pains during the visit to convey the message that he shared the Russians' disapproval of Austria's behavior toward Serbia. While Paléologue characterizes the following interchange as relatively "conciliatory," a dispassionate observer might consider the French President's attitude toward Friedrich Graf Szapary, the Habsburg ambassador to St. Petersburg, as lacking in respect. Poincaré spoke to the envoy as though he were an unruly child who deserves to be punished. "With a little good will," Poincaré scolded the Austrian envoy, "this Serbian business is easy to settle. But it can just as easily become acute. Serbia has some very warm friends in the Russian people. And Russia has an ally, France. There are plenty of complications to be feared."[4]

Paléologue writes that later Poincaré told him that he wasn't satisfied with his conversation with the Habsburg ambassador. The French President said he suspected that the Austrians were planning mischief. "Sazanov must be firm," the President told his envoy, adding that France was behind Russia's policy toward Serbia. The French President naturally expected his envoy to repeat what he had said to the Czar.

Proceeding to a salon where he greeted representatives of minor powers, Poincaré moved down the row of diplomats, shaking hands. The French President paused only once – writes Paléologue – to express "a few words of sympathy" to the Serbian ambassador.[5]

Surely this was a farce. It is unlikely that the French President and his minister were really so concerned for Serbia. The theatrics undoubtedly were intended to woo the Czar to the French cause with a pretense of espousing Russian interests in the Balkans.

The next day (Wednesday, July 22), Paléologue catches the mood of rising excitement in a crowd, assembled at Krasnoye Selo, the parade grounds near St. Petersburg, for a troop review. The ceremony is pompous and solemn, suggesting an empire heading for war.

The Czar, on horseback, accompanies the carriage carrying the imperial party. He is followed by an escort of the grand dukes and aides de camp.

"The sun was dropping towards the horizon in a sky of purple and gold," wrote Paléologue. "On a sign from the Czar an artillery salvo signalled evening prayer. The bands played a hymn. Everyone uncovered. A noncommissioned officer recited the Pater in a loud voice. All those men, thousands upon thousands, prayed for the Czar and Holy Russia."[6]

Paléologue writes of arriving early that evening at a banquet given in Poincare's honor. He finds the Montenegrin princesses, Anastasia and Melitza, wives of Grand Duke Nicholas and Grand Duke Peter, decorating the tables. The black princesses, as they are called,[7] flutter with excitement. Anastasia said: "Today I had a telegram from my father (King Nicholas of Montenegro) in the proper style; he tells me we shall have war before the month is out. What a hero, my father! He is worthy of the Iliad... ."

During the meal, Paléologue, who sat next to Anastasia, reports that "the dithyrambics continued, mixed with prophecies: There is going to be a war... . There'll be nothing left of Austria... . You will get Alsace-Lorraine back. Our armies will meet in Berlin ... Germany will be annihilated... ."[8] Anastasia said she was saving some soil from the French provinces, collected during a visit to the region, and that she used thistles, grown from seed she had gotten in Lorraine, to decorate the table of the guests of honor. No flowers except thistles would do. Then suddenly she stopped talking. The Czar was giving her a disapproving glance.[9]

As some historians have remarked, the Montenegrin princesses did not speak for the Russian government. However, as members of the Romanov family, they had the

Czar's ear in ways that most members of the Russian government did not. It was the Czar, not the government, who had the power to decide for war or peace. While Nicholas II may not really have wanted war, he was heavily influenced by those in his immediate circle, most of whom tended to be long on opinions and short on facts – particularly where Serbia and Austria were concerned.

On the evening of July 23, with Poincaré back on board *La France* where the Austrians considered him unlikely to add fuel to the monarchy's crisis with Serbia, Baron Giesl, the Habsburg minister in Belgrade, delivered the ultimatum to the Serbian government. The Austrians demanded a reply within 48 hours. They had worded their document carefully in the effort to avoid what had happened in 1909 when the Serbs had made what turned out to be equivocal promises to be "good neighbors" with the Habsburgs. Then, all but laughing up their sleeves, the Serbs had immediately continued their efforts to undermine the monarchy. This time the Austrians wanted solid assurances.

The ultimatum, with 10 demands in all, called on Belgrade to stop intrigues against the Habsburg monarchy once and for all. The Austrians required Belgrade to squelch Pan-Serb propaganda campaigns in the press and the schools. Belgrade was to dissolve the *Narodna odbrana* (National Defense) and similar ultranationalist organizations engaging in propaganda against Austria. The Serbian government was required to acknowledge involvement of its army officers and officials in plots against Austria and to purge those individuals known to have participated in such activities. Two demands in particular were to cause an international uproar: Serbia was to allow representatives of the Austrian government to collaborate with Serbian officials in suppressing subversive activities against the monarchy (point 5) and to allow Austrian delegates to join with Serbia in investigating those involved in the assassination plot who were on Serbian territory (point 6).[10]

The Austrian note led to sharp words and flaring tempers when, on the morning of July 24, it landed on foreign office desks. *"C'est la guerre Européenne,"* Sazonov said in greeting one diplomat that morning at the Russian foreign office. It is likely that there was a hint of satisfaction in his voice. The foreign minister immediately telephoned the news to the Czar, who exclaimed, "This is disturbing," and gave orders that he be kept informed as to further developments.[11]

As historian Sean McMeekin's recent archival research confirms, there were, indeed, further developments, secretly put in motion by Sazonov on the morning of July 24. The Russian foreign minister, acting on his own volition, as he was wont, instructed Nikolai Yanushkevitch, the chief of the general staff, to arrange to put the Romanov army on a "war footing." Supposedly this was in preparation for partial mobilization, only against Austria.[12] Claims that the Romanovs intended to go to war solely against the monarchy were patently false. Sazonov knew better than that, too, since he had been involved in the planning for a general European war for more than a year. The Russian military considered Austria and Germany a single enemy. The Russian Council of Ministers, meeting that afternoon, approved Sazonov's initiatives. Then the ministers went much further, agreeing to large-scale mobilization of the Russian army and navy, involving 1.1 million troops and including the Baltic and Black Sea Fleets. A so-called "Period Preparatory for War" was to be instigated in the four military districts nearest the Austrian monarchy. The language was intentionally misleading. This was to be the first phase of full-scale mobilization.

Sazonov wasted no time in embarking on a campaign of deception intended to make the world believe that the blame for the crisis lay with Austria. On July 24, after putting Russia on a war footing, he had lunched at the French Embassy with Paléologue and Sir George Buchanan, the British Ambassador.[13] The Russian foreign minister denounced Austria's conduct as "immoral and provocative." The foreign minister's luncheon companions, unaware that Sazonov and the generals were greasing the wheels for a European war, expressed empathy for Russia and little Serbia. Paléologue reaffirmed his nation's blank check for Russia, vowing total support for the Czar's Balkan policies. Buchanan agreed to try to persuade the British government to rally around the Russians.[14]

Sir Edward Grey, the British foreign secretary, took time from his birdwatching to denounce the Austrian ultimatum, declaring that he had "never seen one State address to another independent State a document of so formidable a character."[15] He made no serious effort to learn the truth about the quarrel involving the Russians and the Austrians, or to inquire into the Habsburgs' reasons for using tough language in their ultimatum to Serbia. Grey depended mainly on Buchanan for his information about developments in St. Petersburg. Buchanan, an ardent Russophile, appears simply to have taken Sazonov's word for what was going on. Sazonov knew that in order to persuade the British to support Russia in the coming war, he had to hide the fact that the Russians were mobilizing and were doing so "without German or Austrian provocation." The Russian foreign minister, writes McMeekin, seems to have succeeded in fooling the British "simply by not telling them."[16]

Neither then nor at any time in the future did Sazonov acknowledge the slightest responsibility for his role in taking the world to war. Recalling the French President's visit from a postwar perspective, Sazonov wrote, "During those three days were taken, in Vienna and Berlin, the mad and criminal decisions which plunged Europe into incredible calamities, covered it with ruins, and arrested for so long the course of its natural development."[17]

To suggest that the war had its origin in decisions made

in Vienna and Berlin during the three days that Poincaré was in St. Petersburg is nonsense. Sazonov, whose actions precipitated the catastrophe, knew that very well. The war that began in 1914 was the last in a series of Balkan conflicts instigated by Russian rulers obsessed with Peter the Great's dream of Byzantium and the Straits. Nicholas II was the third Russian Czar to engage in war with the Ottomans during Franz Joseph's long reign. Russian machinations in the Balkans, all in the hopes of realizing Peter the Great's dream at Constantinople, had brought the Habsburgs and the Romanovs to the brink of war in 1856, in 1878, in 1886-87, and in 1908-09. The Russians increasingly used the Balkan Slavs as proxies against the monarchy. The Balkan Alliance was contrived by the Russians to drive the Turks out of Europe; then, when the time was right, to undermine Austrian interests in the region or even to bring down the monarchy. The Alliance led to two Balkan wars, the second of which left Serbia far more powerful than before, posing a growing threat to the Habsburg monarchy. The Romanovs' thrust toward Constantinople and their perception that the Austrians were standing between them and their historical destiny lay at the heart of the differences between the House of Habsburg and the House of Romanov. The increased German presence in the Ottoman Empire during the decade prior to 1914 gave new impetus to the Russians' fears that they would be forever prevented from planting the Romanov flag at Constantinople. In St. Petersburg what had been a commonplace became a call to arms: "The road to Constantinople lies through Vienna and Berlin."

Saturday, July 25, 1914, was to be a day seared in the memories of many. In St. Petersburg, high society gathered at Krasnoye Selo for one of the major social events of the summer, a full review of the Russian troops. The Czar appeared briefly, then hurried away. The festivities were delayed. Ladies fluttered their fans in the scorching heat and gentlemen fidgeted in their formal clothes. Hours passed.

The Czar and his ministers were said to be in emergency session. Later the military review was cut short. At a banquet that evening there was talk about finally doing something "about Austria." There was raging about "Austrian presumption." At the theater there was a noisy demonstration for war. Then, in the darkness, hoofbeats. The Imperial Guards were returning from Krasnoye Selo where they had been expected to remain for another month.[18]

That night, General Oskar Chelius, Wilhelm II's personal representative to the Czar, sat next to Baron Grünwald, the Czar's chief equerry. Grünwald said, "The situation is very serious. What was decided this noon I am not permitted to tell you. You yourself will soon learn it. But take it from me, it looks very serious." He touched glasses, drank to Chelius's health and said, "Let us hope we shall see each other again in better times."[19]

Nicholas II had approved the decisions of the Council of Ministers at 11 a.m. that day (July 25), just as a troop review was about to get under way at Krasnoye Selo.

A message on July 26, passed on by Paléologue to the French war minister from the French military attaché in St. Petersburg, confirms what the Russian were busy denying. It involves the decisions made the previous day at Krasnoye Selo during the meeting of the Council of Ministers at which the Czar had been present. A decision had been taken to mobilize military districts at Kiev, Odessa, Kazan and Moscow, but that was not all that was decided. The message from the French military attaché continued: "The endeavour is to avoid any measure likely to be regarded as directed against Germany, but nevertheless the military districts of Warsaw, Vilna and St. Petersburg are secretly making preparations. The cities and governments of St. Petersburg and Moscow are declared to be under martial law ... . The minister for war has reiterated to us his determination to leave to Germany the eventual initiative of an attack on

Russia. The information coming to us from Berlin is to the effect that they are disposed there to take this initiative."[20] A telling fact is that this information about secret mobilization is omitted from the French *Yellow Book*, that government's account of events relating to the First World War.

Russia's sheer size made mobilization complicated and slow. The military strategy dating from the First Balkan War offered ways to overcome these complications. As McMeekin has shown, the secret mobilization, to be conducted in stages, was to occur simultaneously with "clever diplomatic negotiations" intended "to lull to sleep as much as possible the enemy's fears."[21] Delaying the inevitable conflict while actively preparing for the war was key to improving the Russian advantage.

For the Czar's generals there was no question about where Russia was heading. General Sergei Dobrorolsky, chief of the mobilization section of the Russian general staff, wrote later that already on July 25, the military "regarded war as a foregone conclusion and the whole deluge of telegrams between the governments of Russia and Germans was only a mise-en-scène of a historical drama."[22]

That evening in Belgrade, minutes before the 6 p.m. deadline, Baron Giesl, the Austrian envoy, received the Serbian reply to the ultimatum. He pronounced it unacceptable. By 6:30 p.m. he had boarded the train and crossed the Danube into the monarchy. Three hours before returning the note to the Austrian minister, the Serbs began mobilizing. Belgrade, separated from Austria by only the Danube, was vulnerable to immediate attack. The Serbs began moving gold, diplomatic and government papers as well as archival documents, out of the capital.[23] They evacuated the munitions depots of the fortress, which Habsburg Empress Marie Theresa had greatly expanded to help defend her empire against the Turks. The garrison, with its full gear, left. Serbia became the first nation to mobilize publicly in the conflict later to be known as the Great War.

At Bad Ischl, Franz Joseph passed July 25 as though it were an ordinary day – or tried to make it seem so.

Albert Freiherr von Margutti, the Emperor's aide-de-camp, said that Franz Joseph did not behave as though he thought the monarchy was on its way to war. He attended to minute details of his household, as he always did when he had visitors. Franz Joseph behaved with his usual courtesy toward the Duke of Cumberland and his family who were guests for the midday dinner. Berchtold, arriving that afternoon, found the Emperor "preoccupied and nervous," but when the two met a few hours later he seemed to have regained his composure. By that time he had received the Serbian reply to the Austrian ultimatum, along with Baron Giesl's message informing him that he considered the Serbian response unacceptable and was departing Belgrade. Margutti wrote that Franz Joseph, upon receiving the news from the Serbian capital, murmured, "The breaking off of diplomatic relations does not necessarily mean war."[24]

Franz Joseph instructed Berchtold to take as long as he needed in analyzing the Serbian response to the Austrian note. The Emperor appeared to be leaving the door ajar for peace. "Nothing meant more to Franz Joseph than the preservation of the peace," Margutti wrote in his memoirs. "It was the *leit motif* of his being."[25] At that same meeting, with war minister Alexander von Krobatin also present, Franz Joseph signed an order for the mobilization of eight military divisions, about half of the Austrian army, to be directed against Serbia and Montenegro.[26] For the Habsburgs mobilization, like severed diplomatic relations, did not necessarily mean war. This was in contrast to the Russian military plan, where general mobilization did mean war, even though that fact was routinely denied in St. Petersburg. None of the mobilized Austrian forces was to be aimed at Russia.

Following the Emperor's instructions, Berchtold took his time in analyzing the Serbian response to the ultimatum before informing the public about the Austrians' reasons for rejecting it. The delay in issuing the explanation was a tactical mistake. The Serbs rushed into print with their side of the story. For many superficial observers their reply seemed conciliatory; others even considered it groveling. Belgrade appeared to agree outright to eight of the 10 Austrian demands. Surely, it was said, this provided grounds for negotiation. However, the Serbs rejected outright the two demands that the Austrians considered essential. They refused to agree to joint efforts to clamp down on insurgent activities directed against the monarchy. More importantly, they refused to allow the Habsburgs to participate in investigating the Sarajevo murders. Vienna demanded this out of certainty that the Serbs never would conduct a serious investigation on their own.

Expressing incredulity at the Habsburgs' audacity in suggesting joint investigative efforts, the Serbs insisted that these demands threatened their sovereignty. Naturally the Serbs did not want Habsburg investigators prowling around Belgrade where, as would later be revealed, the conspiracy reached into the bowels of the government.[27] Several of the Serbs' other answers, while affirmative on the surface, reflected the work of a fine legal staff, agile at inserting qualifiers so that the seemingly concessionary responses were actually meaningless.

By the time Berchtold produced the Austrian response, cries of outrage from the Serbs and their Russian Pan-Slav sympathizers had so deafened Europe that there was little chance of Vienna's point of view being heard. "Poor little Serbia" was about to be crushed, the word was passed on the street: Mother Russia must rush to her rescue.

Almost overnight, the European conversation about the war changed. Common wisdom had it that Austria was using the assassination as a pretext for aggression against Serbia. Soon Germany was being mentioned in the same breath. It became fashionable to portray the Germans and

Austrians as warmongers who were putting the world in harm's way. It wasn't long before the conversation took another turn, with Germany getting the larger share of the blame and Austria being viewed as hardly more than an appendage. Soon Serbia herself was being ignored. Germany became the target of collective rage.

It is easy to understand why Wilhelm II became the whipping boy for those seeking someone to blame for initiating the conflict. The Kaiser was given to irresponsible statements. His marginalia were infamous. He was an imperial enfant terrible, a force of nature, a human tsunami, roiling the political waters wherever he went. But claims that the Kaiser was responsible for taking Europe to war lack a basis in fact. As war loomed, both Czar Nicholas II and Emperor Franz Joseph, who disagreed on almost everything, concurred in their conviction that the Kaiser wanted peace. Wilhelm's urging the Habsburgs to move quickly against Serbia stemmed not from a desire to plunge the continent into war, but rather from his belief that a swift strike by the Habsburgs against the small and dangerous Balkan nation would forestall a widespread conflict involving Russia. The Kaiser's reaction after receiving a copy of the Serbian reply showed that he would have welcomed a peaceful solution to Austria's problem with Serbia.

With his usual impetuousness, Wilhelm II took one look at the Serbian answer and, not bothering with the fine print, pronounced it a great diplomatic success for Austro-Hungary. The Kaiser wrote to his foreign minister, Gottlieb von Jagow, that he was confident that the remaining differences between Austria and Serbia could be settled through negotiation.[28] This enthusiastic response is hardly that of someone who is bent upon a European war. Additionally, the fact that the Germans were still formulating their war aims days after the conflict started shows that they did not expect to go to war at that time.

The German military was meticulous in its planning and would hardly have gone into battle without careful preparation.

At around noon on July 28, Franz Joseph, having received reports of Russian military preparations at Krasnoye Selo, declared war on Serbia. The Emperor still hoped that the Romanovs, against whom the Habsburgs had never previously fought a war, would remain on the sidelines. That was not to be. Izvolsky was to have his revenge.

It took a great deal to cause Emperor Franz Joseph to abandon the peace policy he had pursued during most of his reign, but now, on the eve of his 84th birthday, he had concluded that the Serbian agitation against the monarchy was a mortal threat to the House of Habsburg. Berchtold provides an insightful look at Franz Joseph's thinking in July 1914. The foreign minister wrote that even though the Emperor still wanted peace, "for him there were boundaries – of personal honor, of dynastic tradition, reasons of state."[29]

The Pan-Serbs, egged on by the Russians, had time and again violated those boundaries. The long sessions in which the Emperor and his ministers wrestled with the Pan-Serb problem had eroded Franz Joseph's faith in a peaceful solution to the monarchy's difficulties with its Balkan neighbor. Franz Joseph's decision to go to war in 1914 was not made on the spur of the moment. It was a decision of last resort. For the Emperor, the assassination of Franz Ferdinand provided the ultimate evidence that the monarchy had to be defended or it would be destroyed.

Franz Joseph's continued absence from Vienna during the critical July days has raised questions about his role, or lack of it, in deciding whether to go to war. Was the ailing Emperor in full command of his senses during this period? Was he pushed to declare war by the generals or did he make the decision on his own?

Franz Joseph obviously was not the vigorous and battle hungry young man who had led his troops in Italy in 1859. During the short conflict with Prussia in 1866, realizing his limitations as a military commander, he had stayed away from the battlefield but had kept in close touch with events from Vienna. In July 1914 he was old, he was ailing, and during the waning days of peace, he remained at Bad Ischl, a five-hour train ride from Vienna. Samuel R. Williamson, Jr., suggests that Franz Joseph, deprived of the support of Franz Ferdinand in holding out for peace and "left alone with the generals,"[30] lacked the strength to stay the course and thus opted for war.

Berchtold, who was constantly in touch with the Emperor during those crucial last days, dismisses claims – emanating from what he calls "certain clueless circles" – that the Emperor was a "weak, helpless old man" who was easy to influence. The Emperor "never would have allowed himself to be pressed" on such a matter as going to war, the foreign minister said. According to Berchtold, Franz Joseph had "a clear ability to discern and judge," and made the decision on this "most serious question only with his conscience as his guide."[31]

Since Berchtold's detractors had begun accusing him of being too militaristic, he might have wanted to deflect some of the blame for the war onto the Emperor. However, the foreign minister's statements seem credible. Heinrich von Tschirschky, the German ambassador to Vienna, gives an account of a wide-ranging audience with Franz Joseph occurring on July 2, 1914. The envoy's report, directed to the German chancellor, suggests that the Emperor was remarkably clear-headed. Franz Joseph came to greet him with an elastic step. The Emperor acknowledged that the future looked bleak due to what he terms the growing danger "down under." He declared that it was necessary to examine strategies for the future. It was evident from his remarks that he was surveying the field for allies in a possible war. After discussing the deteriorating situation in Albania, where the Prince designated by the Powers to lead the new nation was proving unequal to his task, Franz Joseph went on to talk about Austria's relations with Italy, with Romania, Bulgaria and Greece, as well as with England and, of course, Germany.[32] The Emperor's analysis of the situation confronting the empire suggests mental acuity rather than weakness.

As a mature ruler Franz Joseph showed a strong, almost stubborn tendency to think for himself, particularly in foreign affairs. He repeatedly put Conrad in his place, informing him that it was he, the Emperor, who made foreign policy. He had done the same in response to General Potiorek's importunings for military action to suppress insurgents in Bosnia-Herzegovina. In the July days of 1914, the Emperor naturally heard from the generals; however, it is unlikely that they had the last word. Nobody in the Habsburg Empire had the power to force Franz Joseph to go to war. The final decision remained in the hands of the monarch himself.

During the last week of July, reports of Russian army activity near the borders of both Germany and Austria arrived in Berlin and Vienna with disturbing regularity. Whenever possible, the Russians flatly denied such reports. When confronted with specific examples of war preparations, Sazonov claimed that the Russians were engaging in partial mobilization, only against Austria. This was not true and Sazonov knew it. Russia never intended to confront Austria without bringing Germany into the conflict. All the Romanov military scenarios treated Germany and Austria as a single entity. This plan of action not only suited the Russians' French allies; it also was exactly what Sazonov wanted. The Limon von Sanders affair, involving a German military presence in Constantinople, had convinced him of the need to fight Germany as well as Austria in order to realize the empire's historic destiny at Byzantium.

The Russians continued to insist that they were, at most, conducting preliminary preparations for war. Actually they were going ahead with full-scale mobilization – phasing it in gradually so that it would be well along by the time general mobilization was actually announced. A pattern of denials, based on carefully parsed semantics, was central to the Russian effort.

On July 26 there was evidence of Russian mobilization along the entire northern front against East Prussia. General Vladimir Sukhomlinov, the Russian minister of war, briefed Bernhard von Eggeling, the German military attaché, that same evening. Eggeling reported that Sukhomlinov gave his word of honor that "not a horse had been recruited, not a reservist called in." The Russian minister said that only in the event that the Austrians crossed the Serbian frontier would the military districts closest to the monarchy – Kiev, Odessa, Moscow, and Kazan – be mobilized. Under no circumstances were the military districts on the German front – Warsaw, Vilna and St. Petersburg – to be mobilized. Eggeling said that upon asking why Russia would mobilize against Austria at all, the war minister shrugged and replied that this was "a matter for the diplomats."[33]

On that same evening, responding to questions from Count Karl Friedrich von Pourtales, the German ambassador to Russia, about a mobilization order said to involve several Russian Army Corps on the empire's western border, Sazonov declared that "he could guarantee that no mobilization order of that sort had been issued." He added that the ministerial council had decided to delay such orders until Vienna had "adopted a hostile attitude toward Russia." Upon being pressed, however, he acknowledged that "certain military measures" were in progress so that the Russians were "not to be taken by surprise."[34]

The Russian pattern of official deceit, promulgated by Sazonov and his associates, characterized the last days of

European peace. Reports arrived in Berlin and Vienna of harbors being mined, telegraph lines being cut. Martial law had been declared in St. Petersburg. Word came that the Russians were mobilizing in distant locations, including Siberia and the Caucasus. M. Boghitschewitch, at the time Serbian *charge d'affaires* in Berlin, wrote in *Kriegsursachen*, published after the war, that upon arriving in the Warsaw district on July 28, he observed extensive Russian mobilization under way. Supply wagons had been sent to their assigned stations and the Russian military had occupied the railroad station in Warsaw. On the German side of the border he saw no signs of mobilization whatsoever.[35] Documents on the world war assembled by Karl Kautsky showed that, between the morning of July 26 and the evening of July 30, the Austrians received 28 reports of Russian military preparations, 16 of them involving the Russian frontier with Germany.[36]

Personal diplomacy, a time-honored method of resolving differences between rulers of Europe's ancient imperial houses, was spectacularly absent during the July crisis. During a visit to the Russian foreign offices on July 28, Buchanan, the British ambassador to St. Petersburg, found Sazonov nearly hysterical over the escalating European crisis. Buchanan suggested the obvious: Why didn't the Czar make a personal appeal to Franz Joseph, asking him to restrict Austria's action within limits that Russia could accept? Sazonov summarily dismissed the idea of personal diplomacy, Buchanan reported. The Russian foreign minister declared that the only way to avoid war was for England to make it absolutely clear that she would join France and Russia if a conflict erupted.[37]

During Franz Joseph's long reign, he and the Romanov czars had often resolved their differences the old fashioned way – by personal letters or by getting together and talking. However, the Austrians' annexation of Bosnia and Herzegovina in 1908 had caused irreconcilable differences between the two imperial houses. The bad feelings were primarily on the Russian side. When war erupted in the Balkans in 1912, Franz Joseph sent Prince Gottfried von Hohenlohe on a peace mission to St. Petersburg in hopes of resolving the crisis. The Habsburg envoy, who had earlier been the monarchy's military attaché in St. Petersburg, was rebuffed in his attempt to improve relations between the two imperial houses. Franz Joseph appears to have decided that efforts to find common ground with the Russian Czar were futile. Nicholas II, basing his opinions mainly on what Sazonov and Izvolsky told him, was convinced that the current quarrel between the monarchy and Serbia was all Austria's fault. The Czar thought the Austrians were bent on dragging Europe into war.

Nicholas II was being "handled." Unfortunately, he was too naive to know it. Perhaps the Czar did not want war. However, he was being forced into it by circumstances for which he bore part of the blame. He had defaulted on his obligations as monarch, allowing his unscrupulous foreign ministers, first Izvolsky and then Sazonov, to lead him and the Russian Empire into a minefield. He had signed documents at Krasnoye Selo on July 25 for the mobilization of more than 1 million troops. Apparently he failed to realize that once the dogs of war were unleashed they could not be easily called off.

In a last minute act of desperation, Nicholas II turned to his friend Willy (Wilhelm II) for help in avoiding the looming disaster. The Czar asked the Kaiser to serve as a go-between with Franz Joseph – to bring the Emperor to his senses, as he thought. A series of messages, known as the "Willy and Nicky" telegraphs, commenced at 1 a.m., on July 29, when the Czar wired the Kaiser requesting him to mediate. The Czar's reply reflects the legacy of hatred toward the Habsburgs handed down through the Romanov family. The Russian ruler's words indicate his conviction that he occupies moral high ground in judging the Balkan crisis: "An ignoble war has been declared to a weak country," his telegram said. "The indignation in Russia shared fully by me is enormous."[38]

Wilhelm II responded immediately, promising his imperial brother that he would approach Franz Joseph in the effort to clear up the misunderstanding between the Romanov and the Habsburg rulers. The Kaiser's remarks show, however, that he thought it was the Czar, rather than the Austrian Emperor, who needed to be brought to his senses. Wilhelm II wrote that he was gravely concerned about the impression Austria's action against Serbia was making in Russia. The "unscrupulous actions" occurring in Serbia over a period of years had finally culminated in Archduke Ferdinand's assassination, the Kaiser's message said. "The spirit that led Serbians to murder their own king and his wife still dominates the country," the telegraph continued. Wilhelm II stressed the common interest of all sovereigns in assuring that those "morally responsible for the dastardly murder" received the punishment they deserved.[39]

The attitude of Nicholas II toward Franz Joseph remained set in stone. This was, after all, the Emperor who had betrayed the Czar's great grandfather, Nicholas I, in the Crimean conflict. This was the Habsburg Emperor who had opposed Romanov interests at the Congress of Berlin, where delegates had taken away most of the territory the czarist army had won during the war with Turkey the previous year. Nicholas II himself had been humiliated by the Emperor's surprise annexation of Bosnia-Herzegovina in 1908. Franz Joseph's scathing letter to the Czar during the annexation controversy hadn't helped matters. The Emperor had minced no words: the Czar was either incompetent or lying, or both, when he claimed that he hadn't given prior approval to Izvolsky's agreement with Aehrenthal at Buchlau. Surely Franz Joseph's words rankled with the insecure Czar. Nothing Wilhelm II or anyone could say swayed the Czar from his conviction that Austria intended to crush "poor little Serbia." Never mind that Serbia was engorged like a tick to twice her previous size with blood spilled during two Balkan wars instigated by Russian agents. And little Serbia still wasn't sated.

The situation spun out of control. On July 28, Franz Joseph declared war on Serbia. He took this action in response to information that the Russians were mobilizing. He hoped to begin and end the conflict with Serbia before the Russians had time to send in their army. The next day the Czar, prompted by the urging of Sazonov and his generals, signed an order for general mobilization. General Dobrorolsky collected the three official signatures required before the order for mobilization could be issued. He rushed to the telegraph office to relay the army's orders. As the order was about to go out the Czar received a telegram from Wilhelm II[40] saying that he believed a direct understanding between St. Petersburg and Vienna was "possible and desirable." The Kaiser said he was doing everything he could toward that end. He warned that Russian military measures would jeopardize his chances as a mediator, a role that he had readily espoused in response to Nicholas II's appeal to his friendship and help.[41]

The Czar rescinded the order for general mobilization and ordered partial mobilization,[42] much to the dismay of General Nikolai Yanushkevich, chief of the military's general staff, and General Sukhomlinov, the minister of war. Russian military officers realized that a European war was inevitable. Partial mobilization might have sounded less threatening than general mobilization, alleviating some of the Czar's fears, but it would leave the Austrians facing a war on two fronts, against the czarist army as well as Serbia. This would force the Austrians to order general mobilization. That, in turn, would require Germany to rise to the defense of her Austrian ally. Ultimately, all Europe would wind up in war.

In a vast empire such as Russia, switching from general mobilization to partial mobilization was a military planner's nightmare. The troops would get in one another's way as they moved into their newly designated fighting positions. Even the logistics of rerouting supply wagons to new locations would cause major problems.

In a three-way telephone conversation, the two generals attempted to convince the Czar that switching to partial mobilization was a terrible mistake. They told Nicholas II that based on the conduct of Germany and Austria, a general war was inevitable.[43] The Czar stood fast. Toward midnight the order for partial mobilization went out over the wires.

Or did it? According to some accounts, the order was never issued. Another source says that Moscow military authorities received and acted on the order just after midnight on July 30.[44]

Wilhelm II continued his mediation. Then, in the early hours of July 30 he received a telegram from the Czar confessing that the Russians had begun preliminary military measures for defense against Austria five days before. The Kaiser went wild. Here he had been attempting to arrange direct talks between St. Petersburg and Berlin while the Russians were mobilizing behind his back. He now was convinced, correctly, that the Russians' interest in mediation was a ploy to give the Czar's forces a head start in the coming conflict. "My work is at end," the Kaiser telegraphed the Czar. The next day, upon learning that red mobilization notices had gone up all over St. Petersburg, Wilhelm II sent the Russians an ultimatum giving them 18 hours to cease mobilization.

Evidence that the Russians lied about mobilization, which was being phased in according to plans developed during the First Balkan War, has recently come to light. We now know that from the beginning of the crisis the Russians had dissembled about their military preparations. Since the ministerial meeting on July 25 they had been secretly mobilizing.[45] As the crisis unfolded they pretended that their measures were intended for a limited war. Russia never planned to go against Austria without bringing Germany into the conflict. For the Russians the way to Constantinople lay through Berlin as well as Vienna.

Unfortunately for the Germans, the Kaiser's hasty ultimatum and consequent declaration of war had damning consequences. By being the first major Power to declare war against another major Power, Germany drew international blame for initiating the conflict. This was exactly what the Russians and the French wanted.

The Austrians were taken aback by Wilhelm II's precipitous action. They learned of the ultimatum only as it was about to be dispatched. Austrian troops were already on trains heading south to Serbia. With a new front opening in Galicia, where German and Russian troops would face off, Austria would be called on to help her ally. Conrad had no alternative but to let his troops continue to their original destination, where many of them would then face redeployment to the north. Thanks to Wilhelm's unexpected move, Austrian troops were marching off to the Great War on the wrong foot.[46]

On the morning of July 30, 1914, the Russian chief of staff and the minister of war decided that the Czar's decision to switch to partial mobilization, made on the evening of the previous day, was untenable. The military men conferred with Sazonov, who agreed. General Yanushkevich telephoned the Czar and pressed him to change his mind and agree to general mobilization. Nicholas II rejected his request. Finally the Czar said curtly that he was ending the conversation. Sazonov, yielding to the generals' importunings, phoned the Czar himself. The foreign minister implored His Majesty to receive him immediately. A long pause followed. Finally Nicholas II agreed to see him at three o'clock that afternoon.

Yanushkevich helped Sazonov prepare for the critical meeting. He was to explain to the Czar that partial mobilization would cause serious dislocation of the army. Sazonov also was advised to tell the Czar that his French friends would be unhappy if their Russian allies failed to honor their obligations. They had, after all, promised to mobilize against Germany as well as Austria. Yanushkevich told Sazonov to phone him as soon as he brought the Czar around so that he could proceed with general mobilization. "After this," said the chief of staff, "I will retire from sight, smash my telephone, and generally take all measures so that I cannot be found to give any contrary orders for a new postponement of general mobilization."[47]

In his memoirs, Sazonov provides his account of the Czar's eleventh-hour conversion to war. Arriving at the Peterhof Palace, he was ushered in to see the Czar, who was alone. The Czar's strain was obvious. Sazonov urged him to agree quickly to general mobilization. The foreign minister claimed that delay was dangerous since German mobilization was already "fairly advanced."[48]

The Russian foreign minister allowed the Czar to persist in the belief that Austria had mobilized against Russia. That was not true. The Habsburgs did not mobilize all of their army until July 31. They made their move only after learning that, on the evening before, the Russians had ordered general mobilization.[49]

Sazonov told the Czar that war could be avoided only if Russia abandoned Serbia. Austria had instigated the war. The Germans, rather than "bringing the Austrians to their senses," were making no effort to do so. Instead, Berlin was demanding that Russia "capitulate before the Central Powers."

Sazonov, exhibiting his masterful talents as a manipulator, played to the Czar's insecurities. He told Nicholas II that the Russian people would consider it unforgivable if he caved in to Germany's demands. They would feel that their good name had been besmirched, the foreign minister told the Czar.

Nicholas II was wracked with misgivings. "This would mean sending hundreds of thousands of Russian people to their death," he said, in a pale voice. Sazanov replied that he, as Czar, would not bear the blame for the precious lives sacrificed to the war. He would not have to answer to God or to his conscience. He could act with a "full conviction of being right." Bloodshed was being thrust on Russia and Europe by enemies "determined to increase their power by enslaving Russia's allies in the Balkans..." Russia had either to unsheathe her sword and defend her interests, or refuse to fight and perish, "covering herself with everlasting shame."[50]

The Czar paced the room, smoking one cigarette after another. The conversation continued for the better part of an hour, with the well-meaning but weak-willed Russian ruler attempting to resist the badgering of his foreign minister. The Czar's instincts were correct, but he eventually succumbed to Sazonov's verbal onslaught.[51] Nicholas II gave him the answer he wanted. Russia would risk a general European war. For the Czar, the matter was now in God's hands.

Sazonov went downstairs to the telephone. He called General Yanushkevich to give him the news. The generals decided to begin mobilization the next day. With the general mobilization order in hand, Dobrorolsky hurried to the main telegraph office. As the general said, it was only necessary to push a button and the whole state would begin "to function automatically with the precision of a clock's mechanism."[52] All the operators were poised at their machines, ready to send the news to every corner of the vast Romanov empire. That evening, "a few minutes after six, while absolute stillness reigned in the room, all the instruments began at once to click."[53] The 20th century's first great war had begun.

The ultimate evidence of the mad consistency of Romanov war aims comes from Nicholas II himself. It is January 1917. Russia is in ruins. The czarist army has suffered millions of casualties. Army garrisons have mutinied. Starving people have broken through bread lines and are looting the stores. The Bolsheviks are rising. The Czar and his family are about to be carted off to Siberia. The Germans send the Czar a peace offer. In response, Nicholas II issues a manifesto to his army: "The time for peace...has not yet come. The enemy has not yet been driven from the occupied territories. Russia has not yet performed the tasks this war has set her, by which I mean the possession of Constantinople and the Straits...."[54]

23 THE PUTIN FACTOR

The Soviet Union, which came into being shortly after the end of the First World War, was a grand social, economic and political experiment that failed. It ended with a thud in 1991, collapsing under its own inertia. Once that occurred, many people in the West lulled themselves into believing that the great Russian bear was awkwardly but steadily stumbling toward democracy and the rule of law, guided by benevolent handlers from the West. Most foreigners failed to understand the vast chasm separating Russia from Western nations that had come of political age during the Enlightenment. Russia never had a tradition of democratic government. For most Russians higher authority was – and is – an unquestioned fact of life.

Vladimir Putin emerged from the shadows to claim his place in history. Many Russians viewed him as a larger-than-life figure, sent by providence to lead his people out of the mire of uncertainty left by the Soviet Union's demise. Although Putin famously said that the collapse of the Soviet Union was the greatest geopolitical tragedy of the 20th century, he showed no signs of wanting to revive the moribund communist system. Instead, after becoming

Russian President in December 1999, Putin laid plans for a new and powerful empire built on the foundations of the House of Romanov but exceeding its influence. The Russian President's 2014 invasion of Ukraine and annexation of Crimea, along with his army's earlier aggression against the tiny country of Georgia, are part of Putin's blueprint for a new Russian century. Putin's dream of imperial greatness is embodied in an ambitious scheme for a Eurasian union involving alliances of mostly totalitarian states that are to serve as a bulwark against the North Atlantic Treaty Organization (NATO) and the European Union.

Vladimir Putin belongs to a rare species among the world's rulers. He is a self-made czar. In photographs, Putin stares at the world from under low-hanging brows, giving the impression that he is plotting something – which is more likely true than not. Those who study him closely say his every move is calculated. He has a talent for deft political moves, allowing him to get what he wants by catching his enemies off guard. He is not a man one would want to cross.

Putin grew up in St. Petersburg (then called Leningrad) in rough surroundings, a world away from the gilded splendor of the Romanov court. He lived with his parents in a working class neighborhood. His family's flat measured a mere 20 square meters. The Putin's shared a tiny kitchen with two other families. The courtyard in front was filled with trash. Young Vladimir became notorious in his neighborhood for street fighting. In fact, he initially was banned from the Communists' Young Pioneers because of his pugilistic tendencies.[1] In spite of this, or perhaps because of it, Putin achieved his early dream of working for the KGB, the Russian spy agency. He was stationed in Dresden in 1989 when the Berlin Wall came down. He is said to have busied himself with destroying incriminating KGB documents as an angry German crowd pressed toward the spy agency's offices.

In 1996, Russian President Boris Yeltsin named Putin head of federal security, a powerful arm of the former KGB. Then, in December 1999, Yeltsin, stepping down from power, chose the 57-year-old Putin to succeed him as President of the Russian Federation. Except for a period from 2008 to 2012, when Putin and his Prime Minister, Dmitry Medvedev, switched titles because of time limits for officeholders, Putin has occupied his country's highest office ever since. Russian election laws, previously calling for presidential elections every four years, now allow the president to serve for six years, with a chance for a second term. This virtually guarantees that Putin will be in power until 2024.

After initially taking office as Russian President, Putin set out to create a myth of himself as czar. Instead of taking his oath in the modernist edifice where the communists held important events, he chose for the ceremony the Kremlin's Great Palace, where the czars once lived. Following Romanov tradition, Putin and his wife, Lyudmila, attended mass at the Kremlin's Annunciation Cathedral. In another move emphasizing his connection to Russia's past, Putin rescued the Romanovs' autocratic czars, Peter the Great, Catherine the Great, Nicholas I and Alexander III from the dustbin of history where they had moldered during the communist era. Putin bestowed full honors on these imperials. Even the last Czar, Nicholas II, who made the fatal decision for war in 1914, was rehabilitated. In September 2000, the hapless ruler was canonized, becoming an Orthodox saint.[2] "This official revival of old imperial pomp and glory coincided with increasingly aggressive behavior vis-à-vis the former Soviet republics,"[3] writes Marcel H. Van Herpen, director of the Cicero Foundation, a pro-EU think tank based in the Netherlands.

In wooing public support, Putin relies on the Romanov pillars of empire – state, church and nation. He poses as a ruler who can take his country back to a world where simple faith is accepted as truth and where he, as czar, is God's representative on Earth. He projects himself as synonymous with the state, potent and unyielding. Putin encourages Russians in the belief that theirs is a unique civilization that must be protected from foreign influences. He cultivates a native brand of xenophobia as a source of political support.

Putin has declared that the "aggrandizement of state powers" must be the goal of every Russian citizen, "and not the aggrandizement of his or her personal freedom or well-being."[4] For him, the individual is a cog in the machine of the state. Following czarist tradition, Putin uses Orthodoxy as a buttress to his power. The Russian President is second to none in his expressions of piety. He consults regularly with his spiritual adviser, a man of God with ultraconservative views. Putin makes a show of regularly attending religious services. He is even said to travel in a consecrated Audi vehicle.

Putin's dreams of imperial glory rival those of Peter and Catherine the Great in grandiosity. However, the Russian President's tactics — so far at least — are much different from those of the early Romanov greats, who sent large armies into the field in search of conquests. Putin, like the later Romanov czars, is using stealth methods enabling him to grow his empire by degrees. These tactics have the advantage of enabling a ruler to gain territory without attracting much attention to the underlying aggression. The Russian President has fomented instability in Ukraine and in other sovereign states adjacent to the Black Sea as an excuse for sending in "peacekeepers" (troops). If forced to withdraw his soldiers, Putin demands concessions for doing so (or pretending to do so). A typical ploy involves covertly keeping special forces on the ground after those troops have feigned withdrawal, in preparation for a future move to seize power. Also, Putin uses vassals (or separatists) as proxies in military skirmishes, calculated to serve Russian imperial interests. These methods are particularly dangerous because they are insidious. The war of 1914 would not have occurred if the Romanovs had not used these methods – against the Habsburgs as well as the Turks in the Balkans.

While Putin takes many of his cues from the Romanovs' military manuals, there is a difference. With his arsenal of nuclear and conventional weapons he has the capacity to do harm that the Romanovs never could have imagined.

Putin launched an assault on Ukrainian sovereignty in late February 2014, when unidentified masked men wearing military fatigues and carrying automatic weapons suddenly showed up on the Crimean Peninsula. The intruders' black uniforms bore no insignias. President Putin scoffed at reporters' suggestions that the men were Russian special agents. Anybody could buy such military uniforms, which were available at bazaars across the peninsula, he told his questioners. The strangers blocked roads, took over government buildings, and occupied two airports. The gun-waving intruders, confronted by terrified residents, claimed they had come to save the local population from fascists who had taken over the Ukrainian capital of Kiev and were heading toward Crimea. A few days later, thousands of uniformed Russian-speaking soldiers, supported by columns of tanks, marched on Crimea's capital, Simferopol. The troops took up positions outside Ukrainian army barracks. They stormed a military hospital, commandeered broadcasting stations and seized the port of Sevastopol. Putin eventually dropped his initial pretense that these were merely local volunteers. The Russian President said he had sent in his military to "restore calm" to the peninsula.

In typical Romanov fashion, the Russian President used political unrest, this time in Kiev, as an excuse for territorial aggrandizement. Protests had erupted in the Ukrainian capital after President Viktor Yanukovych, yielding to pressure from Putin, backed out of a promise to sign a major trade agreement with the European Union. As a result of the protests, Yanukovych fled to Russia. Putin claimed the Ukrainian President's ouster was an illegal coup staged by far right groups.[5] Pro-Russian separatists quickly arranged an illegal referendum in Crimea asking residents to vote on joining the Russian Federation. The referendum ignored international protocols designed to assure that voting is free and fair. Participants in the referendum voted overwhelmingly[6] to join the Russian Federation. Two days later, on March 18, Putin annexed Crimea.

Meanwhile, pro-Kremlin provocateurs entered eastern and southern Ukraine, a region where, in the 1990s, separatist sentiment had sprung up. At that time it failed to gain traction because then-President Boris Yeltsin refused to support it. Putin, on the other hand, provided the separatist proxies with sophisticated arms and military advisers. The region around Donetsk quickly turned into a war zone.

On May 9, Putin arrived by yacht at the Crimean port of Sevastopol, where celebrations marking the end of World War II were under way. When Putin came ashore, Russian naval officers beamed and the crowd roared. The festivities included a spectacular aerobatic performance by Russian fighter jets. It seemed a symbolic moment, a sign that Russia, reduced in significance following the collapse of the Soviet Union, had reclaimed its position as a Great Power.

Although Putin laid out a plan for a "Eurasian union" in an article in *Izvestia* in October 2011, it has attracted little attention outside foreign policy circles. It should be taken seriously. Those close to Putin say he is enthusiastic about the project, officially known as the Eurasian Economic Union, which has five members so far. Besides Russia, these are Belarus, Kazakhstan, Armenia and Kyrgyzstan. The Kremlin is investing heavily in the project, promising member states generous oil and gas subsidies and other assistance.

The Eurasian project is being promoted as a customs union, boasting an integrated market of almost 180 million people. However, its members also are participants in a mutual defense alliance of sorts. Most importantly, perhaps, the Economic Union is intended to stand in moral opposition to the "sinful West," with its despised individualism, its espousal of democratic freedoms and its acceptance of homosexuality and abortion.

The ideologist behind the Eurasian project is a political scientist and pseudo-mystic named Aleksandr Dugin.[7] The founder of an international Eurasian youth organization, he is a hard right-winger and admirer of Benito Mussolini. Dugin, who has close ties with the Kremlin and is said to have acted as Putin's adviser, wants Russia to return to the hierarchical world of the Middle Ages in which authority resides in the hands of God and the czar, the divinity's representative on Earth. Dugin is said to consider human rights a racist idea. He believes that the world is in the end of times, in which a final confrontation will occur between the forces of evil (the West, particularly the United States) and Russia.

Prime Minister Medvedev says he expects the Eurasian Economic Union eventually to include, at the very least, most of the former members of the Soviet Union. He characterizes the future organization as "one big state," which presents problems. While Putin appears willing to concede some authority to other members of the Union, extensive power-sharing is not part of the plan. Putin clearly expects all roads in his new empire to lead to Moscow. Since most of the former Soviet bloc countries enjoy autonomy, they are unlikely to join voluntarily in Russia's latest imperial venture. War almost certainly will be necessary if the Russian President is to achieve his aims.

A major obstacle to Putin's expansionist ambitions is NATO, which has established a presence on territory that the Russian President considers his country's own backyard. Putin has repeatedly expressed anger at the failure of U.S. leaders to abide by promises that they made during negotiations for the reunification of Germany after the fall of the Berlin Wall. During those meetings, the Americans reportedly assured Soviet leader Mikhail Gorbachev that they would not expand NATO eastward. Then, according to the Russians, they went back on their word. In 1999 the Czech Republic, Hungary and Poland were inducted into NATO. In 2004 Bulgaria, Estonia, Latvia, Lithuania, Romania, Slovakia and Slovenia became members. All of Russia's former allies in the Warsaw Pact now belong to what Putin may well consider the enemy camp.

The Russian President, widely viewed as a realist, undoubtedly prefers to build empire without going to war with the West. On the other hand, he appears increasingly willing to risk such a conflict if it is the only way he can achieve his imperialist aims. States located in what the Russians call their "near abroad," meaning lands along the Russian border that were once part of the Soviet bloc, are in danger of being forcibly reintegrated into Putin's empire. Those that are not in NATO – Ukraine, Moldova and Georgia – are particularly vulnerable to being swallowed alive by the Russian bear. However, in spite of being NATO members, Poland and the Baltic states are far from safe from their Russian neighbor.

In August and September 2009 the Russians, angered at a proposal for locating a missile-defense system in Poland, staged military exercises in the Kaliningrad area near that country's border. The maneuvers included a simulated nuclear attack on Poland. The government in Warsaw officially protested the Kremlin's actions. The Poles were right to be worried. Early in his presidency, Putin had revised Russia's military doctrine, cancelling a previous no-first-strike policy for nuclear weapons. He decreed unilaterally that Russia had the right to use these weapons preemptively "if other means of conflict resolution had been exhausted or deemed ineffective."[8]

The little country of Georgia was an early victim of Putin's aggression. On August 8, 2008, the Russian

President and U.S. President George W. Bush were chatting in the VIP section of Beijing's Olympic stadium, known as the Bird's Nest, waiting for the opening ceremonies for the summer games, when Putin received a message. According to one account, the Russian leader "turned pale with rage."[9] His reaction was likely a masterful piece of fakery. Putin is said to have told Bush that on the previous night Georgian troops had launched a surprise attack on Tskhinvali, the capital of South Ossetia, one of Georgia's two breakaway provinces, resulting in some 2,000 casualties. Putin said that Russian troops had entered South Ossetia and its neighboring province, Abkhazia, in response to the Georgian aggression. The Russian President told President Bush it was a "humanitarian intervention." This version of events – that Georgia attacked and Russia responded to the attack – was generally accepted by diplomats and journalists. "The official Russian narrative...was a prime example of active disinformation," something in which Putin, a former KGB agent, excels, writes Van Herpen.

Van Herpen's well-documented account provides evidence that Putin started planning a military intervention in Georgia early in his first term as President. The Russians had gained a foothold in Abkhazia and South Ossetia in the early 1990s by providing the region's pro-Russian separatists with military aid. A cease-fire was arranged, but some Russian troops stayed on. In 2002, Putin's agents, trampling on Georgia's exclusive authority to issue official documents within its borders, began a passport initiative in the two provinces. Suddenly the breakaway regions were teeming with Russian "nationals." The ploy was intended to give the Russians an excuse for later intervention on their citizens' behalf. (The Russians repeated the passport initiative in Crimea a few days before the annexation).

In April 2008, Van Herpen writes, the Russians began covertly positioning themselves for war. Russian "peacekeepers," equipped with heavy artillery and antiaircraft equipment – showed up in Abkhazia. A few weeks later several hundred more Russian soldiers appeared, ostensibly to deliver humanitarian aid. On several occasions Ossetian troops, commanded by Russian officers, fired on Georgian villages in the contested territory. In early August, reports arrived in Tbilisi that five battalions of Russia's 58th Army had crossed into South Ossetia. According to Van Herpen, the Georgians' attack on the night of August 7 came in response to those provocations.

The Russians scored a major triumph in their war. The ethnic Georgians were forced out of South Ossetia and Abkhazia. Then-Russian President Medvedev formally recognized the "independence" of the two regions on August 26, 2008. In practice, the Russians had annexed the provinces. The Russians' progressive encroachment hardly caused a ripple in the international community. (To paraphrase British Prime Minister Neville Chamberlain's infamous remark, Georgia was, after all, a small country about which most of those in the West knew nothing). The war goes on.

In the grand scale of events, what happened in Georgia is relatively insignificant. It is in Ukraine that the battle lines will ultimately be drawn between East and West. The ties between Russia and Ukraine run deep. In AD 988, Vladimir I, the ruler of Kievan Rus, an ancient kingdom that included Russia, Ukraine and Belarus, converted to Orthodox Christianity. Kiev became the spiritual center of what became known as Holy Russia. For many of Putin's subjects, Kiev remains central to Russian national identity. Ukraine's population, totaling some 50 million, is mostly Slav, offering a counterbalance to regions in Russia's east – with their different religions and cultures. In the Russian imperial scheme, Ukraine's size itself is an attraction, since empires are expected to be large. As former U.S. presidential adviser Zbigniew Brzezinski writes, "without Ukraine, Russia ceases to be an empire" – with Ukraine it automatically becomes one.[10] Alexandr Dugin views the struggle over Ukraine in apocalyptic terms. It will be in Ukraine, he says, where the former Soviet states will rise to take on the Western Antichrist. The battle for empire, he says, "is a battle for Kiev."

AFTERWORD: LATER DEVELOPMENTS

The Russians continue to pursue tactics from the Romanovs' military playbook as they proceed with carefully calibrated progressive encroachment in eastern Ukraine. The ongoing low-grade conflict affects the population like a fever, snuffing out stirrings of resistance that otherwise might take hold. Parts of the provinces of Donetsk and Luhansk are now controlled by separatists. The leaders of these regions are puppets with strings pulled by the Kremlin.

A recently completed 11.2 mile highway now connects the Russian mainland with Crimea. The project, a decades-old dream of Kremlin planners, offers a myriad of new opportunities for Russian military adventurism against Ukraine. The highway passes through the Kerch Straits, with its narrow channel connecting the Sea of Azov and the Black Sea. For centuries Ottoman sentries stood guard at the fortifications commanding the Straits, preventing Romanov czars from entering the Black Sea. Now the Russians have control of that strategic corridor.

For Ukraine this means trouble. That country has a long border on the Sea of Azov. It recently completed a large naval base at Berdyansk on the northern coast of the land-locked body of water. The Ukrainians have every right to have access to the facility and to their country's eastern coast. That is in no way guaranteed.

A recent clash between Ukrainian and Russian sailors at Kerch provides a likely harbinger of future trouble. In late November 2018, three Ukrainian vessels — two small armored artillery vessels and a tub boat — attempted to enter the Sea of Azov from the Black Sea. As they neared the passageway, the Russians opened fire, wounding several sailors. The Russians claimed the Ukrainian vessels were "maneuvering dangerously." In a brazen breach of maritime manners, the Russians positioned a large ship sideways in the channel, totally blocking ship traffic. The Ukrainian ships were seized and the sailors were taken to Moscow, where they were jailed for illegally crossing the border.

The Russians, perhaps heedful of the international uproar over their conduct, finally reopened the passage. But the incident sent an ominous message: The Russians are in command at Kerch.

Provocations of this sort could eventually lead to a full-scale war between Russia and Ukraine. Putin may well be hoping for such a conflict.

NOTES TO CHAPTERS

CHAPTER 1

[1] The origin of Peter's boat remains unknown. Perhaps it was English but it is also possible that it was the work of Dutch craftsmen in Russia during the reign of Peter's father, Alexis. Peter later referred to the boat as the Godfather of the Russian Navy. In 1701, Peter had the craft, weighing some 1.5 tons, dragged over rough roads from St. Petersburg to the Kremlin, where it was kept near the Ivan the Great Bell Tower.

[2] James Cracraft, *The Revolution of Peter the Great* (Cambridge, Mass.: Harvard University Press, 2003), 41. See also Eugene Schuyler, *Peter the Great: Emperor of Russia – A Study of Historical Biography* (New York: Charles Scribner's Sons, 2 vols., 1884) v.1, 111-14.

[3] Lindsey Hughes, *Peter the Great: A Biography* (New Haven, Conn.: Yale University Press, 2002), 2-3.

[4] Schuyler, v.1, 10.

[5] Ibid., v.1, 78.

[6] In 1683, Turkish forces set up camp under the walls of Vienna.

[7] Hughes, *Peter*, 10.

[8] B.H. Sumner, *Peter the Great and the Ottoman Empire* (Oxford: Basil Blackwell, 1949), 35.

[9] Schuyler, v.1, 157.

[10] A ceremonial staircase leading into the Palace of Facets in the Kremlin.

[11] Schuyler, v.1, 205.

[12] Ibid., v.1,157.

[13] Ibid., v.1, 247.

[14] Jacob Abbott, *Peter the Great* (New York: Harper & Brothers,

1904), 100-01.

[15] Robert K. Massie, *Peter the Great: His Life and World* (New York: Ballantine Books, 1980), 146-47.

[16] Ibid., 147.

[17] Hughes, *Peter*, 82.

[18] Ibid., 217-18. See also Schuyler, v.1, 300.

[19] Alan Palmer, *The Decline and Fall of the Ottoman Empire* (London: John Murray, 1995), 24-25. From Lord Acton, *Lectures on Modern History*.

[20] Massie, *Peter*, 560.

[21] Ibid., 293. Also Schuyler, v.1., 362.

[22] Schuyler, v.1, 362. See also M.G. Ustryalov, *History of the Reign of Peter the Great* (6 vols., St. Petersburg 1858-1863) v.3, 551-52.

[23] The Turks finally tired of Charles XII's shenanigans and placed him under arrest. In 1714 he decided to leave, traveling incognito back to Pomerania.

[24] Pan-Slavists were nationalists who attempted to get those of that ethnicity to join forces for the common good.

[25] Turkish military leaders.

[26] Edith Durham, *Twenty Years of Balkan Tangle* (London: George Allen & Unwin, 1920), 18-19. The battle occurred in Montenegro, on high ground between Rijeka and Podgorica.

[27] Massie, *Peter*, 572-73.

[28] Ibid., 584-86.

[29] Ibid.

CHAPTER 2

[1] John T. Alexander, *Catherine the Great: Life and Legend* (New York: Oxford University Press, 1989), 8.

[2] Ibid., xvii.

[3] Ibid., 70.

[4] Ibid., 89.

[5] Catherine's last child, fathered by Grigory Orlov, was an infant at the time of the coup.

[6] The Seven Years' War (1756-1763) was a global conflict involving most of the powers of Europe. It was known in America as the French and Indian War.

[7] I have used the conventional English spelling of "Frederick" for Frederick the Great. Other German rulers' names are spelled "Friedrich."

[8] Vincent Cronin, *Catherine Empress of All the Russias* (New York: William Morrow and Company, 1978), 125.

[9] Carolly Erickson, *Great Catherine: The Life of Catherine the Great, Empress of Russia* (New York: Crown Publishers, 1994), 207-09.

[10] *The Memoirs of Catherine the Great,* transl. Mark Cruse and Hilde Hoogenboom. (New York: Modern Library, 2006), lii-liii.

[11] Isabel de Madariaga, *Russia in the Age of Catherine the Great* (London: Phoenix Press, 2002), 203-04.

[12] Alexander, 129.

[13] Referring to the Tatars in Crimea and nearby areas.

[14] Alexander, 131-32.

[15] Ibid.

[16] Cronin, 189.

[17] Madariaga, 207. The date of this note is December 26, 1769.

[18] Ibid., 209.

[19] Ibid., 210.

[20] Ibid.

[21] Alexander, 132-33.

[22] Nancy Mitford, *Frederick the Great* (London: Penguin Books, 1970), 184-85.

[23] Madariaga, 225.

[24] Ibid., 233.

[25] Alexander, 140-42.

[26] Madariaga, 235.

[27] Cronin, 211.

[28] Cronin, 246.

[29] Ibid., 247.

[30] Alexander, 235, 237.

[31] Ibid., 242.

[32] Ibid.

[33] Ibid., 244.

[34] C.A. Macartney, *The Habsburg Empire: 1790-1918* (New York: The Macmillan Company, 1969), 131.

[35] Madariaga, 387-88.

[36] In 1778, Catherine named her second grandson Constantine, after the last Greek Emperor, Constantine Palaeologos, and struck a medal showing the Hagia Sophia on one side and the Black Sea with a star rising over it on the other. Cronin, 250.

[37] Alexander, 247-48.

[38] Ibid., 248.

[39] Ibid., 249.

[40] Ibid., 248.

[41] Madariaga, 366.

[42] Cronin, 249.

[43] The story that Potemkin deceived the Empress with villages of cardboard and painted seaports with painted ships and guns is apocryphal. It is true that at one village, boards were set up so the Empress would not see the paltry huts of the inhabitants. That appears to have been the extent of the deception, although naturally Potemkin planned stops at picturesque villages. It is likely that the story stems from a catty remark by one of Catherine's guests, the Prince de Ligne, who was no admirer of Potemkin.

[44] Cronin, 251.

[45] Madariaga, 394.

[46] A number of historians believe they actually were secretly married.

[47] Alexander, 269.

[48] Macartney, 131.

[49] Ibid., 132.

[50] Ibid., 136.

[51] Grand Duke Constantine was the heir apparent, but he had no wish to reign.

CHAPTER 3

[1] The Napoleonic wars lasted from 1796 until June 1815, when the French ruler finally was defeated at Waterloo.

[2] The Third Coalition.

[3] Prince Adam Czartoryski, *Memoirs of Prince Adam Czartoryski and his Correspondence with Alexander I* (London: Remington & Co. Publishers. 2nd ed., 2 vols., 1888), v.2, 102-03.

[4] Henri Troyat, *Alexander of Russia*, trans. Joan Pinkham (New York: Grove Press, 1982), 86-87.

[5] Ibid.

[6] Ibid., 87.

[7] Ibid.

[8] Czartoryski, v.2, 102-03.

[9] Ibid., 89.

[10] Ibid.

[11] Ibid., 91-92.

[12] Ibid., 92.

[13] Ibid.

[14] Ibid., 92-93.

[15] Ibid., 93.

[16] Ibid., 98.

[17] Palmer, *Ottoman*, 65.

[18] Ibid., 66.

[19] Ibid., 66-67.

[20] Troyat, 102-03.

[21] Ibid.

[22] Ibid.

[23] Harold Nicolson, *The Congress of Vienna: A Study in Allied Unity: 1812-1822* (New York: Grove Press, 1946), 15.

[24] Alan Palmer, *Alexander I: Tsar of War and Peace* (New York: Harper & Row, 1974), 156.

[25] Palmer, *Alexander I,* 160-61.

[26] Palmer, *Ottoman*, 79-80.
[27] Palmer, *Alexander I*, 275.

CHAPTER 4

[1] Nicolson, 54.
[2] Ibid., 171.
[3] Constantin de Grunwald, *La Vie de Metternich* (Paris: Calmann-Levy, 1938), 152.
[4] Adam Zamoyski, *Rites of Peace: The Fall of Napoleon and the Congress of Vienna* (New York: HarperCollins Publishers, 2007), 320.
[5] Nicolson, 175-79.
[6] Ibid., 179-80.
[7] Ibid.
[8] Ibid., 243.
[9] Ibid., 245.
[10] Troyat, 224.
[11] Ibid., 229-30.
[12] Ibid., 230. From *Chateaubriand's Les Memoires d'Outre-Tombe*, centenary edition, Paris, 1948.
[13] Ibid., 231-32.
[14] Ibid., 234.
[15] Ibid., 255.
[16] Nicolson, 251-52.
[17] Ibid., 252.
[18] See Egon Caesar Conte Corti, *Unter Zaren und Gekrönten Frauen* (2 vols., Paris, 1949), v. 2, 82.
[19] Ibid., 193.
[20] Ibid., 201.
[21] Richard Metternich, ed., *Mémoires, Documents et Ecrits laissés par le Prince de Metternich* (8 vols., Paris, 1880-84), v.4, 6. Letter dated April 4, 1823.
[22] Greeks in Constantinople who held high posts under the Turks.
[23] Palmer, *Ottoman*, 85-88.
[24] Ibid., 86-87.
[25] Ibid., 87-88.
[26] Ibid., 230.
[27] Troyat, 282.

[28] Ibid., 244.

CHAPTER 5

[1] Marquis de Custine, *La Russie en 1839* (Paris, 1853), p. 317.
[2] Nicholas's brother, Constantine, was older, and therefore first in line to the throne. However, Constantine had stated repeatedly that he had no desire to be czar. Alexander I concurred with Constantine's decision, but documents naming Nicholas as Alexander I's successor were never made public. This led to the false impression that Nicholas I was a usurper. The name "Decembrists" refers to the month of Nicholas I's accession.
[3] E.M. Almedingen, *The Emperor Alexander II: A Study* (London: The Bodley Head, 1962), 22-24.
[4] Akkerman was later named Ovidiopol to honor an early resident, the poet, Ovid.
[5] Radu R. Florescu, *The Struggle against Russia in the Romanian Principalities: 1821-1854* (Iasi: The Foundation for Romanian Culture and Studies, 1997), 131.
[6] Ibid., 150.
[7] Richard Metternich, *Mémoires*, v.4, 329.
[8] Count Vichy to Metternich, April 24, 1828, *Mémoires*, v.5, 489.
[9] Palmer, *Ottoman*, 98.
[10] John C.K. Daly, *Russian Seapower and 'The Eastern Question,' 1827-41* (Annapolis, Md.: Naval Institute Press, 1989), 16.
[11] Metternich to Apponyi, Nov. 13, 1827, *Mémoires*, v.4, 203.
[12] Metternich to Habsburg Emperor Franz I, Nov. 30, 1827, *Mémoires*, v.4, 432.
[13] Daly, 14.
[14] W. Bruce Lincoln, *Nicholas I: Emperor and Autocrat of All the Russias* (DeKalb, Ill.: Northern Illinois University Press, 1989), 122.
[15] Palmer, *Metternich*, 241-42.
[16] Daly, 18-19.
[17] Florescu, 151.
[18] Lincoln, 125.
[19] Daly, 23-24.
[20] Lincoln, 129.
[21] Daly, 32-33.

[22] Ibid., 33.
[23] Nicholas I told Count Saint-Priest that "Russia was large enough as it was." (Lincoln, 201). It is correct that the Czar wasn't eager to annex any of the small Balkan provinces. Controlling Constantinople and the Straits was his goal.
[24] The Russians also gained full authority over the Chilai outlet. They shared the third outlet, the St. George, with the Turks.
[25] Daly, 86.
[26] Ibid., 87.
[27] Palmer, *Ottoman*, 102.
[28] Daly, 98.
[29] Ibid., 99. The Russians' clever ploy regarding the Straits failed. On July 13, 1841, the Powers revoked the secret provision in the 1833 treaty, replacing it with a convention forbidding war vessels from using the Straits.

CHAPTER 6

[1] Macartney, 232-33.
[2] Fenton Bresler, *Napoleon III: A Life* (New York: Carroll & Graf Publishers, 1999), 86.
[3] T.E.B. Howarth, *Citizen King: The Life of Louis-Philippe, King of the French* (London: Eyre & Spottiswoode, 1962), 162.
[4] Ibid., 183-85.
[5] Metternich to Emperor Franz, July 31, 1830, in *Mémoires*, v.5, 7-11.
[6] Unkiar-Skelessi caused such an international uproar that in 1840 the Russians were forced to accept the fact that it would not be renewed when it expired in 1841. At that time, Nicholas repudiated his claim to a protectorate over the Ottoman Christians and tore up the treaty. The Bosphorus and the Dardanelles were now closed to all foreign warships in time of peace. However, while the Czar forfeited what he had gained from the Ottomans in 1833, he kept all privileges that Russia had won in earlier agreements with the Turks.
[7] Howarth, 242.
[8] Bresler, 210.
[9] Ibid., 216-17.

CHAPTER 7

[1] Louis XVI was sent to the guillotine in 1793. Charles X was driven into exile in 1830. Both kings had claimed divine right as their reason for holding power. Louis-Philippe, on the other hand, had taken his authority not only from God but also from the people.

[2] Macartney, 306.

[3] Eugene Bagger, *Franz Joseph: Eine Persönlichkeits-Studie* (Zürich: Amalthea-Verlag, 1927), 109.

[4] Ibid., 114-15.

[5] Hungary and Austria had different governments, with the Hungarians claiming rights under an ancient constitution that were more liberal than those enjoyed by the Austrians. The Magyars of Hungary were the ruling class even though they were not a majority of the population. These powerful nobles blocked Habsburg attempts to create a central government in which all citizens of the empire would have equal rights.

[6] Jean-Paul Bled, *Franz Joseph* (Oxford: Blackwell, 1992), 36.

[7] Macartney, 324.

[8] Viktor Bibl, *Von Revolution zu Revolution in Österreich* (Wien: Rikola Verlag, 1924), 104.

[9] Macartney, 323.

[10] Ibid., 396.

[11] Ibid., 381-82.

[12] The title "King of Jerusalem" dates to the crusades in the 10th through 13th centuries.

[13] John Van der Kiste, *Emperor Francis Joseph: Life, Death and the Fall of the Habsburg Empire* (Phoenix Mill: Sutton Publishing Limited, 2005), 17.

[14] Ian W. Roberts, *Nicholas I and the Russian Intervention in Hungary*. (New York: St. Martin's Press, 1991), 67.

[15] Joseph Redlich, *Kaiser Franz Joseph von Österreich* (Berlin: Verlag für Kulturpolitik, 1929), 160.

[16] Buda and Pest were separate cities until 1873.

[17] Joseph Alexander Helfert, *Geschichte Oesterreichs vom Ausgange des Wiener Oktober-Aufstandes 1848, Feldzug IV*, (Prague: F. Tempsky, 1886), 393-98.

[18] Arthur Görgei, *My Life and Acts in Hungary in the Years 1848*

and 1849 (New York: Harper's & Brothers, 1852), 196.

[19] Helfert, 212.

[20] Bled, 56-57.

[21] Macartney, 438.

[22] András Geró, *Emperor Francis Joseph, King of the Hungarians* (Wayne, N.J.: Center for Hungarian Studies and Publications, Inc., 2001), 52.

[23] Bled, 58.

[24] General Haynau did the Austrian Empire much harm with his brutal tactics against the Hungarian rebels. Thirteen generals who had opposed the monarchy were executed, as was Lajos Batthyány. The Hungarian public blamed Franz Joseph for what happened, and harbored resentments against the Emperor that time never totally erased.

[25] Geró, 52-53.

[26] Macartney, 430.

[27] Ibid., 429.

[28] Bled, 60.

[29] Görgei, 607.

[30] Roberts, 182-ff.

[31] Bled, 60.

[32] Görgei was allowed to live in retirement in Klagenfurt, Austria., In 1867, he was finally pardoned and permitted to return to Hungary.

[33] Ibid., 60.

[34] Macartney, 431.

[35] Roberts, 190-93.

[36] Ibid., 224.

[37] Ibid., 144, 198.

CHAPTER 8

[1] Heinrich Ritter von Srbik, *Metternich, der Staatsmann und der Mensch* (2 vols., Munich: 1925), v.2, 472.

[2] Ian Fletcher and Natalia Ishchenko, *The Crimean War: A Clash of Empires* (Staplehurst, England: Spellmount, 2004), 9-10.

[3] Trevor Royle, *Crimea: The Great Crimean War:1853-1856* (New York: St. Martin's Press, 2000), 19-20.

[4] Ibid., 34.

[5] Palmer, *Ottoman*, 118. See *Slavic and Eastern Review*, v.27, 1948-9, pp. 139-43.

[6] Lincoln, 331-32. Lincoln is one of Nicholas I's biographers who takes at face value the Czar's disavowal of his interest in seizing Constantinople. He argues that Russia had the chance to do this in 1829 and did not take it; therefore, he concludes, the Czar no longer cherished such ambitions.

[7] Bartolomeo Rastrelli was an architect whose major works included the Winter Palace.

[8] Palmer, *Ottoman*, 119.

[9] Philip Warner, *The Crimean War: A Reappraisal* (Hertfordshire, England: Wordsworth Editions, 2001), 110.

[10] Royle, 38-39.

[11] Ibid., 38.

[12] Egon Caesar Conte Corti, *Unter Zaren und Gekrönten Frauen* (Salzburg-Leipzig: Verlag Anton Pustet, 1936), 90.

[13] Redlich, 128-29.

[14] Ibid., 128-129.

[15] Barker, 8.

[16] Ibid., 10.

[17] Redlich, 128-29.

[18] Ibid., 130-31.

[19] Royle, 122.

[20] Redlich, 131-33. Footnote applies to entire letter.

[21] Ibid., 133.

[22] Ibid.

[23] Corti, *Unter Zaren*, 93.

[24] Ibid., 137.

[25] Redlich, 135-36.

[26] Ibid., 136.

[27] Ibid.

[28] Barker, 11.

[29] Bled, 95. Citing Franz Rauchenberger, *Graf Buol-Schauenstein: Seine Politik im Krimkrieg* (unpublished dissertation, Graz, 1967), 66.

[30] Corti, *Mensch und Herrscher: Wege und Schicksale Kaiser Franz Joseph I zwischen Thronbesteigung und Berliner Congreß* (Graz/Wien: Verlag Styria, 1952), 134.

[31] Redlich, 138-39.

[32] Ibid.

[33] Ibid., 138-41. Nicholas I to Franz Joseph, 4/16 January 1854. Vienna State Archives.

[34] Corti, *Mensch*, 136.

[35] Fletcher, 33.

[36] Corti, *Mensch*, 147-48.

[37] Ibid., 147.

[38] Lincoln, 348.

[39] Barker, 49-54.

[40] Sepoys were Indian soldiers attached to European military operations.

[41] Fletcher, 40. From Alexander William Kinglake, *The Invasion of the Crimea: Its Origin and an Account of its Progress down to the Death of Lord Raglan* (London 1863), v.2, 59.

[42] Royle, 175.

[43] Corti, *Mensch*, 133.

[44] Bagger, 267.

[45] Ibid., 269-70.

[46] Lincoln, 348.

[47] Ibid.

[48] Bagger, 266.

[49] Ibid.

[50] Royle, 86.

[51] Fletcher, 524-25.

[52] Royle, 462-64.

[53] Bagger, 268.

[54] Barker, 285.

[55] Royle, 482.

CHAPTER 9

[1] Virginia Cowles, *The Russian Dagger: Cold War in the Days of the Czars* (New York and Evanston: Harper & Row, 1969), 59-60.

[2] Ibid.

[3] Emanuel Sarkisyanz, "Russian Imperialism Reconsidered," in *Russian Imperialism from Ivan the Great to the Revolution,* ed. Taras Hunczak (New Brunswick, N.J.: Rutgers University Press, 1974), 63-64.

[4] Hunczak, *Russian Imperialism,* 87.

[5] From Pushkin's poem, "To the Slanderers of Russia."

[6] Hunczak, 99-100.

[7] Ibid.

[8] Cowles, 61.

[9] Hunczak, 88.

[10] Exceptionalism worked as a plague in Germany, leading many Germans to follow Hitler in claiming that the superior Aryan culture justified eradication of those they considered *Untermenschen*, including the Jews and the Romanies. Americans also have been guilty of exceptionalist thinking, arguing that American democracy must be spread across the globe as an act of moral beneficence, using force if necessary. American neoconservatives, heavily influenced by German philosophy, used exceptionalism to justify the preemptive war on Iraq.

[11] Noel Malcolm, *Kosovo: A Short History* (London: Papermac, 2002), xlvii. From a memo sent by Belgrade to the Great Powers in early 1913 attempting to justify Serbian control of Kosovo.

[12] Bibl, 204.

[13] Ibid., 320.

[14] Cowles, 60-61.

[15] Ibid., 61.

[16] B.H. Sumner, *Russia and the Balkans 1870-1880* (Hamden/London: Archon Books, 1962), 69.

[17] Cowles, 76-77.

[18] Cowles, 76-79.

[19] Ibid.

[20] Sumner, *Russia*, 71-72.

[21] Ibid., 72.

[22] Ibid., 71.

[23] Durham, *Balkan Tangle*, 18-19.

[24] Ibid.

[25] William Miller, *Travels and Politics in the Near East* (New York: Arno Press and the New York Times, 1971. First publ. London: T. Fisher Unwin, 1898), 59, 71.

[26] Durham, *Balkan Tangle*, 32.

[27] Ibid., 32.

[28] Miller, 42.

[29] Sumner, *Russia*, 108.

[30] Ibid.

[31] Durham, *Balkan Tangle*, 104.

[32] David MacKenzie, *The Serbs and Russian Pan-Slavism 1875-1878* (Ithaca, N.Y.: Cornell University Press, 1967), 20-21.

[33] Ibid., 5.

[34] Malcolm, 58.

CHAPTER 10

[1] Wilhelm I became King of Prussia in 1861 after Friedrich Wilhelm IV died. He was crowned Kaiser of a unified Germany in 1871.

[2] August Fournier, *Wie Wir zu Bosnien Kamen: Eine Historische Studie* (Wien: Verlag von Christoph Reisser's Söhne, 1909), 6.

[3] Corti, *Mensch*, 461.

[4] Ibid. From Schweinitz, *Briefwechsel,* 8. September 1872, 86.

[5] Gyula Andrassy was a Hungarian magnate who sided with the revolutionaries against the Habsburgs during the 1848-49 uprising. As the fighting continued, Andrassy fled to London. He was among 71 rebels hanged in effigy. Returning to Hungary after the revolution, he became active in Hungarian politics. Empress Elisabeth (Sisi), enchanted by the dashing, dark-haired Magyar, became a champion of Hungarian causes that sometimes were at odds with her emperor husband's views. Andrassy pushed through a compromise in 1867 that gave the Hungarian half of the monarchy certain rights not enjoyed by the Austrians. However, Franz Joseph, recognizing Andrassy's considerable abilities, appointed him Foreign Minister of the dual monarchy in 1871. Prince Aleksandr Gorchakov succeeded Nesselrode as Russian Foreign Minister in 1856. He remained bitter at Franz Joseph's failure to support the Romanovs in the military adventure that became known as the Crimean War. He wanted to punish the Austrians for their perfidy.

[6] Fournier, 9.

[7] Corti, *Mensch*, 468.

[8] Corti, *Elisabeth: Die Seltsame Frau* (Graz/Wien: Verlag Styria, 1934), 243.

[9] Corti, *Mensch*, 469. Robilant an Visconti-Venosta. Wien, 9 June 1873. Archiv des Ministeriums des Aussern Rom.

[10] Ibid., 469. Swiss ambassador Tschudi an Cérésole. 8 June, 1873.

Bundesarchiv Bern.
[11] Macartney, 590.
[12] Corti, *Mensch*, 478.
[13] Ibid., 485.
[14] Edmund von Glaise-Horstenau. *Franz Josephs Weggefährte* (Wien: Amalthea-Verlag, 1930), 182-83.
[15] Sumner, *Russia*, 138.
[16] Palmer, *Twilight of the Habsburgs: The Life and Times of Emperor Francis Joseph* (London: Weidenfeld & Nicolson, 1994), 200.
[17] Fournier, 13.
[18] Corti, *Mensch*, 486-87.
[19] Cowles, 76.
[20] Ibid.
[21] MacKenzie, 41.
[22] Sumner, *Russia*, 154.
[23] MacKenzie, 66.

CHAPTER 11

[1] Sir Edwin Pears, *Forty Years in Constantinople, 1873-1915* (New York: D. Appleton and Co., 1919), 16-19.
[2] The present capital of Uzbekistan.
[3] MacKenzie, 88.
[4] Ibid., 97.
[5] Ibid., 116.
[6] Ibid., 112.
[7] Macartney, 591.
[8] Bernard Fürst von Bülow, *Denkwürdigkeiten*, (4 vols., Berlin: Verlag Ullstein, 1930), v. 4, 397.
[9] MacKenzie, 122.
[10] Ibid., 144.
[11] Ibid., 146.
[12] Ibid.
[13] Pears, 16-19.
[14] Peter Stansky, *Gladstone: A Progress in Politics* (New York: W.W. Norton & Company, 1979), 131.
[15] Sumner, *Russia*, 211. See also 205.
[16] Ibid., 207.

[17] Corti, *Mensch*, 494. HHSA, Sept. 11/23.
[18] Ibid.
[19] Corti, *Mensch*, 495.
[20] Sumner, *Russia*, 209.
[21] Corti, *Mensch*, 496.
[22] Ibid.
[23] New style calendar, November 3.
[24] Corti, *Mensch*, 497-98. Tschudi an Bandesrat, Bern, November 4, 1876.
[25] Dated October 5 (old style); October 17 (new style).
[26] Old style calendar – 12 days behind the new style – i.e. by November 12.
[27] MacKenzie, 151. From Jelavich, *Russia in the East*, 31.
[28] Sumner, *Russia*, 221-22.
[29] Ibid., 224-25.
[30] Harold William Temperley, *History of Serbia* (London: G. Bell & Sons, Ltd., 1919), 266.
[31] Ibid., 220.
[32] Sumner, *Russia*, 227.
[33] Ibid.
[34] Ibid., 227-28.

CHAPTER 12

[1] Russia, Austria, Germany, England, France and Italy.
[2] The Czar's concerns about revolutionaries were correct. On March 13, 1881, he would die at the hands of assassins.
[3] Sumner, *Russia*, 252-54.
[4] Ibid., 253-54.
[5] Great Britain, France, Austria, Russia, Germany, and now also Italy.
[6] Sumner, *Russia*, 288.
[7] Ibid., 281.
[8] Ibid., 246.
[9] Ibid., 282. Novi Pazar was the narrow corridor separating Serbia and Montenegro.
[10] Ibid., 281.
[11] Ibid., 258-59.
[12] MacKenzie, 197.

[13] Ibid., 198.

[14] Sumner, *Russia*, 314. Loftus to Derby, Secretary of State for Foreign Affairs, June 20, 1877.

[15] Ibid., 337.

[16] Ibid., 338.

[17] Ibid., 334-35.

[18] Corti, *Mensch*, 492.

[19] Bibl, 360.

[20] Egon Caesar Conte Corti, *The Downfall of Three Dynasties* (London: Methuen & Co., 1934), 236.

[21] MacKenzie, 251.

[22] Corti, *Downfall*, 239.

[23] Ibid., 239.

CHAPTER 13

[1] Edvard Radzinsky, *Alexander II: The Last Great Tsar* (New York: Free Press, 2006), 262.

[2] Corti, *Unter Zaren*, 290.

[3] Tsarigrad (also spelled Tsargrad) is the Slavic name for Constantinople.

[4] MacKenzie, 247.

[5] Sumner, *Russia*, 354.

[6] Czar Alexander II sent Franz Joseph a copy of the preliminary peace agreements that the Russians intended to present to the Ottomans. Franz Joseph was incensed because the Czar's plan broke a promise to the Emperor that the Russians would not create a large Slav state in the Balkans. The San Stefano peace plan called for a huge Bulgarian state under Russian administration.

[7] Sumner, *Russia*, 359.

[8] Corti, *Downfall*, 244.

[9] Ibid., 243.

[10] Corti, *Mensch*, 506.

[11] Ibid., 510. From Festetics *Diary*, May 10, 1878.

[12] Corti, *Downfall*, 240.

[13] Sumner, *Russia*, 398.

[14] The Reichstadt agreements of July 1876 were discussed in the previous chapter.

[15] Sumner, *Russia*, 444-45.

[16] Eduard von Wertheimer, *Graf Julius Andrassy: Sein Leben und seine Zeit* (3 vols., Stuttgart: Deutsche Verlags-Anstalt, 1910-13) v. 3, 109-10.

[17] Ibid., 111.

[18] MacKenzie, 304.

[19] Fürst von Bülow, v.4, 449.

[20] Ibid., 439-40.

[21] Corti, *Mensch*, 511.

[22] Andrassy's fears of retribution from fellow Magyars were valid. On November 5, 1878, the Hungarian Parliament impeached him for occupying the provinces in violation of the Hungarian Constitution. The parliament voted, 170 to 93, against his conviction. However, this showed that he clearly understood and justifiably feared the sentiments of his countrymen.

[23] Wertheimer, v.3, 126.

[24] Corti, *Mensch*, 512.

[25] Bülow v.4, 449.

[26] Bibl, 361.

[27] Corti, *Mensch*, 513.

[28] Ibid.

[29] Luigi Albertini, *The Origins of the War of 1914* (3 vols., London: Oxford University Press, 1952), v.1, 34.

[30] Anatol Murad, *Franz Joseph I of Austria and His Empire*, (New York: Twayne Publishers, 1968), 206.

[31] Sumner, *Russia*, 562. Quoting from Russian sources.

CHAPTER 14

[1] Corti, *Downfall*, 260.

[2] Ibid., 260-61.

[3] Otto von Bismarck, *Gedanken und Errinerungen* (Stuttgart and Berlin: J.G. Gotta'sche Buchhandlung Nachfolger, 1919), 521-22.

[4] Edward Crankshaw, *Bismarck* (Middlesex, England: Penguin Books, 1990), 373. From Wolfgang Windelband, *Bismarck und die Europäische Grossmächte*, 2nd ed., Essen, 1942.

[5] A distant relative of Leo Tolstoy, the author of *War and Peace*.

[6] Corti, *Downfall*, 261.

[7] Radzinsky, 321.

[8] Corti, *Downfall*, 264-65.

[9] Radzinsky, 419.

[10] John Van der Kiste, *The Romanovs: 1818-1959: Alexander of Russia and his Family* (New York: Sutton Publishing, 1998), 44.

[11] Albertini, v.1, 46. See also Macartney, 594-95.

[12] Alfred Pribram, *The Secret Treaties of Austria-Hungary*, (2 vols., Cambridge: Harvard University Press, 1921), v.2, 59.

[13] Ibid., 66.

[14] Macartney, 595.

[15] A.J.P. Taylor, *Struggle for Mastery in Europe 1848-1918* (Oxford: Oxford University Press, 1971), 316.

[16] Macartney, 594-95.

[17] Corti, *Zaren*, 340-41.

[18] Ibid., 41.

[19] Robert D. Warth, *Nicholas II: The Life and Reign of Russia's Last Monarch* (Westport, Conn.: Prager, 1997), 14-15. From V.N. Lamzdorf, *Dnevnik, 1891-92* (Moscow, 1934), 259.

[20] Dominic Lieven, *Nicholas II: Twilight of the Empire* (New York: St. Martin's Press, 1993), 52. From Radziwill, *Intimate Life*, p. 92, and Lamzdorf, *Dnevnik, 1894-96,* pp. 85, 123, 376 and 404.

[21] Hugo Hantsch, *Leopold Graf Berchtold: Grandseigneur und Staatsmann* (2 vols., Graz: Verlag Styria, 1963), 234-35.

[22] Arriving at the Jerusalem Gate, the Kaiser was met by a delegation led by Theodor Herzl, the founder of Zionism, who wanted the Kaiser's support for a Jewish homeland in Palestine. According to Fürst von Bülow, Wilhelm at first was "fire and flame" for the Zionist cause because "he hoped to free his land from many of these not especially sympathetic elements." He changed his mind, however, after the former Ottoman ambassador to Berlin, who was with the German delegation, said the Sultan wanted nothing to do with Zionism or an independent Jewish state. The Kaiser refused the Zionists' attempts for further meetings.

[23] Christian Graf von Krakow, *Kaiser Wilhelm II. und seine Zeit* (Berlin: Siedler Verlag, 1999), 150.

[24] *Grosse Politik*, xix 6237.

[25] *Grosse Politik*, xxxi/xix 6193

[26] Ibid.

[27] *Grosse Politik*, xix 6220.

[28] Ibid.

[29] Ibid.

[30] *Grosse Politik*, xix 6146.

CHAPTER 15

[1] Corti, *Downfall*, 258.
[2] Corti, *Unter Zaren*, 311.
[3] Ibid., 312. (July, 1879).
[4] Corti, *Downfall*, 259.
[5] Corti, *Zaren*, 338. Also Corti, *Downfall*, 296.
[6] Corti, *Zaren*, 340-41. The account comes from a letter to his father, Jan. 28/Feb. 9, 1882.
[7] Ibid., 341.
[8] Corti, *Downfall*, 283.
[9] Ibid., 284.
[10] Ibid., 288.
[11] Ibid., 292.
[12] Ibid., 291.
[13] Ibid., 292.
[14] Oskar Freiherr Mitis, *Das Leben des Kronprinzen Rudolf* (Leipzig: Im Insel-Verlag zu Leipzig, 1928), 292.
[15] Corti, *Zaren*, 373.
[16] *Grosse Politik*, a.a.O. V/66.
[17] A personal union involves two or more states with the same ruler but with separate laws, boundaries, etc.
[18] Corti, *Zaren*, 383.
[19] Ibid., 387-88.
[20] Corti, *Zaren*, 391.
[21] Stephen Constant, *Foxy Ferdinand of Bulgaria* (New York: Franklin Watts, 1980), 71.

CHAPTER 16

[1] Miller,108.
[2] Macartney, 740.
[3] Ibid., 740-41.
[4] Ibid., 742.
[5] Ibid., 745.
[6] Miller, 120.
[7] Macartney, 743-44.

[8] Miller, 120.

[9] Ibid. Miller cited 1895 census figures for Bosnia-Herzegovina showing an ethnically mixed population of 1,568,092 people with 42.94 percent Orthodox Catholics, 34.9 percent Muslims, and 21.21 percent Roman Catholics.

[10] Ibid., 125-26.

[11] Ibid., 156.

[12] Macartney, 743.

[13] Miller, 92-94.

[14] Ibid.

[15] Joseph M. Baernreither, *Fragmente eines Politischen Tagebuches: Die Südslawische Frage und Österreich-Ungarn vor dem Weltkrieg* (Berlin: Verlag für Kulturpolitik, 1928), 54-55.

[16] Miller, 97.

[17] Ibid., 110-11.

[18] Ibid., 140.

[19] Ibid., 100.

[20] Samuel Williamson, Jr., *Austria-Hungary and the Origins of the First World War* (London: Macmillan, 1991), 62-68.

[21] Macartney, 746-48.

[22] Baernreither, 53.

[23] Miller, 118.

CHAPTER 17

[1] Milan would declare himself king of the new kingdom of Serbia in 1882. Note: There is a discrepancy between the spelling of Milan's family name and that of King Peter's family name (mentioned in this chapter).

[2] Pribram v.1, 51.

[3] Ibid., 53.

[4] Bibl, 426.

[5] Feldmarschall Conrad von Hötzendorf, *Aus Meiner Dienstzeit: 1906-1918* (4 vols., Wien: Rikola Verlag, 1922) v.2, 24.

[6] Temperley, 278.

[7] Durham, *Balkan Tangle*, 71.

[8] Temperley, 271.

[9] Durham, *Balkan Tangle*, 74.

[10] Albertini v.1, 138-39.

[11] Ibid., 139.

[12] Ibid.

[13] Bibl, 429.

[14] Ibid.

[15] Bernadotte E. Schmitt, *The Annexation of Bosnia 1908-1909* (Cambridge: At the University Press, 1937), 6.

[16] Durham, *Balkan Tangle*, 158.

[17] In June 1909 Austria and Serbia reached a trade agreement after the Germans threatened war with the Russians if they intervened on behalf of their Balkan vassal.

CHAPTER 18

[1] W.M. Carlgren, *Iswolsky und Aehrenthal vor der bosnischen Annexionskrise* (Uppsala: Almqvist & Wiksells Boktryckeri AB, 1955), 80, 112. Sir Arthur Nicolson's description of Aehrenthal is less flattering. He portrays the Austrian minister as "an unwieldy man, with heavy hapless jaws, a stubble head of hair, and sad turbot eyes." From Constant, 217. He also paints an unflattering portrait of Izvolsky.

[2] Restrictions imposed by the Berlin Treaty prohibited Montenegro from having ships of war and closed Antivari to all military vessels.

[3] Hantsch, v.1, 122.

[4] Ibid., 123-24.

[5] The Russian Foreign Minister's July 2 memo gives a certain credence to Izvolsky's claim. It states that Constantinople and the Straits as well as the annexation of Bosnia and Herzegovina were "eminently" of European concern and "not of a nature to be settled by a separate understanding between Russia and Austria-Hungary." The memo adds that the Romanov government was prepared to engage in discussions of those issues "in a friendly spirit of reciprocity."

[6] Ibid., 123.

[7] Durham, *Balkan Tangle*, 123. Edith Durham tells of a 1905 visit to a small arms factory in Rijeka (a port in the Kvarner Bay, an inlet of the Adriatic Sea, now in Croatia), where she found Russian rifles being retrofitted. She was told the weapons were being prepared for every man in Bosnia and Herzegovina. They were to

be smuggled into the provinces. "The notion of a not distant war with Austria, accompanied by a great Balkan rising, was generally accepted," Durham wrote.

[8] Sidney Bradshaw Fay, *The Origins of the World War*, 2nd ed. (New York: The Macmillan Company, 1936), 369-70.

[9] Ibid., 370.

[10] Macartney, 730.

[11] Malcolm, *Kosovo*, 238; Durham, *High Albania* (London: Edward Arnold, 1909), 223-31.

[12] Durham, *Balkan Tangle*, 193.

[13] Malcolm, *Kosovo*, 237-38.

[14] Edward J. Bing, ed., *The Letters of Tsar Nicholas and Empress Marie* (London: Ivor Nicholson and Watson Limited, 1937. Royalty Digest Reprint, 1995), 236.

[15] Ibid.

[16] Albertini v.1, 247.

[17] Schmitt, 68. Izvolsky had first-hand knowledge that Russia wasn't prepared to go to war at that time. In early February 1908, a few days after Aehrenthal had announced plans for the Sandzak railroad, Izvolsky had begun to make elaborate plans for war. He hoped that the British would join Russia in military action in the Balkans and elsewhere. General Palitsyn, Chief of the General Staff, had warned him that Russia lacked "artillery, machine guns, uniforms." Before entering yet another conflict, the general said, it also would be necessary to restore order in the army and fortresses. This would cost "stupendous sums" and take time. The minister of the navy gave a similar assessment, saying that the Black Sea Fleet needed "sailors, coal, ammunition, guns and mines." M. Kokovtsev, the Finance Minister, complained that neither he nor the whole council "had been kept informed of Izvolsky's warlike and expensive plans." Fay v.1, 371-72. Such unilateral behavior was typical of Izvolsky.

[18] Schmitt, Ibid., 68.

[19] Ibid., 72.

[20] Ibid., 73.

[21] Albertini v.1, 232.

[22] Ibid.

[23] Conrad v.1, 138.

[24] Albertini v.1, 251.

[25] Ibid., 254-56.

[26] Ibid., 255-56.

[27] Ibid.

[28] The Czar might well have looked closer to home if he wanted to find who was looking forward to a war. Pourtales, the German Ambassador to St. Petersburg, passed along Izvolsky's remark to Prince von Bülow on January 16, 1909: "Do not forget one thing: above all the Eastern Question cannot be solved otherwise than by a conflict." From Schmitt, 92.

[29] Schmitt, 92.

[30] Albertini v.1, 274.

[31] Ibid., 274-77.

[32] Ibid.

[33] Ibid., 277.

[34] Schmitt, 187.

[35] Hantsch v.1, 166 ff.

[36] Albertini v.1, 278.

[37] Schmitt, 173-74.

[38] Ibid.

[39] Ibid., 180-81.

[40] The Union of October 17 (Octobrist) party supported a manifesto issued by the Czar on October 30, 1905. It promised civil liberties, a broad franchise, and creation of a legislative body, which was to have limited control over the state budget but none over the executive branch.

[41] Ibid., 188-89.

[42] Albertini v.1, 279-80.

[43] Ibid., 285.

[44] Ibid., 285-86.

[45] Ibid., 283.

[46] Ibid., 291.

[47] Macartney, 785.

[48] Ibid., 785-86.

[49] Albertini v.1, 293.

[50] Ibid., 292-93. Richard Wagner used this Norse legend in *Der Ring des Nibelungen.*

[51] Ibid.

[52] Durham, *Balkan Tangle*, 191.

CHAPTER 19

[1] Fay v.1, 407. See *Grosse Politik*, xxvii, 406 ff.

[2] Albertini v.1, 307-08.

[3] Interestingly, according to news reports of the Duma speech, Izvolsky also mentioned Turkey as a possible member of the federation. Surely the Foreign Minister meant this as a diversionary tactic to disguise his real intentions.

[4] Fay v.1, 400-01.

[5] In 1910, the monarchy finally completed its trade agreement with Serbia, but this did little to improve the relationship between the Serbians and the Hungarians.

[6] Baernreither, *Fragmente*, 126.

[7] Fay v.1, 401-02.

[8] Ibid.

[9] Albertini v.1, 310.

[10] M. Boghitschewitsch, *Kriegsursachen:Beiträge zur Erforschung der Ursachen des Europäischen Krieges mit spezieller Berücksichtigung Russlands und Serbiens* (Zürich: Art Institut Orell Füssli, 1919), 32.

[11] Albertini v.1, 297-98.

[12] Ibid.

[13] Fay v.1, 428.

[14] Friedrich Stieve, *Isvolsky and the World War: Based on the Documents Recently Published by the German Foreign Office* (Freeport, N.Y.: Books for Libraries Press, 1971. First published 1926), 22.

[15] Gina Grafin Conrad von Hötzendorf, *Mein Leben mit Conrad Hötzendorf* (Leipzig: Grethlein & Co., Nachf., 1935), 186-88.

[16] Conrad v.2, 276.

[17] Ibid., 274-76. See also Albertini v.1, 351.

[18] Albertini v.1, 352-53.

[19] Fay v.1, 416-17.

[20] Ibid., 424.

[21] Ibid., 426.

[22] Albertini v.1, 359.

[23] Ibid., 359-61.

[24] Edith Durham, *The Struggle for Scutari (Turk, Slav and Albanian)*, (Memphis, Tenn.: General Books, 2010; first published

1914), 63.
[25] Albertini v.1, 375.
[26] Malcolm, *Kosovo*, 248.
[27] Albertini v.1, 365.
[28] Ibid.
[29] John D. Treadway, *The Falcon and the Eagle: Montenegro and Austria-Hungary, 1908-1914* (West Lafayette, Ind.: Purdue University Press, 1998), 106-07.
[30] Ibid.
[31] Hans Rall, *Wilhelm II: Eine Biographie* (Graz: Styria, 1995), 299.
[32] Albertini v.1, 371.
[33] Stieve, 94. Quoting from Count Max Montgelas, *The Case for the Central Powers*, 54.
[34] Raymond Poincaré, *Memoiren: Die Vorgeschichte des Weltkrieges 1912-1913* (Dresden: Paul Aretz/Verlag, 1928), 331.
[35] Ibid., 332-37.
[36] Poincaré, 338.
[37] Ibid., 338-39.
[38] Fay v.2, 433.
[39] Stieve, 128. Document number 526.
[40] Ibid., 111.
[41] Stieve, 113.

CHAPTER 20

[1] Durham, *Scutari*, 69-70.
[2] Ibid.
[3] Durham, *Balkan Tangle*, 236.
[4] Treadway, 64-65.
[5] Durham, *Scutari*, 80.
[6] Ibid., 236.
[7] Albertini v.1, 377.
[8] Traian Stoianovich, "Russian Domination in the Balkans" in *Russian Imperialism from Ivan the Great to the Revolution*, ed. Taras Hunczak (New Brunswick, N.J.: Rutgers University Press, 1974), 236.
[9] Williamson, 126.
[10] Ibid., 130-31.

[11] Ibid., 125.

[12] During the Buchlau negotiations, Izvolsky had come forward voluntarily with an offer for Austria to acquire the Sandzak. Aehrenthal did not take him up on his offer. By this time the Austrian Foreign Minister had already put in place plans for handing over that vital corridor to Turkey.

[13] A Latin couplet puts it this way: "Let others wage war, but thou/ O happy Austria, marry." The House of Habsburg had its foundations in the 13th century, when family members ruled hereditary lands in the German-speaking Alpine regions. Over time, the Habsburgs increased their holdings through a series of carefully considered marriages. In 1477, Kaiser Friedrich III married off his son, Archduke Maximilian (later Maximilian I), to Maria of Burgundy, at the time the richest heiress in Europe. This marital coup brought Burgundy and the Netherlands under Habsburg control. Maximilian I, following his family's matchmaking tradition, arranged nuptials for his son, Philip "the Handsome," with "mad" Joanna, from Spain's ruling family, bringing Castile, Aragon, and the family's Italian holdings under Habsburg rule. There are debates about whether Joanna was mad. What is not in question is that the Spanish branch of the Habsburg family fell prey to genetic difficulties brought on by intermarriage and eventually died out. The Austrian Habsburgs fared better. In 1515, Kaiser Maximilian I and the Jagiello King Ladislas of Hungary and Bohemia concluded a marriage pact that was to change significantly the imperial map of Europe. Maximilian's grandson, Ferdinand, was betrothed to Anne, the daughter of the Hungarian King. Maximilian's granddaughter, Anne, was to marry Ladislas's son and heir, Louis. The young man came to power as Louis II in 1516, but reigned only 10 years. He died in August 1526, while fighting the Turks in the battle of Mohacs. Ferdinand inherited the kingdoms of Hungary and Bohemia. The Croatians unanimously elected Ferdinand I as their king the following year. The Habsburg Empire, with its territorial boundaries and its multiethnic difficulties, was beginning to take shape.

[14] Hantsch v.1, 388-90. From Berchtold Archive in Buchlau.

[15] Conrad v.1, 127.

[16] Treadway, 130.

[17] Fay v.1, 444.

[18] Hantsch v.1, 385.
[19] Ibid.
[20] Ibid., 387. From Dipl. Schriftwechsel Isvolskys, n. 724.
[21] Durham, *Scutari*, 102.
[22] Ibid., 103.
[23] Ibid., 129.
[24] Conrad v.3, 178.
[25] Ibid., 112.
[26] Ibid., 170.
[27] Ibid., 163.
[28] Ibid., 180-81.
[29] Ibid., 235.
[30] Treadway, 137.
[31] Ibid., 141.
[32] Ibid., 142.
[33] Durham, *Scutari*, 120-21.
[34] Treadway, 142.
[35] Ibid., 143.
[36] Hantsch v.1, 408.
[37] Treadway, 146.
[38] Ibid., 150.
[39] Ibid., 164.
[40] Fay v.1, 446-47.
[41] Stieve, 155-56.
[42] Ibid., 151.
[43] The Triple Entente consisted of France, Russia and Britain. The Central Powers were Austria, Germany, and, eventually, Bulgaria.
[44] Stieve, 163-64.
[45] Hantsch v.2, 471.
[46] Treadway, 161.
[47] Fay v.1, 445-46.
[48] Fay v.1, 464-66.
[49] Williamson, 151.
[50] Ibid., 152-53.
[51] Ibid., 153-55.

CHAPTER 21

[1] Theodor von Sosnosky, *Franz Ferdinand: Der Erzherzog-*

Thronfolger (München und Berlin: Verlag von R. Oldenbourg, 1929), 186-89.

[2] Ibid., 187-89.

[3] Ibid., 189-91.

[4] Ibid.

[5] Fay v.2, 120-21.

[6] Ibid., 44.

[7] Palmer, *Twilight*, 307-08.

[8] Hantsch v.2, 544-45.

[9] Fay v.2, 41.

[10] Willibald Gutsche, *Sarajevo 1914: Vom Attentat zum Weltkrieg,* (Berlin, Dietz Verlag, 1984), 5-6.

[11] Edward Crankshaw, *The Fall of the House of Habsburg* (New York: Penguin Books, 1983), 380-81.

[12] Sosnosky, 209. He identifies the others as Popović, Ilić, Cabrilović and Mehmedbasić.

[13] Fay v.2, 45.

[14] Crankshaw, *The Fall*, 384-85.

[15] Fay v.2, 123-26.

[16] Sosnosky, 205-06. Fay v.2.

[17] Fay v.2, 125.

[18] Sosnosky, 208-09.

[19] Freiherr Albert Margutti, *The Emperor Francis Joseph and his Time*s (London: Hutchinson & Co., 1921) 138-39.

[20] Hantsch v.2, 558.

[21] Ibid., 559.

[22] Ibid.

[23] Telegram to the German Reichskanzler, from the German Ambassador in Vienna, Heinrich von Tschirschky, July 2, 1914. From *Die Deutschen Dokumente zum Kriegsausbruch 1914.* (Berlin: Deutsche Verlagsgesellschaft für Politik und Geschichte- Karl Kautsky collection, 1919), 17-18.

[24] Albertini v.2, 277.

[25] Constant, 293-94.

[26] Hantsch, v.2, 559.

[27] Fay v.2, 204-05.

[28] Hantsch v.2, 565.

[29] Fay v.2, 201.

[30] Franz Joseph to Wilhelm II, *Deutsche Dokumente*, 19-21.

[31] Williamson, 197-98.

[32] Stieve, 187-88.

[33] Ibid., 189.

[34] Ibid.

[35] Ibid., 230-31.

[36] Ibid., 232.

[37] Ibid.

[38] Fay v.2, 148-49.

[39] *Deutsche Dokumente*, I, 53. From a July 8, 1914, report from the German minister in Belgrade to the German Chancellor.

[40] Wiesner did, however, bring some documents back to Vienna for additional study.

[41] Fay v.2, 236.

[42] Ibid., 237-38.

[43] Ibid., 238.

[44] Ibid., 237. fn.

[45] Ibid., 239.

[46] Sosnosky, 192.

[47] Serge Sazonov, *Fateful Years 1898-1916* (Bronx, N.Y., ISHI Press International, 2008. First publ. 1928), 151.

[48] Sosnosky, 193, 229.

[49] Fay v.2, 244.

[50] Ibid., 250.

[51] Cited in Fay v.2, 240.

CHAPTER 22

[1] Maurice Paléologue, *An Ambassador's Memoirs* (3 vols., New York: George H. Doran Company, 6th ed., no date), v.1, 13.

[2] Ibid., 14.

[3] Ibid., 16.

[4] Ibid., 19.

[5] Ibid.

[6] Ibid., 21-23.

[7] Referring to the fact that the princesses were from Montenegro (Black Mountain).

[8] Paléologue, 22-23.

[9] Ibid., 23.

[10] Fay v.2, 271-72. See also Jean Paul Bled, *Franz Joseph*, Transl.

Teresa Bridgeman (Oxford, U.K.: Blackwell, 1994), 310.

[11] Ibid., 289, from Schilling's *Diary*, 28 ff.

[12] Sean McMeekin, *The Russian Origins of the First World War* (Cambridge, Mass.: The Belknap Press of Harvard University Press, 2011), 54.

[13] Fay v.2, 289. The Romanian minister also was at the lunch. He was being courted because the Triple Entente members were seeking the support of that crucially situated Balkan nation in the coming war.

[14] Ibid., 295.

[15] Grey's remarks are quoted in Gilbert Murray's *The Foreign Policy of Sir Edward Grey 1906-1915* (Oxford: At the Clarendon Press, 1915), 15. An ironic twist is that Emperor Franz Joseph in 1878 had supported Serbia's independence from the Ottoman Empire.

[16] McMeekin, 69.

[17] Sazonov, 150.

[18] Fay v.2, 301-03.

[19] Ibid., 301. Chelius to Wilhelm II, July 26, Kautsky Documents, 291.

[20] Albertini, v.2, 592.

[21] McMeekin, 60-61.

[22] Albertini, v.2, 309.

[23] Roderich Gooss, *Das Wiener Kabinet und die Entstehung des Weltkrieges* (Wien: Verlag von L.W. Seidel und Sohn, 1919), 166.

[24] Margutti, 415.

[25] Ibid., 31.

[26] Bled, 311.

[27] Grey later pushed a proposal for a conference of the four Great Powers not directly involved in the controversy. The effort failed. The Austrians insisted that the problems between them and the Serbians should be solved by the two parties involved. They weren't inclined to put their fate in the hands of Germany, France, England and Italy. France was in lockstep with Russia. Italy, although an ally, was a sometime friend, interested mostly in what she could wrest from the situation. England also wasn't being exactly friendly.

[28] Fay, v.2, 420.

[29] Hantsch, v.2, 611.

[30] Williamson, *Op cit.*, 214.

[31] Hantsch II, 612.

[32] *Die Deutschen Dokumente zum Kriegsausbruch 1914*, Kautsky documents (Berlin: Deutsche Verlagsgesellschaft für Politik und Geschichte, 1922), I, 15-18.

[33] Fay, v.2, 324-25.

[34] Ibid., 323.

[35] M. Boghitschewitsch, *Kriegsursachen* (Zürich: Art. Institut Orell Füssli, 1919), 83.

[36] Fay.v.2, 320-21.

[37] Ibid., 295 ff./ Albertini, v.2, 531-32

[38] Ibid., 429.

[39] Ibid., 426.

[40] Sent at 6:30 p.m., July 29.

[41] Fay, v.2, 465. See also *The Kaiser's letters to the Tsar, copied from the government archives in Petrograd and brought from Russia*, ed. by Isaac Don Levine (London: Hodder and Stoughton, 1920).

[42] Albertini, v.3, 143, points out that Austria's entire field army had 50 divisions; 23 of them were marching on Serbia, far from Russian frontiers. Russia's partial mobilization, with 55 infantry divisions, was five more than the entire Austrian army. Information comes from Max Montgelas, *Das Plaidoyer Poincarés*. KSF, February 1928, 161.

[43] Fay, v.2, 465-66.

[44] Ibid., 466.

[45] Williamson, 205.

[46] Ibid., 206-07.

[47] Fay, v.2, 469-70. From Schilling's *Diary*, 64.

[48] This is one of a number of unsubstantiated statements Sazonov made in persuading the Czar to go to war.

[49] Williamson, xv.

[50] Sazonov, 204.

[51] Sidney Harcave, *Years of the Golden Cockerel: The Last Romanov Tsars 1814-1917* (New York: The Macmillan Company, 1968), 412.

[52] Fay, v.2, 481.

[53] Ibid., 473.

[54] Paléologue, v.3, 125.

CHAPTER 23

[1] Masha Gessen, *The Man Without a Face: The Unlikely Rise of Vladimir Putin* (New York: Riverhead Books, 2012), 47-49.

[2] Marcel H. Van Herpen, *The Rise of Russia's New Imperialism* (Lanham, Md.: Rowman & Littlefield, 2014), 53.

[3] Ibid.

[4] Ibid.

[5] While certain rightist elements were involved in the protests, there is no evidence that they were the majority of those who camped out on the Ukrainian capital's main square. Most of the participants wanted an end to rampant corruption at the highest levels of government and they wanted Ukraine to align itself with Western democracies.

[6] Since Crimea's population has a 60 percent ethnic Russian majority, the vote for secession was predictable. This, however, does not mean the referendum was valid.

[7] Iver B. Neumann, *Russia's Europe, 1991-2016: inferiority to superiority* (International Affairs, 2016), 1381-1399.

[8] Gessen, 153-54.

[9] Ibid., 205-06. Russian analyst Pavel Baev described Putin's facial expression upon learning the news from Georgia.

[10] Van Herpen, 248. From Zbigniew Brzezinski, *Strategic Vision: America and the Crisis of Global Power* (New York: Basic Books, 2012), 95.

BIBLIOGRAPHY

Abbott, Jacob. *Peter the Great.* New York: Harper & Brothers, 1904.

Albertini, Luigi. *The Origins of the War of 1914.* 3 vols. Trans. Isabella M. Massey. London: Oxford University Press, 1952.

Alexander, John T. *Catherine the Great: Life and Legend.* Oxford: Oxford University Press, 1989.

Algren, W.M. *Iswolsky und Aehrenthal vor der bosnischen Annexionskrise.* Uppsala: Almqvist & Wiksells Boktryckeri AB, 1955.

Almedingen, E.M. *The Emperor Alexander II: a Study.* London: Bodley Head, 1972.

Baernreither, Joseph. *Fragmente eines Politischen Tagebuches: Die Südslawische Frage und Österreich-Ungarn vor dem Weltkrieg.* Berlin: Verlag für Kulturpolitik, 1928.

Bagger, Eugene. *Franz Joseph: Eine Persönlichkeits-Studie.* Zürich: Amalthea-Verlag, 1927.

Barker, A.J. *The War Against Russia: 1854-1856.* New York: Holt, Reinhart & Winston, 1971.

Bibl, Viktor. *Von Revolution zu Revolution in Österreich.* Wien: Rikola Verlag, 1924.

Bierman, John. *Napoleon III and his Carnival Empire.* London: St. Martin's Press, 1988.

Bing, Edward J. *The Letters of Tsar Nicholas and Empress Marie.* London: Ivor Nicholson and Watson Limited, Royal Digest Reprint, 1995.

Bismarck, Otto von. *Gedanken und Errinerungen.* Stuttgart and Berlin: J.G. Gotta'sche Buchhandlung Nachfolger, 1919.

Bled, Jean-Paul. *Franz Joseph.* Trans. Teresa Bridgeman. Oxford: Blackwell, 1994.

Boghitschewitsch, M. *Kriegsursachen: Beiträge zur Erforschung der Ursachen des Europäischen Krieges mit spezieller Berücksichtigung Russlands und Serbiens.* Zurich: Art. Institut Orell Füssli, 1919.

Bresler, Fenton. *Napoleon III: A Life.* New York: Carroll & Graf Publishers, 1999.

Bülow, Bernard Fürst von. *Denkwürdigkeiten.* 4 vols. Berlin: Verlag Ullstein, 1930.

Conrad, Field Marshall von Hötzendorf. *Aus Meiner Dienstzeit:*

1906-1918. 4 vols. Wien: Rikola Verlag, 1922.

Constant, Stephen. *Foxy Ferdinand of Bulgaria.* New York: Franklin Watts, 1908.

Corti, Egon Caesar Conte. *Elisabeth: Die Seltsame Frau.* Graz/Wien: Verlag Styria, 1934.

—. *Mensch und Herrscher: Wege und Schicksale Kaiser Franz Joseph I zwischen Thronbesteigung und Berliner Congreß.* Graz/Wien: Verlag Styria, 1952.

—. *The Downfall of Three Dynasties.* Transl. L. Marie Sieveking and Ian F.D. Morrow. London: Methuen & Co., 1934.

—. *Unter Zaren und Gekrönten Frauen.* Salzburg/Leipzig: Verlag Anton Pustet, 1936.

Cowles, Virginia. *The Russian Dagger: Cold War in the Days of The Czars.* New York and Evanston: Harper & Row, 1969.

Cracraft, James. *The Revolution of Peter the Great.* Cambridge, Mass.: Harvard University Press, 2003.

Crankshaw, Edward. *Bismarck.* Middlesex, England: Penguin Books, 1990.

—. *Maria Theresa.* London: Longmans, 1996.

—. *The Fall of the House of Habsburg.* New York: Penguin Books, 1983.

Cronin, Vincent. *Catherine: Empress of All the Russias.* New York: William Morrow and Company Inc, 1978.

Daly, John C.K. *Russian Seapower and 'The Eastern Question,' 1827-41.* Annapolis, Md.: Naval Institute Press, 1991.

Die Deutschen Dokumente zum Kriegsausbruch 1914. (Kautsky documents). Berlin: Deutsche Verlagsgesellschaft für Politik und Geschichte, 1922.

Donia, Robert J. *Islam under the Double Eagle: The Muslims of Bosnia and Herzegovina, 1878-1914.* New York: Columbia University Press, 1981.

Durham, Edith. *The Struggle for Scutari (Turk, Slav, and Albanian).* Memphis, Tenn.: General Books, 2010. First published 1914.

—. *Twenty Years of Balkan Tangle.* London: George Allen & Unwin, 1920.

Erickson, Carolly. *Great Catherine: The Life of Catherine the Great, Empress of Russia.* New York: Crown Publishers, 1994.

Fay, Sidney Bradshaw. *The Origins of the World War*. 2nd ed. New York: The Macmillan Company, 1936.

Fletcher, Ian and Ishchenko, Natalia. *The Crimean War: A Clash of Empires*. Staplehurst, England: Spellmount, 2004.

Florescu, Radu R. *The Struggle against Russia in the Romanian Principalities: 1821-1854*. Iaşi: The Foundation for Romanian Culture and Studies, 1997.

Fournier, August. *Wie Wir zu Bosnien Kamen: Eine Historische Studie*. Wien: Verlag von Christoph Reisser's Söhne, 1909.

Friedjung, Heinrich. *Österreich von 1848 bis 1860*. 2 vols. Stuttgart und Berlin: J.G. Cotta'sche Buchhandlung Nachfolger, 1912.

Geró, András. *Emperor Francis Joseph, King of the Hungarians*. Wayne, N.J.: Center for Hungarian Studies and Publications, Inc., 2001.

Gessen, Masha. *The Man Without a Face: The Unlikely Rise of Vladimir Putin*. New York: Riverhead Books, 2012.

Glaise-Horstenau, Edmund von. *Franz Josephs Weggefährte*. Wien: Amalthea Verlag, 1930.

Gooss, Roderich. *Das Wiener Kabinet und die Entstehung des Weltkrieges*. Wien: Verlag von L.W. Seidel und Sohn, 1919.

Görgei, Arthur. *My Life and Acts in Hungary in the Years 1848 and 1849*. New York: Harper's & Brothers, 1852.

Gutsche, Willibald. *Sarajevo 1914: Vom Attentat zum Weltkrieg*. Berlin: Dietz Verlag, 1984.

Hantsch, Hugo. *Leopold Graf Berchtold: Grandseigneur und Staatsmann*. 2 vols. Graz: Verlag Styria, 1963.

Harcave, Sidney. *Years of the Golden Cockerel: The Last Romanov Tsars 1814-1917*. New York: The Macmillan Company, 1968.

Harris, David. *A Diplomatic History of the Balkan Crisis of 1875-78*. Stanford, Calif.: Stanford University Press, 1936.

Helfert, Joseph Alexander. *Geschichte Oesterreichs vom Ausgange des Wiener Oktober-Aufstandes 1848, Feldzug IV*. Prague: F. Tempsky, 1886.

Hötzendorf, Gina Gräfin Conrad von. *Mein Leben mit Conrad von Hötzendorf*. Leipzig: Grethlein & Co., 1935.

Howarth, T.E.B. *Citizen-King: The Life of Louis-Philippe, King of the French*. London: Eyre & Spottiswoode, 1961.

Hughes, Lindsey. *Peter the Great: A Biography*. New Haven: Yale University Press, 2002.

—. *Russia in the Age of Peter the Great*. New Haven: Yale University Press, 1998.

Hunczak, Taras. *Russian Imperialism from Ivan the Great to the Revolution*. New Brunswick, N.J.: Rutgers University Press, 1974.

Jelavich, Barbara. *Russia's Balkan Entanglements 1806-1914*. Cambridge: Cambridge University Press, 2004.

Klyuchevsky, Vasili. *Peter the Great*. Trans. Liliana Archibald. Boston: Beacon Press, 1958.

Lafore, Laurence. *The Long Fuse: An Interpretation of the Origins of World War I*, 2nd ed. Long Grove, Ill.: Waveland Press, 1971.

Lieven, Dominic. *Empire: The Russian Empire and its Rivals*. New Haven: Yale University Press, 2000.

—. *Nicholas II: Twilight of the Empire*. New York: St. Martin's Press, 1993.

Lincoln, W. Bruce. *Nicholas I: Emperor and Autocrat of All the Russias*. DeKalb, Ill.: Northern Illinois University Press, 1989.

Macartney, C.A. *The Habsburg Empire 1790-1918*. New York: The Macmillan Company, 1969.

MacDonogh, Giles. *Frederick the Great*. London: Phoenix Press, 2000.

MacKenzie, David. *The Serbs and Russian Pan-Slavism 1875-1878*. Ithaca, N.Y: Cornell University Press, 1967.

Madariaga, Isabel de. *Russia in the Age of Catherine the Great*. London: Phoenix, 2003.

Malcolm, Noel. *Bosnia: A Short History*. London: Papermac, 1996.

—. *Kosovo: A Short History*. London: Papermac, 2002.

Mansel, Philip. *Louis XVIII*. London: John Murray, 2005.

Margutti, Freiherr Albert. *The Emperor Francis Joseph and his Times*. London: Hutchinson & Co, 1921.

Massie, Robert K. *Peter the Great: His Life and World*. New York: Ballantine Books, 1980.

Mazower, Mark. *The Balkans: From the End of Byzantium to the Present Day*. London: Phoenix, 2000.

McConnell, Allen. *Tsar Alexander I: Paternalistic Reformer.* Arlington Heights, Ill.: Harlan Davidson, Inc., 1970.

McLynn, Frank. *Napoleon: A Biography.* London: Pimlico, 1997.

McMeekin, Sean. *The Russian Origins of the First World War.* Cambridge, Mass.: The Belknap Press of Harvard University Press, 2011.

Medlicott, W.N. *History of the Near Eastern Settlement: 1878-1880.* Hamden, Conn.: Archon Books, 1963.

Miller, William. *Travels and Politics in the Near East.* New York: Arno Press and The New York Times, 1971. First published London, T. Fisher Unwin, 1898.

Mitford, Nancy. *Frederick the Great.* London: Penguin Books, 1973.

Mitis, Oskar Freiherr von. *Das Leben des Kronprinzen Rudolf.* Leipzig: Im Insel-Verlag zu Leipzig, 1928.

Murad, Anatol. *Franz Joseph I of Austria and His Empire.* New York: Twayne Publishers, 1968.

Murray, Gilbert. *The Foreign Policy of Sir Edward Grey: 1906-1915.* Oxford: At the Clarendon Press, 1915.

Nicolson, Harold. *The Congress of Vienna: A Study in Allied Unity: 1812-1822.* New York: Grove Press, 1946.

Paléologue, Maurice. *An Ambassador's Memoirs*, 6th ed. 3 vols. Trans. F.A. Holt. New York: George H. Doran Company, undated.

Palmer, Alan. *Alexander I: Tsar of War and Peace.* New York: Harper and Row, 1974.

—. *Metternich: Councillor of Europe.* London: Phoenix, 1997.

—. *The Decline and Fall of the Ottoman Empire.* London: John Murray Ltd., 1993.

—. *Twilight of the Habsburgs: The Life and Times of Emperor Francis Joseph.* London: Weidenfeld & Nicolson, 1994.

Pears, Sir Edwin. *Forty Years in Constantinople, 1873-1915.* New York: D. Appleton and Co., 1916.

Poincaré, Raymond. *Memoiren: Die Vorgeschichte des Weltkrieges 1912-1913.* Dresden: Paul Aretz Verlag, 1928.

Pribram, Alfred. *The Secret Treaties of Austria-Hungary: 1879-1914*, 2 vols. Trans. J.G. Darcy Paul and Denys P. Myers. Cambridge: Harvard University Press, 1921.

Radzinsky, Edvard. *Alexander II: The Last Great Tsar.* New York:

Free Press, 2005.

Rall, Hans. *Wilhelm II: Eine Biographie*. Graz: Verlag Styria, 1995.

Redlich, Joseph. *Kaiser Franz Joseph von Österreich*. Berlin: Verlag für Kulturpolitik, 1929.

Roberts, Elizabeth. *Realm of the Black Mountain: A History of Montenegro*. Ithaca, N.Y.: Cornell University Press, 2000.

Roberts, Ian W. *Nicholas I and the Russian Intervention in Hungary*. New York: St. Martin's Press, 1991.

Royle, Trevor. *Crimea: The Great Crimean War: 1853-1856*. New York: St. Martin's Press, 2000.

Sazonov, Serge. *Fateful Years 1909-1916*. Bronx, N.Y.: ISHI Press, 2008. First published, 1928.

Schmitt, Bernadotte E. *The Annexation of Bosnia 1908-1909*. Cambridge: At the University Press, 1937.

Seton-Watson, Hugh. *The Russian Empire 1801-1917*. Oxford: Clarendon Press, 1967.

Sosnosky, Theodor von. *Franz Ferdinand: Der Erzherzog-Thronfolger*. München und Berlin: Verlag von Roldenbourg, 1929.

Stansky, Peter. *Gladstone: A Progress in Politics*. New York: W.W. Norton and Company, 1979.

Stieve, Friedrich. *Isvolsky and the World War: Based on the Documents Recently Published by the German Foreign Office*. Freeport, N.Y.: Books for Libraries Press, 1971. First published, 1926.

Sumner, B.H. *Peter the Great and the Ottoman Empire*. Hamden, Conn.: Archon Books, 1965.

—. *Russia and the Balkans, 1870-1880*. Hamden/London: Archon Books, 1962.

Taylor, A.J.P. *The Struggle for Mastery in Europe 1848-1918*. Oxford: Oxford University Press, 1971.

Temperley, Harold William. *History of Serbia*. London: G. and Sons, 1919.

Thomson, Gladys Scott. *Catherine the Great and the Expansion of Russia*. New York: Collier Books, 1965.

Treadway, John D. *The Falcon and the Eagle: Mongenegro and Austria-Hungary 1908-1914*. West Lafayette, Ind.: Purdue University Press, 1998.

Troyat, Henri. *Alexander of Russia: Napoleon's Conqueror*. Trans.

Joan Pinkham. New York: Grove Press, 1982.

Van der Kiste, John. *Emperor Francis Joseph: Life, Death and the Fall of the Habsburg Empire.* Phoenix Mill, England: Sutton Publishing Limited, 2005.

—. *The Romanovs: 1818-1959. Alexander of Russia and His Family.* Phoenix Mill, England: Sutton Publishing Limited, 1998.

Van Herpen, Marcel H. *The Rise of Russia's New Imperialism.* Lanham, Md. : Rowman & Littlefield, 2014.

Warner, Philip. *The Crimean War: A Reappraisal.* Hertfordshire, England: Wordsworth Editions, 2001.

Warth, Robert D. *Nicholas II: The Life and Reign of Russia's Last Monarch.* Westport: Prager, 1997.

Wertheimer, Eduard von. *Graf Julius Andrassy: Sein Leben und seine Zeit.* 3 vols. Stuttgart: Deutsche Verlags-Anstalt, 1913.

Williamson, Samuel R., Jr. *Austria-Hungary and the Origins of the First World War.* London: Macmillan, 1991.

Zamoyski, Adam. *Rites of Peace: The Fall of Napoleon and the Congress of Vienna.* New York: Harper Collins, 2007.

INDEX

abdications
  Charles X (King of
    France), 95
  Ferdinand I (Emperor of
    Austria), 105, 106
  Franz II (as Holy Roman
    Emperor), 56–57
  Louis-Philippe I (King of
    France), 100–101
  Milan I (King of Serbia),
    253–54
Abdul Hamid II (Ottoman
  Sultan), 171, 183, 188, 267
Abdulaziz (Ottoman Sultan),
  170–71
Abdulmejid I (Ottoman
  Sultan), 121, 125
Abkhazia, 395, 396
Adrianople (Edirne), 88, 199,
  310, 327, 329
  Treaty of, 88–90, 90
Aehrenthal, Count Lexa von,
  260–63, 272, 273–74, 297–
  98, 422
  and) Izvolsky, Aleksandr,
    273, 276–77, 280
  and Bosnian crisis, 266,
    283, 284
  Buchlau bargain, 276–77,
    278–79
agriculture, 248, 258–59, 290–
  91
Aix-la-Chapelle, Congress of,
  73–74
Akkerman, Treaty of, 84, 85–
  86
Aksakov, Ivan, 143–44, 148–
  49, 184, 194–95
Albania, 266–67, 301–2, 330–
  31

Montenegrin invasion, 311,
    312–13
  Scutari, 313, 318, 319–20,
    321–22, 323–24
  Serbian invasion, 313, 323,
    330–31
Aleksei Nikolaevich,
  Czarevitch of Russia, 223
Alexander I (Czar of Russia),
  48, 49, 66–67
  and Austerlitz (Slavkov),
    Battle of, 49–50, 52–55,
    55–56
  autocracy, 74–75
  Bucharest, Treaty of, 62
  at Congress of Vienna, 65,
    66–67
  conservatism, 74–75, 77–
    78
  death, 81
  diplomacy, 79–80
  and Friedrich Wilhelm III
    of Prussia, 50, 57–58
  Greek War of
    Independence, 75–76
  Holy Alliance, 72–73
  interventionism, 74–75
  'liberalism', 67, 74
  and Metternich, 67–68,
    73–74, 74, 75, 80
  military strategy, 51–52,
    53–54
  and Napoleon I, 59–60,
    60–62
  public image, 55–56
  religious beliefs, 70–72,
    74–75, 80
  Russo-Turkish War (1806–
    12), 58–59, 62
  territorial demands, 67–68,

70
Tilsit, Treaties of, 59–60
and Treaty of Guarantee,
70
War of the Sixth Coalition,
63
War of the Third
Coalition, 49–50, 51
Alexander I (King of Serbia),
254–56, 256, 333
Alexander II (Czar of Russia)
accession, 139
and Alexander of
Battenberg, 232, 233
assassination, 215–17
Balkan policy, 142, 168,
174
and Bismarck, Otto von,
197–98
and Bosnia and
Herzegovina, 263, 272
criticism of, 214–15
diplomacy, 191, 204–5
and Franz Joseph I, 179–
81, 196–98
League of the Three
Emperors, 158–59, 159
militancy, 212
military strategy, 200–201
and Ottoman Empire, 183,
187
Ottoman Empire, war
against, 173, 178–80,
180, 181–82, 183–84,
213
and Pan-Slavism, 144, 149,
168, 213
Reichstadt negotiations,
173–75
revenge, desire for, 195
and Russo-Turkish War

(1877–78), 193
and Serbian-Ottoman war,
183
and Wilhelm I (German
Emperor), 179, 212
Alexander III (Czar of
Russia), 148, 216, 217
and Alexander of
Battenberg, 233–36,
238–39
and Bismarck, Otto von,
217–18
death, 221
Franco-Russian Alliance,
221
and Franz Joseph I
(Emperor of Austria),
220, 238
and Russo-Turkish War
(1877–78), 193
Alexander of Battenberg
(Sandro), 199–200, 235,
238–39, 239, 231–39
and Alexander II (Czar of
Russia), 232, 233
and Alexander III (Czar of
Russia), 233–36, 238–39
as ruler of Bulgaria, 231–
32, 234–36
and Russia, 234, 235
Alexander of Hesse, 202–3
Alexandra Feodorovna,
Czarina (Alix of Hesse),
222–23, 362
Alexis I of Russia, 3
alliances, 49–50, 49–50, 79–
80
Austro–Serbian Alliance,
237–38, 252–53, 254
Buchlau bargain, 262–63,
266, 276–77, 278–79

Index

Dual Alliance, 212, 214,
219
France-Ottoman, 58–59
Franco-Russian Alliance,
221, 223–24
Holy Alliance, 72–73, 80
League of the Three
Emperors, 161, 204–5,
214, 218–19
Russo-German, 238
Serbia and Montenegro,
172
Serbo-Bulgarian, 258
Triple Alliance, 214, 288,
337–38
Triple Entente, 225–26,
338, 360
Anastasia of Montenegro,
Princess, 326, 364–65
anathemas, 57–58, 76
Andrassy, Gyula, 159, 161,
188–89, 192–93, 205, 240,
243, 414, 418
Congress of Berlin (1878),
206, 207–10
Reichstadt negotiations,
174–75, 205
Anhalt-Serbst, Prince
Christian August of, 25
Anhalt-Serbst, Princess
Johanna Elisabeth of, 25
Anhalt-Serbst, Princess
Sophia Augusta Frederica
of. See Catherine II of
Russia
annexation, of Crimea, 39–40,
43, 47, 391
anti-Semitism, 57–58
Antivari (Bar), 262
Apis. See Dimitrijevic,
Colonel Dragutin

Arakcheyev, Aleksei, 80–81
Archangel, 7
Armenia, 327–29
army (Austro-Hungarian),
135, 243, 280–81, 320
maneuvers, in Bosnia, 333,
334, 339
army (British), 136
army (Bulgarian), 235, 236
army (French), 49, 62
army (Ottoman), 130–31, 350
army (Russian), 24, 72, 80–81,
281, 320
and Balkan Alliance, 304
Crimea, invasion of, 391
and Crimean War, 134–35
Danubian Principalities,
occupation of, 126
defeats, military, 4–5, 9,
19–20, 57–58, 136
and Hungarian Revolution,
114, 117
Ismailovsky regiment, 24
Kuban Host, 39
mobilization, 366–67, 368–
69, 369–70, 376–78,
381–82, 382–83
Napoleonic Wars, 51
Preobrazhensky regiment,
24
Russo-Turkish War (1768–
74), 31, 36
Russo-Turkish War (1828–
29), 87, 88
Russo-Turkish War (1877–
78), 199–202
Semenovsky regiment, 24
victories, 192
assassinations, 207, 253, 337
Alexander I (King of
Serbia), 255–56, 256,

333
Alexander II (Czar of
    Russia), 215–17
Elisabeth of Austria, 107
Franz Ferdinand,
    Archduke of Austria,
    256, 334–36, 340–42
Gregorius V (Ecumenical
    Patriarch), 76–77
Michael III (Prince of
    Serbia), 252
Paul I (Czar of Russia), 48
Peter III (Czar of Russia),
    29
Petrovic, Karadjordje, 155
Sophie (Duchess of
    Hohenberg), 340–42
atrocities, 312, 320–21
Auffenberg, Moritz von, 314
Augustus III of Poland, 30
Austerlitz (Slavkov), Battle of,
    52–55
Austria, 50, 63–64, 65–70,
    102–3, 105–6
Austria-Hungary. *See also*
    Habsburg Empire
    army, 243
    Austro–Serbian Alliance
        (1881), 237–38, 252–53
    Balkan Alliance,
        implications of, 302,
        303–4
    Balkan policy, 316–17, 343
    Bosnia/Herzegovina,
        annexation, 190–91,
        197, 205, 207, 218, 268–
        71
    Bosnia/Herzegovina,
        occupation, 207–10,
        242–50, 257–58
    Buchlau bargain, 262–63

Budapest conventions,
    190–91
Congress of Berlin, 210–11
and Danube (river), 130
Dual Alliance, 212
and First Balkan War, 313–
    15, 324–25, 325
and Franz Ferdinand,
    death of, 344–45, 346,
    353
German declaration of
    war, 383
July Crisis, 344–50
large Slav state, opposition
    to, 153, 189, 197, 205–6
League of the Three
    Emperors, 161, 204–5,
    214, 218–19
militancy, 273–74, 280–81,
    372
mobilization, 371
and Montenegro, 151–52,
    153, 210, 325
neutrality, 181, 190, 192–
    93, 201, 205
and Ottoman Empire,
    188–89, 279–80
Pig War, 258–59, 290–91
and Russia, 188–89, 203–4,
    266
and Russo-Turkish War
    (1877–78), 192–93
Sandzak of Novi Pazar,
    return of, 267
and Serbia, 237–38, 252–
    53, 253, 254, 257, 280–
    81, 353
Serbia, case for war
    against, 347–48, 348–50
Serbia, declares war on,
    374–76, 381

Serbia, ultimatum to, 357–
58, 365, 370, 371–72
and Serbian invasion of
Albania, 331–32
and Serbo-Bulgarian War,
237–38
territorial ambitions,
assumed, 315–16, 317
Treaty of Berlin, 270–71,
283
Treaty of Good
Neighborliness, 290
Triple Alliance, 214
Austrian Empire. *See also*
Habsburg Empire
and Danube access, 90–91
Austerlitz defeat, blamed
for, 55–56
at Congress of Vienna, 68
constitution, 103
and Crimean War, 138, 140
France and Great Britain,
treaty with, 69
'Greater Austria' campaign,
140
Russian criticism of, 148–
49
Second Italian War of
Independence, 289
uprising, 102–3
Austro-Prussian War, 158
Austro–Serbian Alliance,
237–38, 252–53, 254
autocracy, 223, 254, 387
Alexander II (Czar of
Russia), 74–75
Charles X (King of
France), 96
Habsburg Empire, 100
Metternich, Prince
Klemens von, 66, 67

Nicholas I (Czar of
Russia), 82–83
Putin, Vladimir, 389
Azov, 8, 10, 11, 13, 20, 31
Azov campaigns, 7–9
Azov, Sea of, 1, 10, 13, 31
Bagrationovsk (Eylau), 57–58
Balkan Alliance, 289–90, 292,
302–4, 305–8, 330
Balkans. *See also* Albania;
Bosnia; Bulgaria; Dalmatia;
Greece; Herzegovina;
Kosovo; Macedonia;
Moldova; Montenegro;
Romania; Serbia; Slovenia;
Wallachia
Austrian territorial
demands, 218
Christian population, 32,
301
First Balkan War, 310–11
nationalism, 21–22
nonintervention policy,
161
Ottomanization of, 301
and Pan-Slavism, 151–54
power, balance of, 164–65
railroad development, 265–
66
Reichstadt negotiations,
174
restructuring of, 188–89,
202, 210, 218
Russian invasions of, 70
Russian territorial claims,
79, 123, 218
Russification of, 195–96
and Russo-Turkish War
(1710), 17, 18–20
Sandzak of Novi Pazar,
267, 291, 310, 316, 329,

427
Slav population, 33
territorial boundaries, 318
and Young Turks
government, 301–2
Bar (Antivari), 262
Batak, 177
Battenberg, Alexander of. *See*
Alexander of Battenberg
Batthyany, Lajos, 103
battles
Austerlitz (Slavkov), 52–55
Chesme (Çesme), 33–34
The Field of the Sultan's
Felling (Montenegro),
151
Leipzig (Battle of the
Nations), 63
Navarino, 84–86
Poltava, 15–17
Sinope, 131
Ulm, 49
Zenta, 12
Belgium, 98
Belgrade, 354
Berchtold, Count Leopold,
222, 260, 273, 280, 298,
338, 349, 357–58
and First Balkan War, 314,
324–25, 325
and Franz Ferdinand,
death of, 343, 344
and Franz Joseph I
(Emperor of Austria),
374, 375
Berchtold, Nandine, 260
Berlin, Congress of, 206–11,
272
Berlin, Treaty of, 210–11,
262, 270–71, 276, 283
Bessarabia, 62, 83, 196, 202,

210
Bethlehem, 120, 121
Bismarck, Herbert von, 238
Bismarck, Otto von, 60, 158–
59, 179, 182, 233–34
and Alexander II (Czar of
Russia), 197–98
and Alexander III (Czar of
Russia), 217–18
Congress of Berlin, 206,
207
dismissal, 221
Dual Alliance, 212, 219
League of the Three
Emperors, 214, 218–19
'Reinsurance Treaty', 219–
20, 240
Triple Alliance, 214
Björkö, Treaty of, 227–30
Black Hand (Serbian
nationalist group), 333,
334, 340–42, 354, 356
Black Sea, 1
Livadia (palace), 178–79
Ottoman control of, 30
Russian access to, 7–9, 20–
21, 84
shipping access to, 90–91,
91–92
Bludova, Countess
Antoinette, 143, 149
Boghitschewitch, M., 378
Bohemia
Karlovy Vary (Carlsbad),
260
Konopiste, 338
Prague, 104, 106
Bonaparte, Napoleon. *See*
Napoleon I
Bosnia, 162–63, 163, 164,
202, 243–44, 257–58, 323,

357
Austria-Hungary
  annexation, 190–91,
  197, 205, 207, 218, 268–
  71
Austria-Hungary army
  maneuvers, 333, 334,
  339
Austria-Hungary
  occupation, 207–10,
  242–50, 257–58
Ilidze, 338, 339
rebellion (1875), 166, 167,
  170
Reichstadt negotiations,
  174–75
Sarajevo, 246, 247, 339–42
Tarcin, 334, 339
Bosnian crisis, 270–83
Bosphorus, 92, 93
Boyar Duma, 10–11
Brancovo, Constantine, 19–
  20, 20
Britain. See Great Britain
Brünn (Brno), 51
Buchanan, Sir George, 366–
  67, 367, 378
Bucharest, Treaty of (1812),
  62, 83
Bucharest, Treaty of (1913),
  329–30, 343
Buchlau (Buchlovice), 260
Buchlau bargain (Austro-
  Russian agreement), 262–
  63, 266, 276–77, 278–79
Budapest conventions, 190–
  91, 196
Bulgaria, 88, 127, 170, 202,
  210, 234–36, 320, 394
  Alexander of Battenberg,
    231–39

army, 235, 236
and Austria-Hungary, 349
and Balkan Alliance, 302–3
Batak, 177
and Crimean War, 134–35
Eastern Rumelia, 236, 238
Ferdinand I, 240–41, 262,
  320, 349
First Balkan War, 310
and Greece, 303
independence, 187–88,
  202, 262
and Macedonia, 252–53
massacres in, 177–78
and Montenegro, 303
and Pan-Slavism, 291
Plevna, 194, 195
and Russia, 154, 191
as Russian vassal state,
  185–86, 187, 189, 195–
  96, 197, 218, 231–32
and Russo-Turkish War
  (1877–78), 192, 193–94,
  194, 195
Second Balkan War, 327
and Serbia, 258, 302–3
Serbo-Bulgarian War, 236–
  38
Treaty of Bucharest (1913),
  329
and Treaty of San Stefano,
  202, 205
Varna, 87
Bulgars (ethnic group), 329
Bülow, Prince Bernhard von,
  229, 281–82, 282, 285
Buol, Karl Ferdinand von,
  137–38, 197
Burian, Baron Stefan, 257
Byzantium. See
  Constantinople

Cabrinovic, Nedjelko, 335
Cantemir, Dimitrie, 19, 20
Caprivi, Count Leo von, 221
Carlsbad (Karlovy Vary), 260
Castlereagh, Viscount (Robert
    Stewart), 69, 70
Catherine I of Russia, 20
Catherine II of Russia
    (Catherine the Great), 22,
    23–47
    accession, 23–24
    and Crimea, 43, 44–45
    death, 47
    Habsburgs, alliance with,
        40–43
    Kuchuk Kainarji, Treaty
        of, 36–37
    marriage, 25–27
    militarism, 24–25, 30, 42–
        43
    religious beliefs, 26
    Russo-Turkish War (1768–
        74), 32–33, 36–37
    Russo-Turkish War (1787–
        92), 45–47
Catholicism, 13, 120–21, 144,
    246, 249, 321
Çesme (Chesme), Battle of,
    33–34
Cetinje, 32–33, 152, 311, 312,
    324
Charles X (King of France),
    95, 96
Charles XII (King of
    Sweden), 15–17, 402
Charykov, N.V. (Nikolai
    Valerievich), 271, 299, 300
Chelius, General Oskar, 369
Cherkasky, Prince Vladimir,
    187
Cherniaev, General M.G.,

    171–72, 175–76
Chesme, Battle of, 33–34
Chikova, Princess Vasilisa,
    143
Chotek, Sophie (Duchess of
    Hohenberg), 337, 338, 339,
    340–42
Christianity. *See also* Eastern
    Orthodox Church
    Balkan, 32, 33, 244, 246,
        249, 301
    Catholicism, 13, 120–21,
        144, 246, 249, 321
    and Islam, 18
    as minority religion, 141,
        164, 166, 170, 301
    persecution of members,
        164, 321
Ciganovic, Milan, 334, 354–
    55, 356–57
Codrington, Sir Edward, 85
colonization, 38–39, 43–45
Concert of Europe, 73–74
Confederation of the Rhine,
    56
Congress of Aix-la-Chapelle,
    73–74
Congress of Berlin, 206–11,
    272
Congress of Poland, 98
Congress of Troppau, 74
Congress of Verona, 75
Congress of Vienna, 63–64,
    65–70
conservatism, 74–75, 77–78
conspiracies, 33–34, 48, 215–
    17, 238–39, 333–36, 340–
    42, 353–57
conspiracy theories, 338
Constantinople, 2, 14, 350, *See
    also* Turkish Straits

Castle of the Seven
    Towers, 30
and Christianity, 120–21,
    150
in First Balkan War, 310
Russian claim to, 15, 72–
    73, 128
Russian desire for, 2, 24–
    25, 192, 293, 352, 367–
    68, 386
Russian Embassy, 15, 30,
    126
Russian failure to capture,
    199–202
Russian military presence
    in, 91–93, 124–25
Young Turk Revolution,
    266, 268–69
Constantinople Conference,
    185–87, 189–90
Cossacks, 39, 114
coups. *See also* assassinations
    alleged, 391–92
    Decembrist revolt, 82–83
    against Paul II (Czar of
        Russia), 48
    against Peter III (Czar of
        Russia), 23–24, 29
Crimea, 44–45
    and Catherine II of Russia,
        43, 44–45
    colonization of, 43–45
    Kerch, 10, 12–13, 14
    Kherson, 39
    Ottoman Empire,
        controlled by, 30, 39–40
    Russian annexation of, 39–
        40, 43, 47, 391
    Russian invasion, 388
    Sevastopol, 43–44, 45, 139,
        391, 392

Simferopol, 391
Crimean Tatars, 2, 4, 7–8, 44
Crimean War, 91, 119–30,
    130–41
Croats (ethnic group), 105
Czartoryski, Adam, 50
Czech Republic, 394
    Austerlitz (Slavkov), Battle
        of, 52–55
    Bohemia, 104, 106, 260,
        338
    Brünn (Brno), 51
    Buchlovice (Buchlau), 260
    Karlovy Vary (Carlsbad),
        260
    Konopiste, 338
    Moravia, 50, 51, 52–55,
        105, 106, 260
    Olmütz (Olomouc), 50,
        105, 106
    Opava (Troppau), 74
    Prague, 104, 106
Dalmatia, 162–66
Danilevsky, Nikolai, 149–50
Danube (river), 19, 36, 37, 84,
    90–91, 130, 134
Danubian Principalities
    (Moldavia and Wallachia),
    31, 62, 76, 83–84, 84, 140–
    41, 141
    and Austrian Empire, 136,
        140
    hospodars, 18, 19–20, 62
    Ottoman rule of, 34–35,
        58–59
    and Russia, 34, 83, 84, 124,
        126, 128, 136
    and Russo-Turkish War
        (1710), 17, 18, 19–20
    and Russo-Turkish War
        (1828–29), 86–87

Dardanelles, 88, 89–90, 93, 127, 300
Dashkova, Catherine, 29
Decembrist revolt, 82–83
Detroit, Karl (Mehmed Ali Pasha), 207
Dibich-Zabalkansky, Count Ivan (Hans Karl von Diebitsch), 88
Dimitrijevic, Colonel Dragutin ('Apis'), 256, 333, 334, 356–57
diplomacy, 78, 290
    Alexander I (Czar of Russia), 79–80
    Alexander II (Czar of Russia), 191, 204–5
    and Bosnian crisis, 279–83
    Franz Joseph I (Emperor of Austria), 274–79, 318
    Grey, Sir Edward, 271, 283
    Nicholas I (Czar of Russia), 93–94
    Nicholas II (Czar of Russia), 277–78
    personal, 274–79, 318, 378
    Peter I of Russia (Peter the Great), 11–13, 14–15
    Wilhelm I (German Emperor), 158–59, 159, 197–98
    Wilhelm II (German Emperor), 226–27, 278, 279, 379–80, 381, 382
Disraeli, Benjamin, 206
divine right monarchy, 96, 120, 409
Dnieper (river), 8, 9, 20
Dodecanese islands, 300–301
Dolgoruky, Major General Yuri V., 32, 33

Don (river), 8, 10
Dostoevsky, Fyodor, 146
Dual Alliance (Austria and Germany), 212, 214, 219
Dugin, Aleksandr, 393, 396–98
Durazzo (Durres), 313
Durham, Edith, 269, 285–86, 312
Dusan, Stefan (King of Serbia), 155
Eastern Orthodox Church
    anathemas, 57–58, 76
    anti-Catholicism, 144
    in Bosnia-Herzegovina, 257–58
    in Bulgaria, 127
    in Constantinople, 2
    holy places, access to, 15, 121, 124, 125
    as minority religion, 143–44
    in Montenegro, 153
    in Ottoman Empire, 77, 78–79, 125, 127
    persecution of members, 77–78, 311
    and Russia, 121, 125, 141
    Slavophilism, 144
    xenophobia, 5–6
Eastern Rumelia, 236, 238
Edirne (Adrianople), 88, 199, 310, 329
    Treaty of, 88–90, 90
Edward VII (King of United Kingdom), 225–26, 270, 271
Eggeling, D. von, 377
Egypt, 91
Elisabeth Alexeievna, Czarina (Louise of Baden), 81

Elisabeth of Austria
(Elisabeth of Bavaria, Sisi),
107, 160, 414
Elizabeth of Russia, 22, 23,
25
England. *See* Great Britain
Erfurt, 60–62
Essad Pasha, 324
Estonia, 394
ethnic cleansing, 320–21
ethnic identity
Serbs. *See also* Pan-Serbism
ethnic identity, 107, 111–12,
242, 246, 338, 409
Bulgars, 329
Croats, 105
Magyars, 105
Serbs, 105, 164–65
Eurasian union, 388, 392–93
Evelyn, John, 11–12
exceptionalism, 145–47, 291,
413
executions, 116
Eylau (Bagrationovsk), 57–58
Fadejev, Rostislav
Andreievich, *Opinion on the
Eastern Question*, 150–51
Feodor III (Czar of Russia), 3
Ferdinand I (Emperor of
Austria), 97, 98, 100, 105,
106
Ferdinand I (King of
Bulgaria), 240–41, 262,
320, 349
First Balkan Crisis, 270–83
First Balkan War, 310–11,
317–26
First World War, 361
and Austria-Hungary, 361,
371–73, 374–76, 381
and Germany, 372–74,

379–80, 383
and Great Britain, 367, 378
origins, 367–68
and Russia, 366–67, 368–
70, 376–78, 379, 381–
83, 383–85
and Serbia, 370
Serbia, ultimatum to, 361,
365
France, 89, *See also* Napoleon
I
and Alsace-Lorraine, 227
Austerlitz (Slavkov), Battle
of, 52–55
Austrian Empire and Great
Britain, treaty with, 69
and Balkan Alliance, 304–6
Charles X, 95, 96
at Congress of Vienna, 69
and Crimean War, 127, 134
Germanophobia, 304–5
Grande Armée, 49
and Hungarian Revolution,
114
July Revolution, 95, 96
Louis Napoleon III, 120,
121, 137, 141
Louis-Philippe I, 96–97,
100–101
Napoleon II, 63
Napoleonic Wars, 405
Napoleonic Wars, 49–64,
67–68
Ottoman Empire, alliance
with, 58–59
revolution (1848), 100–101
and Russia, 62, 307–8, 308,
328–29, 360, 366–67
and Serbia, 363
spies/spying, 52
Triple Entente, 225–26,

360
and Turkish Straits, 268
Franco-Prussian War, 158
Franco-Russian Alliance, 221,
    223–24
Franz Ferdinand, Archduke
    of Austria, 177, 256, 274,
    314–15, 316–17, 338, 344
    assassination, 256, 334–36,
        340–42
    in Bosnia, 333, 336–37,
        338–39
Franz II (I) (Holy Roman
    Emperor/Emperor of
    Austria), 63, 65, 98
    abdication as Holy Roman
        Emperor, 56–57
    death, 100
    Holy Alliance, 72–73
    Münchengrätz (Mnichovo
        Hradiste) Agreements,
        98–99
    and Napoleonic wars, 49–
        50, 50
    Pressburg, Treaty of, 54–
        55
Franz Joseph I (Emperor of
    Austria), 54, 94, 106–7
    accession, 106
    and Alexander I (King of
        Serbia), 254
    and Alexander II (Czar of
        Russia), 179–81, 196–98
    and Alexander III (Czar of
        Russia), 220
    and Hungarian Revolution,
        108–10
    assasination plot, 337
    Balkan policy, 166–67,
        173–74, 174, 316
    and Bosnia and

Herzegovina,
    annexation of, 263–64,
    274, 275–79
Buchlau bargain, 278–79
and Crimean War, 137–38,
    274
Dalmatia, visit to, 162–66
diplomacy, personal, 274–
    79, 318
Dual Alliance, 214
and First Balkan War, 314–
    15, 324–25
foreign policy, 128
and Franz Ferdinand,
    death of, 341–42, 344,
    346
and Hungarian
    Constitution, 111–12
Hungarian throne, deposed
    from, 112
League of the Three
    Emperors, 158–59, 159
mediator, 129
and Milan I (King of
    Serbia), 252
monarchy, commitment to,
    107–8, 112
neutrality, 201
and Nicholas I (Czar of
    Russia), 107–8, 112–13,
    113–14, 113–14, 125–
    26, 127, 128–30, 131–
    33, 135
and Nicholas II (Czar of
    Russia), 274–79, 318–
    20, 379, 380–81
peace policy, 240, 278–79,
    344, 371, 379
Reichstadt negotiations,
    173–75
and Russia, 107–8, 113–14,

161–62, 203–4, 239–40
and Scutari crisis, 322–23
Second Italian War of
Independence, 289
and Serbia, 347–48, 371
and Serbo-Bulgarian War,
237–38
and Treaty of San Stefano,
202–3
and Turco-Italian War,
296, 298
and Wilhelm I of
Germany, 157–58
and World War I, 374–76
Franz Joseph I of Austria
birth, 97
Franz Karl, Archduke of
Austria, 97
Frederick Augustus I of
Saxony, 68
Frederick II of Prussia
(Frederick the Great)
and Catherine II of Russia,
34, 40
and Joseph II (Holy
Roman Emperor), 40–
41, 41
and Peter III (Czar of
Russia), 23, 27, 28
and Poland, partition of,
35
Russo-Turkish War (1787–
92), 46
Friedland (Pravdinsk), 57–58
Friedrich III (German
Emperor), 220
Friedrich Wilhelm III of
Prussia, 50, 57–58, 59–60,
65, 72–73, 98–99
Friedrich Wilhelm IV of
Prussia, 110, 136–37

Georgia, 90, 388, 394–96
Germany, 56–57, 60, *See also*
Frederick II of Prussia;
Friedrich III; Wilhelm I;
Wilhelm II
and Austria, 212, 214
Austria-Hungary, support
for, 348
Balkan Alliance,
implications of, 303–4
Berlin, 110
Björkö, Treaty of, 227–30
and Bosnian crisis, 281,
285
Dual Alliance, 212
Erfurt, 60–62
League of the Three
Emperors, 161, 204–5,
214, 218–19
militarism, 372–74
navy, 226
and Nicholas I (Czar of
Russia), 182
Ottoman army, training of,
350
Prussia, 46–47, 50, 57–58,
60, 110, 150
rebellions/revolutions, 98,
110
'Reinsurance Treaty', 219–
20, 221, 240
and Russia, 219–20, 221,
238, 240, 353, 376–77,
382, 383
Saxony, 68
Triple Alliance, 214, 288,
337–38
unification, 158
Giesl, Baron, 365
Gladstone, William, 177–78
Golitsyn, Prince Vasily, 4–5

Golovin, Count Fyodor, 8

Gorchakov, Aleksandr, 146, 149, 159, 161, 174, 182, 206, 207, 414

Gorchakov, General Mikhail, 134

Gordon, Patrick, 7, 8–9

Görgei, Arthur, 111, 115–16, 410

Grabez, Trifko, 335–36

Grande Armée (Napoleonic French Army), 49

Great Britain, 11–12, 72, 89, 114, 121–22, 136, 367
  at Congress of Vienna, 69
  and Crimean War, 127, 134
  Navarino, Battle of, 86
  and Ottoman Empire, 93, 177–78, 182–83, 350
  and Russo-Turkish War (1877–78), 192, 202
  and Turkish Straits, 268, 271

Great Northern War, 15–17

Greece, 33, 79, 90, 252–53
  and Balkan Alliance, 303
  and Bulgaria, 303
  Dodecanese, Italian control of, 300–301
  First Balkan War, 310
  Philike Hetairia ('Society of Friends'), 75, 76
  Second Balkan War, 327

Greek War of Independence, 75–76, 84–86

Gregorius V (Ecumenical Patriarch), 76–77

Grey, Sir Edward, 271, 283, 367

Grinevitsky, Ignoti, 216

Grünwald, Baron, 369

Gurko, General Josif, 192

Habsburg Empire, 12–13, *See also* Austria-Hungary; Austrian Empire
  and Balkan nationalism, 21–22
  Catherine II, alliance with, 40–43, 46–47
  and Danubian Principalities, 34–35
  German territories, loss of, 56–57
  and Ottoman Empire, 34, 35
  and Russia, 13
  Russo-Turkish War (1768–74), 31
  Russo-Turkish War (1787–92), 46–47
  Treaty of Karlowitz, 12

Habsburg monarchy, 427, *See also* Ferdinand I; Franz II (I); Franz Joseph I; Joseph II; Maria Theresa
  abdications, 56–57, 105, 106
  criticism of, 338
  and Holy Roman Empire, 56–57
  opposition to, 116, 333–34
  reputation, 100, 106, 116, 284
  Romanov antipathy to, 14, 55–56, 79–80, 107–8, 217, 220
  Romanovs, alliance with, 4–5, 276
  succession, 97, 106

Hartwig, Nicholas, 292, 293, 345

Havlicek, Karel, 146–47

Haynau, General Julius Jacob
von, 113, 116, 410
Herzegovina, 162–63, 163,
164, 202, 243–44, 357
Austria-Hungary
annexation, 190–91,
197, 205, 207, 218, 268–
71
Austria-Hungary
occupation, 207–10,
242–50, 257–58
and Montenegro, 167, 311,
323
Mostar, 248, 339
rebellion, 166, 167, 170
Reichstadt negotiations,
174–75
and Treaty of San Stefano,
202
High Porte. *See* Porte
Hohenlohe-Schillingsfürst,
Prince Gottlieb zu, 318–19
Holstein-Gottorp, Princess
Johanna Elisabeth of, 25
Holy Alliance, 72–73, 80
Holy League, 4–5, 12–13
Holy Roman Empire, 56–57
holy war (jihad), 76, 85–86, 86
hospodars, 18, 19–20, 62
Hötzendorf, Conrad von,
296–97, 298, 314, 343–44
Hübner, Alexander, 195
Hungary
revolution, 410
Hungary, 98, 103, 111–12,
208, 258, 394, 409
revolution, 104–5, 108–10
Revolution, 110–16
Hungary. *See also* Austrian
Empire; Austro-Hungary;
Habsburg Empire

Hunkar-Iskelesi Treaty, 94, 99
Hunkar-Iskelesi, Treaty of,
408
Ianushkevich, Nikolai, 383,
384, 385
Ignatiev, Nikolai, 185–86,
189, 191, 201, 205–6
Ilic, Danilo, 336
Ilidze, 338, 339
Islam, 18, 44, 244, 246–47,
248–49, 314–15
Islamophobia, 2, 57–58, 314–
15, 320–21
Istanbul. *See* Constantinople
Italy, 74–75
Piedmont, 289
Racconigi Bargain, 287–89
rebellions, 98
Second Italian War of
Independence, 289
Triple Alliance, 214, 288,
337–38
Turco-Italian War, 296,
300–301
Venice, 32
Verona, 75
Ivan V of Russia, 3, 5, 10, 21–
22
Ivan VI of Russia, 21–22
Izmir (Smyrna), 89
Izvolsky, Aleksandr, 260,
264–65, 266, 267–68, 269–
70, 271, 294, 295, 300, 423
and Aehrenthal, Count
Lexa von, 273, 276–77,
280
Armenian question, 327–
29
and Balkan Alliance, 289,
292, 302, 307
and Bosnia/Herzegovina

annexation, 272–73,
276, 282–83
Buchlau bargain, 271–72,
276–77, 278–79
and First Balkan War, 315–
16, 317
and France, 293–94, 307–
8, 360
Pan-Serbism, 272–73
Racconigi Bargain, 287–89
and Russian access to
Turkish Straits, 298–300
Japan, 263
Jassy, 31
Jassy, Treaty of, 47
Jerusalem, 120, 121, 224–25
jihad (holy war), 76, 85–86, 86
Jones, John Paul, 45–46
Joseph II (Holy Roman
Emperor), 35, 40–43, 44,
46
Jovanovic, Misko, 336
July Crisis, 344–50
July Revolution (France), 95,
96
Kallay, Benjamin, 245
Karlovy Vary (Carlsbad), 260
Karlowitz, Treaty of, 12
Katar, Bay of, 323
Kaunitz, Wenzel Anton von,
35
Kazikerman, 8
Kerch, 10, 12–13, 14
Kherson, 39
Kiev, 4, 391
Kinsky, Count, 12–13
Kirk-Kilisse (Kirklareli), 310,
329
Kollar, Jan, 145
Konopiste, 338
Korcula, 338–39

Kosovo, 202, 310, 329
Kossuth, Lajos, 104–5, 110–
11, 111, 112, 113, 114–15
Krasnoe selo, 363–64, 368–69
Krepost (frigate), 14
Krizanic, George, 144–45
Krobatin, Alexander von,
314, 371
Krüdener, Baroness Julie von,
70–72, 72–73
Kuchuk Kainarji, Treaty of,
36–37, 83, 124
Kütahya, Peace Agreement
of, 93
Kutuzov, General Mikhail,
51–52, 53–54
Laguiche, General de, 360
Lamsdorf, Vladimir, 229
Latas, General Omar Pasha,
131
Latour, Theodor von, 106
Latvia, 394
Lazarev, Admiral Mikhail, 92
League of the Three
Emperors (Austria,
Germany, Russia), 161,
204–5, 214, 218–19
Lefort, Francis, 8
Leipzig, Battle of, 63
Leopold II (Holy Roman
Emperor), 46–47
liberalism, 67, 74, 103, 252
Libya, 288, 296, 300–301
Lithuania, 394
Livadia (palace), 178–79
Loftus, Lord Augustus, 182–
83, 192
London Ambassadors'
Conference, 317–18, 321–
22, 323, 325, 330–31
London Conference (1877),

191
London, Treaty of, 326
Louis Napoleon III (Emperor
    of France), 120, 121, 137,
    141
Louise of Baden (Elisabeth
    Alexeievna, Czarina), 81
Louis-Philippe I (King of
    France), 96–97, 100–101
Macedonia, 237, 252–53,
    266–67, 349
Mackenzie, Admiral Thomas,
    43–44
Magyars (ethnic group), 105,
    111–12, 208, 338, 409
Mahmud II (Ottoman
    Sultan), 76, 78–79, 85–86,
    86, 88–89, 91–93
Maly, Stepan (Stephen the
    Little), 32–33
Maria Theresa (Holy Roman
    Empress), 31, 35, 41
Marie Alexandrovna (Czarina
    of Russia), 143–44, 148,
    149, 203, 217
Marie Louise of Austria, 62
Masaryk, Professor Tomas,
    284
Mashin, Draga (Obrenovic),
    254–56, 256, 333
Medvedev, Dmitry, 389, 393,
    396
Mehemet Ali (Pasha of
    Egypt), 91, 92, 93
Mehmed Ali Pasha (Detroit,
    Karl), 207
Mehmed Said Pasha (Grand
    Vizier, Ottoman Empire),
    299
Melitza (Milica) of
    Montenegro, Princess, 326,

364–65
Menschikov, Aleksandr, 124–
    25, 126
Metternich, Prince Klemens
    von, 66, 78, 85, 93, 95–96,
    103
    and Alexander I (Czar of
        Russia), 67–68, 73–74,
        74, 75, 80
    autocracy, 66, 67, 100
    and Concert of Europe,
        73–74
    Münchengrätz (Mnichovo
        Hradiste) Agreements,
        98–99
    and Nicholas I (Czar of
        Russia), 84, 98–99, 108
Michael III (Mihailo
    Obrenovic, Prince of
    Serbia), 252
Midhat Pasha, Ahmed Sefik,
    188
Milan I (King of Serbia), 237–
    38, 252, 251–53, 253–54
Milanovic, Milovan, 290–91
militarism, 168, 372–74
    and Pan-Slavism, 149,
        150–51
    Russian, 24–25, 30, 42–43,
        80–81, 178
Milyutin, Dmitry, 201
Mnichovo Hradiste
    (Münchengrätz)
    agreements, 98–99, 110,
    113
Moldavia, 19–20, 40, 58–59,
    83, See also Danubian
    Principalities
    Bessarabia, 62, 83
    Jassy, 31
    Ottoman rule of, 58–59

Russian protectorate, 90
and Russo-Turkish War
  (1710), 17
and Russo-Turkish War of
  1768–74, 31
monarchy, 95–96, 98, 107–8,
  134, *See also* Habsburg
  monarchy; Romanov
  monarchy
constitutional, 103
divine right, 96, 120, 409
succession, 27, 97, 106
Montenegro, 32–33, 125,
  151–54, 164–65, 267, 311
Albania, invasion of, 311,
  312–13, 322
and Buchlau bargain, 262
and Austria-Hungary, 151–
  52, 153, 210, 325
and Balkan Alliance, 303
Bar (Antivari), 262
Bosnia/Herzegovina,
  threatens, 323
and Bulgaria, 303
First Balkan War, 310,
  311–13
and Herzegovina, 167, 311,
  323
independence, 202
and Ottoman Empire, 172
and Pan-Slavism, 291
Reichstadt negotiations,
  174
and Russia, 153, 151–54,
  325–26
and Russo-Turkish War
  (1710), 17, 18
and Scutari, 323–24, 325–
  26
and Serbia, 153, 164–65,
  172, 303, 329

territorial gains, 210
torture, 320–21
Treaty of Bucharest (1913),
  329
and Treaty of San Stefano,
  202
Moravia
Austerlitz (Slavkov), Battle
  of, 52–55
Brünn (Brno), 51
Buchlau (Buchlovice), 260
Olmütz (Olomouc), 50,
  105, 106
Morocco, 226–27, 227
Moscow, 6
Moscow Slavic Benevolent
  Committee, 143–44
Mostar, 248, 339
Muhammed Ali. *See* Mehemet
  Ali (Pasha of Egypt)
Münchengrätz (Mnichovo
  Hradiste) Agreements, 98–
  99, 110, 113
Murad V (Ottoman Sultan),
  171
Muslims, 314–15, 320–21,
  330
Mustafa II (Ottoman Sultan),
  2, 4, 12
Napoleon I (Emperor of
  France, Napoleon
  Bonaparte), 47–48, 49, 69–
  70
and Alexander I (Czar of
  Russia), 59–60, 60–62
Austerlitz (Slavkov), Battle
  of, 52–55
Brünn (Brno), occupation
  of, 51
Confederation of the
  Rhine, 56

defeat of, 63
military strategy, 52–53
Ottoman Empire, alliance
 with, 58–59
peace negotiations, 54–55
Prussia, invasion of, 57–58
Russia, invasion of, 62
Tilsit, Treaties of, 59–60
Vienna, occupation of, 50
Napoleon II, 63
Napoleonic Wars, 49–64, 67–
 68, 405
 Austerlitz (Slavkov), Battle
  of, 52–55
 Russia, invasion of, 62–63
 Third Coalition, 49–50,
  51–52
 Tilsit, Treaties of, 58–60
 Vienna, fall of, 50–51
Narodna odbrana (National
 Defense, Serbia), 292–93,
 356, 365
Narodnaya Volya (Will of the
 People), 215–17
Natalya, Czaritsa of Russia
 (Natalya Kirillovna
 Naryshkina), 3
National Defense (*Narodna
 odbrana*, Serbia), 292–93,
 356, 365
nationalism, 107, 177
 and Pan-Slavism, 142–43,
  145–47
 Serbian, 171–72, 256, 270,
  333, 365
NATO (North Atlantic
 Treaty Organization), 393–
 94
Navarino, Battle of, 84–86
navy (Austro-Hungarian), 323
navy (British), 89, 202, 323

navy (French), 89
navy (German), 226
navy (Italian), 323
navy (Ottoman), 84–86, 350–
 51
navy (Russian), 1–2, 7, 20–21,
 92, 140–41, 366–67
 Black Sea Fleet, 43–44, 92,
  351–52
 establishment, 7, 10–11,
  13–14
 Russo-Japanese War, 263
 Russo-Turkish War (1768–
  74), 30–31, 31–34
 Sinope, Battle of, 131
 Turkish Straits, access to,
  260–61, 263, 265, 266
Nelidov, Aleksandr, 284–85
Neman (river), 59–60
Neratov, Anatoly, 299
Nesselrode, Karl, 80, 98–99,
 123–24
neutrality, 219–20
 Austria-Hungary, 181, 190,
  192–93, 201, 205
 Austrian Empire, 137–38,
  181
Nicholas I (Czar of Russia),
 54, 82–94, 127, 161–62,
 407
 autocracy, 82–83
 Balkan policy, 128
 and Constantinople, 124–
  25
 Danubian Principalities,
  occupation of, 126
 death, 94, 139
 Decembrist revolt, 82–83
 diplomacy, 93–94
 and Eastern Orthodox
  Church, 121

and Franz Joseph I
(Emperor of Austria),
107–8, 113–14, 125–26,
127, 128–30, 131–33,
135, 138, 274
Habsburg Empire, military
support for, 110, 114,
117
and Hungarian Revolution,
110, 114, 117
Hunkar-Iskelesi Treaty, 94
and Metternich, 84, 98–99,
108
military strategy, 121–22,
124–25
Münchengrätz (Mnichovo
Hradiste) Agreements,
98–99
Navarino, Battle of, 84–86
Ottoman policy, 83–84,
87–88, 91–92, 122–24,
124, 128
Russo-Persian War (1826–
28), 86
Russo-Turkish War (1828–
29), 86–87, 88–90
and United Kingdom,
121–22
Nicholas I of Montenegro
(Nikola, Nikita), 152–53,
164–65, 303, 310–12, 324,
325–26
Nicholas II (Czar of Russia),
216–17, 221–22
and Austria-Hungary, 315–
16
and Balkan Alliance, 304
and Bosnian crisis, 263,
266, 272, 273, 275–79
Buchlau bargain, 276–77,
278–79

canonization, 389
diplomacy, 277–78
European war, case for,
351–52, 353
and Franz Joseph I
(Emperor of Austria),
274–79, 318–20, 379,
380–81
manipulation of, 222, 223,
227–28, 379
Poincaré, Raymond, visit
of, 360, 362
Racconigi Bargain, 288–89
Treaty of Björkö, 227–30
and Wilhelm II (German
Emperor), 379–80
and World War I, 379–80,
381–82, 383–85
Nikolai Nikolaevich, Grand
Duke of Russia, 193, 199–
202, 204
North Atlantic Treaty
Organization (NATO),
393–94
Novosiltsev, Nikolai, 55–56
Obrenovic, Draga (Mashin),
254–56, 256
Obrenovic, Milos, 155
Obreskov, Aleksei, 30
Ochakov, 8
Olmütz (Olomouc), 50, 105,
106
Opava (Troppau), 74
Oranienbaum, 29
Orlov, Aleksei Fyodorovich,
93–94, 133
Orlov, Count Aleksei, 23, 29,
31–32, 33
Orlov, Count Grigory, 23, 29,
30–31
Orthodox Church. *See*

Eastern Orthodox Church
Osman Pasha, General, 194, 195
Ottoman Empire, 1–2, *See also* Constantinople; Turkish Straits
  Akkerman, Treaty of, 84
  and Alexander II (Czar of Russia), 183, 187
  and Austria-Hungary, 188–89, 279–80
  and Balkan Alliance, 302, 303, 305–6, 305–6
  Black Sea, control of, 30
  Bosnia, rule of, 243–44
  and Bosnian crisis, 208, 270, 279–80
  Bucharest, Treaty of, 62
  Bulgaria, atrocities in, 177–78
  Congress of Berlin (1878), 207, 209–10
  Constantinople Conference (1876-7), 190
  constitution, 188, 285–86
  Crimea, control of, 30, 39–40
  Danubian Principalities, rule of, 34–35, 58–59
  defeats, military, 12, 33–34, 192, 310
  defense capabilities, 350–51
  and Eastern Orthodox Church, 77, 78–79, 125, 127
  Egypt, threats from, 91
  European territory, loss of, 310, 330
  France, alliance with, 58–59
  and Germany, 350
  Gregorius V, Patriarch, murder of, 77
  and Habsburg Empire, 34, 35
  Herzegovina, rule of, 243–44
  instability, 170–71, 351
  Mehmed Said Pasha (Grand Vizier), 299
  and Metternich, 78
  Moldavia, rule of, 58–59
  and Montenegro, 172
  and Napoleon I, 58–59
  navy, 84–86, 350–51
  and Nicholas I (Czar of Russia), 83–84, 87–88, 91–92, 122–24, 124, 128
  and Russia, 15, 34, 42–43, 58–59, 83–84, 91–93, 298–300
  and Serbia, 155, 172, 183
  'Sick Man of Europe', 42, 84–85, 122–23, 123–24, 170–71, 351
  sovereign rights, 209–10
  Sublime/High Porte, 14–15, 30, 125, 126
  Treaty of Bucharest, 70
  and Treaty of Guarantee, 70
  Treaty of Karlowitz, 12
  and United Kingdom, 93, 177–78, 182–83, 350
  victories, military, 19–20, 194
  Young Turks, 285–86, 301
Ottoman Empire, Sultans
  Abdul Hamid II, 171, 183, 188, 267

Abdulaziz, 170–71
Abdulmejid I, 121, 125
Mahmud II, 76, 78–79,
    85–86, 86, 88–89, 91–93
Murad V, 171
Mustafa II, 2, 4, 12
Selim III, 58–59, 72
Ottoman Empire, wars
First Balkan War, 310–11
Navarino, Battle of, 84–86
Russo-Turkish War (1710),
    16–20
Russo-Turkish War (1768–
    74), 30–31, 31–34, 29–
    34, 36–37
Russo-Turkish War (1787–
    92), 45–47
Russo-Turkish War (1806–
    12), 58–59, 62
Russo-Turkish War (1828–
    29), 86–87, 88–90
Russo-Turkish War (1877–
    78), 191, 192–95, 195–
    98, 199–202, 274–75
Second Balkan War, 329
Turco-Italian War, 296,
    300–301
Ottomanization, 285, 301,
    311
Palacky, Jan, 145
Paléologue, G.M., 360, 362–
    63
Palmer, Alan, 165
Panin, Nikita, 29
Pan-Serbism, 253, 257, 263,
    267, 272–73, 345
and Austria-Hungary, 252,
    365, 374
Pan-Slavism, 145, 142–56,
    167, 171–72, 184
and Alexander II (Czar of

Russia), 144, 149, 168,
    213
Balkan, 151–54, 151–54,
    154–56, 175–77, 290,
    291–92
and exceptionalism, 145–
    47
Moscow Congress (1867),
    147–48
and nationalism, 145–47
origins, 144–45
Romanov support for,
    143–44, 148
Russian, 145–47, 149–50,
    150–51, 172–73, 175–
    77, 291–92
and Russo-Turkish War
    (1877–78), 192
Serbian, 154–56, 175–77,
    290
Paris Peace Conference
    (1919), 355
Paris, Treaty of, 140–41
Pasha, General Omar, 131
Pasic, Nikola, 253, 257, 273,
    313, 329–30, 331, 353–54,
    354
Paskevich, Field Marshal Ivan
    (Duke of Warsaw), 114,
    115
Paul I (Czar of Russia), 27,
    47–48
Peter I (King of Serbia), 255–
    56, 354
Peter I of Russia (Peter the
    Great), 3, 1–22
Azov campaigns, 7–9
defeats, military, 9, 19–20
diplomacy, 11–13, 14–15
Great Northern War, 15–
    17

legacy, 21–22
and Montenegro, 151
navy, establishment of, 7,
  10–11, 13–14
and Russo-Turkish War
  (1710), 16–20
shipbuilding, 9–10
Western Europe, attitude
  to, 6, 11–12
Peter III (Czar of Russia), 22,
  25–27, 27–29, 29, 47
Petrovic, Danilo, 151
Petrovic, Karadjordje, 155
Petrovic, Nikola. *See* Nicholas
  I of Montenegro
Piedmont, 289
Pig War, 258–59, 290–91
Pius VII, Pope, 72
Pleshcheyevo, Lake, 3
Plevna, Siege of, 194, 195
Pogodin, Michael, 143–44
Poincaré, Raymond, 304–6,
  307, 308, 328, 358, 360–61,
  361–65
Poland, 29–30, 35, 50, 68, 69,
  98, 394
Poltava, Battle of, 15–17
Poniatowski, Stanislaus, 30
Porte (Ottoman Empire
  government), 14–15, 30,
  125, 126
Potemkin, Grigory, 37–38,
  43–44, 45, 404
Potiorek, General Oskar, 313,
  339, 340, 341, 355–56
Pourtalès, Friedrich von, 377,
  424
Prague, 104, 106
Pravdinsk (Friedland), 57–58
Pressburg, Treaty of, 54–55
Princip, Gavrilo, 334–35,

335–36, 341–42, 356
propaganda, 290, 317
Protasova, Countess Natalia,
  143
Prussia, 46–47, 50, 57–58, 60,
  68, 110, 150, *See also*
  Frederick II
Prut (river), 19, 126, 192
Prut, Treaty of, 20
Putin, President Vladimir,
  389–90, 394, 387–98
Racconigi Bargain, 287–89
Radical political party
  (Serbia), 253, 257, 273
Rasputin, Grigory, 223
rebellions/revolutions, 98,
  102–3
  Berlin, 110
  Bosnia, 166, 167
  Eastern Rumelia, 236
  France (1830, July
    Revolution), 95, 96
  France (1848), 100–101
  Herzegovina, 166, 167, 170
  Hungary, 104–5, 108–10,
    110–16
  Prague, 104
  Russia (1825, Decembrist
    revolt), 82–83, 407
  Russia (1881), 214–17
  Serbia (1804–17), 155
  Serbia (1883), 253
  Vienna, 102–3, 105–6
  Young Turk Revolution,
    266–67, 268–69, 269
refugees, 166
Reichstadt negotiations, 188–
  89, 196
'Reinsurance Treaty', 219–20,
  221, 240
religion, 13, 18, 70–72, 76,

78–79, 85–86, 86, 247, *See also* Christianity; Eastern Orthodox Church; Islam

revolutions. *See* rebellions/revolutions

Rhodope Mountains, 170

Rodic, Gavrilo, 163

Romania, 33, 202, 210, 327, 394

Romanians (ethnic group), 338

Romanov monarchy, 27, 134, *See also* Alexander I (Czar of Russia); Alexander II (Czar of Russia); Alexander III (Czar of Russia); Alexis I of Russia; Catherine I of Russia; Catherine II of Russia; Elizabeth of Russia; Feodor III of Russia; Ivan V of Russia; Ivan VI of Russia; Nicholas I (Czar of Russia); Nicholas II (Czar of Russia); Paul I (Czar of Russia); Peter I of Russia; Peter III (Czar of Russia)

Habsburgs, alliance with, 4–5, 276

Habsburgs, antipathy to, 13, 14, 55–56, 79–80, 107–8, 217, 220

reputation, 197–98, 214–17, 264

Romanov, Aleksei Petrovich (Czarevich), 13

Rose, Colonel Hugh, 124

Rudolf, Crown Prince of Austria, 107, 240

Rumyantsev, General Pyotr, 36, 37, 40

Russia, 273, *See also* vassal states

Akkerman, Treaty of, 84

and Austria-Hungary, 188–89, 234–35, 238, 315–16, 315–16, 317, 330, 366, 380–81

Balkan policy, 21–22, 195–96, 264–65

Björkö, Treaty of, 227–30

and Bosnia and Herzegovina, 266, 281, 284–85

Buchlau bargain, 262–63

Budapest conventions, 190–91

and Bulgaria, 154, 185–86, 187, 189, 191, 218

Congress of Berlin (1878), 211

Constantinople Embassy, 126

Constantinople, claim to, 15, 72–73, 128

Constantinople, desire for, 2, 24–25, 192, 293, 352, 367–68

Crimea, annexation of, 39–40, 43, 47, 391–92

and Danube (river), 84, 90–91, 134

Danubian Principalities, control of, 83, 84, 90, 136

Danubian Principalities, occupation of, 34, 124, 126

defeats, military, 4–5, 9, 19–20, 194–95

expansionism, 393

and First Balkan War, 315–

16
Franco-Russian Alliance,
    221, 223–24
and Franz Ferdinand,
    death of, 344–45
French invasion of, 62
Georgia, 394–96
and Germany, 219–20,
    221, 238, 240, 353, 376–
    77, 383
Krasnoe selo, 363–64,
    368–69
League of the Three
    Emperors, 161, 204–5,
    214, 218–19
and Milan I (King of
    Serbia), 251–52
militarism, 80–81, 178,
    394–96
mobilization, 369–70, 376–
    78, 383–85
and Montenegro, 153,
    151–54, 321, 323, 325–
    26
and Nicholas I of
    Montenegro, 311
opposition to, 204
Ottoman policy, 83–84,
    87–88, 91–92, 91–93,
    122–24, 124, 128, 188–
    89
and Pan-Slavism, 145–47,
    149–50, 172–73
Poincaré, Raymond, visits,
    358
poverty of, 187
and Prussia, 150
'Reinsurance Treaty', 219–
    20, 221, 240
revolutionaries, 214–17
Russification, 215

and Serbia, 155, 251–52,
    279–80, 281, 326–27
St. Petersburg, 24, 23–24,
    28, 216, 305
Turkish Straits, access to,
    260–61, 263, 265, 266
and Ukraine, 38–39, 391
victories, military, 192
Western Europe, attitude
    to, 387, 393
Russia, wars
    Crimean War, 91, 119–30,
        130–41
    Russo-Japanese War, 263
    Russo-Persian War (1826–
        28), 86
    Russo-Turkish War (1710),
        16–20
    Russo-Turkish War (1768–
        74), 30–31, 31–34, 29–
        34, 36–37
    Russo-Turkish War (1787–
        92), 45–47
    Russo-Turkish War (1806–
        12), 58–59, 62
    Russo-Turkish War (1828–
        29), 86–87, 88–90
    Russo-Turkish War (1877–
        78), 191, 192–95, 195–
        98, 199–202, 274–75
    and World War I, 352,
        350–53
Rysakov, Nikolai, 216
Sahin Giray. See Shagin-Girei
    (Sahin Giray, Crimean
    Khan)
Sail, The (newspaper), 148–49
Salisbury, Lord (Robert
    Gascoyne-Cecil), 204
San Giovanni de Medua
    (Shëngjin), 313, 323

San Stefano, 199–200

San Stefano, Treaty of, 202–3, 205

Sanders, Liman von, 350

Sandzak of Novi Pazar, 267, 291, 310, 316, 329, 427

Sarajevo, 246, 247, 339–42

Saxony, 68

Sazonov, S.D. (Sergei Dmitryevich), 294, 299–300, 315–16, 319, 326–27, 327
and Austria-Hungary ultimatum, 366
and Balkan Alliance, 307
and Franz Ferdinand, assassination of, 356
and Poincaré, Raymond, 305–6, 360
and Serbia, 331, 352–53
and World War I, 350, 351–52, 361, 366–67, 367, 377, 383, 384–85

Schemua, Blasius, 313

Schönbrunn Convention, 161

Schuwalow, Count Paul, 238

Schwarzenberg, Felix von, 110, 115, 116

Schweinitz, General Hans Lothar von, 182

Scutari, 313, 318, 319–20, 321–22, 323–24

Second Balkan War, 327, 329–30

Second Schleswig War, 158

Selim I Girayn (Crimean Khan), 4–5, 7–8

Selim III (Ottoman Sultan), 58–59, 72

Serbia, 62, 84, 154–56, 167, 210, 251–57, 347–48, See
also Pan-Serbism
Albania, invasion of, 313, 323, 330–31
and Austria-Hungary, 252–53, 353–54, 357–58, 365, 370, 371–72
Austro–Serbian Alliance, 237–38, 252–53, 254
and Balkan Alliance, 289–90, 302–3
Black Hand (nationalist group), 333, 334, 340–42, 354, 356
and Bosnian crisis, 270, 272–73, 273, 283
Budapest conventions, 190–91
and Bulgaria, 258, 302–3
exceptionalism, 291
expansionism, 329–30
First Balkan War, 310, 313
and Franz Ferdinand, assassination of, 354, 353–57
Greater Serbia, 171–72, 267, 289–91
Habsburgs, threat to, 343
and Hungary, 290–91
independence, 202
mobilization, 370
and Montenegro, 153, 164–65, 172, 303, 329
Narodna odbrana (National Defense), 292–93, 356, 365
nationalism, 171–72, 256, 270, 333
Ottoman Empire, war against, 172, 175–77, 183
Pig War, 258–59, 290–91

Reichstadt negotiations, 174
and Russia, 168, 175–77, 254, 279–80
and Russo-Turkish War (1710), 17
seaport, desire for, 313, 315
Second Balkan War, 327
torture, 320–21
Treaty of Bucharest, 329
Treaty of Good Neighborliness, 290
and Treaty of San Stefano, 202
vassal state, 352–53
Serbo-Bulgarian War, 236–38
Serbs (ethnic group), 105, 164–65, 284
in Bosnia-Herzegovina, 242, 249–50, 257–58
Pan-Serbism, 252, 257, 272–73
Sevastopol, 43–44, 45, 139, 391, 392
Seven Years' War, 28, 27–28
Seymour, Sir Hamilton, 122–23
Shagin-Girei (Sahin Giray, Crimean Khan), 39–40, 42
Shëngjin (San Giovanni de Medua), 313, 323
Sheremetev, Boris, 8
Shipka Pass (Bulgaria), 192
shipping, 9–10, 11
Black Sea, 90–91, 91–92
Danube (river), 84, 130
Turkish Straits, 84, 260–61, 263, 265, 266
Silesia, 74
Silistra, 134, 135, 136

Simferopol, 391
Sinope, Battle of, 131
Sixth Coalition, War of, 63
slavery, 7–8
Slavkov. See Austerlitz
Slavophilism, 144
Slavs (ethnic group), 33, 104, 148–49, 208, See also Pan-Slavism
Slivnitza, Battle of, 237
Slovakia, 394
Slovenia, 394
Smyrna (Izmir), 89
Sophia Alekseyevna (Regent of Russia), 3–4, 4–5
Sophie (Duchess of Hohenberg, Sophie Chotek), 337, 338, 339, 340–42
Sosnosky, Theodor von, 356
South Ossetia, 395, 396
Soviet Union (U.S.S.R.), 387
Spain, 75
spies/spying, 52, 290, 294
St. Petersburg, 24, 23–24, 28, 216, 305
St. Vitus Day (28 June), 340
Steed, Wickham, 338
Stefan Dusan (King of Serbia), 155
Stieve, Friedrich, 328
Stolypin, P.A. (Pyotr Arkadyevich), 271
Straits, Turkish
Bosphorus, 92, 93
Dardanelles, 88, 89–90, 93, 127, 300
Russian access to, 84, 260–61, 263, 265, 266, 298–300, 408
Sublime Porte. See Porte

Sukhomlinov, Vladimir, 377
Sumner, B.H., 165
Sweden, 15–17
Szapáry, Friedrich Graf, 363
Taganrog, 10–11, 11, 13, 20, 31, 81
Tankosic, Voja, 256, 334, 354–55
Tarcin, 334, 339
taxation, 245–46
terrorism, 292–93, 333, 334–36, 340–42
Third Coalition, War of, 49–50, 51, 54–55
Tilsit, Treaties of, 59–60
Timmerman, Franz, 1
Tisza (river), 12
Tisza, Count Stephen, 331, 349, 357
Tittoni, Tommaso, 288
Tolstoy, Count Dmitry, 215
torture, 320–21
Totleben, Count Eduard, 204
treaties, 15, 34, 69, 279–80
    Adrianople (Edirne), 88–90, 90
    Akkerman, 84, 85–86
    Balkan Alliance, 302–3
    Berlin, 210–11, 262, 270–71, 276, 283
    Björkö, 227–30
    Bucharest (1812), 62, 83
    Bucharest (1913), 329–30, 343
    Budapest conventions, 190–91, 190–91, 196
    Final Act of Congress of Vienna, 69
    Hunkar-Iskelesi, 94, 99, 408
    Jassy, 47

Karlowitz, 12
Kuchuk Kainarji, 36–37, 83, 124
Kütahya, 93
London, 326
Münchengrätz (Mnichovo Hradiste) Agreements, 98–99, 110, 113
Paris, 140–41
Pressburg, 54–55
Prut, 20
Racconigi Bargain, 287–89
'Reinsurance Treaty', 219–20, 221, 240
San Stefano, 205
Schönbrunn Convention, 161
Tilsit, 59–60
Treaty of Good Neighborliness, 290
Treaty of Guarantee (Congress of Vienna), 70
'Vienna Note', 129
Trinity Lavra of St. Sergius, 5
Triple Alliance (Austria, Germany and Italy), 214, 288, 337–38
Triple Entente (France, Russia and Great Britain), 338, 360
Tripoli, 288, 296
Troppau (Opava), Congress of, 74
Tsarigrad. See Constantinople
Tschirschky, Heinrich von, 375–76
Turco-Italian War, 296, 300–301
Turkey, 210, 310, 327, 329, See also Constantinople;

Ottoman Empire
Turkish Straits, 351
  Bosphorus, 92, 93
  Dardanelles, 88, 89–90, 93,
    127, 300
  Russian access to, 84, 260–
    61, 263, 265, 266, 298–
    300, 408
U.S.S.R. See Union of Soviet
  Socialist Republics
  (U.S.S.R.)
Ukraine, 37–38, 38–39, 40,
  396–98
  Kherson, 39
  Kiev, 4, 391
  Ochakov, 8
  Russian invasion, 388, 391
Ukraintsev, Emilian, 14–15
Ulm, Battle of, 49
Union of Soviet Socialist
  Republics (U.S.S.R.), 387
United Kingdom. See Great
  Britain
United States of America
  (U.S.A.), 139–40
Vardar River Valley, 316
Varna, 87
vassal states, 151, 176–77,
  202, 262, 330
  Bulgaria, 185–86, 187, 189,
    195–96, 197, 218, 231–
    32
  Serbia, 352–53
Venice, 32
Verona, Congress of, 75
Victoria (Queen of Great
  Britain), 122, 225–26
Victoria, Princess of
  Germany (Princess Adolf
  of Schaumburg-Lippe),
  233–34

Victoria, Princess Royal
  (German Empress), 225–
  26
Vidin, 134
Vienna, 50, 63–64, 65–70,
  102–3, 105–6
  Congress of, 63–64, 65–70
'Vienna Note', 129
Voronezh, 10
Vorontsov, Elisabeth, 28, 29
Vukotic, Petar, 164
Wallachia, 17, 19–20, 31, 58–
  59, 90, 131, See also
  Danubian Principalities
wars
  Austro-Prussian War, 158
  Crimean War, 91, 119–30,
    130–41
  First Balkan War, 317–26
  Franco-Prussian War, 158
  Great Northern War, 15–
    17
  Greek War of
    Independence, 75–76,
    84–86
  jihad (holy war), 76, 85–86,
    86
  Napoleonic, 49–64, 67–68,
    405
  Pig War, 258–59, 290–91
  Russo-Japanese War, 263
  Russo-Persian War (1826–
    28), 86
  Russo-Turkish War (1710),
    16–20
  Russo-Turkish War (1787–
    92), 45–47
  Russo-Turkish War (1806–
    12), 58–59, 62
  Russo-Turkish War (1828–
    29), 86–87, 88–90

Russo-Turkish War (1877–78), 274–75

Russo-Turkish War (1877–78), 191, 192–95, 195–98, 199–202

Second Balkan War, 327, 329–30

Second Italian War of Independence, 289

Second Schleswig War, 158

Serbian-Ottoman, 172, 175–77, 183

Serbo-Bulgarian War, 236–38

Seven Years' War, 28, 27–28

Sixth Coalition, 63

Third Coalition, 49–50, 51, 54–55

trade, 258–59, 290–91

Turco-Italian War, 296, 300–301

World War I, 304, 361

Welden, General Ludwig Baron von, 112, 113

Wellington, Duke of (Arthur Wellesley), 86

Werder, General August von, 179

Weyrother, Franz von, 53–54

Wiesner, Dr. Friedrich von, 354–56

Wilhelm I (German Emperor), 157–58, 207, 213–14, 414

and Alexander II (Czar of Russia), 179, 212

death, 220

as mediator, 158–59, 159, 197–98

Wilhelm II (German Emperor), 60, 220–21, 270

Anglophobia, 225–26

Austria-Hungary, support for, 348

diplomacy, lack of, 226–27

expansionism, 227

and Franz Ferdinand, Archduke of Austria, 338, 346–48

and German navy, 226

Jerusalem, tour of, 224–25, 419

as mediator, 278, 279, 379–80, 381, 382

Morocco, visit to, 226–27

and Nicholas II (Czar of Russia), 223–24

Russia, ultimatum to, 382

and Serbia, 347, 380

Treaty of Björkö, 227–30

and World War I, 373–74

Will of the People (*Narodnaya Volya*), 215–17

William III (King of England), 12

Windisch-Graetz, Prince Alfred, 104, 106, 108–10, 112

Winter Palace, 24, 28, 216

World Exhibition (1873), 160

World War I, 304, 361

and Austria-Hungary, 361, 371–73, 374–76, 381

and Germany, 372–74, 379–80, 383

and Great Britain, 367, 378

origins, 367–68

and Russia, 366–67, 368–70, 376–78, 379, 381–83, 383–85

and Serbia, 370

Serbia, ultimatum to, 361, 365
xenophobia, 5–6, 142–43
Yanukovych, Viktor, 391–92
Yeltsin, Boris, 389
Young Turks, 266–67, 268–69, 269, 285–86, 299, 301–2, 311
Ypsilanti, General Aleksandr, 76
Zenta, Battle of, 12
Zerajic, Bogdan, 337

ABOUT THE AUTHOR

Maggie Ledford Lawson is an American professor and an
award-winning investigative reporter who has lived in
Prague since 1994.

Born in Morristown, Tennessee, Lawson majored in
German at the University of Tennessee, where she was
valedictorian of her graduating class. She holds a Ph.D.
from the University of North Carolina at Chapel Hill, with a
specialty in 19th-century British literature. She continued her
German studies at the Goethe Institute in Munich under a
Fulbright grant.

Lawson taught at various institutions, including the
University of North Carolina at Chapel Hill; the University
of Alabama in Huntsville; Armstrong State College in
Savannah; and George Mason University, in Fairfax,
Virginia. She later covered Capitol Hill for Roll Call
newspaper and Congressional Quarterly. After moving to
Prague with her husband, Don Hill, a senior editor for
Radio Free Europe/Radio Liberty, she wrote for The
Prague Post.

CPSIA information can be obtained
at www.ICGtesting.com
Printed in the USA
BVHW070832171119
564070BV00001B/202/P